Understanding School System Administration: Studies of the Contemporary Chief Education Officer

Understanding School System Administration:

Studies of the Contemporary Chief Education Officer

Edited by

Kenneth Leithwood and Donald Musella

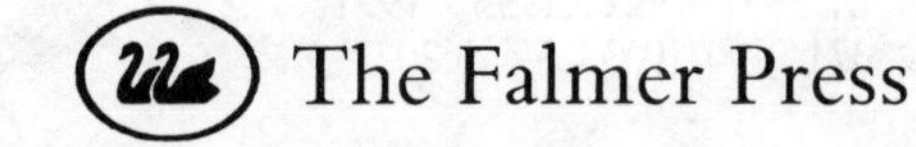

The Falmer Press
(A member of the Taylor & Francis Group)
London · New York · Philadelphia

UK The Falmer Press, 4 John St., London, WC1N 2ET
USA The Falmer Press, Taylor & Francis Inc., 1900 Frost Road, Suite 101, Bristol, PA 19007

First published 1991

British Library Cataloguing in Publication Data
Understanding school system administration: studies of the contemporary chief education officer.
1. Education. Administration
I. Leithwood, K.A. (Kenneth Arthur) II. Musella, Donald
379.15

ISBN 1-85000-869-8
ISBN 1-85000-870-1 (pbk)

Library of Congress Cataloging-in-Publication Data
Understanding school system administration: studies of the contemporary chief education officer/edited by Kenneth Leithwood and Donald Musella.
p. cm.
Includes bibliographical references and index.
ISBN 1-85000-869-8: — ISBN 1-85000-870-1 (pbk.):
1. School superintendents — Canada. 2. School management and organization — Canada. I. Leithwood, Kenneth A. II. Musella, Donald F.
LB2831.726.C2U53 1991
371.2'001'0971 — dc20 90-19766
CIP

Printed in Great Britain by Burgess Science Press, Basingstoke on paper which has a specified pH value on final paper manufacture of not less than 7.5 and is therefore 'acid free'.

Contents

Acknowledgments vii

Foreword viii

Notes on contributors x

Chapter 1 Introduction: A Framework for Understanding School System Administration 1
Kenneth Leithwood and Donald Musella

Section A: Chief Education Officers' Practices and Effects

Chapter 2 Setting, Size and Sectors in the Work Environment of Chief Education Officers 23
Derek J. Allison

Chapter 3 Policy Administration as Rhetoric: One Leader and His Arguments 42
Richard G. Townsend

Chapter 4 The Influence of Chief Education Officers on School Effectiveness 78
Donald Musella and Kenneth Leithwood

Chapter 5 Negotiating the Master Contract: Transformational Leadership and School District Quality 96
Linda LaRocque and Peter Coleman

Section B: Why Chief Education Officers Act As They Do

Chapter 6 Components of Chief Education Officers' Problem Solving Processes 127
Kenneth Leithwood and Rosanne Steinbach

Chapter 7 The Values and Beliefs of Ontario's Chief Education Officers 154
Mark Holmes

Chapter 8 Administrative Artifacts: Inferring Values From the Physical Culture of the CEO's Office 175
Stephen B. Lawton and Joyce Scane

Chapter 9 Pride and Privilege: The Development of the Position and Role of Chief Education Officers in the United States and Canada 209
Derek Allison

Section C: Fundamental Challenges for Chief Education Officers

Chapter 10 A Delicate Balance: Leadership or Stewardship 241
Mark Holmes

Chapter 11 Centralize, Decentralize, Control and Liberate: CEO's Views of Restructuring School Systems 273
Stephen B. Lawton and Joyce Scane

Chapter 12 Assessing Organizational Culture: Implications for Leaders of Organizational Change 287
Donald Musella and John Davis

Chapter 13 Conclusion: Preparation for Becoming a Chief Education Officer 306
Kenneth Leithwood and Donald Musella

Index 336

Acknowledgments

The research reported in this book is substantially based on a project undertaken by faculty in the Educational Administration Department of the Ontario Institute for Studies in Education (OISE). Funded for two years by the Social Sciences and Humanities Research Council of Canada, the focus of the research emerged over a six-month period from a series of (sometimes heated) discussions among faculty. Not everyone who participated in these discussions is reflected among the authors of this book, although their contributions were significant, nevertheless. In particular, we acknowledge a debt to Alan Brown, Thom Greenfield, Gerald McLeod, and Susan Padro.

Our work was enriched considerably by a number of non-OISE colleagues, as well. Several of these people are included among the contributors of this book (Derek Allison, Peter Coleman, Linda La-Rocque). The confluence of their work with ours was fortunate and its inclusion expands the scope and value of the book significantly.

Finally, an invitational conference concerned with the CEO's role was held at the mid-point of our work (also funded by SSHRC, in part) seeking critical feedback and as a way of additionally stimulating our thinking. We are indebted to those who gave us the benefit of their reactions in that context, although we cannot name all of them here. We can acknowledge, however, those not already mentioned who presented papers at that conference: Robin Farquhar, Tom Fleming, and Arthur Blumberg.

Kenneth Leithwood and Donald Musella
Ontario Institute for Studies in Education

Foreword

The work of the Chief Education Officer (CEO) in Canada is not well understood; at present it constitutes an enigma, perhaps largely because it is invisible to most. And yet, one suspects that the work must be important; otherwise, one wonders why it would be so relatively well compensated and why so many competent and ambitious educators would aspire to take it on. Thus, this role would seem to offer a prime object for the attention of curious scholars and, given its existence for several decades, the virtual absence of such attention until recently is somewhat dismaying.

Fortunately, however, within the past few years this role seems to have been discovered by a few serious students of educational administration, and they are gradually uncovering some of its mysteries (e.g., *The Canadian School Superintendent*, OISE Press, 1989, to which the present volume is something of a sequel — albeit set largely in Ontario, but with considerable generalizability beyond that Province). The project which gave rise to this book was driven primarily by a desire to facilitate the improvement of CEO practices largely through enhancing understanding of the role (its nature, causes, and consequences) and the work it involves. The contents collectively represent a significant contribution to knowledge of a subject which is important not only in itself but also in its relationships to numerous associated fields such as school effectiveness, comparative administration, international education, organizational culture, leadership theory, and change processes, to mention but a few. There is much here of value, then, to scholars and practitioners in numerous areas, but especially to those with a primary interest in educational administration.

This volume comprises the presentation of several distinctive but related empirical studies and opinion pieces. It constitutes perhaps the most thorough and wide-ranging presentation of the CEO role ever published in a single volume; and yet, it stimulates one's curiosity and desire to explore the subject further. It is characterized by an unusual degree of coherence for such a multiple-author undertaking, thanks to the common conceptual framework which loosely integrates the interestingly varied perspectives from which the different writers approach their topics. It is not a unified book, but there is considerable articulation among its several components; and it offers a good example of the values in collaborative, interdisciplinary, coordinated team research which could not possibly be undertaken by a lone scholar.

Herein the reader will find a remarkably wide-ranging treatment of the role — from fundamental principle to office furniture, from individual idiosyncrasies to international trends, from confusion to certainty, from trivial to earth-shaking, from thought to action, and from past to future. Underlying all of this diversity is a sustained respect for theory and conceptualization as the authors endeavour to describe, explain, and anticipate the CEO's behaviour, its causes and consequences. The book represents a bold and comprehensive analysis of an important role and the behaviour of its incumbents, incorporating consideration of the impact on CEO practice of interactions between and among internal thought and value processes and external institutional and environmental characteristics. As well, it presents and tests a number of conceptual models, provides worthwhile new information and knowledge, yields proposals for both policy and practice, generates numerous suggestions for future research, and proposes some crucial needs for professional preparation. It ranges organizationally from description and analysis to explanation and projection; and in format the abstracts preceding most chapters permit informative sampling by the selective reader who prefers not to devour the entire work, while the appended references demonstrate conscientious efforts to review, and provide helpful guides to accessing substantial bodies of relevant literature.

What emerges is the portrait of a role that seems highly complex in nature, demonstrably impactful in important ways, and situationally dependant on both personal and contextual variables. The volume conveys as well the sheer joy inherent in hard work to achieve worthwhile results, thereby offering some encouragement to both those who currently occupy the CEO role and those thinking of taking it on.

This book, then, should be welcomed as a positive contribution, not only to understanding of the role, but also to facilitating and encouraging improvement in its practice. As the authors reveal repeatedly throughout the volume, there is much more to be learned and done in the interest of improving the practice of CEOs in Canada. Here we have a significant step in that direction, and one awaits with some eagerness the promised third volume in this distinctive trilogy.

Robin H. Farquhar, President
Carleton University

Notes on Contributors

Derek Allison, University of Western Ontario, London, Ontario.

Peter Coleman, Simon Fraser University, Burnaby, British Columbia.

John Davis, Educational Administration Department, Ontario Institute for Studies in Education.

Mark Holmes, Educational Administration Department, Ontario Institute for Studies in Education.

Linda LaRocque, Department of Educational Administration, Faculty of Education, University of Alberta, Edmonton, Alberta.

Stephen Lawton, Educational Administration Department, Ontario Institute for Studies in Education.

Kenneth Leithwood, Educational Administration Department and Centre for Leadership Development, Ontario Institute for Studies in Education.

Donald Musella, Educational Administration Department and Centre for Leadership Development, Ontario Institute for Studies in Education.

Joyce Scane, Educational Administration Department, Ontario Institute for Studies in Education.

Rosanne Steinbach, Centre for Leadership Development, Ontario Institute for Studies in Education.

Richard G. Townsend, Educational Administration Department, Ontario Institute for Studies in Education.

Chapter 1

Introduction: A Framework for Understanding School System Administration

Kenneth Leithwood and Donald Musella

This is a book about Chief Education Officers (CEOs) — what they do, why they do it and some of the consequences of their work. It is about CEOs in the contemporary context, although chapter 9 provides compelling evidence regarding the influence of historical tradition on contemporary practice. In this respect the book might be read as a logical next step after *The Canadian School Superintendent* (Boich, Farquhar and Leithwood, 1989), a body of work substantially focused on the evolution of the CEO's role across the regions of Canada. Indeed, we hope the present book eventually will be part of a trilogy, research for the third book being in the planning stages as we completed this manuscript.

Like *The Canadian School Superintendent*, this book is the product of many minds. Multiauthored books usually offer the insights to be gained by exploring a phenomenon from a number of different vantage points. It is often difficult to discern in such books, however, what those different vantage points add up to. What is usually missing, when this is the problem, is a shared framework. Under the best of circumstances, such a framework allows the insights offered by different perspectives to be accumulated into a relatively more holistic appreciation for the object of inquiry. The research reported in the subsequent chapters of this book was guided more or less directly by the same framework. Indeed most of the chapters are based on research carried out in the context of one large-scale, two-year research project coordinated by ourselves.

In the remainder of this chapter we outline the broad purposes for the book and identify several of the more significant variations among the chapters in how these purposes were interpreted. We then describe the framework which was used to better understand the CEO's role in school system administration. As part of our argument for the usefulness of this framework, we also provide a relatively comprehensive review of relevant previous empirical research.

An important feature of this book is its domination by data from one of Canada's provinces, Ontario. Several chapters (5 and 9) are based on non-Ontario data and the authors of all chapters make significant links between their data and research carried out elsewhere. Nevertheless, the Ontario context is a sometimes subtle and sometimes quite explicit feature of the research. To what extent does this limit the value of the book for those who wish to make use of its ideas for their own purposes outside Ontario? Primarily, it is readers who must answer this question for themselves (i.e. do the ideas seem 'plausible' in the readers' context?) To help the reader, however, we point out that most educational research is context bound in exactly the same way as this book is. For example, Murphy and Hallinger's (1986) study of superintendents in effective school districts was undertaken in the context of California. Furthermore, such research rarely purports to be representative of the population from which it was drawn; one would not attempt to claim that Ortiz and Hendrick's (1987) case studies of three superintendents in any way represented the population of California superintendents of which they were members, never mind US superintendents more generally.

There are two features of the Ontario-dominated research context we think are especially noteworthy, however. First, Ontario is a Canadian province and, as Allison notes in chapter 9, historical traditions in Canada may have created a context in which Canadian CEOs' work is different than the context for US CEOs in at least several significant ways. An example of such a difference is the value associated with local district or board control. Second, Ontario school systems, on average, are relatively large as compared with many systems in other parts of Canada and the United States and CEOs included in our research were often from such large organizations. As we shall see subsequently, variations in organizational size are strongly related to variations in the practices of CEOs. With the notable exception of Coleman and LaRocque's research in British Columbia (chapter 5) then, extrapolations of our research results to the work of CEOs in relatively large school systems would be less hazardous then extrapolations to very small school systems.

Purposes for the Book

The role of the Chief Education Officer (CEO) is an enigma to most people. Indeed, writing in a US context, Crowson (1987) refers to the role as 'puzzling'. It is a role probably understood well only by experienced trustees, a few scholars and those with personal experience in or very close to the role. Many parents consider the person in charge, the final court of appeal on matters concerning their child's education, to be their local school principal. To the public at large, the local 'superintendent' or 'director' is a gray personage whose outlines are barely visible on the fringes of the media spotlight occupied by the elected school board chairperson. To teachers, their CEO is a distant authority figure, usually part of the cast on stage at school opening (or closing) ceremonies and whose infrequent visit to their school has the curious power to stimulate a flurry of pre-visit tidying-up on the part of the principal. For their part, principals view the CEO as preoccupied with 'politics' and see little connection between that preoccupation and the more fundamental educational problems to which they devote their efforts.

That the work of the CEO is not well understood should not be surprising — it is invisible to most. In contrast, for example, everyone has been a student and, because of that experience, has observed something of the work of teachers. Nor should it be surprising that the value of CEOs' work is viewed with skepticism by some. Such scepticism concerning those in authority is widespread both in our society and internationally. Political leaders, medical practitioners, police officers and lawyers are all subject to more searching and more critical scrutiny than was the case in earlier times. There are occasions when the scepticism seems justifiable. The corrupt and the incompetent are exposed; the tyrant is overthrown. But is the scepticism always or even generally justified? Mikhail Gorbachev's Russia, Margaret Thatcher's Britain, Lee Iaccocca's Chrysler and Konrad Black's Daily Telegraph are all examples of major change, none admired by everyone, attributable in large part to the skill and determination of a power administrator.

Whether one adopts an optimistic or pessimistic perspective on the motives and consequences of the work of those who act as chief executives, it is difficult to deny that such work has consequences. These consequences are often substantial, touching the lives of many within the organization and often outside, as well. And this is reason enough for efforts, such as those described in this book, to learn more about the nature, causes and consequences of what one group of CEOs do. In this respect, the research reported in this book may be viewed as a contribution to a comparative literature on the work of CEOs across different types of organizations. Examples of this literature include Mintzberg (1973), Peters and Waterman (1982), Kanter (1983) and Hambrick (1988). But a more ambitious purpose was the main stimulus for the collective work contained within these covers. Even though, as a group, the researchers who carried out this work differed widely in their degree of optimism concerning the typical consequences of what CEOs do, the majority were nevertheless driven by the goal of contributing to the 'improvement' of CEO practices.

In making the case for the importance of more research on the CEO,

Jones (1987) cites a handful of empirical studies in which significant relationships were demonstrated between CEO practices and student outcomes. Such evidence is important in establishing the possibility and estimating the magnitude of CEO impact. But these data provide few insights about the complex chain of mediating relationships accounting for such impact. Accordingly, as a reading of subsequent chapters illustrates, no single dependent (or mediating) variable has been selected as the criterion for defining the meaning of improvement. For Coleman and LaRocque (chapter 5), instructional effectiveness and cost-effectiveness are empirically linked criteria. Townsend (chapter 3) and Musella and Leithwood (chapter 4) might see improvement in terms of greater influence by the CEO on the actions of others. Making decisions more reflective of the values represented by the public will and by minorities would likely be evidence of 'improvement' for Holmes (chapters 7 and 10) while Lawton and Scane (chapter 8) might like to see even deeper commitment to the individual child. More effective problem solving processes would count as improvement for Leithwood and Steinback (chapter 6); for Musella and Davis (chapter 12), greater influence on school system culture and through such culture, changes in other school system characteristics.

Just as the researchers adopt different perspectives on the meaning of improvement, so too do they hold quite different assumptions about what knowledge is required to foster such improvement. Allison explains variation in typical CEO practices in terms of different historical traditions (chapter 9) and work contexts (chapter 2); Lawton and Scane attempt something very similar with respect to CEO values. This strategy of understanding and explaining normal practice assumes that improvement depends on better appreciating the reasons for typical practice; given such appreciation, CEOs may themselves be empowered to find ways of working more effectively. This assumption is decidedly noninstrusive and leaves open a panorama of alternative specific actions that might be taken toward improvement. Townsend (chapter 3), Leithwood and Steinbach (chapter 6), Holmes (chapter 10) and Coleman and LaRocque (chapter 5) generate knowledge based on the work of exceptional, representative or highly effective CEOs. This strategy assumes that inferences about improvement can be made with greater certainty from knowledge about 'effective' rather than from 'typical' practice. This assumption is relatively intrusive. It implicitly, if not explicitly, prescribes models for others to emulate (although that is decidedly not Holmes' intention in chapter 10), thereby substantially reducing the panorama of alternative actions for improvement. Yet more intrusive, however, are the assumptions underlying the work of Musella and Davis (chapter 12) and Leithwood and Musella (chapter 13). Those chapters assume that it is knowledge of the specific change strategies themselves

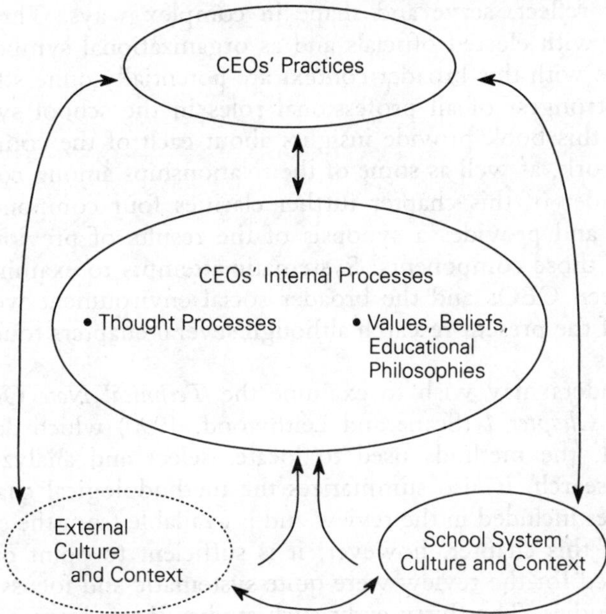

Figure 1.1 A Framework for Understanding the Nature, Causes and Consequences of What CEOs Do

that is required for improvement and such knowledge is what those chapters provide.

Previous Research and the Framework for this Book

Overview

Figure 1 depicts the primary components and relationships in the research on which this book is based. CEOs' values, educational philosophies and beliefs are part of the explanation for CEOs' practices, as are rational thought processes and problem solving strategies; these two components together (internal processes) seem likely to explain much of what CEOs do. Furthermore, on some occasions practices may flow largely to and from one or the other; an integrated set of internal processes may inform or be informed by a CEO's practice on other occasions. A CEO's overt practices interact with the larger organizational culture and context, one that is potentially shaped by what the CEO does and most certainly shapes the CEO's values, philosophies, and beliefs, rational thought processes and overt practices. Finally, figure 1 acknowledges that school systems are themselves embedded in a broader social culture and context which they reflect, serve and shape in complex ways. Through their interactions with elected officials and as organizational symbols, CEOs' relationships with this broader context are potentially quite strong, most likely the strongest of all professional roles in the school system. The chapters in this book provide insights about each of the components in this framework, as well as some of the relationships among components. The remainder of this chapter further clarifies four components of the framework and provides a synopsis of the results of previous research germane to those components. Systematic attempts to examine relationships between CEOs and the broader social environment were beyond the scope of the present research although several chapters touch on these relationships.

Some readers may wish to examine the *Technical Note On Literature Review For Chapter 1* (Scane and Leithwood, 1990) which describes, in some detail, the methods used to locate, select and analyze relevant, previous research. It also summarizes the methodological characteristics of the studies included in the review and is available from the editors. For purposes of this chapter, however, it is sufficient to point out that the methods used for the review were quite systematic and focussed only on empirical studies. The thirty-eight such studies located provided uneven amounts of evidence in respect to the components of our framework: only one study was relevant to CEOs' educational philosophies, values, and beliefs and only six studies examined CEO thought processes and problem solving strategies. In contrast, CEOs' practices were the object of inquiry in twenty-four studies and eighteen studies were located which directly or indirectly provided data about the CEOs' relationship to organizational culture and context.

Values and Educational Philosophies and Beliefs

This component of our framework is premised on the not very startling assumption that what a CEO wants to do (in whatever way that desire is manifested) is one important influence on what is done. More than fifty years ago, Chester Barnard (1938) espoused a compelling argument of the links between values and executive action. His argument also anticipated the results of current research demonstrating the explanatory power of organizational culture and suggesting its dependence on the moral character of the CEO (Stout, 1986). Nevertheless, Barnard's work resulted in very little follow-up by others until quite recently. The reason appears to have been a preoccupation with rational explanations of administrative practice stemming from the influence of Simon (1957). His pioneering work recognized that 'decision-making is the heart of administration', and from this vantage point, he set out to explore 'the logic and psychology of human choice'. The flaw in this orientation is not so much its narrowness, for choice is certainly a fundamental and unavoidable dynamic in the making of organizational and administrative realities. Rather, the weakness stems from Simon's own choice to explore only the factual basis of choice and to ignore value and sentiment as springs for human action. Because science could not speak to the 'ethical content' of decision making, Simon eliminated values from his putative science of administration. Thereafter he was content with his struggle to predict and control decisions purely from their 'factual content'. Factual propositions cannot be derived from ethical ones by any process of reasoning, nor can ethical propositions be compared directly with the facts — since they assert 'oughts' rather than the facts. Since decisions involve valuations of this kind, they too cannot be objectively described as correct or incorrect. Efforts have been made more recently to redress the absence of attention to the role of values and beliefs in administration. These efforts largely have been of a theoretical nature. Greenfield (1986), Hodgkinson (1978) and others have argued, for example, that conventional administrative science has increasingly obvious failures which arise for the simple reason that essential questions of administration are not scientific at all. They are philosophical. Organizations are a nexus of freedom and compulsion, asserts Hodgkinson. As invented social realities, they are both created and manipulated. Creation and manipulation are part of the task of the administrator. The central realities of administration are moral issues — issues that have often been camouflaged behind a facade of facts and procedures that helps to remove any sense of responsibility. To choose and to acknowledge responsibility for one's choice is often a risky way of living. It may require standing with those who are defined as heretics by a powerful and possibly vengeful authority. In organizational politics and administrative affairs, the acknowledgment of clearly chosen values can be dangerous. But their acknowledgment enables us to reflect upon our values. And in thinking about our lives, we may come to recognize that our decisions represent something beyond the decisions themselves; they bespeak a value and perhaps a commitment.

By this time, arguments for greater consideration of values in explaining administrative practice are becoming both repetitive and redundant. What seems necessary to move forward is empirical research designed for two related purposes. One purpose, as Stout suggests, is 'to map the terrain of [CEO] values' (1986, p. 204). Stout cited one study by Gross *et al.* (1958) suggesting that superintendents have different values which he defined as 'predispositions' to behave in ways classified as moralistic, expedient or moralistic-expedient. A handful of recent studies comparing CEOs in typical school districts with those in effective school districts also suggests value differences.[1] This research suggests, in addition, that CEOs in effective districts have a commitment to educational excellence and value consensual decision-making.

A second purpose for empirical research on CEOs' values is to better understand the nature and strength of the link between such values and CEOs' practices. The same research cited above implies strong links between CEOs' values and relatively predictable patterns of practice designed to foster school and school system objectives. These practices include the use of 'controls'— both bureaucratic controls (for example, procedures for student testing) and cultural controls (for example, symbolizing personal commitment to the district's mission by visibly allocating time to key tasks). The amount of available research concerning value-practice links, nevertheless, is extremely limited. As Stout (1986) points out; '. . . only a small beginning has been made in answer to the question of how executive values become manifest in executive action and the mechanisms [or practices] which executives use to influence the work of the organization' (p. 284).

Because of the limited research available to either 'map the terrain' of CEO values or understand their consequences for what CEOs do, research in this book addressed five questions:

- What are the educational belief systems of CEOs?
- To what extent do CEOs' belief systems affect educational decisions made in school systems?
- What other values, beliefs or sentiments underly the decision-making of CEOs?
- To what extent are CEOs aware of the values influencing their choices?
- How are these other values, beliefs and sentiments reflected in the decision-making of CEOs?

The first two and the fourth of these questions are addressed by Holmes directly in chapters 7 and 10. Coleman and LaRocque in chapter 5, Lawton and Scane in chapter 8 and Leithwood and Steinbach in chapter 6 address the remaining questions.

Thought Processes and Problem-Solving Strategies

A second important set of influences on what CEOs do is their thought processes and problem-solving strategies. Clearly, to consider such processes independent from values, beliefs and philosophies is to make a distinction that has limited meaning in reality. Values, for example, are pervasive and direct overt attention to some issues rather than others. Thoughts are imbued with feelings based on prior experiences and these feelings can cause us to respond positively or negatively to ideas sometimes without reference to the 'objective' quality of those ideas. It is useful, nevertheless, to separate these two components of our framework to simplify the research process. Eventually, as chapter 6 illustrates, modelling the problem solving of CEOs requires fitting the two components back together again.

Our prior discussion of CEOs' educational philosophies, values, and beliefs drew attention to the historical preoccupation of educational administration research with rational processes. Nevertheless, this preoccupation has not generated much empirical data concerning the internal, cognitive bases of such processes. This is especially the case for CEOs. Our review of the modest amount of relevant research suggested that effective CEOs are claimed to demonstrate high degress of cognitive flexibility (Wirt, 1987; McMurray and Bentley, 1987). Successful CEOs also have been reported to possess reasonably detailed cognitive images (or visions) of what they would like their organization to become and the processes for getting there (Coleman and LaRocque, 1987; Ortiz and Hendrick, 1987). These results, however, fall far short of providing a reasonable understanding of CEOs' thought processes.

Since the mid '70s a substantial body of research on teacher thinking has accumulated (for example, Clark and Peterson, 1986). Similarly, there has been a growing body of evidence concerning the 'strategic thinking' of senior administrators of non-educational organizations (for example, Srivastva, 1983; Schwenk, 1988). In both cases, this research has been based largely on information processing models of how the mind works (for example, Voss *et al.*, 1983). Results of this research suggest that much of the variation in problem-solving processes can be explained by the extent to which the solver possesses crucial background knowledge relevant to the problem; by the context for problem solving; and by the solver's initial classification and interpretation of the problem. Based on this orientation to human thinking, research reported in subsequent chapters addressed three questions:

- What is the nature of CEOs' problem-solving, including the range of types of problems that CEOs face; the components of the process used to solve a problem; and the way CEOs classify problems?
- Are there differences in CEOs' problem-solving processes depending on: characteristics of the problem; context of the problem (i.e., whether it is solved alone or in a group); and characteristics of the solver?

- Are there differences between CEOs and school administrators in the type of problems with which they are faced and the demands made on their problem-solving processes (i.e., the importance of context in shaping problem-solving processes)?

These questions are addressed most directly in chapter 6 by Leithwood and Steinbach. Townsend's analysis in chapter 3 is also relevant, however.

CEOs' Practices

The research reflected in this book is unbalanced, some would say, in its attention to CEOs' internal processes. In our view, this is justified on the grounds that such processes stand between the external environment experienced by CEOs, whether the school system or broader environment, and CEOs' practices. Such processes, as we have already pointed out, serve as screens or sense-making mechanisms giving rise to CEOs' actions; knowledge about such processes provides explanations for why CEOs act as they do.

Nevertheless, it is the CEO's practices themselves that are experienced by others and account for whatever impact CEOs have on their school systems. It is important to know, then, what it is that CEOs do. Indeed, the goal of improving CEOs' contributions to their school systems depends more precisely not just on knowledge of what CEOs do but a fuller appreciation of (a) how variations in CEOs' internal processes are related to variations in CEOs' practices; and (b) how such variations in practices effect the nature and extent of impact that CEOs have on their school systems.

Murphy and Hallinger (1986), Pitner and Ogawa (1981), Bridges (1982) and Crowson (1987) have concluded, from their own independent research reviews, that little is known about these basic questions regarding CEO practices. Our own literature search turned up some twenty-one relevant empirical studies, a substantially larger number than was available for the other components of our framework. These studies were of three types. Six studies involved direct and detailed observation of the work of CEOs, usually for a period of more than a week.[2] Nine studies inquired about CEO job functions (but from quite diverse perspectives).[3] The nature and amount of influence exercised through selected CEO practices was the focus of ten studies.[4]

The six observational studies, two Canadian and four US, had their genesis, for the most part in Mintzberg's (1973) influential studies of managers in different organizational contexts. Results from the most recent of these studies, carried out by McLeod (1984) in Ontario, are representative of much of what has been found through this type of research. In this study, CEOs were reported to work at a 'torrid pace' in response to numerous interruptions and frequent switches in their focus of attention. On the other hand, 'long hours pass with the same person immobilized during attendance at scheduled meetings' (p. 175). Verbal communication is the dominant activity of CEOs, about half initiated by them. Duignan (1980) reported that the CEOs in his sample averaged thirty-eight different activities each day, of which 65 per cent lasted less than ten minutes each. Managerial and executive work, as distinct from educational leadership, best characterized the substance of CEO activities in Duignan's (1980) study. Based on similar evidence, Pitner and Ogawa (1981) characterized the CEO as a mediator, as someone 'who acts to manage and, thereby, to influence the processes by which shared meanings are constructed' (p. 50). While such studies provide rich detail about the day to day activities of administrators, they are not well designed to capture the most significant acts engaged in by such people, (which, by definition, do not occur often). Nor are such studies well suited to the development of an understanding of how many small actions, seemingly trivial when considered independently, may accumulate to have non-trivial consequences over an extended period of time. Indeed, recent research offers that as the most plausible explanation of principals' effects (for example, Dwyer *et al.*, 1983; Leithwood and Montgomery, 1986) and we believe it is worth pursuing with CEOs as well. In order to explore this explanation, it is necessary to examine patterns of CEOs' practices over large segments of time.

The results of the nine studies of CEOs' job functions support two claims. First, CEOs and those in other roles with whom CEOs work (including school board members) often hold different understandings of what CEOs do and ought to do: such differences, if not resolved, may hamper the CEO's effectiveness. Second, an overriding function of the CEO is the management of conflict between different groups with vested interests in the school system. The amount of conflict to be managed, however, is not excessive as compared with senior executives in similar types of organizational contexts (for example, city planners). Nor do CEOs appear to feel beleaguered by such conflict.

Of the ten studies concerned with CEO influence strategies, six described such strategies as used in representative school systems presumably by 'typical' CEOs. These studies described CEOs' use of both formal mechanisms of bureaucratic authority (or influence) and more interpersonally-based influence strategies. Formal strategies include the means used by CEOs to control inputs to schools and classrooms, behavior of school and school system personnel and school and district output. Input controls include, for example, the allocation and flow of financial resources, allocation of time, provision of curricular materials and the distribution of students across schools and classes. These controls, although mediated by school and classroom characteristics, appear to have a significant indirect impact on the educational experiences of students, although they are not perceived as intrusive by teachers; they are substantially under the CEO's direction.

Behavior controls include supervision and evaluation practices as well as other procedures, rules and regulations which staff are expected to follow. Evidence suggests that, typically, neither teachers nor principals perceive their behavior to be severely constrained by such controls. Yet there is also evidence that these controls may account for much more of what principals and teachers do than they perceive. While probably an extreme case, Crowson and Morris (1985) found such controls to consume 50 per cent of the time of Chicago principals, for example. These controls are readily accessible to CEOs. Output controls, the final type of formal bureaucratic influence strategy are perceived, at least by principals, to be extensively used by CEOs. Such controls include student achievement testing, public opinion and the like.

CEOs also use less formal influence strategies based more on interpersonal relations than on sources of bureaucratic authority. The more obvious of these strategies, according to Pitner and Ogawa (1981), stem from CEOs' ability to control a significant portion of their own work, to initiate new ideas and activities and to place demands on others through schedules, emphasizing promptness and delegating work. Less obviously, CEOs are reported to exercise influence through the persuasiveness of their extensive communications. CEOs also use careful timing of initiatives in order to create the best opportunity for their initiatives to succeed. Sometimes they create diversions, as well, to draw attention away from issues about which they wish to act decisively, (read 'without much interference from others').

In addition to studies of influence strategies used by typical CEOs, our literature search uncovered five studies of strategies used by CEOs in exemplary school systems. How CEOs exercised 'instructional leadership' was the the specific question addressed by these studies. Results of these studies do not differ dramatically from results of the six studies reviewed above. However, CEOs in exemplary school systems, as compared to other CEOs, appear to attend to instructional improvement more actively and personally and to use a more extensive array of those bureaucratic and culture-building influence strategies available to them for this purpose. A greater degree of coherence is evident in the direction suggested by their influence strategies. For example, the in-service of teachers is directed at developing qualities needed to implement the clearer vision of effective CEOs which they pursue within what Coleman and LaRocque (1987) refer to as norms of consensuality.

Research reported in subsequent chapters adds to the knowledge reviewed here about CEO practices by addressing three questions:

- What are the practices in which CEOs engage and which are of greatest significance for others?
- To what extent are variations in CEO practices related to organizational context?
- What strategies are used by CEOs to influence others and what is their perceived effect?

Allison addresses the first two of these questions in chapters 2 and 9. Townsend speaks to the first question in chapter 3, Leithwood and Musella address the third question in chapter 4 as do Coleman and LeRocque in chapter 5; chapter 5 is also relevant to the first question.

Organizational Context and Cutlure

By organizational context, we refer to school system size, ways in which the system is organized, its geographical location, the makeup of its student body and possibly other relatively 'tangible' features of the system. Organizational culture has been defined in many ways (reviewed in chapter 12). Schein's definition, sufficiently comprehensive for our purposes, characterizes culture as:

> . . . a pattern of basic assumptions — invented, discovered or developed by a given group as it learns to cope with its problems of external adaption and internal integration — that has worked well enough to be considered valid and, therefore, to be taught to new members as the correct way to perceive, think and feel in relation to those problems. (Schein, 1985, p. 9)

An organization's culture is less tangible than its context but not less powerful in shaping the activities of organizational members. Together, culture and context are intended to be inclusive conceptual nets capable of catching whatever lurks inside the boundaries of the school system influencing or being influenced by the CEO. And that is the rationale for incorporating this component into our research framework.

It seems likely that research to date has captured only a small proportion of what will eventually be considered important about context and culture in explaining the causes and consequences of what CEOs do. Based on that limited research, we are able to partially answer two questions. One question is: What features of organizational context appear to shape the activities of CEOs? Our literature review located seven studies relevant to this question.[5] These studies support the claim that variations in what CEOs do is partly explained by school systems' organizational structure (flatter organizations permit and encourage greater CEO involvement in schools and greater attention to curriculum and instructional decisions). Also influencing what the CEOs do is the ethnic makeup of the student body; school system size (as school systems increase in size, there is a tendency for CEOs' priorities to shift from day-to-day operations and perhaps curriculum and instructional concerns to schoolboard management); and the relative geographical isolation of school systems (less cosmopolitan, isolated school systems present more tractable problems to CEOs who wish to implement progressive educational changes).

A second question addressed by previous research, in a very limited way, is: What are the characteristics of effective school system cultures? Answers to this question suggest strong parallels with the characteristics of effective school cultures identified in recent research by Little (1982), Rosenholtz (1989), Lieberman (1988) and others. Among the seven relevant studies[6] included in our review, Coleman and LaRocque (1987) offer the most succinct synopsis of these characteristics. The culture or 'ethos' (to use their term) of effective districts has a focus on learning, — or what Berman and McLaughlin (1979) refer to as the 'primacy of delivery concerns' (p. 62) — is committed to ongoing instructional improvement and fosters a norm of accountability among schools for such learning and improvement. Effective district cultures show respect for students and staff (a 'caring focus') and create a strong commitment to effort, effort devoted to doing the best job possible for students. Such district cultures also value extensive community involvement. Additional aspects of effective school system culture identified in the studies reviewed include consistency in directions and policies, openness to ideas from outside the system, high levels of trust and cohesiveness among organizational members and at least temporary feelings of organizational stability.

In subsequent chapters, we add to what is known about the relationships between CEOs, practices and organizational culture and context by addressing four questions:

- What features of organizational context influence the work of CEO's? Why? In what ways?
- What qualities are associated with productive school system cultures?
- What CEO practices seem most useful in consciously shaping school system cultures?

The first of these questions is addressed by Allison in chapter 2: the remaining questions by Coleman and LaRocque (chapter 5) and by

Musella and Davis (chapter 12). Among others, Townsend (chapter 5) touches upon these questions between the lines, obliquely.

Conclusion

During the course of this research we have become impressed by the potential for leadership available to CEOs. We have also become impressed with the dramatic variation among CEOs in their exercising of that potential. Some CEOs clearly put their imprint on their organizations, are visibly helpful to most of their colleagues in their organizations and are a major explanation for the quality of the educational services provided to students. CEOs such as these, however, are few in number. Many more seem to be 'minding the shop', for the most part, with most of their time devoted to managing their boards. Doing the CEO's job well is no mean feat. It takes an extraordinary level of commitment, skill, stamina and persistence. Where do CEOs find such resources? Not, it would seem, in any formal preparation programs, since few such programs exist. Yet we know that beginning CEOs cannot afford the luxury of many mistakes. Unlike architects, who sometimes make their first blunders in designs for remote off-shore locations, Canadian CEOs usually spend their whole careers within one province; so there's no getting away from reputations that travel intra-provincially and fast. We also know that CEO effectiveness is nourished by ongoing learning opportunities that on-the-job experiences may not afford (Rosenholtz, 1989). For this reason, we devote the concluding chapter (13) of the book to the preparation needs of CEOs.

Notes

1 The studies included Alpin (1984), Murphy and Hallinger (1986), Rosenholtz (1989), Coleman and LaRocque (1987), Jones (1987) and Iannoccone (cited in Stout, 1986).

2 Included among these studies were Duignan (1980), Larson *et al.* (1981), Morris (1979), Patterson (1975), Pitner and Ogawa (1981) and McLeod (1984).

3 These studies included Salley (1979–80), Baker (1984), Willower and Fraser (1979–80), Bart (1981), Cox (1976), Duea and Bishop (1980), Blumberg (1985), Fast (1986) and Zeigler, Kehoe and Reisman (1985).

4 See Jones (1987), Murphy and Hallinger (1986), Peterson, Murphy, and Hallinger (1987), Awender (1985), Pitner and Ogawa (1981), Gamoran and Dreeban (1986), Floden, *et al.* (1988), Peterson (1984).

5 See Rosenblum and Louis (1981), Carr (1987), Baker (1984), Duea and Bishop (1980), Cox (1976), Salley (1979–80) and Fast (1986).

6 The studies were by Berman and McLaughlin (1979), Coleman and LaRocque

(1987), Ortiz and Hendrick (1987), Rosenblum and Louis (1981), Crowson and Morris (1985), Murphy and Hallinger (1986) and Peterson, Murphy and Hallinger (1987).

References

ALPIN, M.D. (1984) 'The values guiding the operational practices of a suburban superintendent', paper presented at the annual meeting of the American Educational Research Association, New Orleans.

AWENDER, M.A. (1985) 'The superintendent school board relationship', *Canadian Journal of Education*, 10, 2.

BAKER, J.F. (1984) 'The superintendent's role: An analysis of expectations for public school superintendents as reported by superintendents, school board members, high school principals, high school teachers, elementary principals, and elementary teachers in Colorado', *Dissertation Abstracts International*, 44, 8.

BARNARD, C. (1938) *The Functions of the Executive,* Cambridge, MA, Harvard University Press.

BART, M.J.S. (1981) 'The role and function of boards of education and school superintendents as reflected in the perceptions of members of both groups in selected school districts in Arizona', *Dissertation Abstracts International*, 41, 10.

BERMAN, P. and MCLAUGHLIN, M.W. (1979) *An Exploratory Study of School District Adaptation,* Santa Monica, CA, Rand.

BLUMBERG, A. (1985) *The School Superintendent: Living with Conflict,* New York, Teachers College Press.

BOICH, T.W., FARQUHAR, R.H. and LEITHWOOD, K. (1989) *The Canadian School Superintendent*. Toronto, OISE Press.

BRIDGES, E.M. (1982) 'Research on the school administrator: The state of the art, 1967–1980', *Educational Administration Quarterly* 18, 3, pp. 12–33.

CARR, J.C. (1987) 'Effects of structural complexity on administrative role demands', paper presented at the annual meeting of the American Educational Research Association, Washington.

CLARK, C.M. and PETERSON, P.L. (1986) 'Teachers' thought processes' in WITTROCK, M.C. (Ed.) *Handbook of Research on Teaching* (3rd edn) New York, Macmillan.

COLEMAN, P. and LAROCQUE, L. (1987) 'Reaching out: Instructional leadership in school districts', Vancouver, Simon Fraser University, mimeo.

COX, R.R. (1976) 'A study of the perceptions of teachers, principals and school board members about the real and ideal behaviors of public school superintendents in Nebraska Class III school districts', *Dissertation Abstracts International*, 37, 4009A.

CROWSON, R.L. and MORRIS, V.C. (1985) 'Administrative control in large city school systems: An investigation in Chicago', *Educational Administrative Quarterly*, 21, 4, pp. 51–70.

CROWSON, R.L. (1987) 'The local school district superintendency: A puzzling administrative role', *Educational Administration Quarterly*, 23, 3, pp. 49–69.

CUBAN, L. (1976) *Urban School Chiefs Under Fire.*Chicago, IL.: University of Chicago Press.

DUIGNAN, P. (1980) 'Administration, behavior of school superintendents: A descriptive study', *Journal of Educational Administration*, XVIII, 1.

DUEA, J. and BISHOP, W.L. (1980) PROBE Examines Time Management, Job Priorities and Stress Among Public School Superintendents. Practical Research into Organizational Behavior and Effectiveness (PROBE), Cedar Falls, Iowa.

DWYER, D., LEE, G., ROWAN, B. and BOSSERT, S. (1983) *Five Principals in Action*. San Francisco, CA, Far West Laboratory.

FAST, R.G. (1986) 'Perceptions, expectations and effectiveness of school superintendents in Alberta and Pennsylvania as reported by principals and board members', State College, PA, unpublished doctoral dissertation.

FLODEN, R.E., PORTER, A.C., ALFORD, L.E., FREMAN, D.J., IRWIN, S., SCHMIDT, W.H. and SCHWILLE, J.R. (1988) 'Instructional leadership at the district level: A closer look at autonomy and control', *Educational Administration Quarterly*, 24, 2, pp. 96–124.

GAMORAN, A. and DREEBAN, R. (1986) 'Coupling and control in educational organizations', *Administrative Science Quarterly*, 31, pp. 612–32.

GREENFIELD, T.B. (1986) 'Representing organization theory with a human face: The search for a human and humane understanding of administration', paper presented to the annual meeting of the American Educational Research Association, San Francisco.

GROSS, N., WARD, M. and MCEACKERN, A. (1958) *Explorations in Role Analysis*. New York, John Wiley.

HAMBRICK, D. (Ed.) (1988) *The Executive Effect: Concepts and Methods for Studying Top Managers*, London, JAI Press.

HART, A. (1984) 'An exploration of the effects of superintendents on the instructional performance of school districts', unpublished doctoral dissertation, University of Utah.

HODGKINSON, C. (1978) *Towards a Philosophy of Administration*, Oxford, Basil Blackwell.

IANNACCONE, L. (1981) 'Superintendents made a difference', *The School Administrator*, September, 16.

JONES, B.W. (1987) 'Teacher and principal perceptions of instructional climate and the instructional leadership of superintendents in selected Ohio school districts', a dissertation at Miami University (mimeo).

KANTER, R.M. (1983) *The Change Masters*, New York, Simon and Schuster.

LARSON, L.I. and others. (1981) *The Nature of a School Superintendent's Work,* Final technical report on a study for the National Institute of Education, Washington, D.C.

LEITHWOOD, K. and MONTGOMERY, D. (1986) *Improving Principal Effectiveness: The Principal Profile,* Toronto, OISE Press.

LIEBERMAN, A. (Ed.) (1988) *Building a Professional Culture In Schools,* New York, Teachers College Press.

LITTLE, J. (1982) 'Norms of collegiality and experimentation: Workplace conditions of school success', *American Educational Research Journal,* 19, pp. 325–40.

MCLEOD, G. (1984) 'The work of school board chief executive officers', *Canadian Journal of Education*, 9, 2, pp. 171–90.

MCMURRAY, A.R. and BENTLEY, JR. E.L. (1987) 'Situational leadership: Conscious criteria applied in educational leaders' decisions', paper presented to the annual meeting of the American Educational Research Association, Washington.

MINTZBERG, H. (1973) *The Nature of Managerial Work*, New York, Harper and Row.

MORRIS, J.R. (1979) 'Job(s) of the superintendency', *Educational Research Quarterly*, 4, 4.

MURPHY, J. and HALLINGER, P. (1986) 'The superintendent as instructional leader: Findings from effective school districts', *Journal of Educational Administration*, 24, 2, pp. 213–36.

OGWAW, R. and HART, A. (1983) 'The effect of principals on the instructional performance of schools, paper presented to the annual meeting of the American Educational Research Association, Montreal.

ORTIZ, F. and HENDRICK, W. (1987) 'A comparison of leadership styles and organizational cultures: Implications for employment equity', *Journal of Educational Equity and Leadership*, 7, 2, pp. 146–60.

PATTERSON, W.N. (1975) 'A day in the life of Berkeley Superintendent Dick Foster', paper presented to the annual meeting of the American Educational Research Association.

PETERS, T.J. and WATERMAN, R.H. (1982) *In Search of Excellence: Lessons From America's Best Run Companies*, New York, Harper and Row.

PETERSON, J.D., MURPHY, J. and HALLINGER, P. (1987) 'Superintendents' perceptions of the control and coordination of the technical care in effective school districts', *Educational Administration Quarterly*, 23, 1, pp. 79–95.

PETERSON, K.D. (1984) 'Mechanisms of administrative control over managers in educational organizations', *Administrative Science Quarterly*, 29, pp. 573–97.

PITNER, N.J. and OGAWA, R.T. (1981) 'Organizational leadership: *The case of the school superintendent', Educational Administration Quarterly*, 17, 2, pp. 45–65.

ROSENBLUM, S. and LOUIS, K.S. (1981) *Stability and Change: Innovation in an Educational Context*, New York, Plenum Press.

ROSENHOLTZ, S. (1989) *Teachers' Workplace,* New York, Longman.

SALLEY, C. (1979–80) *Superintendents' Job Priorities Administrator's Notebook*, 28, 1.

SCANE, J. and LEITHWOOD, K. (1990) 'Technical note on literature review for chapter 1', Toronto: The Ontario Institute for Studies in Education, mimeo.

SCHEIN, E.H. (1985) *Organizational Culture and Leadership*, San Francisco, CA, Jossey-Bass.

SCHWENK, C.R. (1988) 'The cognitive perspective on strategic decision making', *Journal of Management Studies*, 25, 1, pp. 41–56.

SIMON, H. (1957) *Administrative Behavior* (2nd edn) New York, The Free Press.

SRIVASTVA, S. (1983) *The Executive Mind.* San Francisco, CA, Jossey Bass.

STOUT, R. (1986) 'Executive action and values', *Issues In Education*, 4, 3, pp. 198–214.

VOSS, J.F., GREEN, T.R., POST, T.A. and PENNER, B.C. (1983) 'Problem solving skills in the social sciences', in BOWER, G.H. (Ed.) *The Psychology of Learning and Motivation*, New York, Academic Press, pp. 165–213.

WILLOWER, D.J. and FRASER, H.W. (1979–80) 'School superintendents and their work', *Administrator's Notebook,* University of Chicago, 28, 5.

WIRT, F.M. (1987) *'Administrators' perception of policy influence: Conflict management styles and roles',* paper presented to the annual meeting of the American Educational Research Association, Washington.

ZEIGLER, H., KEHOE, E. and REISMAN, J. (1985) *City Managers and School Superintendents,* New York, Praeger.

Section A

Chief Education Officers' Practices and Effects

Chapter 2

Setting, Size and Sectors in the Work Environment of Chief Education Officers[1]

Derek J. Allison

Research dealing with the role and work of CEOs is briefly reviewed in this chapter and a conceptual model of their work environment presented. This model identifies three main work sectors: board, system and community. The nature of each sector is outlined and potential differences in the way in which CEOs may orient themselves toward and actively administer each is discussed. Personal style, institutional setting and organizational size/administrative complexity are identified as contingent factors influencing the way in which CEOs relate to each sector. Findings from recent Ontario research are used to illustrate the model, but connections are also made to research conducted in other North American settings.

This chapter examines the work and the work environment of Chief Education Officers in Ontario with reference to variations in the size of the school systems administered. The discussion is based on data gathered during a policy oriented study of Ontario superintendents (Fullan, *et al.*, 1987), which investigated the roles and responsibilities of the full range of central office administrative positions in order to recommend changes to the Province's supervisory officer certification process. Although the final report of the original study naturally considered the role of CEOs, its overall objectives and purpose precluded a tightly focussed analysis of a single administrative position. The principal investigators provided access to the original data on CEOs to facilitate such an analysis, additional details of which are contained in Allison and Allison (1988). The account of the work of Ontario CEOs that is presented here draws directly on the insights gained during that reanalysis and on those offered in McLeod's (1984) earlier observational study of sixteen Ontario CEOs.

Setting

Ontario is the largest, richest and most populous of the Canadian provinces. Despite the vastness of its total area of over one million square kilometres, the great bulk of the current population of more than nine million is concentrated along and around an 800 kilometres long axis extending from Ottawa, the national capital, to Windsor at the southwestern tip of Lake Erie. This rich agricultural, commercial and industrial corridor is served by schools operated by large area county and city school boards. Geographically this region has the aspect of a great arrowhead thrusting some 500 miles below the 49th parallel, which forms the boundary between Western Canada and the United States. Settlement in the middle north of the province follows a rough arc from Ottawa, through Sudbury, then along the north shore of Lake Superior to Thunder Bay, some 1400 kilometres distance. Provincial schools in this region are administered by very large area district boards, which service networks of widely separated small communities. With the exception of a few isolated settlements served by small school jurisdictions the far north is virtually unsettled.

Whereas the formative history of the American superintendency is characterized by ambiguity and conflict (Blumberg, 1985; Tyack and Hansot, 1982), the Ontario directorship evolved from a much more stable tradition of school administration (Allison and Wells, 1989). As discussed in more detail in another chapter, the British-derived political and administrative institutions established in the formative decades of this originally Loyalist province fostered an acceptance of centralized authority that was contrary to the 'Town Meeting' rooted notions of local political autonomy which predominated in the 'older colonies' to the south. Key legislation enacted in 1850 and 1871 laid the foundations for the development of a centralized system of school administration which endured until the 1960s, vestiges of which still remain. For almost a century, town and country schools were administered and supervised by a corps of centrally regulated inspectors. Chief administrators of city school systems were directly employed by local boards, but their appointment was contingent on certification and approval by the Ministry. All school system administrators became locally employed with the establishment of the current large area school boards in 1969, but the practice of centralized certification examinations remains in effect and all supervisory officer appointments must still be approved by the central authority.

Under current legislation all Ontario school boards with a total enrollment of 2000 or more students are required to appoint a director of education to serve as chief education and chief executive officer (Ontario, 1980, S. 253). In practice all of the 112 boards[2] enrolling more than 1200 students have a director, as do three boards enrolling fewer students. The *Education Act* further specifies that directors shall, 'within policies established by the board, develop and maintain an effective organization and the programs required to implement such policies' (S.253[2]). System job descriptions typically specify that directors will advise the board on policy matters, ensure the effective administration of the system and provide leadership. It is also common practice for many Ontario boards to assign the additional legal title and duties of Secretary to the director's position. This additional function gives directors (subsequently referred to as CEOs) legal responsibility for board minutes and typically gives them charge of preparing the board agenda.

The Data

The original Fullan, *et al.* (1987) study was based on data gathered from a sample of Ontario school systems drawn so as to ensure appropriate representation on the basis of size (enrollment), geographic location, and constitution (public/separate, anglophone/francophone). In each of the selected systems, interviews were held during 1985–1986 with the CEO, the chairperson of the board and some or all central office supervisory officers (SOs), depending on total numbers. Interviews lasted about one-and-a-half hours and were based on standardized protocols. CEOs were interviewed according to the standard supervisory officer schedule (*ibid*, pp. 207–9). Career trajectory and demographic data were collected through a short pre-interview questionnaire. The discussion presented here is based on coded questionnaire data from twenty-two CEOs supplemented by a reanalysis of eighteen of the original interview transcripts.

Size

Ontario school systems vary widely in size, those employing CEOs ranging in enrollment from approximately 1000 students to over 100,000, the median enrollment being 8700. Such large size variations obviously reflect proportional variations in the complexity of internal organizational structures and other related factors which could be expected to be associated with differences in the nature of the work environment and activities of CEOs. In order to explore this possibility during the reanalysis, the sample school systems were grouped into three size categories: Small (<10,000 students), Large (10,000 – 50,000) and Very Large (>50,000). Using this classification, seven of the twenty-two CEOs discussed here administered small school systems (SSS), eleven large systems (LSS) and four very large school systems (VLSS).[3] This 'sample' provides an inverse proportional representation of the population of Ontario CEOs, accounting for 57 per cent of the VLSs CEOs ($N = 7$), 22 per cent of those in LSS ($N = 50$), and 12 per cent in SSS ($N = 58$). The distribution of the respondents across these categories did, however, allow for within-group patterns of responses to be considered and for comparisons to be made across the overall size range.

All but two of the twenty-two CEOs considered here were men.[4] All had been teachers and most had spent at least several years as principals. Most had had considerable central office administrative experience in positions other than that of CEO, the total sample reporting a median of 7.2 years of experience in such positions. Only two members of the sample had served as CEOs of other systems prior to assuming their current post, which is consistent with McLeod's (1984) identification of an Ontario tradition discouraging lateral mobility among CEOs. Most of the CEOs considered here, then, were well experienced and seasoned educational administrators who had likely attained their professional apogee.

Analysis and Limitations

The transcript reanalysis sought to identify commonalities, contrasts and conceptual themes in the way the CEOs described and discussed their work and, where possible, to relate these to the organizational size of the school systems. Particular attention was paid to the responses given to interview questions which asked CEOs to identify the most important aspects of their job, the major responsibilities and tasks involved, the people and groups dealt with, and the relative influence of these others on the way in which CEOs structured their work. Comments dealing with these and related matters were noted, compared, counted, grouped and regrouped using the guidelines for the interpretation of qualitative data discussed by Miles and Huberman (1984).

Some of the interview transcripts were far more detailed than others, and this unevenness in the data could have distorted the findings in some respects. This limitation was borne in mind during the analysis and attempts were made to cross-check the conceptual 'patterns, themes or "Gestalts"' (*ibid*, p. 216) that emerged as the work progressed. There were limited opportunities for triangulation within the data, however, and it has not been possible to test the representativeness of emergent conceptual patterns through further interviews designed to feed back themes and images to the CEOs concerned or to others. These limitations, together with the relatively small size of the data set examined, should be borne in mind when considering the findings reported below.

Work Patterns

General Patterns

The image of the CEO's work life which emerged from the reanalysis of the Fullan *et al.*, interview data was generally similar to that presented in Mintzberg's (1973) influential study of executive work and reaffirmed in subsequent studies of school chiefs in other jurisdictions (for example, Duignan, 1980; Pitner and Ogawa, 1981; Willower and Fraser, 1979). On the whole the directors reported a work week of between forty and eighty hours, with most of this time being spent in interaction with others.

The transcripts contained references to tasks and duties which embodied or reflected aspects of Mintzberg's ten interrelated managerial work roles, namely the three interpersonal roles of figurehead, leader and liaison; the three informational roles of monitor, disseminator and spokesperson; and the four decisional roles of entrepreneur, disturbance handler, resource allocator and negotiator (pp. 167–70). But while there was some evidence in the transcripts of the 'brevity, variety and fragmentation' that Mintzberg (1973, p. 32) found to be so characteristic of managerial work, these qualities did not appear to dominate the work of Ontario school chiefs to the same degree as in the case of the executives studied by Mintzberg, or the school superintendents studied by Pitner and Ogawa and Duignan. Similarly, while it was clear that the work of these Ontario CEOs was, as in the case of other studies, primarily concerned with communication of various kinds, and that the basic 'tools' through which they conducted their work were the five basic media identified by Mintzberg (mail, telephone, unscheduled and scheduled meetings and tours), Ontario school chiefs appear to spend more of their time in regularly scheduled meetings than the subjects of previous studies. Duignan (1980), for example, reported that his eight Alberta superintendents spent roughly a quarter of their time in unscheduled, and a quarter in scheduled meetings, while Pitner's six California superintendents spent aggregates of 9 per cent and 46 per cent of their time in unscheduled and scheduled meetings respectively (Pitner and Ogawa, 1981). McLeod's (1984) published report of his study of Ontario directors, however, has them spending half to two-thirds of their working week in 'protracted meetings, usually involving large numbers of participants' (p. 175).

Timed observational data were not gathered in the original Fullan *et al.*, study, but the interview data support, and in some ways extend, this finding. CEOs typically reported that they had regularly scheduled administrative committee meetings several times a week as well as frequent, often daily, meetings with colleagues and in some cases trustees, plus, of course, regular board and board committee meetings. Ontario boards typically schedule one evening a week for regular meetings during the academic year, alternating standing committee and full board meetings every other week. Most of the CEOs, nonetheless, reported blocking out two or more evenings a week for meetings, with one sometimes being reserved for public relations functions in the community. Whether a schedule such as this results in Ontario school chiefs typically spending a greater proportion of their time in scheduled meetings than their counterparts in other jurisdictions is not, however, entirely clear. Mintzberg (1973), for instance, reported that the single school superintendent in his study spent 75 per cent of his time in scheduled meetings.

Even so, attendance at a large number of formal and semi-formal scheduled meetings will logically reduce the overall amount of brevity and fragmentation in the work of CEOs, and this might well explain why these commonly noted characteristics of managerial work were not readily apparent in the interview transcripts, especially as a fair proportion of the scheduled meetings attended by CEOs will be board or committee meetings of record wherein business will be conducted with appropriate structure and formality. Regardless, being at and in a multitude of time-tabled meetings is clearly the staple of a CEO's working life.

Work Patterns and System Size

Mintzberg also noted that chief executives of larger organizations typically attend slightly more scheduled meetings, and that these generally last longer and involve more participants, than those in smaller organizations. The transcript reanalysis found a similar pattern in the case of Ontario CEOs, particularly with regard to evening meetings. Whereas most of the SSS CEOs typically reported that they were engaged in meetings two to three nights a week, all three VLSS CEOs declared that they frequently attended meetings three to four evenings a week, one noting that during busy weeks he would have meetings every night of the week. Similarly, while some CEOs of small and large systems explained that they tried to keep their weekends free, others, and most particularly those in larger systems, reported that they often attended scheduled meetings during weekends.[5] One of the VLSS chiefs, for instance, explained that he had regularly scheduled meetings on two Saturdays and one Sunday each month. Some of the CEOs who declared that they attempted to keep their weekends free also noted that they would often spend part of this 'free time' engaged in paperwork, while one of the VLSS chiefs specifically explained that he always reserved Sunday afternoon for 'homework'. Others made similar references to Sunday as a kind of 'sanctuary day' free of formal commitments which allowed them to catch up with outstanding work and reading.

Sectored Work Environment

Analysis of the transcripts suggested that the CEOs tended to sector their work environment and their responsibilities into three domains: board, system and community. Each of these sectors appeared to represent a different but reciprocal action arena with a distinct set of obligations and objectives.

Different CEOs reported spending more or less time and care on one or another sector. In several cases CEOs understood that the board expected them to tighten up certain aspects of system operations and as a consequence of this 'commission' from the board they deliberately involved themselves more in the workings of the system. Others believed that it was important to better represent the system to the community and thus they tended to place more emphasis on this sector, taking care to develop good links to community groups. In another case a CEO confided that he gave hardly any attention to the community sector except for necessary ceremonial events, preferring to 'leave all that to the trustees'. The relative emphasis placed on the three sectors also appeared to be related in some respects and in varying degrees to the size of the system. Additional details are discussed below, but in general activities involving the board and community sectors figured more prominently in the transcripts from LSS and VLSS directors, while SSS chiefs appeared to be more directly concerned with system operations. Yet regardless of the relative emphasis each CEO placed on one or another of these sectors, most seemed to perceive each as a distinct domain. More importantly, they also appeared to share a common understanding that the elements of one sector should not, ideally, intrude in an uncontrolled manner on another. Thus, in addition to regarding each sector with a different gaze, they were generally concerned to keep them apart.

This general desire to keep the elements of each sector in their proper place was most evident at the interface between the board and the system sectors. As expressed by one CEO, this is essentially a matter of 'buffering' the system from the trustees. This is not to imply that the CEOs attempted to sabotage or otherwise disrupt the implementation of board policies. On the contrary, the transcripts showed CEOs as having a strong sense of loyalty toward official system policy. Indeed, they recognized a clear duty to implement properly constituted board directives; but at the same time they recognized a collateral duty to help the board make good policy and try and head off decisions and actions, particularly by individual trustees, that they believed would unnecessarily endanger the operation and health of the system. Consequently, many of the interview transcripts contained an implicit, and at times explicit, distinction between the corporate board and its constitutionally supreme authority on one hand, and trustees as fallible individuals on the other.

The Board Sector

The interview data did not directly illuminate the way in which CEOs interacted with the board in its corporate manifestation. From clues in these data and McLeod's account, however, it would seem that if things are going well the CEO's main task during formal meetings will be to ensure that all the necessary props and actors are at hand and hope that the talk and action does not diverge too far from the roughly drafted script. Control of board meetings, of course, resides with the chairperson, but the transcripts suggest that there will likely be a close working relationship between this key individual and the CEO.

CEOs and Chairpeople

Many CEOs commented on the importance of the relationship and their frequent meetings with the chairperson to discuss the general state of affairs and the business of the next board meeting. Often, it appears, meetings between the chairperson and CEO revolve around the agenda for the next board meeting during which both content and procedure are reviewed, and potential problems and possible solutions are discussed. Semi-formal review meetings of this kind may occur weekly, but in some instances CEOs and chairpeople meet much more regularly. One of the VLSS chiefs, for instance, reported that he met with his chairperson every day, while five of the other CEOs also mentioned that they met or talked to their chairperson 'most days'.

Trustees

Many CEOs, and particularly those of Large and Very Large systems, also reported a great deal of interaction with other trustees. To some degree this may have been an outcome of the timing of the research and the phrasing of key questions in the interview protocol. Most of the interviews were conducted shortly after school board elections, and many CEOs commented on the need to socialize the new trustees to their role — a revealing comment in itself. Unfortunately, interview questions designed to probe responsibilities and roles also asked respondents to frame their answers with regard to their work 'over the last two months'. Nevertheless, it would seem that many of the CEOs, particularly those in larger systems,met frequently with trustees to answer questions regarding system operations and discuss Ministry policy, community developments and, of course, board business and political issues. This aspect of a CEO's work appears to be less dominant in smaller systems, trustees being identified far less frequently in the SSS transcripts when the respondents were asked to discuss the extent to which they worked with different individuals and groups. Even so, individual and small group meetings with trustees is clearly a delicate aspect of a CEO's work, for he or she cannot afford to be suspected of taking sides in political struggles between trustees. One of the VLSS interviewees was particularly candid on this point and took care to point out that he was scrupulously open and above board in all such encounters.

Strong collaborative data on the importance of the relationship between the CEO and board members emerged in the answers trustees gave in response to being asked their expectations for the CEO. As expressed in the Fullan *et al.* (1987) report, trustees said that they wanted:

> ... good and complete information from the [CEO], but even more they want advice, recommendations, and direction. This expectation seems to be paramount, as was expressed by virtually all trustees we interviewed. One trustee suggested a further refinement, the [CEO] 'getting trustees to recognize the implications of their own ideas'. In other words the CEO is to protect trustees from the unanticipated consequences of their own actions ... [Also] trustees assume the [CEO] will inform them of the *political* consequences of the policies they suggest, but it involves more than just this. As one trustee put it, 'I expect the [CEO] to anticipate moves on the part of various trustees and others in the system, and have a motion in mind that would satisfy the various elements'. (p. 78)

Flight Plans

Clearly advice and guidance of such magnitude and sensitivity cannot be given in the fishbowl of a public meeting and must, perforce, be sought 'backstage', hence the previous reference to the roughly drafted script for formal meetings of the corporate board. This tentative outline will not necessarily have been drafted by the CEO and chairperson alone, for each trustee will likely anticipate his or her part and that of others as well as the general ebb and flow of debate. Even when the outcome of a vote is unpredictable, the alternatives to be decided will likely have been consensually culled to eliminate the unpalatable, perhaps during the committee of the whole discussion that many Ontario boards hold *in camera* immediately prior to their public meetings. In such a scenario, the function of the CEO is analogous to that of an air traffic controller equipped with an intermittently functioning and somewhat unreliable radar set. He has a fair idea of the location, route and probable destination of each trustee, and he and the chairperson will likely have drafted rough flight plans and discussed possible emergency procedures. But there is always the risk of turbulence, especially if unpredictable elements intrude. Moreover, political expediencies can result in trustees making sudden inflight manoeuvres.

Difficulties

The details of managing the board sector can be complex, especially given the number of trustees, often fifteen or more, that sit on the larger Ontario boards and the emergence of the 'full-time' trustee (Hickcox, 1974). It would also be incorrect to imply that the relationships between CEOs, the corporate board and individual trustees are always respectful and orderly. The interview data suggest that tension and conflict can be inescapable aspects of the CEO's work, especially when a board is divided along political lines or trustees involve themselves with system elements, frequent references to both of these contingencies being found in the transcripts, particularly those from CEOs of VLSS. Nevertheless, the account given above is believed to approach the truth of the matter, although it does not fully apply to all situations. One CEO of a large system, for instance, declared that he did not spend a lot of time with trustees because 'we do our dealings at board meetings, not behind the scenes'.

The System Sector

As would be expected, CEOs also reported that they interacted frequently with their supervisory officers and school based personnel, this being, of course, the prime means by which they manage the system itself. Working with and through senior colleagues is obviously another important medium through which CEOs draft the scripts, rehearse key parts and ensure the readiness of essential props in preparation for meetings with the corporate board and its committees. McLeod's (1984) composite vignette captured this aspect of work with senior staff well:

> In the conference room Alex and his superintendents work through each agenda item for tonight's meeting.... What will the trustees say to our recommendation on the next item? The [CEO] draws his aides' attention to a particular document. At this time it is potentially too explosive to take to the board. Reroute it through channels! ... The [CEO] wants a briefing on agenda item #3. He knows that it falls within the Superintendent of Business's bailiwick. Yet trustees like to quiz their CEO on whim it seems. Besides, his subordinate will benefit from this rehearsal. Alex takes his turn at giving background information.

He explains the budget situation . . . [and] . . . counsels his superintendent on how to present the figures to trustees. After 70 minutes and scrutiny of 13 agenda items, the administrators disperse. (p. 181)

In addition to the obvious similarity to a dress rehearsal, this slice of a CEO's work life shows clearly how he must meld his private knowledge of trustees' 'flight plans' with the administrative workflow of the system, while at the same time ensuring all the necessary reports and information will be on hand and that his people are well briefed and primed for their performances.

Direct and Indirect Management

Nevertheless, most of a CEO's work meetings with his subordinate administrators appear to have a tighter focus on the internal operations of the system. In the smaller systems, CEOs reported that they were of necessity directly involved with one or more aspect of system operations. One SSS chief, for example, talked about his personal involvement in teacher evaluations, another his work implementing a new elementary school computer program and several others their responsibilities for contract negotiations with teachers and non-professional staff. As noted previously, CEOs of smaller systems appear to spend less time in scheduled meetings, and from the transcript analysis they tend to manage system affairs primarily through individual contacts with other SOs and principals.

Functional and structural differentiation in larger systems ensure that system operations are attended to by subordinates, with the co-ordination and supervision of school and system operations in the larger systems being handled by senior SOs, and in the largest by deputy directors. In LSS and VLSS much of the CEO's system sector work is typically conducted in and through regularly scheduled 'cabinet' meetings with senior SOs, 'council' meetings with larger groups of system administrators, often including principals, as well, of course, through discussions with individual superintendents or ad hoc groups of colleagues. These various internal meetings are the media through which most CEOs of larger systems appear to manage the flow of information, issues, and decisions in the organization, and they also provide the main means by which they keep in touch with events, happenings and developments. Several CEOs described this aspect of their work as 'supervising the other SOs', and it would seem that each meeting or encounter allows the CEO to review the status of various issues, projects, processes, and proposals, and if necessary, give additional instructions or advice. New problems or concerns are also identified, categorized, solved, delegated or otherwise assigned a place within the administrative workflow.

Principals

Three-quarters of the CEOs reported that they also had direct dealings with principals. Some CEOs reported that they met regularly with specific groups of principals, while others said that they only dealt with principals 'on demand'. Principals figured more prominently in the SSS transcripts, and it appears that CEOs of smaller systems typically rely on and interact more frequently with their principals than is the case in larger systems with their greater numbers of central office administrators. One SSS CEO explained that he used his principals as consultants, while two others specifically identified principals as the group which had the greatest impact on their work. None of the LSS or VLSS CEOs, however, mentioned principals in their responses to this question, all nominating either trustees or supervisory offers as the group having the greatest impact on their work.

School Visits

Brief meetings with principals were also mentioned as a feature of school visits, with half of the CEOs offering specific comments on this aspect of their work. Three of the LSS transcripts and two of those from VLSS revealed that the CEOs concerned had attempted to deliberately integrate school visits into their regular work activities. One LSS chief declared that he visited one school each week, another that he visited three schools a month. Similarly, one VLSS director said 'Tuesday is school day', another that he tried for half-a-day each week in schools. Three of the SSS chiefs also specifically mentioned school visits, but in two of these cases the CEOs complained that they had difficulty in finding the time to 'get out to the schools', a problem that was clearly exacerbated by the very large geographical area of some systems. This was also a factor in the third instance, but in this exceptional case that CEO explained that because he was new to the system he had made it a priority to personally visit every classroom. Thus, while some CEOs of both large and small systems saw school visits as an important aspect of their work, the demands of other responsibilities and the greater travelling distances involved appeared to make this more difficult in the smaller systems.

Other specific aspects of the CEO's work that appeared in the transcripts were the generic administrative tasks of making decisions, solving problems and resolving conflicts.Little specific information was given in the transcripts on the kinds of decisions, problems and conflicts that they handled personally. It would appear, however, that many concern or arise directly from managing the administrative workflow, while others are rooted in disturbances in the board and community sectors, or are associated with an intrusion of one sector into another.

Difficult Relationships

One interesting point here was that when asked to identify groups with whom they had particularly difficult relationships, CEOs of Small and Large systems typically identified two or three or more such groups, whereas the VLSS directors named very few, if any, such groups. One VLSS chief said that he had recently had a difficult experience with the caretakers' union, but that that particular problem was not part of his formal responsibilities and he had chosen to become personally involved in resolving the matter. Another simply declared that he did 'not really' have any difficult relationships. One SSS chief gave a similar answer, but all others and all the LSS chiefs identified groups with whom they had what appeared to be continuing difficulties. The most frequently mentioned were teacher federations (unions) and other employee unions, some respondents explaining that contract negotiations and grievances were particularly troublesome.

The Community Sector

All but one of the transcripts contained comments dealing with work and responsibilities outside of the system and board sectors. Taken together these comments defined and encompassed four environmental precincts, as it were, each of which can be taken as constituting a sub-sector of the community oriented activities engaged in by CEOs.

Public Relations

Nine of the CEOs made specific reference to 'PR work' of one kind or another. The LSS CEOs appeared to be more concerned with and active in this area. One declared that he spent 'a lot of time doing PR work in the community', another that he 'does a lot of community PR stuff'. For the most part this would seem to consist of maintaining contact with and making presentations to what one described as 'education related groups and service groups'. One CEO said that he regularly made 'forty-fifty presentations a year', and this may not be atypical for CEOs who place a high priority on this precinct of the community sector. Specific references were also made to 'ratepayers', and one to the 'communities', meaning the different towns and other settlements within the boundaries of the system. On this point, the CEO in question explained that 'we're going to nail them for increased taxes so we need their support'.

There were far fewer references to public relations activities in the SSS and VLSS transcripts, and those that were made tended to have a different flavour. Two SSS CEOs, for example, cited their involvement in preparing newsletters as an illustrative instance of their public relations work while another confessed that he didn't like to speak to public groups and thus did very little. None of the VLSS chiefs talked specifically about 'PR' work, but each made references to the importance of representing the board to the community, particularly through attendance at community oriented school activities and symbolic and ceremonial events such as civic functions, dinners, retirement and funerals. As expressed by one VLSS chief, 'senior administration *has to be seen* to be meeting the needs of the community' (my emphasis).

Interagency Liaison

The establishment and maintenance of formal or semi-formal working contacts with local agencies also emerged as an aspect of a CEO's community oriented activities. Here emphasis is placed on the exchange of information relevant to the operation of the system and, particularly in the smaller systems, the direct management and coordination of inter-organizational relationships between the system and various community agencies. One specific example given was the management of shared facilities, a task which has gained increased importance and complexity in smaller systems with the advent of government funding for Roman Catholic high schools and the entrenchment of French language education rights. Other examples mentioned in the transcripts included liaison with social and municipal agencies.

Parents

Perhaps surprisingly, only four of the transcripts made specific references to parents, but in each case the relevant comments portrayed parents as a distinct element within the external environment. Also in each case, their references associated parents with problems of one kind or another. One CEO, for example, described his relationship with parents as primarily one of handling complaints, another explained that he saw his role toward parents as being 'available and understanding', while another declared somewhat ruefully that 'parents think I can solve all problems'.

Professional Community

Finally, there was clear evidence in the transcripts that the CEOs devoted some of their scarce time to maintaining contact with their professional colleagues and peers, and gathering intelligence at conferences and other information oases. Few specifics were given, but it would seem that attendance at Ministry briefings and participation in professional activities provide important vehicles for both gathering and exchanging information. No reliable measure on how much time CEOs spend on this aspect of their work was available, but one declared that he regularly devoted 10–15 per cent of his time to 'out-of county' activities. Some CEOs complained that they were caught in a 'catch-22' in this part of their work, for while it was necessary for them to spend time out-of-system to gain the up-to-date information demanded by trustees, some of their political masters also wanted 'their' CEO to be available to them at all times.

Discussion

Three broad and related points emerge from the analysis reported above. First, the work and role of Ontario CEOs as represented in the data discussed here broadly conforms to previous analyses of executive work and that of school system chiefs in particular. As noted at the outset of the analysis and illustrated throughout the account of the findings, the descriptions which CEOs gave of their work reflected the managerial roles identified by Mintzberg (1973) as well as the nature and texture of the work done by the executives he studied and the school superintendents studied by others. Given the differences between the historical, organization and institutional contexts of Ontario directors and American superintendents discussed elsewhere (Allison and Allison, 1988; Allison, 1988; Chapter 9), this is itself a notable finding.

Generalism

Second, while there were clear similarities between the findings of this and earlier work, at the same time the description and analysis of the work of Ontario CEOs offered here also helps illustrate other aspects of executive work which were not stressed in previous studies. One synthesizing concept which helps capture some key elements of the CEOs orientation to their work environment is provided by Hodgkinson's (1978) notion of generalism. He has argued that whereas management is essentially a specialism, administration is a generalism. He further refined this point by noting that the chief executive is the organization's 'specialist in generalism' (p. 17). As such he or she is naturally more concerned with ends than means; with the broad coordination of effort, rather than the handling of specific functions; with the future than the present, and with planning rather than reacting.

Such characteristics were threaded through the account of CEO's work offered above, and seem particularly evident in the ways in which

CEOs relate to and integrate elements within the board, system and community sectors of their work environment. Their interactions with each of these sectors provide them with unique opportunities to accumulate information and develop in their minds a broad but complex image of the system which is more detailed and complete than that held by others. Their unique knowledge of each of the three sectors together with their broad general understanding of the organization enables them to explain, interpret and relate each sector to the others. In addition, their role requires them to use their unique knowledge to balance, arbitrate and when possible harmonize many diverse and often inherently conflictual expectations and demands. In essence, they must use their specialized generalist understanding of the organization and its operations to guide, integrate and choose between the specialized specialist understandings and interests of others. (Also see chapter 6 on this point)

This view is supported by pertinent findings in the original Fullan *et al.* (1987) report. In the course of analyzing the work of all the supervisory officers interviewed, the researchers developed three summative style dimensions: system-driven vs school driven; reflective vs fire-fighting and generalist vs specialist (pp. 81–5). As would be expected, CEOs were found to be dominantly system oriented, but they were also strongly reflective and overwhelmingly generalist in orientation. Their subordinate superintendents, on the other hand, were rated consistently lower on all three dimensions.

Size

Finally, while there would appear to be broad similarities in the work environment of Ontario CEOs, a number of size related differences in both the nature of the work and the emphasis placed on particular tasks and relationships were noted. Thus, while the construct of a sectored work environment appeared to accurately account for the way in which CEOs in Small, Large and Very Large systems structured their activities and understood their main tasks and responsibilities, differences in the emphasis which CEOs placed on their dealings with each sector and differences in the ways in which they interacted with each appeared to be at least partially related to the organizational size of the system. Other factors such as the administrative style of the CEO concerned, his or her personal values, specific directives or policies of the board and so forth, would account for some of the differences but the size of the system and related structural and environmental factors seem to offer a more consistent and parsimonious explanation for some of the patterned differences noted. The tendency for CEOs of SSS to be involved in managing some discrete operational aspects of the system while those in larger systems concentrate on coordinating and supervising the work of supervisory officers provides one of the more obvious examples. The greater emphasis which many CEOs of LSS appeared to place on managing the board sector and participating in public relations activities might constitute another, as might the more ceremonial involvement of VLSS CEOs in the community sector and the way in which they appear to be able to resist entanglement in difficult relationships with groups with which the board and other administrators must deal.

Spectrum of Abstraction

Size related differences in the work of CEOs can be related to the notion of generalism discussed above with the assistance of an empirically based theory advanced by Jaques (1976). His scheme recognized the existence of a profound disjunction between the administration of what he calls direct command and general command systems. In Jaques' words, the heart of this difference involves

> the step from work and management based upon concrete modes of thought to work and management based on abstract modes of thought. No longer can the chief executive or manager perceptually encompass the whole of this task, even by imaginal scanning. He must be able to detach himself sufficiently from the concrete situation to be able to gain a rounded perspective and grasp it by means of conceptually formulated information. (p. 318)

Jaques' theory also contemplates the existence of higher and more abstract levels of imaginal complexity in the administration of particularly large organizations. His notion of general command systems is quite similar to Hodgkinson's idea of generalism, and taken together the two views suggest a spectrum of conceptual abstraction in the governance of organizations ranging from concrete, material and specialist emphasis and orientations in smaller systems to more indirect, abstract and generalist modes in larger systems.

There are problems in matching Jaques organizational size categories to school systems, but the administration of at least the smaller systems in the SSS category used there could be taken as embodying elements of his direct command systems. As such, Jaques' theory and the notion of a spectrum of conceptual abstraction offers a basis for interpreting and relating the size related differences noted above. Moreover, the VLSS could be recognized as Stratum 4 and 5 organizations in Jaques' scheme, in which case his theory predicts that the CEOs of these particularly large systems would be required to work at even higher levels of abstraction and generalization. No clear test of this hypothesis was possible with the data considered here, but the findings reported above would appear to provide some support for such a view. Nevertheless, the Jaques-Hodgkinson notion of a size related spectrum of conceptual abstraction and generalism in the orientation of chief school officers to their work environment would appear to offer a potentially profitable avenue for future research, especially as it embodies profound implications for the education and selection of school chiefs of different sized systems.

Conclusion

Despite the limitations of the data considered in the reanalysis reported here, the findings and explanatory images discussed appear to offer useful insights into the work of Chief Education Officers. Although relatively simple and not particularly novel, the construct of a sectored work environment developed in this paper appears to be solidly anchored in the data and could well provide a useful framework for future work. The possible effect of organizational size and related factors of the administration of school systems and how chief school officers orient themselves to their work environment also seems worthy of further study, and the notion of a spectrum of abstraction and generalism outlined above may prove useful in this respect. Yet regardless of the conceptual frames which may guide future work in this area, the important point would seem to be that we seek ways to better understand how chief administrators understand their world and their work.

Notes

1 A previous version of this chapter entitled 'Exploring the work of school chiefs: The case of the Ontario director of education ', appeared in *The Alberta Journal of Educational Research,* 1989, XXXV, 4, pp. 292–307.
2 Excluding the Metropolitan Toronto School Board.
3 The eighteen original interview transcripts on which the bulk of the detailed analysis reported here was based were distributed across these size categories as follows: Seven from SSS, eight from LSS and three from VLSS.
4 Male pronouns are used throughout the discussion of the transcript reanalysis in order to avoid inadvertently identifying the two women CEOs in the sample or attributing quotations to them.
5 One partial exception here concerns some of the northern SSS where the directors noted that regular board meetings were held on Saturdays.

References

ALLISON, D.J. (1988) '*Ontario directors and American superintendents: A study of contrasting cultures and contexts*', Paper presented to the Department of Educational Administration, University of Alberta.

Allison, D.J. and Allison, P.A. (1988) 'Discovering the Ontario school chief: Insights from the Fullan, Park and Williams study of supervisory officers', *Proceedings of the Conference 'The Chief School Officer'*, Centre for Executive Studies, Department of Educational Administration, Ontario Institute for Studies in Education, Toronto, Ontario, pp. 73–132.

Allison, D.J. and Wells, A. (1989) School supervision in Ontario' in Boich, J.W., Farquhar, R.H. and Leithwood, K.A. (Eds) *The Canadian School Superintendent*, Toronto, OISE Press, pp. 69–114.

Barnard, C. (1938) *The Functions of the Executive*, Cambridge, MA Harvard University Press.

Blumberg, A. (1985) *The School Superintendent: Living with Conflict*, New York, Teachers College Press.

Duignan, P. (1980) 'Administrative behavior of superintendents: A descriptive study', *Journal of Educational Administration*, 18, 1, pp. 5–26.

Fullan, M.G., Park, P.B., Williams, T.R., Allison, P., Walker, L. and Watson, N. (1987) *The Supervisory Officer in Ontario: Current Practice and Recommendations for the Future,* Toronto, Ontario, Ontario Ministry of Education.

Hickcox, E.S. (1974) 'The trustee and the administrator', *Education Canada*, pp. 34–8.

Hodgkinson, C. (1978) *Towards a Philosophy of Administration*, Oxford, Blackwell.

Jaques, E. (1976) *A General Theory of Bureaucracy*, London, Heinemann.

McLeod, G.T. (1984) 'The work of school board chief executive officers', *Canadian Journal of Education*, 9, 2, pp. 171–90.

Miles, M.B. and Huberman, A.M. (1984) *Qualitative Data Analysis,* Beverly Hills, CA, Sage.

Mintzberg, H. (1973) *The Nature of Managerial Work,* New York, Harper and Row.

Ontario (1980) *Education Act*, revised Statutes of Ontario, Chapter 129. (Office Consolidation, August 1988).

Pitner, H.J. and Ogawa, R.T. (1981) 'Organizational leadership: The case of the school superintendent', *EducationalAdministration Quarterly*, 17, 2, pp. 45–65.

Tyack, D. and Hansot, E. (1982) *Managers of Virtue: Public School Leadership in America, 1920–1980*, New York, Basic Books.

Willower, D.J. and Fraser, H.W. (1979) 'School superintendents on their work', *Notebook*, 28, 5.

Chapter 3

Policy Administration as Rhetoric: One Leader and His Arguments

Richard G. Townsend

Based on participant observations, over much of a year, of an outstanding Director of Education, this account put its subject into his institutional setting, still a fairly rare approach for a single-actor study in the politics of education. The norm for research on the powerful is to tell how time is spent doing the job, what his/her views are, how the executives fight in battles, and whom he/she likes or dislikes. Seldom is an effort made to tell how much or how little he or she tries to persuade others of policy directions. With this attempt to study a Director functioning with fellow educators, secretaries, and custodians, the chapter is a study of a man interacting with various work groups.

Administration may have preceded rhetoric — indeed my old teacher Lewis Mumford (1967) has argued that the first humans integrated large-scale public affairs through such administrative activities as planning, organizing, scheduling and controlling before they even learned how to speak. Today, however, as top administrators work through contextual persuasion to affect people, the coordinating of activities hinges to some extent on the quality of a leader's skills in argumentation.

In this chapter, I explore aspects of the policy discourse for one executive, seeing him as a something of a stand-in for other peak administrators. Little serious work has been done in this realm. Traditional students of public policy tend to prefer explaining allocations in terms of long-term forces such as political culture, class, ideology, presence of unions, and levels of problem-solving knowledge. If these scholars comment at all on 'the rhetorical', it is as insincere, decorative, extravagant or manipulative talk. Likewise, leadership consultants give higher priority to attributes such as persistence, stability, and 'concept of the total' than to a policy administrator or leader's 'mere' rhetoric. In contra-distinction to these forebears, I propose to conceptually link the domains of leadership, policy and oral rhetoric.

Bases in Three Domains

Writers within the vast prescriptive literature on leadership see the executive as prompting events to happen, if she or he stays well informed, takes risks, focuses time and energy, facilitates log-rolling, creates winning coalitions, and appreciates that any altering of others' preferences at best occurs only gradually (for example, Bennis, 1976; Wrapp, 1984). Texts in the field of educational administration (for example, Immegart, 1988) are among the most hopeful that leaders can indeed make a difference; presumably, in certain situations a positional leader's values, traits, styles, articulations of purposes, and alignments to expectations of outside forces can non-coercively direct and coordinate others' means and ends. Interpreters of empirical studies have found that appointed leaders of schools can have impact in certain kinds of issues (internal and routine policy decisions) within certain kinds of communities (larger and more heterogeneous ones) (Boyd, 1976b; but also see Lutz and Iannaccone, 1978; and Burlingame, 1988). However, a number of other modern analyses are more pessimistic about the impacts of leadership (Burns, 1978; Edinger, 1976; Hocklin, 1977). There, unless they happen to appear at one of history's 'forking points' to act as institutional embodiments of purpose, very senior executives are perceived as so constrained by institutional, political, psychological, and other variables that they have relatively little scope within which to act (Paige, 1977; McLeod, 1988). Just as well too that rulerships are contained, some observers might add: a leader can over-simplify, become obsolescent in information, adapt irrelevant criteria for policy-making, lose a sense of proportion, sacrifice a value base, and so on.

A rather different perception has been developed of late among a number of non-traditional students of public policy who emphasize the autonomy of the state (Downs, 1967; Block, 1980; Poulantzas, 1978; Gogh, 1979; Pal, 1987). Those who occupy state positions are thought to possess their own values, powers, material bases, and insights. Neither dominated by capitalists or labor, these public authorities can be regarded as self-interested maximizers, pursuing personal prestige as well as income and their sense of morality through expansions of their services to diverse publics. Empirical spadework is necessary to conform or disconfirm this conceptual lead, but this view of the state *is* promising as it opens up the possibility of public managers expressing their own creativities and dispositions, perhaps becoming leaders for the good, right and just life. A unique quality of institutional leadership, or statesmanship, may reside then in ways of defining and justifying organizational policy. State policies, then, would more than simply reflect the ruling class and those long-term movements of society that traditional policy students have noticed. A role would exist after all for human agency.

At bottom, my assumption is that human agency is reflected in rhetoric. As means of persuasion, rhetoric taps public hopes and fears, helps to unify audiences, promulgates communal values, and demonstrates the orator's self-consciousness of his or her role and station (Ryan, 1988). Also in argumentation, a leader is involved in a process of policy construction, finding good reasons for public actions, helping to bring focus to the behavior of organizational members, projecting identities for his or her guidelines for public action. On the premise that such mobilizations of support are worth analyzing, here I explore one policy administrator's argumentation.

In effect, I am maintaining that policy administration is a process of arguing. In a democracy, officials do not simply make policies; if they have reasons, they have to give them. Like politicians who offer constituents justifications for their votes or akin to lobbyists who represent their causes as serving public interests, elite administrators have to put forward the assumptions that undergird their claim. This rhetoric can deter critics — even if the grounds are afterthoughts, intended to rationalize decisions taken on other reasons. More specifically, students of argumentation (for example, Toulmin, 1958; Freeley, 1976) would hold that at least six categories are vital. The reader should not despair if she or he does not quite 'connect' with all of this listing; while it is more than a jumping-off point, the key pillars are the fourth and fifth categories (*Warrant* and *Backing*).

1 *Relevant information*, i.e., evidence from policy problems, alternatives, actions, outcomes and performances; these data can be in the form of conclusions, expressed needs, generalized statistics, and so forth.
2 *Claim*, i.e., the conclusion of the policy argument, typically the subject of disagreement or conflict among different segments of the community. When a policy claim follows the presentation of information, the claim implies 'therefore'. For example, if semestering is more efficient and effective (*relevant information*), it follows therefore that secondary schools should forego teaching courses for short periods over year-long bases, i.e., half-year courses should be scheduled for extended periods of the school day. Hence, policy claims are the logical consequence of policy-relevant information.

3 *Qualifier*, i.e., the degree to which the arguer is certain about a claim, ranging from 'Definitely' to 'Probably Not'.
4 *Warrant*, i.e., the assumption which permits an argument to move from relevant information to claim. One explanatory warrant: the concentrations afforded by semestered courses are the best way to ensure that students master assigned materials. The role of the warrant is to carry information to a claim about which there is dissensus, thus providing a reason for accepting the claim.
5 *Backing*, i.e., an additional assumption that may support a warrant which may not be accepted at face value. A backing enables a policy advocate to step back further and state underlying assumptions. For semestering fewer courses over a single term, the start of an explanatory backing could be 'less is more', i.e., if scheduling allows longer lessons, teachers can work at greater depth every day with students. A motivational backing for educators is: 'With fewer students each term, semestering would mean you'd get to know your students better and have fewer discipline problems.'
6 *Rebuttal*, i.e., an anticipated objection to a claim. Against semestering, a rebuttal might be that semestering undercuts certain subjects like instrumental music where practice throughout a year-long course can facilitate the acquisition of greater skill. Of course, this objection itself can be rebutted; students who participate in community bands can extend their skills over the whole year.[1]

Students of rhetoric have interpreted and applied these distinctions,so that policy warrants and backings can now be separated into at least seven modes or frames: method-centred, intuitive, ethical, causal, motivational, parallel case or comparative, and authoritative (Brockriede and Ehninger, 1960; Rein, 1976; MacRae, 1976; Dunn, 1981).[2] I do not maintain that certain modes are more highly valued than others.

For a second example of the structure of an argument, consider this drastically abbreviated reasoning for one reform in education. Chauvinists may declare that the following arguments are a smokescreen for women's self-interest, but I believe that real values which are unconnected to any obvious short-term interest, are at stake.

Figure 3.1. Diagram of a Short Argument for Affirmative Action

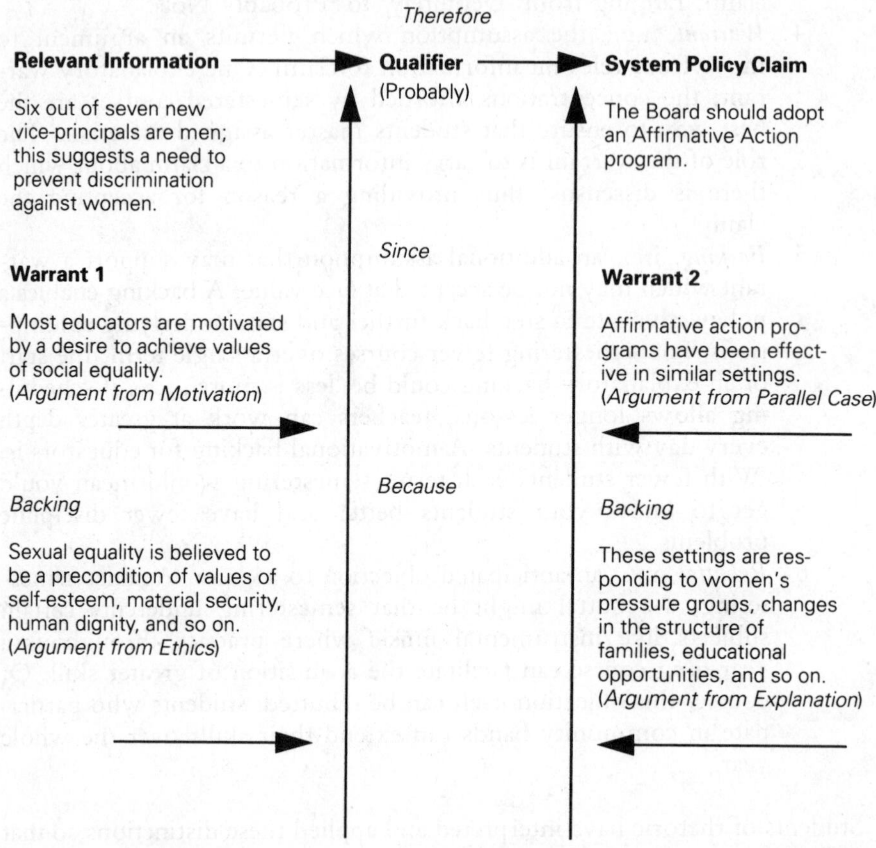
Therefore
Relevant Information
Six out of seven new vice-principals are men; this suggests a need to prevent discrimination against women.
Qualifier
(Probably)
System Policy Claim
The Board should adopt an Affirmative Action program.
Since
Warrant 1
Most educators are motivated by a desire to achieve values of social equality.
(Argument from Motivation)
Warrant 2
Affirmative action programs have been effective in similar settings.
(Argument from Parallel Case)
Because
Backing
Sexual equality is believed to be a precondition of values of self-esteem, material security, human dignity, and so on.
(Argument from Ethics)
Backing
These settings are responding to women's pressure groups, changes in the structure of families, educational opportunities, and so on.
(Argument from Explanation)

Below, elements of argumentation are introduced separately and more fully.

Even though the scholarly literature for several decades has carried the idea of the policy process as a succession of distinct phases (Dror, 1968; May and Wildavsky, 1978; Hogwood and Gunn, 1984), so far as I know, little work connects these phases to acts of leadership, especially leadership in and for schools. Hodgkinson's value paradigm (1978) is a notable exception and a few studies (for example, Begley and Leithwood, 1989) have built upon that important sorting of values of preference, consequence, consensus and freely chosen principle in policy-making and managing. Even more unstudied is an executive's rhetoric about issues during policy stages. While agreement does not exist on the number of these stages through which an issue may pass, a convention is that at the very least the policy cycle includes formulation, implementation, and evaluation. While a school administrator may make a big deal about the difference between policy and administration, to her and him the dividing lines between these stages often may appear artificial, not demarcations that she or he consciously employs when reacting to (and defining for school board members) a new problem in the field. Nevertheless, this trilogy of phases is employed below for heuristic purposes.

But first let me introduce the 45-year-old Director of Education whose rhetoric I start to dissect. Examples of his argumentation comprise most of this chapter. That detailing necessarily is idiosyncratic and situation-specific, and some readers will find my treatment boring, especially since (as it happens) a fairly complimentary portrait of an administrator emerges. Those only interested in glimpsing a brief outline of the most critical of my conclusions about argumentation can turn directly to the penultimate section, 'Leadership, Policy, and Argument'.

Wally Beevor, Policy Administrator

Wally Beevor is, as a group of secondary students said in a musical tribute to him, 'energetic, ruggedly handsome, [with a] friendly handshake, silvery hair, a friendly smile ... and sparkling eyes.... a really cool dude'. Also, he is one of Canada's dozen or so most widely known chief executive officers for elementary and secondary schools. To begin, Beevor is celebrated for having developed in the 1970s, while at the Lakehead Board in a corner of northern Ontario, a widely-copied plan for deferring salaries. Through it, teachers have the option of taking 80 per cent of their earnings each year over four years so that, in the fifth year, they are free from duties while earning their same income. Installing this scheme at a time of declining enrolments, Beevor initially sought to reduce layoffs of teachers. But when the numbers of students began climbing upwards again, his salary-holdback arrangement was turned into a tool for professional development: teachers used the plan to take fifth-year sabbaticals, sometimes to travel, to go to graduate school, or to learn more about themselves by trying out new ventures. At the provincial level, Beevor also had captured some attention by initiating 'single-team bargaining' at the Lakehead. Instead of adversarial teams facing each other during contract talks, representatives of labor and management were expected to (and apparently did) peaceably sit around a common table jointly settling problems. Remote as northerly Lakehead may seem in a jurisdiction as vast and truly far-flung as Ontario — after all, in area this province is larger than eight Czechoslovakias, or four United Kingdoms, or one-and-a-half Texases — Beevor's reputation for achievement, for organization, and for deflating contention would have preceded him to any board in that province.

By the time I caught up with him in Burlington for this study, Beevor had moved to the south-central part of Ontario and to the Halton

Board of Education, one of Canada's fifteen largest. For a large suburban/exurban county encompassing five somewhat competitive towns, he was administering eighty-two schools, 43,000 students (for most of whom discipline was not a major problem), and 5500 staff (some were using that salary-holdback scheme). Early on, Beevor had caused some stir across the province for firing, demoting, and transferring to 'Siberia' certain administrators he had inherited; 'ruthless' was the characterization made by those who thought that the protective Ontario 'way' was to cool out officials less abruptly and visibly. (Back in Lakehead too he had replaced senior administrators whom, it was said, 'did not sing from the same songbook' as he.) But six years later when we met, he seemed to be doing well in Halton: over 75 per cent of a group of citizens polled for a Board survey had given his organization a performance rating of A or B. To that realm, Beevor had not succeeded in importing single-team bargaining; Halton, after all, is fiscally conservative, and undercapitalized. It is a place where 'we count paper clips for God's Sake' and where even the idea of collective bargaining could be anathema to a former trustee who has said that 'letting teachers bargain is like letting the monkeys dish out the peanuts'. Yet in any event, for the most part, Beevor's tenure had been marked by peaceably-settled negotiations, a spinoff perhaps of his upbeat style. Differing from a number of other Ontario executives in local spotlights, he is not a mean person.

Over the course of a year and with no set framework in mind, as a 'shadow' I observed Beevor interact with individuals at various levels of his organization. Additionally, I queried over forty-five persons who had first-hand knowledge of 'life with Beevor'. My data-gathering was brought to a close in 1988 when Beevor resigned from Halton to accept a provincial posting as Assistant Deputy Minister of Education, in charge of a large division for initiating learning programs. I suspect that his new colleagues find him as I did, usually easy-talking but not verbally garrulous.[3]

In my hearing, Beevor never mentioned those analytical terms I introduced in the preceding section, i.e., claim, warrant, backing, value-critical, parallel case, and so forth. And he was as surprised as I that, in the end, my participant observations (including notes of various debates he got into) led to a codifying of a portion of his argumentation. Beevor probably would be surprised too if I were to depict him as a particularly original Herbert-Simon-like thinker on policy and leadership; much of what I heard Beevor say is reminiscent of the most recent treatises on management and on involving personnel at all levels in all functions (for example, Peters and Waterman, 1982; Newberry, 1987). If Beevor has a special handle on leadership, it seems to me that one part of that quality is his oral skill in claiming, for policy sake, that different things should be included in or excluded from various categories.

Though this study of a central leader's harnessing of rhetoric to policy may point in a fresh direction, this chapter still will disappoint readers looking for research based on a larger population than just one man. Yet profiles of single leaders do have their didactic strengths too, among which are their capacities for exploring new themes and for starting to bring alive detailed textures of particular circumstances. In the spirit of that case tradition but also cognizant of the methodological issues encountered when 'boswelling' a high official (MacPherson, 1985), I selectively present fragments of that texture in Halton. I am trying to develop an image that, although it is based on one administrator's unique experiences, catches the spirit of other policy leaders' language and action. This account further has the distinct advantage of being about a highly gifted and articulate administrator, something which a number of accounts are not (for example, Walcott's ethnography of the bland 'Ed Bell', 1971). (Had my findings turned out to be less sympathetic, I might have had to disguise the study's location and persons.)

A limitation of this study is that it does not acknowledge other gifted and articulate people at all levels in Halton, for example, teachers, support staff, principals, superintendents, ratepayers, trustees. Equally short shrift is given to historical antecedents to Beevor's tenure. Those pre-1981 circumstances and those gifted persons probably would do very well for any leader. For his part, Beevor recognizes that much of his success, if not his rhetoric, is fueled by others. A leader interacts with other leaders, in the process being coopted into new views — but that perspectives is not treated here either.

Finally, I recognize that I am not dealing with the whole gamut of leadership. With great oversimplification, Blanchard and Johnson (1984) propose these steps for leaders: (i) *tell* (what to do); (ii) *show* (how to do); (iii) *let* the follower try; (iv) *observe* performance; and (v) *praise* progress or *redirect*. This construction of reality is only about the very first step, telling.

Selected Arguments During Policy Formulation

Helping to choose problems for public action, articulating the professionals' criteria and priorities, and communicating to staff a Board's purposive interventions within an issue-area — these are crucial tasks that school executives undertake in policy formulation. Given that problems are multiple and that resources for their resolutions are scarce, competition among idea champions at this particular phase can be fierce. Even if absenting themselves from the remainder of the policy flow, winners at this stage achieve a crucial victory just by delineating problems that governments take hold of. In this phase, Beevor argues primarily but not exclusively on the bases of method and of value-criticism.

Arguing from Method

For more than a decade, Halton had had annual Aims and Objectives, a Priorities and Expenditures Committee to sort out various needs, an Innovations Committee which travelled across North America searching for good ideas, and task forces (for example, for teacher evaluation, primary education, leadership development) which looked ahead to imminent problems and opportunities. One of Beevor's contributions has been to sophisticate and refine this planning process. To a degree, he has done this by winning the debate over what is the valid method for defining situations, for debating right and wrong, and for placing one's preferred definitions onto the Board's crowded agenda. The central machinery of Beevor's administration includes 'situational analyses' and 'goal settings' which lead to highly visible 'policy developments' which become operationalized into 'five-year plans', budgets, and implementation activities. Through series of meetings, which can begin at the school, mission statements are floated, tested against precedents and available baseline or system data, and worked-over for consistency with other policies. More reactions now are elicited from more people on more committees. In his era at Halton, he introduced a language of how policy formulations become accepted (once different interests have negotiated ideas through those aforementioned hurdles of situational analyses, goal-settings, mission-statings, and other consistency-bringing steps). It is this procedure, incidentally, that has helped to give Beevor the reputation as being 'all process', a charge not supported by my data about his substance here.

With the help of Lorne Downey, a professor at the University of British Columbia and an authority on goals of school governance[4], Beevor made the claim (not long after his arrival) that Halton needed such an elaborate approach. To coax various political and bureaucratic interests to accept his meta (or transcending) routine, Beevor could point to his own situational analysis of the Halton Board he had just joined. Some friction at the Board table was common, trustees often ratifying proposals only by the slimmest of margins. Reportedly, a segment of these and other officials did not feel actively involved in orchestrating the system's future. And as his visits with principals seemed to prove, certain schools were not altogether buying into initiatives of the central office. Insiders seemed widely respectful and loyal to the Board's first two Directors, Jim Singleton from 1969–75 and Em (for Emerson) Lavender from 1975–81, but as with all the other systems that periodically chose to import top executives from outside the organization, Halton had reached a point in 1981 where 'new motivation, new communication, and a breath of fresh air seemed attractive'. Also appearing to need attention, according to the relevant information of some, was (i) the consultation process that Lavender particularly had been nurturing; and (ii) relationships, especially between the system and the media, between the business and pedagogical functions, between the centre and the periphery (i.e., some superintendents were not seen as facilitators).

To build confidence that any fragmentation could be overcome and that rational improvement was possible, Beevor and Downey held a seminar for the Board, stressing that their model for long-term policy development would help the trustees 'anticipate needs rather than respond to sudden issues'. By writing policy that would dovetail the best ideas from all levels, order and a systematic approach would be brought to organizational practice. (As backing to that method-centred warrant, Beevor pointed to a number of other school jurisdiction, such as Lakehead, that had capitalized on trustees' preferences for a greater 'feel' for their organization and for 'a legitimate route to achieve personal goals with the Board's corporate structure'. In evoking those systems' evidently successful routines for more extensive policy-making, Beevor presented backing in the parallel-case mode, to be discussed in another section below.)

In time, that overarching meta-policy passed, unanimously. By representing Halton's needs as he did, Beevor had made necessary his particular procedures for finding and resolving predicaments. The collection of new data evolved systemically. Before long, the size of the organization's policy manual mushroomed. Timelines for staff to achieve priorities became more explicit. While it would be misleading to suggest that all actors had ownership of the policies that emanated from the new process, sufficiently large elements of the community appeared to be, in the phrase of one member, 'working as a team'. Helpfully too, a number of 'uncooperative and obstreperous' trustees, belatedly unsympathetic to this meta-method, removed themselves from the Board.[5]

Typically, Beevor does not support those who attempt an end-run around his consultation-oriented and data-rich process. For example, at a planning retreat with his superintendents, Beevor had occasion to tell an idea champion for Effective Schools that:

> O.K., ——, you're very intense and committed on this [proposal for a data system for the pilot Effective Schools program] and we don't want you to be discouraged by our direct feedback. Our discussion is intended to help. What we want to do is make a good product even better.... But your idea has come down the street too soon ... You've gotten too far ahead of us.

Those words came after other members of his administrative council, including Beevor, had turned down a proposal for which groundwork evidently had not been laid. 'Organizations', Beevor later reflected, 'have a way of dulling the outrider', and the high-profile and innovative Superintendent championing that data-system proposal had failed to clear a costly but still somewhat nebulous idea with principals, who in turn had not had much of a chance to explore the idea's ramifications with their staffs. To propel that notion forward to the next round of annual budgeting, the idea champion would have to come back, armed with more data, after more consultation with more committees. Or as that Superintendent recognized (after Beevor had asked him point-blank, 'As a result of our discussion, what are you going to do?'), 'The system needs something more that you can lay your hands on.' The outrider had accepted the dynamic that the system operates according to the meta-policy.[6]

Arguing Claims From Intuition

For all his reliance on the logic of his 'This is how we'll decide' meta-process, Beevor has been known occasionally to ignore evidence. He can argue instead for new policies on the basis of what 'hits' him in the organization. Pointing out, as he likes to do, that 'good judgment can't be legislated', he recognizes a place for subjectivity and tacit knowledge in policy formulation. In Pascal's terms, 'the heart has its reasons, which reason does not know'. Curiously, my interviewees did not seem to feel that their claims violated the Board's shared norm of consultation.

Thus, for example, when one official inquired about the initiation of an Award of Excellence for an outstanding principal with the leading question, 'Did this go through the [meta-] process?', Beevor first replied in terms that left no doubt about who was in charge, 'No, I just did it'. Aware, though, that because he 'felt like it' was an insufficient standard of judgment, Beevor went on, 'We've talked about it before, talked about it a lot' (*relevant information*). Then looking around the room and perhaps appreciating that policy formulation does not invariably require his meta-process' elements for gradually clearing of a host of channels, he gave his intuitive warrant. 'We just didn't seem to be getting anywhere', Beevor smiled and next delivered this rebuttal to his take-charge action: 'This Award policy *is* an exception . . . so, I hope in time the system develops formal criteria for it'. As he well realized, a test of his standard of judgment was whether it could be applied consistently, i.e., did Beevor's spotlighting of an innovative principal mean that anyone else who could claim that certain 'spark' was entitled to that special honor too? But before that matter got worked-out 'in time', Beevor's inner mental state (insight, judgment, understanding, gut feeling) was telling him, '*Now* is the season to salute that secondary principal. She helped turn around that school from the one to avoid to the system's "in" school'.

Superintendents tell of other times when Beevor argues on the basis of intuitive and personal judgment. Often the occasions seem to be ones where new symbols of caring are created as he 'cut through' red tape. Without objective data and the elaborate routines of his meta process, for example, he portrayed an across-the-Board need for a special mid-year occasion to 'showcase' student achievement, just as he backed procedures for a Tragic Events Response Team, shortly after some youths were killed at a railroad crossing. While this Team approach could be justified as faciliating a rational division of labor among school people interested in helping such youths' family, friends, and teachers cope with that kind of tragedy, what associates remember is Beevor's intuitive emphasis that a Team would most sensitively enable different grievers' needs to be met. In another move his critics saw as intuitive, he was less successful when he tried to cut the Curriculum Office's staff by 10 per cent. Affected staff reversed that effort reputedly by enlisting trustees on their side (with consequentialist concerns like 'Do you realize that now there'll be no music consultant?').

Available data suggest, however, that such intuition definitely is not his central mode in any policy phase: he realizes that recognizing someone simply because he 'felt like it' is unlikely to win much support. 'I try for an approach that's rational', Beevor shrugs with an explanatory assumption, ostensibly referring in part to the rationality he has tried to program into the system via the meta process' strategic planning. 'But', he adds, 'we don't operate in a rational world'.

Arguing From Ethics

In this popular mode of argument, warrants and backings are posited that are value-critical. That is, policy ideas are highlighted for their goodness or badness, the rightness or wrongness of their consequences, the fairness or unfairness of their principles and burdens. In part, Beevor has been able to defend his meta-policy approach to policy formulation principles and on the ethical grounds that it is democratic in its inclusiveness.

Beevor recognizes the old saw about 'giving each person his due' as tapping into a powerful drive for egalitarian order (*relevant information*). Yet he lives 'too much of my life getting ready for Board meetings' to advance a claim for the pure democracy of, say, the New England town meeting. Beevor's explanatory warrant against such wholesale participatory democracy for his Board's governance is that all of Halton's residents could not participate in policy-making. Although Beevor recognizes that values are not derived from facts and numbers, here is an explanatory backing with such 'objectivity': if each of Halton County's 281,000 individuals were given five minutes of speaking time, at least 9780 days, day and night, would be consumed in resolving any one issue. Yet, and here is where an ethical argument for representative democracy comes in, Beevor warrants that his trustees are committed enough democrats to weigh any policy proposal presented by anyone. He has a more specific ethical backing too: while such deliberations complicate those trustees' jobs and his, ethically it would be 'wrong' to define in advance which problems are dealt with, which options are given status.

In that vein, one responsibility that Beevor has *not* delegated is appraising the 140 or so situational analyses, which he requests as part of his meta-process, from internal units (for example, schools, educational psychologists, bus drivers) and external groups (for example, chambers of commerce, university women's clubs, childrens' aid societies). In an era when the provincial government has not particularly boosted community involvement in policy development, he looks for answers to questions like this: 'What did the Halton system do last year that you liked?' and 'What needs should the system address in the coming year?' Once this relevant information is collected, members of these associations have told me that Beevor gets back to them personally with thanks and with claims like 'You know, maybe we ought to have a policy on that.'

These situational analyses are fed into the system's forementioned planning process, a process that has committees of board members, administrators, and educational specialists (drawing upon their specialized competences and vested responsibilities) consciously and publicly trying to address diverse concerns. Granted, the relevant data generated by these situational analyses sometimes are incomplete and partial. Yet by way of making an explanatory warrant supporting a claim that his Board operates as a representative democracy, Beevor points out that any absence of perfect information leaves Board members free to decide whether their own judgments, rather than the expressed will of other stakeholders, should be honored. Before citizens groups, he is a thorough enough debater to round out his argument, providing a rebuttal to his conception of grassroots democracy: although it may not happen often, local decisions always can be overturned or amended by senior levels of government.

Beevor concludes that the meta-process is flexible and adjustable for crises. Yet as an annual budget is about to be brought forward, he is unenthusiastic about reopening the process to those who have not been involved in discussions to date — when that date includes more than a year of hauling and pulling for agreements (*claim*). With the policy-relevant information that a need exists to 'treat likes alike', Beevor gives the ethical warrant that by avoiding the give-and-take of the Board's rules for moving an idea through the system, johnny-come-latelys would be unfairly and suddenly advantaged in policy formulation. Value-critically, he backs this point by indicating that the values of the many, not just of the process' late-comers, simultaneously ought to be satisfied.

The ethical point has been made that Beevor's meta-process enables the better informed and more articulate to impose their wills on the weaker. Conceivably, those 'in the know' can conceptualize their concerns with just the 'right' sophistication to relevant committees at just the 'right' moments of choice-making. That, in essence, is the core of an argument made some years ago by a group of secondary students who held that they had been penalized by *not* knowing the system was developing a smoke-free policy. The system's policy did not derive, these students said, from the explicit consent of the governed students. Protagonists for 'butting out', being more informed about Board norms and routines, had well-crafted situational analyses and had seized timely moments to carry the day against smoking. In reaction, those protesting students had an ethical declaration of their own: in a democracy, no individual, not even one who smoked, should become merely an instrument of the will of another (or of a board). These students then went beyond argumentation: they blocked vehicular traffic in front of their school, hoping to catch headlines and promote a policy that was more 'legitimate' in reflecting the views of 'the people' (their student selves).

Not by a long shot did they succeed in undoing the ban on smoking: the system's established process of government by elected representatives, working in tandem with committees, prevailed. As the disappointed students learned, 'You don't go to a higher level until you've exhausted the one just above you.' That, from Beevor's organization, was a claim about democracy as well as about bureaucracy; the not-yet-adult students were shown to have such unequal standing compared to elected Board members, a common explanatory warrant, that their claims for equal governance were deemed inappropriate. But then, consistent with another ethically grounded argument that the purpose of democracy is not to make policy-making simpler but to make it more adequate, Beevor won another claim: the system employed an outside expert to survey students on assorted dimensions of their schooling. System-wide encouragement was given as well for secondary students to meet after school with teachers to explore the smoke-free rationale. From an ethical angle, Beevor could and did maintain that the Board's policy was not completely right or satisfying *until* at least its dissenters could consider the value-critical position of those who categorize smoking as 'doing harm to self and others'.

Selected Arguments During Policy Implementation

Beevor's world *is* rational to the extent that once trustees approve a policy, staff engage in the detailed design of associated programs. As elsewhere, adherences to standards are necessary as are regularities of results.

In asking how on-the-ground activities actually 'fit with policies', Beevor exploits value-critical arguments. For instance, he justifies approving of 'five or six requests per year' for secondary students to attend schools outside their neighborhoods on the ethical grounds of freedom of choice. 'When the application gets to me, principals know

I'll grant it', he says. 'I feel it's a good thing. Basically, I'm an open-boundaries man'. Other portions of his arguments in policy implementation are cast in method-centered terms, for example, 'If ____ [an influential trustee] had his way, that teacher would be out of the system tomorrow.... The thing is, the process [of dismissal] doesn't work that way'. However, more of Beevor's arguments in this policy phase are made in causal and pragmatic terms, considered next.

Arguing From Cause

After several passing mentions to it above, at last we come to a separate treatment of the mode where explanations help to advance a claim. In causal arguments for policy installation (as in other policy phases), warrants and backings about a situation or stakeholder are related to a phenomenon's powers (*causes*) and results (*effects*).

Almost from the start of his Halton career, a 'problem' for Beevor was his physical distance from co-workers and the public. In formal rhetoric, his relevant information fastened on the tucking-away of his given office in an out-of-the-way space on the second floor of the Board's central office. According to his explanatory warrant as the 'new boy on the block', he needed to be astraddle many information channels, the better to inform and to be informed. A relationship existed, he explained to anyone who would listen, between propinquity and accessing information. For productivity, his office needed to be shifted downstairs to the middle of the first floor, near the main door. (Indeed, he decreed, that whole lobby had to be refurbished and made more inviting to the public.) As additional warrant to that claim, Beevor reminded colleagues that a leader symbolically can make himself a compass point for change by creating an event. His backing was that through that shift of office space, the 'word' would go out that he was no backroom boy — purportedly, his door was open. In time, through that door came vice-principals, leaders of home and school associations, librarians, part-time cleaning women, real estate agents wanting to know about the system's operations, and others who (I repeatedly was told) had not been so beckoned to a newcomer's central office before.

Reasoning from cause to effect, from warrant to claim, Beevor secondly tried to improve information flow by reasoning that if he had fewer tiers between himself and program people, he would be more 'in the picture'. With the relevant generalization that he needed more valid information from even more sources, Beevor began claiming the right to hold weekly breakfast meetings with elected executives of various other power groups. (Some outside these groups deprecated these 'cosy' and 'elite' breakfasts.) The first Tuesday of a month, he would convene at a

Burlington restaurant with officials from a principals' association. A week later, he would chat over his morning meal with spokespersons for the system's social workers and psychologists. The third week, he would converse with officials for the secretaries' organization. And so on.

At first, these chats appeared threatening to superintendents. Beevor's slicing through the pyramidal structure was seen as flying in the face of (bureaucratic) theory on how to manage, and these staff and line subleaders feared they might have to 'run interference on' new programs before they had sufficient resources and infrastructure. In several well-noticed instances outside that breakfast circuit, instead of aligning himself with those superintendents, Beevor had sided with principals or even with parents who had 'good ideas'. Now, the story goes, these superintendents feared that — over a fried egg and orange juice with their subordinates at the Harvester Restaurant — their new Director might undermine superintendental authority, possibly redirecting their rulings. When Beevor started bringing issues back from those breakfasts and seemed attentive to performance requirements defined by other stakeholders, the eight or so superintendents were concerned that their Director was extending the flattening of the hierarchy that his predecessor, Lavender, had initiated by eliminating the post of Deputy Director. Channels were being bypassed. With needs and resources of their own, these senior administrators were owed, as Beevor soon realized, a fuller explanation.

From an information and value base, he argued that the system had become so large that he could not singly process all the germane considerations about people and situations. Of course superintendents and the system's middle managers were indispensable in selecting what was vital; that was why he had delegated real authority and responsibility to them and why they could allocate a small percentage of their time for special projects (like Effective Schools) that they felt strongly about. That also was why he also was going to make use of such management tools as lateral transfers and secondments. But, as data worked their way up the organization's ladder, Beevor warranted that bias inevitably crept in, interfering with effective administration. To reduce bias and to facilitate unity, declared that he had to understand the 'truth' experienced by staff at other levels — and, to demonstrate his orientation towards change, he had to send a signal that the success of the organization depended on the people in the front lines. (Actually, Beevor did not speak so pompously about 'sending a signal', but that's seems to have been part of what he had in mind.) By talking with those in the front lines, he did not intend to undercut superintendents, but he had to 'fight the rumor mill' that surrounds every head office. Organizations, Beevor's backing concluded, 'do not work just through formal channels but through informal ones, and anyone who thinks otherwise is naive'.

In time, superintendents' concerns waned; breakfast meetings continued. At them, the first-level bureaucrat and the third or fourth level bureaucrats would open with banter, then shift into more business-like discussions. Three items, each with causal aspects:

- Over breakfast, the five members of the executive for the elementary group of principals might relay their puzzlement, say, over whether custodians or principals had the final word once the school day was over. In response, Beevor might first argue from authority, specifically the legal status of the province's Education Act which accords after-school responsibility to principals. That said, he might argue at greater length in an explanatory mode, i.e., if the principal is to coordinate the school's outreach to the community, then he or she has to have the discretion to make the facility's after-hours commitments.

- The next week, the eight members of the executive for the custodians might wonder (among other topics) what to do at night about a parent volunteer who consumes liquor on school premises at students' basketball games. By way of justifying his rejection of 'anybody boozing at school', Beevor might reply with an argument touching upon the cause and ethics of civility, i.e., 'Volunteer or not, a parent like that is out of line. He's a guest at a particular kind of public institution. If he "cracks one", he's not being consistent with the institution's expectations for guests.' In this exchange, Beevor also might refer to community standards, providing a warrant that is a parallel case (assuming a similarity among public places) that the parent volunteer 'wouldn't walk through the Burlington Mall doing that'. Finally, with an authoritative warrant, Beevor might mention (1) the policy manual's prohibition of liquor at student functions and (2) the need to provide a standard of safety and care for the school's clients, but usually those by-the-book references would be brief.

- During the following Tuesday morning get-together, the executive for the schools' secretaries might convey the fact that they were upset with commercial salespersons who maintain that they have central-office approval to sell luggage, cookbooks, pantyhose, and other items on school premises. From the time that issue emerged, here is an abstract of a cause-and-effect Beevorism: 'If this sort of open-sesame is offered all manner of merchants, mall owners will cry foul. Staffs and students could be distracted during work.' Out of that discussion, new procedures were introduced to reinforce the Board policy of restricting commercial business on school property.

And so Beevor, advocate for policy claims, would hear and speak to assorted themes. Sometimes he would promise to get back to these fellow-breakfasters with information they wanted 'by tomorrow noon'. At other times, he would propose a strategy, for example, 'Either we share the responsibility with the County Health Officer or we put pressure on him to increase his responsibility (for hair lice).' Occasionally too, Beevor would urge those elected executives to approach other people within the system, and 'If you don't have success with them', he would remark, 'let me know'.

Then over a second cup of coffee, Beevor would share his outlooks about a miscellany of matters — about the high fees required for a day's work by the system's lawyers ('1500 big ones'), about 'working the numbers' for maximum grants from the province, about "educating the trustees" to think comprehensively, about revisions demanded by women teachers in groundrules for Halton's leadership course, and so forth. These parts of breakfast sessions mostly were high on information-sharing — without formal warrants, backings, or policy claims.[7] All the same, some of the cause-and-effect dynamic typically lurked within Beevor's observations. At one point, as an example, he speculated about a newly-formed alignment of trustees, 'They've isolated themselves.... They're perceived as having the power to get what they want (*relevant information about implementing the Board's school-closure policy*).... But I suspect they won't succeed, the Board won't keep the school open (*claim*).... Their presentation was very weak (*explanatory warrant*) ... They didn't strike when the iron was hot (*explanatory backing*)'.

Arguing From Motivation

A policy should be adopted for one of two reasons — because of the motivating power of its goals inspiring those who are supposed to execute the policy) *or* because the policy matches values of those who have to live with it. That is the wellspring of the rather pragmatic mode of arguing from motivation.

The reader should be cautioned, particularly if she or he has moments of cynicism and hard-boiledness (or even medium-boiledness), in the motivational frame, Beevor almost sounds like an exhortative page from a human relations textbook written in the trusting 1960s, when he reached maturity in small-town eastern Ontario. Beevor's words also have resonances with a civics lecture spreading the value that in addition to legitimate collective decisions for allocation, sacrifices and reductions should be acceptable to those involved. Perhaps a faith in this benign ideal of collegiality, of pulling together, and of the willingness to share power, is requisite for stirring others?[8]

In one of his most insistent motivational arguments, Beevor talks up the virtues of administrators, before they even start a job, developing plans of action for school improvements. From trustees, superintendents, principals, teachers, janitors, and cafeteria staff, Beevor would have newly-appointed officials elicit answers to such questions as, 'What are your overall impressions of this school's operation? How are important decisions made here? What basic qualities are you looking for in the new incumbent? How can we help each other to be successful?' Responses should become grist for preparing several-month action plans, ones which then are shared with those colleagues who had been interviewed.

Often Beevor combines a cause-effect warrant with a motivational one. The shorthand version for his claimed Entry Plan goes something like this: 'If you don't hear out others, you don't get a chance to try to change their minds.' Alternatively, 'I've found that the best way to influence others is to demonstrate that you can be influenced — in feelings, attitudes, beliefs, futures. So while you're trying to influence me, I'm trying to influence you.' Beevor's longhand warrant is that by so demonstrating that he or she is looking for assistance, an incoming principal is assumed to spur other people to appreciate that they are genuine parts of the school team, thereby (it is hoped) boosting their support for the whole system and its policies. By swapping ideas with stakeholders, the principal affirms their human dignity as well as their sense of self-esteem and self-confidence. As the principal interacts through this medium to better know the alternatives that are available, she or he is mustering information for intelligent choices. Simultaneously, useful feelings of loyalty and solidarity in the community are being deepened among those whom the principal has been caring enough to consult. By consequence, in Beevor's argument, that principal no longer comes across as a remote, impersonal figure.[9] (Principals who fumbled this approach were not especially supported by Beevor.)

Beevor's reasoning is laced, of course, with a certain psychological practicality. The explanation underlying the Entry Plan is that when individuals do not understand reasons behind a policy, they retreat into cynicism, resistance and alienation. Beevor's backing is that only if the individual is valued as part of the policy world is he or she likely to comprehend school objectives and problems, and only then is that individual likely to cooperate in realizing the policies that ultimately are made. Within Beevor's motivational theme, the mature principal realizes that if she or he cannot build upon interviewees' ideas for an Entry Plan, those interviewees deserve a close and honest reckoning of why, a recounting of which specific forces in the arena mitigate in what way against the adoption of the interviewees' ideas.[10]

Arguing From Parallel or Comparative Cases

In my observation, Beevor makes two basic sorts of comparative arguments for policy implementation. Most commonly, he tells associates about specific programs in other jurisdictions throughout the province or nation. Some of his allusions are to business too — a decade ago, Beevor flirted with the idea of becoming a management consultant for corporations, and he keeps up with that literature. To defend Halton's existing administrative structure, he contrasts articulations of Halton's families of schools (*relevant information*) with other boards' more sprawling, 'disjointed', and costly bureaucracies (*parallel case or comparative warrant*). To plant a seed for the sort of reform he hopes that Halton can adopt, his warrant sometimes may be that Halton faces problems and opportunities similar to those of other boards and 'smart' industries. It is no secret, for instance, that he very much wanted Halton to produce a research newsletter as service-oriented for classroom teachers as two other boards in the region had; in this argument, other jurisdictions' outreach in this particular regard make Halton look less than first-rate.[11]

A variation of comparing parallel implementations in different settings is an argument based on experiences of the same organization across time. The claim then becomes that past policies should move the organization towards adopting particular courses of action, usually those which are only marginally different from the status quo. An example? Exploiting the relevant information that Halton had adopted in the 1970s a Management-By-Objectives (MBO) approach and a 'Manager's Letter' as part of a confidential evaluation with each administrator, Beevor tied the MBO more explictly into the Manager's Letter. Some weight also was placed on self-evaluation. A warrant for this policy is derived from the across-time assumption that present-day Halton has accountability needs similar to those recognized through earlier decisions.

Selected Arguments During Policy Evaluation

As with other school districts, when Halton's Board passes a policy, a date is set for its fundamental review, usually within three to five years. Officials then explore whether stronger contenders exist for the policy's resources elsewhere. They ascertain whether that policy should be revised, downgraded in priority, or terminated. Along the way, questions are asked about whether the policy, as implemented, seems successful in achieving desired outcomes.

For his part, Beevor tries to look not just at the policy itself — 'Policy changes fail', he muses, 'either because of the *P*rocess or the *P*roduct or the *P*erson'. Informally and formally, he seems to evaluate all of these three P-lettered components with the full gamut of argumentative modes. By way of a brief reprise of all the previously cited frames, I review an example or two of each.

Thus, on the basis of relevant information from budget sources and with a warrant in the method-centred mode, Beevor claims that a provincial process for disbursing funds for capital development is too 'secretive'; the techniques of the money-dispensers are not open enough for a democracy, a point that shades into ethical and explanatory warrants. (He thus was continuing the tradition of Halton Directors to bash Ministry financing, i.e., the Mowat Block raises expectations while lowering resources for people in the field.) As critically, Beevor evaluates Halton's process for selecting heads and new teachers (Halton's student population is growing): he senses that the people on each of the half-dozen or so interview panels are applying their own idiosyncratic standards; consistency is at risk. Later he brings in an expert to train panelists to ask the same sorts of questions and thus to rate candidates on a common scale. Eventually, problems arise with that expert's product too: some panelists do not use the set questions or ratings; they go with their own particularistic hunches. With consistency still uncertain, Beevor, his team, and the outside expert meet to evaluate the possibility that their new method of choosing staff is more form than substance. Is there a better way? Might hiring become more of a 'bottom-up' process, where teachers screen applications, interview, conduct on-site evaluations, and determine the finalists? If this collegial approach were adopted, what new problems would ensue?

One example of a value-critical evaluation of policy sprang from a routine whereby Gideon Bibles were distributed to children in Grade Five, a matter that other boards also have had to deal with of late. The relevant information: schools requested that parents sign and return a specific form if they did not wish their children to receive Bibles through an in-class distribution. One year, parents in two families independently complained about this practice to Beevor. Their warrants were that this particular distribution of Gideons splits children into Christian and non-Christian groups while giving subtle authority to Christian beliefs. Beevor agreed with those parents' categorizations and, shortly afterwards, trustees agreed that the existing practice had to be modified. In due course, problems are likely to emerge from this resolution too. But, at present, parents seem satisfied in having the shoe on the other foot, so to speak: now if they want their child to receive a Bible, parents are to sign a form and the distribution occurs in an area other than a classroom (during recess or after school). For backing, Beevor and Pauline Laing, his Superintendent of Curriculum, argued that while an ethnocultural policy had yet to be hammered-out through Halton's meta-process, immediate steps had to be taken so complaints would not escalate into full-fledged battles over racism, minority rights, equality of opportunity for immigrant children, and lack of role models drawn from minorities within ranks of Halton's educators (Woods, 1988). Not surprisingly, the overriding ethical warrant for putting the onus on the parents whose children are to receive the Bible was equality of treatment for children of different faiths.

Only rarely does an executive from of a large board get a chance to address an International Congress of Mathematics Educators — conventional wisdom is that districts as sizeable as Halton's are too complex for Directors to assume direct responsibility for the sort of instructional leadership in which such math specialists are interested. The system's coordinator for math, Brendan Kelly, was among those who were instrumental in shepherding through the system a pace-setting and intricate change in math evaluation. But it was Beevor, for his reputation as a 'doer' with a hands-on sense of Halton's math changes, whom the aforementioned International Congress invited to Budapest.[12]

Over in the Hungarian capital and elsewhere, when arguing for his evaluation format for math, Beevor routinely articulates relationships between cause and effect (see, for instance, Beevor and Russell, 1988). He reminds listeners of problems a teacher sees when a board requires external testing of her or his class' learnings — if associated with low scores, then the teacher faces public embarrassment or reprimand. Any teacher-to-teacher comparisons of results may be bandied about recklessly, hurting reputations. Since such scores may be attributable to societal factors beyond the teacher's control, Beevor insists that it is high time an approach is in place which goes some distance to protect the anonymity of staff within schools. He holds that if individual teachers are not identified in the process, the validity of the testing data can be maintained. Appreciating that this sort of testing may be a difficult point for some teachers to accept, Beevor does not argue for immediate acceptance: in the words of Howard Russell, an OISE professor who was his testing consultant, Beevor does not push the innovation 'beyond its natural pace. He allows time for the idea to sink in. He accepts opposition to the good idea in order to help give attention to it and to help clarify it.'

Beevor also discourses about Halton's grade-level surveys that now produce across-the-system figures on average percentages of numerical, geometrical, and algebraic items that have been taught. When the district's evaluators learn, for instance, that only 35 per cent of their math instructors have taught Item Number 29 (involving coordinate geometry), curriculum-writers are charged with devising more specific outcome-oriented materials to help 100 per cent of the teachers deliver lessons on that Item. With these kinds of interactions and valuings of professional development, Beevor maintains the focus is more on curriculum-monitoring than on people-monitoring.

In fairness, it should be noted that this explanatory warrant has not been enough to persuade *all* of Halton's staff and trustees. Attesting to the point that problems are not so much solved as superseded by other problems, a Department Head points to the contradiction that students' achievements scores are available at the school level; *if* the school is small and *if* only one teacher is responsible for a tested subject, a problem may be created in that the evaluations' results do not altogether achieve the promised anonymity. Questioning of this evaluation comes too from several trustees, keen to root out any incompetent, who want to make the very comparisons that teachers and their unions want to avoid.

Argumentation is so bred into Beevor's bone that in conversations about these evaluations of curriculum policy, Beevor also regularly uses arguments of the parallel or comparative case. Besides referring to the nine other Ontario boards also involved in the aforementioned survey of math curriculum, he vouches the backing that similar approaches have been taken by authorities in Japan and sections of the US. True, he does not go so far as to say that Halton's policy evaluation is suitable because similar jurisdictions find that this form of curriculum-monitoring is worthwhile and successful, but that implication reasonably can be inferred.

Behind some of his other evaluations of policy is an intrinsic appreciation of the motivational power of values and intentions. A strong example of a motivational warrant appeared when Beevor reacted to a news announcement that a high-school facility belonging to a public board (in nearby Hamilton) was to be transferred, with no compensation, to a Catholic board in need of student places. This policy stemmed from a controversial law (Bill 30) providing governmental support for the full funding of Catholic secondary education, a funding which Separate School supporters in Ontario had long sought and which was prompting heavy student enrolments which the Catholics' systems could not handle without portables. Beevor, who had just heard about the imminent transfer on the radio in his old and somewhat dishevelled-looking station-wagon,[13] provocatively evaluated the 'hand-over-the-building' policy as a pocketbook issue that might be applied to his own system:

> Not that we're looking for a fight with our Separate School colleagues who need facilities too, but when Public School rate-payers paid 72 per cent of a facility *(relevant information)* we'd like to get 72 per cent of its value *(claim, with implied warrant that the money-saving values of Halton taxpayers should be respected)*. . . . I don't know though if the Board wants to pursue that, and the provincial government may tell us to cool our heels, though. We'll have to see what unfolds (*rebuttal*).

As far as I could notice, Beevor's trumpet call 'worked' with his small audience — these educators moved forward in their chairs and their eyes seemed to light up with the 'it's-our-money' motivation. Nonetheless with his balancing remark about 'cooling heels', Beevor revealed an awareness that others may be less animated by his pitch. Perhaps speaking within the assumption that even his preferences about the transfer can change, he seemed open to learning from the new provincial policy (which ultimately 'found' funds for purchasing at market value new Catholic facilities).

The authoritative mode, which celebrates the achieved or ascribed status of authorities such as experts or insiders, usually is not explicitly and singly used by Beevor. But implicitly he does call upon those outside sources, for in the midst of an evaluative discussion about a policy problem, he will not hesitate to drop a name. Hence, midway through a discussion where he has evaluated Halton as obsolescent with regard to mainstreaming, it is not unusual for Beevor to cite a British psychologist who, two months earlier, had made a favorable impression at a Professional Development day, for example, 'You know what Mortimore says on this? . . . About having low expectations? That's our problem.' Weeks later, in another discussion about student learning, Beevor may bring closure by referring to that incisive Briton with a different context for a different assembly, for example, 'As Supervisory Officers (SO), it would be good for us to sit in on Mortimore's classroom for three months. But then', he smiles broadly almost as if he would be giving away the shop, 'who'd do the SO work?' Then in a subsequent month, Beevor may say to a union activist, 'There are a lot of people around with good ideas. . . . Did you see that article by Peter Mortimore?'. Certain of Beevor's referents are to other internationally known workshop-presenters whom he has lined-up for Halton, for example, Warren Bennis, Richard Beckhard, Howard Gardner, William Purkey.

Beevor explains his expert-invoking rhetoric itself by citing an authority (if an unnamed writer can be considered an authority). 'I once read', he remembers, 'that the greatest changes come when you take advantage of other people's initiatives'. When those others are well-regarded as highly-qualified producers of advice, in effect Beevor boosts his own policy evaluations.

Leadership, Policy and Argument

'I'm like [the detective-attorney] Perry Mason, piecing things together', Wally Beevor once said of himself. From the representative data I have reported on this widely interactive man, I hope to suggest that this chief executive officer is versatile in his 'piecing-together' of elements of argumentation. What I have not adequately suggested, though, is how Beevor combines these rhetorical ways of reasoning. One illustration of that point can be one of his own personal policies that impacts his organization's credibility and collective ends. But first, a little background.

At backyard picnics and at various clubs or restaurants in his pre-Halton days at the Lakehead, Beevor had spent time bridge-building with trustees and staff. During post-mortems of Board meetings, 'the Director and his potentially major protagonist resolve[d] more conflict after midnight than can be generated before' (Nelson, 1980). After an especially stormy, paternalistic, and go-slow-with-reform past, the Lakehead crew was at last innovating and developing a sense of togetherness. The camaraderie of such informal occasions at Lakehead enabled the Director and his wife to build support for new policy directions. When Beevor moved to Halton and acting on concerns he had picked up on at breakfast meetings, however, he made a clean break from such close relationships. Weekdays, he was quick with energetic 'Helloes', seeming to treat all with the same heartiness, and he won points by being able to address by name each teacher in various work groups. Like his predecessors and like fellow-directors, he might have his afternoon coffee with a purchasing agent or a media technician and he might help staff when their cars broke down in front of the central office. He still popped up, unannounced and 'bouncy', in schools to talk with principals (but not so much with teachers or students) about particular topics. Weeknights, he was active in executive sessions getting a sense of the whole Board's confidence levels and leanings on hot issues. Weekends, he would have friendly chats with staff he happened to bump into at the Bi-Way Discount store or at the antique furniture auctions he loved to patronize. But when it came to post-mortems and to parties, Beevor remained apart. If he accepted an invitation to a social function, he would stay only briefly. And he did not invite back.

Once I heard him justify this strikingly different-from-Lakehead style. Let me diagram his rationales for this marked shift in relationships with followers in figure 3.2. Beevor made no explicit argument with a parallel-case referrent to another board, but implicitly his pitch was a recognition that Lakehead's circumstances were different than Halton's. According to some who have observed him over the years, in Halton 'the Beevor' too was different — he was more playful, had even better interpersonal skills, was more attuned to family, and so forth.

As might be expected in a world where solving one problem only gives rise (if we're lucky) to more interesting difficulties, this particular policy transformed a recognized problem into one of lesser magnitude — a few staff told me that, while they very much respected their personable Director, sometimes he seemed to keep his social self overly distant. They wanted 'to hoist a few' with him, to hobnob with him in school staff rooms, to make his famed 'open door' policy for more rank-and-file folks.

Figure 3.2 Diagram of an Argument on Not Mixing Business and Socializing

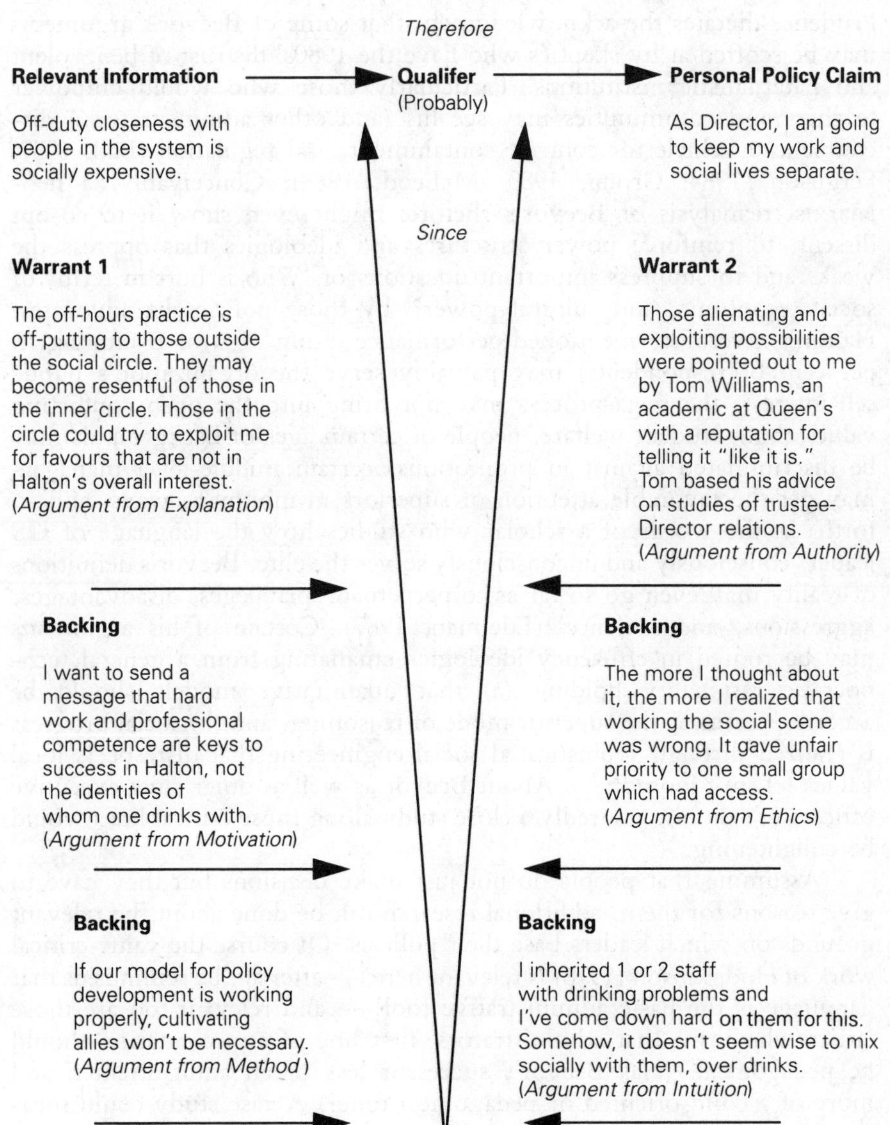

Therefore
Relevant Information
Off-duty closeness with people in the system is socially expensive.
Qualifer
(Probably)
Personal Policy Claim
As Director, I am going to keep my work and social lives separate.
Since
Warrant 1
The off-hours practice is off-putting to those outside the social circle. They may become resentful of those in the inner circle. Those in the circle could try to exploit me for favours that are not in Halton's overall interest. (Argument from Explanation)
Warrant 2
Those alienating and exploiting possibilities were pointed out to me by Tom Williams, an academic at Queen's with a reputation for telling it "like it is." Tom based his advice on studies of trustee-Director relations. (Argument from Authority)
Backing
I want to send a message that hard work and professional competence are keys to success in Halton, not the identities of whom one drinks with. (Argument from Motivation)
Backing
The more I thought about it, the more I realized that working the social scene was wrong. It gave unfair priority to one small group which had access. (Argument from Ethics)
Backing
If our model for policy development is working properly, cultivating allies won't be necessary. (Argument from Method)
Backing
I inherited 1 or 2 staff with drinking problems and I've come down hard on them for this. Somehow, it doesn't seem wise to mix socially with them, over drinks. (Argument from Intuition)

More Theoretical Work Needed

Prudence dictates the acknowledgment that some of Beevor's arguments may be scoffed at by skeptics who have the 1980s' distrust of benevolent and paternalistic institutions. Particularly those who would empower teachers and communities may see his (and other administrators') discourse as a vehicle for control, containment, and regulation (Ball, 1987; Ferguson, 1984; Gronn, 1983, McLeod, 1988). Conceivably, a neo-Marxist reanalysis of Beevor's rhetoric might even show it to co-opt dissent, to reinforce power structures and ideologies that oppress the weak, and to suppress important questions of 'Who is hurt in terms of social, economic, and cultural power?' by those policies he advocates. Halton's heretofore-mentioned performance rating of A or B (among 75 per cent of respondents) may palpably serve the organization's public self-interest, the meta-process may not bring into the open conflicting values about student welfare, people of certain ages or backgrounds may be discriminated against in promotions, certain middle-level managers may get the favorable attention of superiors in inhumane ways, and so forth. In the words of a scholar who studies how the language of US leaders consciously and unconsciously serves the elite, Beevor's definitions of reality may even go so far as to perpetuate 'privileges, disadvantages, aggressions, and violence' (Edelman, 1987). Certain of his arguments may be rooted in efficiency ideologies emanating from a general technocratic rationality holding (a) that quantitative models should be accorded status as the superior mode of reasoning, and (b) social progress is realized through sophisticated social engineering that disrespects local values (cf. my footnote[10]). About Beevor as well as other chief executive officers of schools, assuredly a close study along those critical lines would be enlightening.

Assuming that people do not just make decisions but they have to give reasons for them, additional research can be done about the relevant grounds on which leaders base their policies. Of course the value-critical work of Hodgkinson (1978) is relevant here, — after all, he reminds us that 'language is the basic administrative tool' — and relevant too are those critics who insist that administrators' first line of argumentation should be pedagogical. (Has Beevor's successor less of an adult-oriented and more of a child-oriented or pedagogical tone?) A case study could measure the persuasiveness of Beevor's arguments on their audiences, possibly gauging the impact of his rhetoric as opposed to other recognized skills of his — in diagnosis, delegating, following-through, trouble-shooting, creating rewards, taking risks, and so forth. Perhaps too a researcher could find a relationship between the quality of the reasons that Beevor uses on the one hand with his policy successes and with his policy controversies (some might say 'failures') on the other hand;[14] is there a difference? With or without premeditation, does he use different modes to reach different kinds of people? (My hunch is that he does, for example, in Budapest, he pitched his math-testing plan to a learned audience in terms of change theory, while back home he sold the plan to teachers in terms of professional development in the right places at the right time.) Beevor's effectiveness in defending his positions against legitimate criticism also might be compared to other admired administrators in and outside of local education. 'Who do policy administrators at different levels of government talk to, about what, when, and how?' might be a still broader research topic. Through study, rhetorical rules for success for influencing chief executive officers also might be traced. The place of the public in judging rhetorical examples of principle, vision and silence needs attention as well; how is deliberative government affected by executive argumentation (Tulis, 1987)?

Yet from Beevor's exemplar, perhaps enough has been said to suggest that policy administration can include more than the expression of goals, power, rights or interest. Vision, analytic capability, and soundness are often seen as the prerequisites for an organizational leader, but she or he also could use impetus, impulse, and push for articulating that vision, capability, and soundness. Through argumentation, top bureaucrats are not simply entertaining themselves and others with haphazard verbiage as opposed to sober statements. To move from this chapter's descriptive nature to a wee bit of prescription, the data on Beevor suggest that the several modes of warrants and backings may help other leaders defend their institutions' integrity and share their senses of reality to move their organizations through the policy cycle. It might even prove worthwhile for administrators consciously to try diversifying their reasons, thereby making as complete a case for their claims as possible. Even going so far as to diagram an important argument might turn out to be wise homework (see figures 3.1 and 3.2).

A case can be made, then, that argumentations help pinpoint the existence of policy problems. With attention to the structure of persuasive reasoning, a policy administrator may be able to help others realize that the problems may be categorized in ways that makes them susceptible to resolution through certain kinds of implementations. Through careful and intelligent rhetoric about policy evaluations, people in talk-intensive roles of leadership can elaborate the character of those new problems that almost inevitably arise out of efforts to deal with old ones. Put another way, administration is not just a role that is neutrally played out, but a rhetorical practice that has the capacity to affect how others interpret policies. These, anyway, are a few 'rhetorical' points for building a general theory of leadership in educational policy.

Notes

1 Because of space limits and because the particular leader whom I observe does not use many of these elements within his own arguments, references in this chapter to *rebuttals* are minimal.

2 Dunn (1981) also distinguishes the *argument from analogy* where claims are based on assumptions that relationships (not cases themselves) among two or more policies are essentially similar. In this report, this mode is not highlighted.

3 Initially, the rhetorical identity I found was of a man who seldom is cynical — as he ages or in private, he may yet become suspicious but only a few times in the course of scores of lengthy conversations have I heard him imply that there may be a gap between another person's words and actions. Beevor also is not given to detecting cabals or small cliques as dictating policy. He weaves between generalizations and particularizations, becoming most detailed in talking about fiscal responsibility and financial planning (reportedly Halton has recently pioneered in financing school modernizations with debentures). Historical allusions definitely are not his style — just once did I hear him speak of an semi-historical antecedent, widespread doubling-shifts in Ontario schools in the 1960s. In my log notes, he seems as future-oriented as presentistic, just as he tends to emphasize the practically feasible as opposed to the distant utopian. These verbal characteristics, which previously have been parts of delineations of the talk and belief systems of politicians (Putnam, 1973; Townsend, 1988), *in and of themselves* are not especially interesting, for they do not violate any expectations we may have of superordinate administrators.

4 Downey has since written a helpful, prescriptive book on this meta-process (1988) *Policy Analysis in Education,* Calgary, Detselig.

5 Have Beevor's arguments for the meta-policy been accepted? My trustee-interviewees volunteered that the process now in place for a half-dozen years, is appreciated as 'efficient' and 'philosophically sound'. 'Local policies are not introduced', one board member told me, 'unless there is an 80 per cent chance of approval'. 'Communication and motivation is improved', another trustee said.

Even so, the process is not trotted out as a virtue by those trustees who have had 'a long struggle' to advocate the interests of their community's schools (sometimes these concerns are as concrete as a pot-holed parking lot or poor facilities for student lunches). Although 'the committee is the place for the trustee to be effective' (one trustee's estimate), another thinks the debate at certain standing committees can be superficial, with individual items being insufficiently probed. She adds that administrators can be 'too set in their ways' when it comes to developing alternatives. A former Board member also points out that, for all the process' emphasis on committee deliberation, Beevor still has to lobby with trustees on a one-to-one basis for a few selected causes. This ex-trustee is not fretful over that lobbying, so much as he is commenting on leadership efforts that he thinks appropriate for a Director.

Administrators generally seem to value the procedures Beevor has installed through devices such as the process' policy manual — 'We know what to do all the time, there's criteria for performing our roles', one principal says. Subject-matter consultants appear to appreciate the meta-process too, although one comments with acerbity on its relentless focusing:

> At the Board, Beevor always looks clean — he doesn't put issues on the agenda unless they've already gotten a lot of support. *[Interviewer: How's that?]* Oh, he tells SOs, 'It's your report, and if you don't seek input from others before taking it forward, you may run into trouble.' ... If trustees start shooting down a policy proposal at a public meeting, there's always the chance Beevor may do what he did a couple of times at Lakehead — jump in and bawl out the presenter.

None of my informants recalled any such chastisements from Beevor at public meetings of the Halton Board (some key officials did remember public confrontations with the Director at Administrative Council meetings, in offices, or even in public corridors, though — about performances that he regarded as inadequate). (Not surprisingly, for this he was resented by these he bawled out, by those whose careers he nipped, and by those loyal to those who were so dumped upon. Rather, at Board sessions, consistently Beevor has stood back and let the trustees handle controversies.) 'The trustees retain the ultimate authority and accountability for the system', I heard him explain more than once. Even in the face of 'badly conceived' decisions, Beevor keeps his silence. One Superintendent explains, 'Whatever trustees decide, it's not the end of the world. We can always go back next time with more facts and try making things right... The system allows for that.'

Although hostility and anxiety initially greeted certain new curriculum guidelines associated with the meta-process (but also attributable to the provincial Ministry), the sense that I kept getting was that staff are adapting many of the initiatives than the Board had enacted. A teacher attributed this shift to 'the policy and Beevor continuing the policy of providing money for professional development and teacher interaction ... It wasn't just the principal "walking through" the document with you any more.' A Department Head remarked that 'We were able to exercise more control of mandated change'. This observation was depicted as a virtue, as if the process was overcoming twists of fate that prevented staff from controlling their own destinies.

In the view of a number of rank-and-file teachers that I talked with, however, the meta-process means cogitating, however cursorily, about what the Board wants, and then — if those wants approximate what the staff wants — putting into practice their own versions of the policy. 'Otherwise, it's a waste of time', one such educator says, recalling the teacher's everyday power to close the door, to remain quite unaffected by new policy, but to claim that 'Yes, sir, the policy is being implemented'. Another explains occasional non-compliance with Board policy as stemming from a meta-process that is not 'messy' enough. The routine is seen to favor those who speak the system's technocratic language of objectives, alternatives, and criteria:

> Everytime we get together to discuss anything, we have to have to develop a mission statement. You get tired of having to think in those terms, of having to put things on paper. We want to throw up over that *(gestures with fingers to mouth, as if inducing vomit)*. The process is all terribly rational, some of us don't think that linearly. *[Interviewer: Linearly?]* You know, what you do when you move very sequentially through a series of logical steps. Right-brainers feel like their intuitions aren't valued unless they can be quantified and systematized and objectified ... Heavy.

I have not heard Beevor address that discontent with any policy argument, value-critical, method-oriented, or whatever. What I have heard is that his energetic successor has redirected this process a bit so that, as one Superintendent says, 'We're smiling more now'.

6 Nobody has called the routine infallible. Beevor himself tells how the process broke down when the Board rejected a long-in-the-making Outdoor Education policy that would have necessitated buying recreation acreage. From this episode, Beevor's reflection was that the presentation of the proposal was ill-timed, coming within days of Halton's residents receiving their tax bills. 'The public was on the phone complaining to trustees about higher school costs', Beevor says, 'and voting *No* to Outdoor Education gave trustees a chance to hang tough against bigger budgets.... When we put Outdoor Ed on the agenda, we didn't even think of the fallout from the tax hike'. From this, the listener gets two distinct impressions: (1), Beevor will not make that tax-bill mistake again; and (2), timing of presentations will become a touchstone in his meta-process.

7 Beevor's fellow-breakfasters especially seemed to appreciate his understandings of doings at the provincial level, especially his critique of the Ministry for, say, its 'unrealistic' or 'paradoxical' formulas for calculating numbers of classrooms and its curriculum guidelines that 'need to be simplified'. Beevor could also praise provincial mandarins for getting a new grant program through the legislature and, of more importance, generally reducing its rule-making for local boards. In these provincial ruminations too, outcroppings surfaced of a mentality attuned to argumentation: 'Not enough secondary principals are preparing themselves for board-level policy-making', he concluded one morning out of his experience on a provincial panel for picking Supervisory Officers. (By policy in the Education Act, SOs are empowered to become superintendents and directors). Beevor mentioned how mostly elementary principals are securing those credentials *[relevant information]* with the result that 'A vacuum is being created in terms of sensitivity to secondary problems ... Secondary people are being put on the sidelines *(implementation claims)*. There must be a perception that a high-school principal has less hassle, more actualization, than an SO' *(warrant explaining the claim)*.

8 A genesis of the argument in this section was Beevor's beginning work in education, during the 1960s as a sports coach (a background some of his teachers sneered at). 'I always consulted parents in what the team was doing.... It's natural for me to think of bringing stakeholders on board ... People lose their enthusiasm and so you try to keep them committed.' This

thrust toward human development was furthered, he says, by his work as a learner and then as a teacher of small-group relations at the National Training Laboratory (NTL) in Bethel, Maine.

9 Entry Plans are now not just commonplace in Halton — I heard a new secretary talking about her own Entry Plan — but throughout Ontario education. From other districts, I have had principals *qua* masters' students at OISE, for instance, refer to them uncomplainingly as sensitizing them to make a good first impression on the job. Across the province, Beevor is credited with advancing this format for leaders trying to understand the culture with which they are dealing before they start to administer. In assorted forums, Beevor talks widely about how he himself had used such an approach, interviewing people in Halton and then producing a six-month plan for action, before taking up the Director's day-to-day tasks. 'It's worked for me', he explains when he voluntarily sends an Entry Plan packet to each newly-appointed director in the province.

10 For what it may be worth, my reading of Beevor is that he did not see the Entry Plan or his various other participatory mechanisms as slick stratagems to engineer consent or to mislead individuals into thinking they have influence when actually he preserved all critical decisions to himself. To begin, in my view, in itself the meta-process — with its accent on consultation — did not necessarily strengthen his own power. (To be sure, the possibility exists that its communitarian ideal was corrupted during the working-out of policies, but a different kind of study would be required to discover that.) Then too, other insightful people in the system tended to reduce Beevor's authority and any propensities he might have had towards error. In this regard, on one of numerous occasions when I saw him influenced by others, he was almost alone among members of a scheduling committee arguing (with an explanation about possible adverse reaction from parents and trustees) that Halton's classes should begin the same day, not the day after, as the rest of the province's schools. But educators of the scheduling committee wanted September 5 to be a 'Let's-pull-our-act-together' professional development day for staff. Although he was not persuaded by their rationale, in the end Beevor was influenced by the higher procedural consideration that the decision was quite legitimately within the committee's purview, not his; if the Board wanted to over-rule that collegial decision, it would. As it happened, the Board didn't over-rule, and parents did not mobilize against the committee's determination.

My observation is that, more often than not, Beevor leaves the norms of the Entry Plan's attention to others. At meetings about implementation, rather than asserting (as some directors might), 'That's my decision', conciliatorily he might lean over at various times to respect others' needs with 'Can you live with that?', 'Is this causing any difficulty?', and 'Are you happy with the arrangement?'. Beevor spins his glasses to allow, 'Hmmm, we hadn't thought of that'. He looks up from a report to remark, 'What are these teachers telling us?'. He tries to take hold of another's input, 'There's something to what you say. Help us. Can you rephrase that?'. At times, Beevor does not hesitate to confront other positions — 'I don't see it that way', 'I find that approach distasteful', 'That's *dumb* — if I may say that in the privacy of this meeting' and 'You're destroying the evidence' — but my data suggest that, adhering to a central NTL lesson at Bethel, Beevor at least *tries* to separate the problem from the person.

From details he has told me about staff in particular schools (a 'dynamic' art teacher at Maplehurst, a consultant on computers 'with immediate credibility', a 'spectacular' drama teacher at Lord Elgin, *et al.*), by and large he appears to want to keep the field clear so that people of creative intelligence can be motivated towards implementing policies that satisfy the self and the organization. Still, in the event of a clash of interests and should some way out not be found, Beevor explains: as an accountable official, he believes that preferences of individual staff members (for example, for assignments to particular schools or classes) should be considered after needs specified by the organization, i.e., its peak leaders.

Importantly, some would contest this position, seeing it as one that is based on science and rationality with its depiction of organizations as real entities. Another position, rooted in philosophy, views 'the organization' as only a fiction, a constructed reality, merely a concept that is acted out. In this reckoning, the organization is people doing things around a set of values and purposes; rather than necessarily always putting the organization first and foremost, the administrator needs to work alongside others to better understand the purposes and means that bring these people together in right decisions about their situations. On this perspective, see for instance Greenfield (1985) and Hodkinson (1978).

11 In a discerning study of the organizational premises at the Lakehead Board during Beevor's tenure there, Nelson (1980) has pointed to this administrator's 'magpie' quality. Beevor himself calls this activity 'tail-gating' onto others' ideas from any source that might give educators ammunition to do what they think suitable for education. From his contacts, Beevor 'finds and brings home ideas, skills, concepts, and people' (Nelson, 1980). In Halton, I saw this same proclivity. For instance, Beevor gave a group of communications consultants, with decades of experiences with hundreds of school boards south of the border, one of their first Canadian contracts. (Granted, that decision did trigger problems — nationalists complained that Canadian communication experts were being ignored, but Beevor explained that those Canadian consultants had no in-school experience and their bids were higher.) One final example of Beevor as would-be tail-gator: when he thought that this particular study of mine would be a comparative one of two boards' operations — a participant observer can be open to anything — he wanted me to hurry-up and please release my not-yet-drafted and still-unconceptualized findings; he had assumed that I was a much faster writer than I am able to be. Hoping for comparisons, Beevor thought that Halton might 'pick the plums' of some other Board's implementation strategies. 'If I come across anything "out there" that's relevant', he said, 'I ask myself, "How can I bring it home for Halton?"'. This approach is not unprecedented among Halton CEOs; for instance founder Singleton used to say, in valuing others' contributions he would boast 'gold is where you find it'.

12 Halton, regarded in some circles as a 'lighthouse district', probably would have arrived at this policy evaluation without Beevor, but my reading of the situation is that his entrepreneurship accelerated and set details.

13 Perhaps reflecting a ratepayers' or an agrarian perspective that city educators

can be overpaid spendthrifts, portions of Halton appear to have 'a strong thing' against administrators who drive conspicuously expensive cars. For instance, spokespersons for the custodians' union chide an administrator who drives a red Porsche. Founding Director Singleton somewhat 'got back' at such old-line critics, who in 1969 were skeptical that anyone could be worth his $29,000 annual salary: he flaunted around the community in an old but still-stylish Rolls-Royce.

14 The latter included the protracted turmoil about closing Perdue School, a lack of spark in certain high schools, a timid immersion program (French never exceeds 50 per cent) which does not give children a 'language bath', a disproportionate prevalence in administration of males (from a particular secondary school and from certain fields), one of the province's highest pupil-teacher ratios — curious for a region now so affluent — and, not least, a perceived over-whelming of staff with policy initiatives that are associated with the central office. About this last matter of policy overload, one teacher told me:

> We have three Assistant Superintendents in the central office and each has their own Vision. Each says "Grow, Grow, Grow." Gary says we're doing a 12-year program in 6 years.... The troops are drowning. ...Can't do everything.

Almost a half-dozen other staff, wearily, voiced this theme too. Beevor was aware of that burn-out, and unlike other directors I've overheard, he did *not* harp that 'Teachers are always belly-aching', or that 'Administrators inevitably are under-appreciated'. Recurrently he warned his superintendents that 'We should be careful not to over-commit ourselves', or 'We didn't achieve all of last year's policy levels', and so forth. Interestingly, Robert Williams, an insider former Superintendent and his successor as Halton's Director, has been moving the system toward a greater decentralization which would 'empower' overloaded school staffs to set more of their own policy levels. Those grassroots, though, are still expected to work through the meta process' assorted steps.

References

BALL, S. (1987) *The Micro-politics of the School: Towards A Theory of School Organization*, London, Methuen.

BEGLEY, P.T. and LEITHWOOD, R.A. (1989) 'The influence of values on school administrator practices', *Journal of Educational Administration and Foundation*, 4, 2, pp. 26–39.

BENNIS, W. (1976) *The Unconscious Conspiracy: Why Leaders Can't Lead*, New York, Amacom/American Management Associations.

BLANCHARD, K. and JOHNSON, S. (1984) *Putting the One Minute Manager to Work*, New York, Benkley Books.

BLOCK, F. (1980) 'Beyond political autonomy: State managers as historical subjects,' in Miliband, R. and J. Saville (Eds). *The Socialist Register*, London, The Merline Press.

Boyd, W.L. (1976) 'The Public, the professionals, and educational policy making: Who governs?', *Teachers College Record*, 77, 4, May, pp. 539–77.

Brockreide, W. and Ehninger, D. (1960) 'Toulmin on argument: An interpretation and application', *The Quarterly Journal of Speech*, 46, pp. 44–53.

Burlingame, M. (1988) 'The politics of education and educational policy: The local level' in Boyan, N.J. (Ed.) *Handbook of Research on Educational Administration*, New York, Longman pp. 439–51.

Burns, J.M. (1978) *Leadership*, New York, Harper and Row.

Downs, A. (1967) *Inside Bureaucracy*, Boston, MA, Little Brown.

Dror, Y. (1968) *Public Policymaking Reexamined*, San Francisco, LA, Chandler.

Dunn, W.N. (1981) *Public Policy Analysis: An Introduction*, Englewood Cliffs, NJ, Prentice-Hall.

Edelman, M. (1987) *Constructing the Policy Spectacle*, Chicago, IL, University of Chicago Press.

Edinger, L.J. (1976) 'Editor's Introduction' in Edinger, L.J. (Ed.) *Political Leadership in Industrialized Societies: Studies in Comparative Analysis.* Huntington, NY, Robert E. Krieger Publishing, pp. 1–25.

Ferguson, K. (1984) *Feminist Case Against Bureaucracy*, Philadelphia, PA, Temple University Press.

Freeley, A.J. (1976) *Argumentation and Debate: Rational Decision Making* (4th ed.) Belmont, Wadsworth Publishing.

Gogh, I. (1979) *The Political Economy of the Welfare State,* London, Macmillan.

Greenfield, T.B. (1985) 'Theories of educational organization: A critical perspective' in Husen, T. and Postlethwaite, T.N. (Eds) *The International Encyclopedia of Education: Research and Studies,* Oxford, Pergamon, pp. 5240–51.

Gronn, P. (1983) 'Talk as the work: The accomplishment of school administration', *Administrative Science Quarterly*, 28, pp. 1–21.

Hocklin, T.A. (1977) 'The Prime Minister and political leadership: An introduction to some restraints and imperatives' in Hocklin, T.A. (Ed.) *Apex of Power: The Prime Minister and Political Leadership in Canada* (2nd ed.) Scarborough, Prentice-Hall, pp. 2–21.

Hodgkinson, C. (1978) *Towards a Philosophy of Administration*, Oxford, Basil Blackwell.

Hogwood, B.W. and Gunn, L.A. (1984) *Policy Analysis for the Real World*, Oxford, Oxford University Press.

Immegart, G. (1988) 'Leadership and leader behavior' in Boyan, N.J. (Ed.) *Handbook of Research on Educational Administration*, New York, Longman, pp. 259–77.

Lutz, F. and Iannaccone, L. (Eds) (1978) *Public Participation in Local School Districts,* Lexington, MA, Lexington.

McLeod, G.T. (1988) 'Dynamic leadership and the organizational imperative: Implications for educational administration' in Schwartz, A. (Ed.) *Challenges to the Management of Canadian Education,* Toronto, Ontario, Canadian Education Association, pp. 40–53.

MacPherson, R.J.S. (1985) 'Some problems encountered "Boswelling" elite educational administrators', *The Canadian Administrator*, 14, 4, pp. 1–6.

MacRae, D., Jr. (1976) *The Social Function of Social Science*, New Haven, CT, Yale University Press.

May, J.V. and Wildavsky, A. (Eds) (1978) *The Policy Cycle*, Beverly Hills, CA, Sage.

Mumford, L. (1967) *The Myth of the Machine*, New York, Harcourt Brace Jovanovich.

Nelson, N. (1980) *A Study of Creation and Control of Policy*, Thunder Bay, Ontario, Lakehead University.

Newberry, A. (1987) 'A decimal measure of effective leadership', *The Canadian School Executive*, April, pp. 26–7.

Paige, G.D. (1977) *The Scientific Study of Political Leadership*, New York, The Free Press.

Pal, L. (1987) *Public Policy Analysis: An Introduction*, Toronto, Methuen.

Peters, T.J. and Waterman, R.H. Jr. (1982) *In Search of Excellence*, New York, Harper and Row.

Poulantzas, N. (1978) *State, Power, Socialism*, London, New Left Books.

Putnam, R. (1973) *The Beliefs of Politicians: Ideology, Conflict, and Democracy in Britain and Italy*, New Haven, CT, Yale University Press.

Rein, M. (1976) *Social Science and Public Policy*, Baltimore MD, Penguin.

Ryan, H.R. (1988) *Franklin D Roosevelt's Rhetorical Presidency*, Westport, CT, Greenwood Press.

Toulmin, S. (1958) *The Uses of Argument*, Cambridge MA, Cambridge University Press.

Townsend, R.G. (1988) *The Politick For Schools*, Toronto, Ontario, OISE Press.

Tulis, J.R. (1987) *The Rhetorical Presidency*, Princeton, Princeton University Press.

Woods, L. (1988). 'The case of the Gideon bible', unpublished paper.

Wrapp, H.E. (1984) 'Good managers don't make policy decisions', *Harvard Business Review*, July–August, pp. 8–21.

Chapter 4

The Influence of Chief Education Officers on School Effectiveness

Donald Musella and Kenneth Leithwood

Four questions guided the study of chief education officers described in this chapter: What is the nature and extent of their influence on selected factors contributing to student growth in schools? Is there a relationship between types of influence strategies used by chief education officers and extent of their influence? What achievements are attributed to chief education officers? How might chief education officers increase their influence on education? Data to address these questions were collected in Ontario through a survey carried out with sixty-nine chief education officers and a total of 762 other respondents in five other roles. Results indicate extensive perceived influence of chief education officers on school system factors through the use of a broad array of influence strategies. Specific implications for improved practice are identified.

The 'effective schools movement', in spite of its faddish qualities, has forcefully reminded us of our central purposes as researchers and educational administrators. It has also challenged the pessimism underlying our neglect in searching more creatively for causal links between various levels and types of administrative action and 'bottom line' outcomes for students. There is a danger in the movement, however. It is the danger of being seduced into acting as though the school somehow exists as a closed system; that the qualities contributing to student growth within the school unit lie entirely within the schools' control. Of course, we know that is not true. Centra and Potter (1980), for example, synthesize evidence concerning the effects of school size, family background, teacher salaries, PTR, and the like on student achievement.

Coleman's (1986) recent study of such conventional school system correlates of achievement, in British Columbia, continues to find support for their effects – although the study includes some real surprises. Nevertheless, Coleman concludes that these conventional variables leave at least

30 per cent of the variance in test scores between districts unexplained. We appear to know relatively little about how school systems and, in particular, how their chief education officers[1] influence school effectiveness. This lack of knowledge was the stimulus for our study, conducted in Ontario under contract with the Ontario Association of Education Administrative Officials (OAEAO). We began with four general questions: What is the extent of influence of chief education officers, as compared to other educator groups, on selected educational factors? Is there a relationship between the type of influence strategy used and the extent of perceived influence? What significant achievements were perceived to be attributed to the leadership of chief education officers? How might chief education officers increase the extent of influence on education?

Framework

The framework used to guide the study included four sets of factors considered (with widely differing degrees of certainty) to be capable of significantly affecting student learning; also included were six categories of administrative influence that may change or modify the conditions of these factors.

Factors Affecting Student Learning

A considerable body of evidence from teacher effectiveness and school effectiveness research has accumulated in support of the direct effects on various types of learning of the 17 school and classroom factors incorporated into the framework. This evidence is reviewed extensively in Leithwood and Montgomery (1986) and we make no attempt to replicate that review here. The ten classroom factors included:

- The Teacher
  Which teacher teaches which students.
- Program Objectives and Emphasis
  The objectives or outcomes the teacher works toward with students, including the emphasis the teacher places on different types of objectives.
- Instructional Behaviours of the Teacher
  The teaching strategies or instructional methodologies engaged in by the teacher, including the types of learning activities these strategies are designed to provide for students.

- Materials and Resources
  The types and amount of material and resources available and the uses made of these.

- Assessment, Recording and Reporting Procedures
  The ways in which the teacher assesses, records, and reports student performance, achievement, and experiences.
- Time/Classroom Management
  The way time is allocated and the things that the teacher does to get and keep the students focussed on the learning task. This includes student discipline and control.

- Content
  The subject matter, themes, or topics encountered by the students in their programs.

- Physical Environment
  The organization and appearance of the physical environment of the classroom.
- Interpersonal Relationships in the Classroom
  The role model provided (exhibited) by the teacher and the nature of the relationships both between the students and the teacher and between students and students in the classroom.

- Integration
  The nature and degree of integration between the objectives of programs within and across programs and grades.

School-wide factors incorporated into the framework were as follows:

- Human Resources
  The functions, assignments, and roles of people in the school and classroom (including decisions about which teachers teach what grades and subjects; the role of the psychologist, the janitor.)

- Material and Physical Resources
  Uses to be made of space, material resources, and student products (including the use of playground, open/closed areas, displays of student work).

- Relationships with Community
  The form and substance of communications and relationships with the community.
- Extra Curricular and Intra-mural Activities
  The nature and degree of organized out-of-classroom (area) experiences for the students.

- Relationships among Staff
  The adult role models provided by staff as individuals and as they interact with one another; and form and substance of communications among staff.
- Relationships with Out-of-school Staff
  The form and substance of communications and relationships with out-of-school system staff (for example, consultants).
- Teacher Relationships with Students While Out of the Classroom
  The nature of the relationships that the teachers develop with the students in the playground, halls, etc., and the role model provided by the teachers in these relationships.

The framework also incorporated eleven system factors. Evidence of the potential link between these factors and student growth or factors mediating student growth varies in quality and amount among these factors. Fairly convincing evidence is available concerning:

- Staff development programs (for example, Courter and Ward, 1983)
- Teacher evaluation practices (for example, Lawton *et al.*, 1986)
- System morale and climate (for example, LaRocque, 1983).

Effects of the remaining system factors are more speculative. Nevertheless, we included them because a plausible argument could be constructed, in each case, for at least substantial impact on other intervening variables at the classroom or school level, if not direct impact on students.
These factors included:

- Administrator evaluation practices
- Teacher selection and promotion practices
- Administrator selection and promotion practices
- Trustee-teacher relations
- Trustee-administrator relations
- Board-community relations
- Administrator-teacher relations
- Program evaluation practices.

Finally, four provincial factors were included in the framework. Educational funding is a variable related to student learning in a controversial way; although positive relationships are usually reported, they are weak. Further, Coleman (1986) found a negative relationship in British Columbia leading him to conclude that effective school systems were often resource-lean. Provincial policy and legislation, two further factors, have self-evident effects on what as well as how much students learn. As an example from Ontario, Bill 82 (special education legislation) has resulted in a more stimulating educational environment for special students in many school systems. Board-Ministry relations is the final provincial factor.

Types of Administrative Influence

The categories of influence that administrators may bring to bear on educational factors, incorporated in our framework were based on Duke's (1986) conception of the aesthetic properties of leadership. The behaviour of a person, according to Duke, 'does not constitute leadership until it is perceived to do so by an observer' (p. 14). Duke then identifies four properties he believes to be valued in leaders by Western industrial nations — direction, engagement, fit and originality:

- **Direction.** In the presence of a leader people have a sense of direction and appreciate the reasons for that direction. Uncertainty and surprise are minimized.
- **Engagement.** In the presence of a leader people's feelings, thoughts and aspirations are captured. They find meaning in the activities.
- **Fit.** Leaders' actions appear to be in tune or congruent with the times and the culture in which they work, including the guiding values in that culture.
- **Originality.** The capacity of a leader to capture people's imagination through the uniqueness of their ideas, programs and the like.

In order for these properties of leadership to become evident to people, Duke suggests that the leaders be perceived as having the ability to communicate ideas in simple language; the ability to coordinate the actions of many people to a common purpose; and the ability to transform vision into reality (design).

The detailed questions guiding our research emerged largely from this framework relating types of leadership influences to categories of factors potentially affecting student outcomes. For example, which factors are chief education officers perceived to influence? How does that influence compare to the perceived influence of principals, teachers, trustees[2] and other administrators? Which types of influence do chief education officers use? Which are perceived to have the most effect on different types of factors? Do people in different roles perceive the nature and type of influence of the chief education officer differently? We also asked about chief education officers' achievements and what they might do to increase their impact.

Method

A questionnaire survey was used to collect information about the research questions. Prior to the distribution of questionnaires, each chief education officer (Director in Ontario) was sent a letter requesting permission to include their school board in the study. For various reasons, twelve directors indicated that their board (i.e., district) was not to be included. Sixty-three public school and forty separate school boards[3] agreed to participate in the study. All respondent groups, except Ministry education officers, were selected from within these 103 boards.

Questionnaires were sent to all those CEOs who agreed to participate (103). Twenty-five questionnaires were sent to a senior Ministry official for distribution to this number of education officers.[4] A random sample of 228 superintendents[5] (168 public and sixty separate) were selected from a provincial total of approximately 450. This included between one and five superintendents in eighty-eight of the 103 boards. No less than two or more than three trustees were included from each board. However, the choices within each board were made randomly. Questionnaires were sent to 104 public, forty-five separate and forty-seven francophone trustees.

The sample of thirty school boards (sixteen public and fourteen separate), from the overall sample of 103 boards, used in the selection of principals and teachers was chosen to satisfy a number of criteria. First, the sample had to represent school boards (1) from all regions of Ontario, (2) of both types (public and separate), and (3) of all sizes. Second, it had to be of sufficient size to allow reasonably reliable inferences using parametric statistics. The sample of boards was as follows:

Type	Region	Numbers
Public	Northern	4
	Western	2
	Central	8
	Eastern	2
		16

Separate	Northern	3
	Westen	2
	Central	7
	Eastern	2
		14

One criterion was basic to the selection of samples of individuals within boards; that is, a sufficient number had to be selected from each board for reliable estimates to be made of school board characteristics that required aggregated data. Whenever possible, two elementary and two secondary schools were selected in each board. Six principals decided not to participate in the study. In four of these cases, the schools were replaced by another one in the same school board. In two cases a secondary school had to be selected from another school board. Questionnaires were sent to sixty elementary and fifty-four secondary school principals; further, these principals each were sent ten questionnaires to be distributed randomly to teachers in their schools.

The number of questionnaires distributed along with number of returns and return rate were as follows:

			%
CEOs	103	69	(67)
Education Officers (Ministry of Education)	25	11	(44)
Superintendents	228	124	(54)
School Trustees	196	40	(20)
Elementary/Secondary Principals	114	80	(70)
Teachers	1140	507	(44)

Two major limitations were imposed on the design of the study. One was the limitation set by the funds available. More extensive sampling and the use of interviews were not possible. Further, the condition of complete anonymity of respondent prevented any follow-up to the initial mailing, as well as the use of questions which might indirectly disclose the identity of the respondent.

Data were analysed in order to indicate:

- the influence of CEOs on classroom, school-wide, system and provincial factors, as perceived by those in various roles
- the relative influence of CEOs, as compared with other roles, on classroom, school-wide, system and provincial factors
- the ways in which CEOs, as compared with those in other roles, go about exercising influence (influence strategies)

- the relationship between the amount of perceived influence on each category of factor and the type of influence strategy
- the relationship between degree and type of influence exercised and size, based on number of students, and years of educational experience of the respondents
- recommendations for improved CEO practices.

Results

Amount of Influence

Those in different roles perceived the amount of CEOs' influence quite differently. These differences varied depending on the category of factor. For the most part, those outside the school (CEO, Ministry, trustee, superintendent), perceived the CEO as having greater influence on classroom factors (mean rating = 2.7 out of a possible highest rating of 5.0) than those inside the school (mean ratings = 1.7) although neither groups believed this influence to be high. This same pattern of perception was reported for school-wide factors (mean ratings of 2.9 and 2.0). The CEOs' influence on system factors was perceived as relatively high by all groups (mean rating = 3.9); trustees and CEOs perceived CEOs as having the most influence on these factors (4.3 and 4.2 respectively) and principals awarded them the least influence (3.4). In relation to provincial factors, CEOs' influence was rated 3.5 overall. CEOs perceived themselves as having less influence than other groups, 2.8 as compared with a mean rating of 3.7 by others.

The general pattern evident in these data is unsurprising. Greatest influence was awarded to those most closely associated by role with each category of factor: teachers were viewed as having greatest influence on classroom factors, principals on school-wide factors, CEOs on system factors and Ministry officials on provincial factors, for example. Overall, principals and CEOs were awarded the greatest influence, Ministry officials and trustees, the least. Superintendents and teachers were perceived as having a moderate degree of influence.

A more detailed analysis of the relative influence of each role on each of the four categories of factors considered separately was conducted, as well. The relative influence of each role was arrived at by computing the mean of the scores of all the respondents on each factor (for example, sum the scores of all the responses on one factor and divide by the total number of respondents from all groups in the study). The result permits a comparison of the total respondents' perception of the influence of each group on each factor within the four categories of factors.

Classroom factors

The results of a comparison of the relative influence of the different roles on classroom factors indicated that: (1) teachers had the most influence on all the factors except assigning students to teachers and on resources and physical environment; principals had results similar to teachers for these two factors, and (2) for most factors, the ranking of influence from high to low by group was teachers, principals, superintendents, and CEOs, with Ministry education officials and trustees having least influence.

School-wide factors

In relation to school-wide factors: (1) principals, superintendents and CEOs had the highest influence (in that order) on human resources; (2) compared to the other five groups the principals' group had the highest influence on human resources, facilities, community relations, and relationships with out-of-school professional staff; and (3) education officers were perceived to have the least influence on each of the factors.

System factors

For this category of factors, CEOs, superintendents and trustees were perceived as having high influence and principals, teachers and Ministry education officers having relatively low influence. CEOs were rated highest in influence on administrator evaluation practices, administrator selection and promotion procedures, and trustee-administrator relations; they were rated lowest on administrator-teacher relations and program evaluation practices.

Provincial factors

CEOs and Ministry education officers were perceived equally as having the highest influence of the six groups. Education officers had the highest influence on provincial educational policy and educational legislation, while CEOs had the highest on school board-Ministry relations.

A summary of the roles perceived to have the highest and lowest influence is provided in figure 4.1.

Nature of Influence

Respondents were asked to rate, on a four point scale, the six methods of influence described in our framework used by those in different roles (3 = major method; 2 = occasional method; 1 = rarely used method; 0 = don't know).

With the exception of the CEO, each respondent provided his/her perception of three roles — CEO (director), one other, and his/her own. CEOs were asked to respond to two other roles, as well as their own. The following combinations were used:

Table 4.1 Roles Perceived to Have the Highest and Lowest Influence

Classroom Factors	Highest	Lowest
Which teacher teaches which student	Principal	Ed. Officers
Program objectives and emphasis	Teacher	Trustee
Instruction practices	Teacher	Trustee
Types and amounts of instructional resources available	Principal	Ed. Officers
Student evaluation practices	Teacher	Trustee
Classroom management practices	Teacher	Trustees/ Ed. Officers
Subject matter content	Teacher	Trustee
Physical environment	Teacher/Principal	Ed. Officers
Interpersonal relations	Teacher	Ed. Officers
Integration of objectives across different subjects or topics	Teacher	Trustee

School Factors	Highest	Lowest
Human resources	Principal	Ed. Officers
Facilities	Principal	Ed. Officers
Relationships with parents and the broader school community	Principal	Ed. Officers
Extra-curricular activities	Teacher	Ed. Officers
Relationships among teachers and other staff in school	Teacher	Ed. Officers
Relationships with out-of-school professional staff	Principal	Ed. Officers
Relationships between teachers and students while outside class	Teacher	Ed. Officers

- CEOs: Education Officers and Trustees
- Education Officers: CEOs and Trustees
- Superintendents: CEOs and Trustees
- Trustees: CEOs and Principals
- Principals: CEOs and Superintendents
- Teachers: CEOs and Principals

Because of the different number of participants in each role, and because each participant was asked to respond only to three roles, it was not possible to compare each role's perception of every other role. However, it was possible to compare the means of the methods of influence among the six groups and to compare the methods of influence used by CEOs, as perceived by respondents in each of the roles.

Results suggested that CEOs, superintendents, principals and teachers 'occasionally' to 'frequently' make use of most types of influence. As well, trustees and Ministry officials only 'rarely' to 'occasionally' were perceived to use any of the types of influence examined.

Results also suggested, that CEOs most frequently were perceived to exercise leadership through providing a sense of direction, coordinating the actions of people, generating a sense of involvement and communicating. Less often were CEOs believed to provide unique, innovative ideas or assist in helping people interpret policies or events.

Relationships

The relationship between the six methods used by CEOs to influence people and the perceived extent of influence was arrived at by correlating the mean ratings of each method of influence with the mean ratings of each of the classroom, school-wide, system, and provincial factors. The purpose of this analysis was to explore, in a tentative way, whether CEOs' impact might be greater on some factors as compared with others depending on the method of influence they were perceived as using. While the study could not answer such a cause and effect question by its design, it might well indicate avenues for further inquiry. Results of our initial analysis do not contribute much to this purpose, however, and hence we do not provide a detailed description of the data summaries. Correlations between all methods of influence and most factors were statistically significant and, with several exceptions, in the same range (approximately .25 to .40). This lack of discrimination may be traced back to the lack of variation in ratings given the CEOs' use of the six different methods of influence.

The relationship between methods of influence and classroom factors was significant with all four groups of factors. However, the highest relationships were as follows:

1 Providing a sense of direction	•	Student evaluation practices
2 Getting people involved	•	Instructional practices and student evaluation
3 Facilitating integration of ideas	•	Instructional practices and student evaluation
4 Orchestrating activities	•	Student evaluation practices
5 Providing new ideas and initiatives	•	Instruction practices
6 Communicating meaningfully	•	Instruction practices and student evaluation

The relationship between methods of influence and school-wide factors indicated that 'relationships among teachers and other staff in school' correlated the highest with *all* of the methods of influence. In examining the relationship between methods of influence and system factors, the highest correlations were with 'program evaluation practices' and 'staff development programs', and the lowest with 'administrator selection and promotion practices'. The relationship between methods of influence and provincial factors indicated highest correlations with 'school board-Ministry relations'.

CEOs' methods of influence were unrelated to the size of their boards. More experienced respondents were less inclined to attribute influence to CEOs than were those with less experience.

Significant Achievements

Table 4.2 summarizes responses concerning significant achievements attributed to CEOs, in eight focal areas of leadership. These areas included Fiscal, Personnel, Public Relations, Program, System, Personal, Policy and Trustee. These are post-hoc categories. The numbers of people whose responses are summarized vary from responses to the questionnaire, as a whole. Some people offered no response to this question (123 teachers, nine principals, ten superintendents, two trustees and two directors). Some people responded 'no comment' or 'do not know' (thirty-six teachers) and others said that they could not attribute any significant achievement to the director (sixty-nine teachers, four principals, five superintendents, two trustees).

Considerable unanimity across roles is evident in the responses concerning the nature of the leadership provided by CEOs within each leadership focus. This perspective on leadership (the properties of leadership perceived as helpful by others) is consistent with assumptions underlying Duke's (1986) aesthetic model of leadership. Data in table 4.2 can be used to assess the extent to which the leadership properties identified in that model have any empirical grounding.

There is considerable evidence in table 4.2 to support the value attributed to providing a sense of direction. Achievements associated with System and Policy leadership constitute such evidence (for example, goal setting, focus, vision). Achievements identified as Program leadership also support the importance attached to originality on a leader's part (for example, new program development, increased standards). Duke's conception of leadership also entails 'the transformation of vision into reality' (p. 22) through organizational design. Achievements related to both Fiscal and Personnel leadership seem closely related to such transforming purposes (for example, staff development, acquiring funds). Achievements in communicating the intentions and programs of the school system through Trustee and Public Relations leadership and through policy interpretation support Duke's construct related to effective communication. Finally, orchestration seems to be the intent of some achievements in Personnel leadership (for example, reorganization, delegation).

Table 4.2 Significant Achievements Attributed to CEOs

Leadership Foci	Teachers (N = 302)	Principals (N = 67)	Superintendents (N = 109)	Trustees (N = 35)	Ed. Officers (N = 11)	Directors (N = 64)
fiscal leadership	• setting priorities • acquiring funds • efficient expenditure practices • school closures and new facilities	• setting priorities • school closures and new facilities	• setting priorities • acquiring funds • school closures and new facilities		• setting priorities	
personnel leadership	• staff development • staff acquisitions • reorganization	• staff development and evaluation • reorganization • improved morale	• staff relations • delegation of responsibility • accountability • reorganization	• staff relations		• staff development and evaluation • selection and promotion • morale and motivation • delegation and reorganization • team building
public relations leadership	• improve visibility and communication with community and schools	• improve visibility and communication with community and schools	• improve visibility and communication with various groups			

program leadership	• new program developments • revision • increased standards • increased resources	• develop, implement and revise programs	• develop, revise implement new programs • increase standards • increase resources	• new and revised programs		• new program development and implementation • program excellence • program review initiative
system leadership	• goal setting and planning • system maintenance	• goal setting and planning • smooth operations	• provide a focus or vision • system credibility	• provide a focus or vision • goal setting and planning	• goal setting	• provide a focus • goal setting and planning • goal attainment
personal leadership	• concern for others	• concern for others	• recognize others		• policy implementation	
policy leadership	• policy development review and interpretation	• policy development, implementation and clarification	• policy development and implementation		• improve trustee-staff relations	
trustee leadership	• improve trustee-teacher relations • trustee education	• improve trustee-staff relations • trustee education	• improve trustee-staff relations			

The data however, do not appear to address properties of leadership which Duke labels 'Fit' and 'Engagement' (only CEOs, for example, identified improving morale or motivation as an achievement).

Improving Practices

Respondents were asked what they would recommend the CEO do to increase his or her positive impact 'on education in your board'. A total of twenty-five different suggestions were offered by 396 teachers, sixty-three principals, 117 superintendents, thirty-five trustees, eleven education officers and fifty-four directors. Of these, seven were offered by at least several people in three or more roles:

- visit schools (mentioned by those in all roles)
- increase accessibility to staff (four roles)
- communicate more with the community (four roles)
- delegate more tasks and decentralize decision-making more (four roles)
- increase efforts on trust and team building (four roles)
- consult more with staff (three roles)
- make more effort to clarify the mission of the school system (three roles)

Concerns for school visits, increased accessibility, team building, consultation and the like, suggest a strong desire by respondents to participate more in the decision-making some CEOs appear to retain for themselves. These data may be interpreted as a clue for CEOs wishing to engage their staffs more in the mission of the school system. Engagement was one of the properties of leadership notably absent from the significant achievement attributed to CEOs in the previous section.

Respondents were also asked how CEOs might increase their provincial impact. Thirteen types of suggestions were made by 241 teachers, forty principals, seventy-six superintendents, thirty-nine trustees, eleven education officers and forty-eight directors. Of these, five were offered by those in three or more roles:

- increase contact with Minister, Ministry officials and possibly members of parliament (all roles)
- become more visible with the community and in the public media (five roles)

- develop more contacts with other CEOs and boards (five roles)
- regularly participate in professional development activities (three roles)
- increase involvement in CEOs' professional association (three roles).

Four of these suggestions appear to concern the CEO's role in communication — both shaping and advancing the interest of the school system by building a broader base of support for its activities in the province.

Conclusion

Three results of the study are, in our view, especially noteworthy and their implications warrant consideration by way of conclusion. First, CEOs in Ontario, at least, were perceived to have high levels of influence on school system factors, as a whole. This influence was greater than the perceived influence of those in any other role — marginally more than that of superintendents and significantly more than those in the remaining roles examined. CEOs' influence was perceived to be almost as high in relation to provincial factors but diminished substantially as school and classroom factors were considered. Second, CEOs were perceived to be exhibiting all the properties of leadership (or using all methods of influence) identified in Duke's (1986) theory of leadership. Further, they were perceived to be making more extensive use of each leadership property (or influence method) than those in any other role examined in the study. Finally, in spite of the high ratings awarded CEOs for their personal efforts in generating involvement or engagement among other members of the school system, respondents clearly wanted a larger piece of the decision-making action. What implications do these results have for CEOs in their future efforts to contribute to school effectiveness? Our answers to this question necessarily draw on data beyond the study. The first implication is that CEOs should continue to focus on their perceived strength. By this we mean that CEOs should focus their efforts even more directly on school system factors. At least a significant number of these factors play a vital role in shaping the condition of classroom and school factors known to directly affect the quality of education for students. There is little question, then, that through these factors, CEOs can have a powerful, albeit indirect, effect on improving school effectiveness; it also seems likely that CEOs are often the only people in a position to actually alter the condition of school system factors.

Based on evidence outside this study, we also believe that CEOs would do well to focus on a selected set of school system factors, at least in the short run. Our nominations for selection here are based, in part, on evidence which suggests that (a) the most cost-effective strategy for school improvement at present seems to be improving school administrator effectiveness (see, for example, recent work by Robinson and Wittebols (1986), comparing the effects of this strategy with lowering class size or providing teacher in-service); (b) approximately 40 per cent of school administrators in Canada will be retiring over the next eight years. These data argue strongly for investment of considerable effort in school system factors involving the preparation, selection, appraisal and continuing professional development of school administrators. Further, we suggest that the objective of such effort should be the creation and implementation of policies consistently based on a coherent conception of growth in school administrator effectiveness suitable to the school system. This recommendation might be summed up as 'place your bets on middle management'.

Our final suggestion is to 'be a coach and a referee but not a player'. This suggestion emerges from the strong sentiment expressed by respondents for a more active role in decision-making and more opportunity to communicate with the CEO about what they are doing. Reconciling this sentiment with data acknowledging CEOs' personal efforts to involve and engage staff, we think requires some basic restructuring of typical school system decision-making roles and responsibilities. Toward this end, we find attractive the recent efforts by a number of school systems in the country to shift the locus of decision-making control to the school level in the form of 'school-based planning' or 'school based curriculum development'. With this shift, of necessity, must come a much clearer set of expectations for what schools are to be accountable for (and hence attention must be given to system program evaluation) as well as much more control over hiring, budgeting, staff development and the like.

Such a move seems entirely consistent with conditions in some Canadian provinces at present (although not all school systems in those provinces). The most crucial of these conditions include a substantial pool of available curriculum resources on which schools can draw, an increasingly sophisticated school administrative and teaching staff, and a demonstrated willingness on the part of Ministries of Education to legitimate school level initiative. We believe that there is also a growing recognition that the aggressive actions of the Ministries and boards in some provinces to generate and disseminate curriculum policies has created an impossible list of 'priorities' at the school level. It is no longer possible, even if we thought it desirable, to conceptualize the school's task as policy implementation — there are just too many policies. Instead we must reconceptualize the task as school improvement — a task defined most fundamentally in terms of the goals of education espoused for the provinces. In accomplishing such a task, new policies are not ends in their own right, they are potential means to be used or not depending on their potential value in the school's context. In sum, then, this recommendation involves clarifying the rules of the game for schools, blowing the whistle when the rules are violated and helping school staffs learn how to play the game more skillfully.

Notes

1 Throughout the chapter we use the term Chief Education Officer (or CEO) to refer to the most senior administrator of a school system. In Ontario, this position is designated Director. In most Canadian provinces and the US states the same position is designated Superintendent.
2 Trustees are elected members of the public equivalent, in the US, to school board members.
3 In Ontario, separate school boards are publicly-funded Roman Catholic school boards.
4 In the US, senior state education agency personnel would be the equivalent of Ministry of Education education officers in Ontario.
5 Equivalent, in the US and most provinces to Assistant Superintendents.

References

CENTRA, J.A. and POTTER, D.A. (1980) 'School and teacher effects: An interrelational model', *Review of Educational Research*, 50, pp. 273–91.

COLEMAN, P. (1986) 'School districts and student achievement in British Columbia', *Canadian Journal of Education*, 11, 4, pp. 509–21.

COURTER, R.L. and WARD, B.A. (1983) 'Staff development for school improvement' in GRIFFIN, G.A. (Ed.) *Staff Development,* Chicago IL, University of Chicago Press.

DUKE, D. (1986) 'The aesthetics of leadership', *Educational Administrator Quarterly*, 22, 1, pp. 7–28.

LAROCQUE, L. (1983) 'Policy implementation in a school district: A matter of chance?', Burnaby, British Columbia, Simon Fraser University, Mimeo.

LAWTON, S., HICKCOX, E., LEITHWOOD, K.A. and MUSELLA, D. (1986) 'Development and use of performance appraisal of certificated education staff in Ontario school boards', 1, Ontario, Ministry of Education.

LEITHWOOD, K.A. and MONTGOMERY, D.J. (1986) *Improving Principal Effectiveness: The Principal Profile*, Toronto Ontario, OISE Press.

ROBINSON, G.E. and WITTEBOLS, J.H. (1986) *Class Size Research: A Related Cluster Analyses for Decision Making*, Arlington, VA, Educational Research Services, Inc.

Chapter 5

Negotiating the Master Contract: Transformational Leadership and School District Quality

Linda LaRocque and Peter Coleman

In this chapter, the authors draw on data from an extensive study of nine effective school districts and CEOs in British Columbia to provide a description and explanation of the leadership provided by those CEOs. Such leadership is termed 'transformational' and its purpose is to develop a productive district culture or ethos. To give culture a more active meaning the metaphor of a master contract is introduced. Within the metaphor, transformational leadership is a process of continuously negotiating and refining the goals, norms and values on which the practices of organizational members are based. Exceptionally effective CEOs demonstrate exceptional commitment to a vision of what their districts should provide to students as well as consensual norms for decision-making in the context of negotiating the master contract.

Superintendents who are effective educational leaders create an organizational ethos based upon two fundamental values: first, they value service to clients; second, they value mutual respect within the educational community (teachers, parents, and students) and in particular between educational professionals. Such leaders attempt to shape the norms and practices (ethos) of the organizations in which they work to reflect these congruent values. Far from lacking conviction, such leaders proselytize at every opportunity for their beliefs.

We will argue that these leaders reconcile, in their work, the apparently competing basic values of executive leadership and representativeness (Kaufman, 1963). Their strong convictions make them charismatic leaders of the traditional type. But since part of their creed is a norm of mutual respect (and hence an expectation of interactive or mutual influence), their beliefs and practices are not immutable, particularly with respect to practice. Such leaders play their part in the organization by developing a 'master contract' which 'includes the organization's self-image' (Smircich, 1983, p. 348, citing the work of Harris and Cronen, 1979).

In developing this thesis we begin with a brief sketch of recent trends in the politics of education apparently common to the US and Canada, and of some current ideas about leadership and change, and then elaborate and we hope justify our view by presenting some data, and inferences from them, drawn from a study of school districts in British Columbia, Canada.

Power and Leadership in Educational Organizations

In 1977 it was apparent to some that a major power shift was underway in Canadian education:

> In recent years, power (or reliable influence) in education has become more widely distributed. Net losers of power in Canada have been provincial governments, trustees, and administrators; net gainers have been teachers and their associations, special interest group of various kinds, parents, and to some extent students. (Coleman, 1977, p. 79)

This trend in Canada paralleled a power shift in the US, in which the major losers of influence were educational administrators (Hanson, 1976, p. 93). There the trend was said to reflect a shift in public value orientations. Kaufman's (1963) influential analysis of state and local governments in the US suggested that there were three basic value positions with respect to bureaucratic organizations: representativeness, technical competence, and executive leadership. The power-shift in education in the two countries could be seen as an emphasis on the public value of representativeness, at the expense of the other two.

Administrators in both the US (Hanson, 1976) and Canada (Coleman, 1977) felt relatively powerless, caught in a narrow 'zone of tolerance' (Boyd, 1975) between competing interest groups, including teachers' unions. These were flexing the muscle of newly won bargaining rights, perhaps more effectively in Canada than in the US (Canadian teacher salaries seem to be about 15 per cent higher than those in the US in terms of purchasing power; Lawton, 1987).

Those with a strong belief in the efficacy of executive leadership expected that this shift in power would have strong negative consequences for educational quality. In the absence of centralized authority the implementation of positive changes in public education would slow, it was thought, to an even more leisurely pace than in previous decades. Others, however, argue that removing the dead grasp of 'downtown' from such schools as Kennedy High School could only be positive (Lightfoot, 1983, p. 113).

Members of the latter group, including ourselves, took heart from the work of such organizational theorists as Tannenbaum, who pointed out that 'the total amount of control exercised in a group or organization can increase, and the various participants can acquire a share of this augmented power. Conversely, the total amount of control can decrease, and all may share the loss' (1962, p. 247). Tannenbaum argued that in organizations which deliberately set out to increase the size of the influence-pie, the greater degree of mutual influence lead, in certain circumstances, to more effective performance.

A more 'principled' case for mutual influence in educational organizations has recently been argued by Guttman (1989). We need democratic education because 'the policies that result from our democratic deliberations will not always be the right ones, but they will be more enlightened — by the values and concerns of the many communities that constitute a democracy — than those made by unaccountable educational experts' (p. 185).

The touchstone used by Guttman in testing the desirability of 'representativeness', that it promotes accountability to a larger degree than other governance forms, is important. Effectively she is asserting a hierarchy of values in which representativeness serves a greater good, accountability. This point becomes central to our empirical argument later.

Power and Change in Educational Organizations

Leadership in educational organizations has long been defined as initiating change (Lipham, 1964, p. 122). Thus it is not surprising that the conflict between executive leadership and mutual influence has been reflected in studies of change implementation in education. Summarizing such work, Coleman and LaRocque (1987) contrast 'left-side' and 'right-side' views of educational change. The first, left-side view, is based on a 'machine bureaucracy' (Mintzberg, 1979) view of organizations, on a rational decision-making model of policy formation, and on the belief that if a policy statement is clear there will be an 'irresistible unfolding' (Wildavsky, 1979) in the implementation process. Such views stress the importance of strong and decisive executive leadership exercised through centralized policy decisions. Sergiovanni (1987) describes this view of educational organizations as 'this tidy and orderly clockworks mindscape', which

> simplifies the task of school management. A leader need only control and regulate the master pin and wheel, and all the other

> wheels and pins will move responsively and in concert. The clockworks mindscape imbues management with a sense of power and control, which in part accounts for its attractiveness. (p. 118)

Right-side views, on the other hand, adopt a 'professional bureaucracy' (Mintzberg, 1979) view of organizations, in which administrators 'manage uncertainty' (McPherson, Crowson and Pitner, 1979), assume and accommodate the play of political influence in policy formation (Boyd, 1975), and expect implementation to be a matter of mutual adaption, that is, of mutual influence.

A case study of a change attempt based on left-side views is summarized thus: 'It is ironic to see in our study that behind the formal hierarchy each level of authority is unsure of what is going on below or how to intelligently intervene. This dilemma extends all the way from Washington to the classroom' (Hargrove *et al.*, 1981, p. 122). The best-known case studies of successful implementation (Huberman and Miles, 1984) reveal a 'supported enforcement' scenario. Strong central leadership results from commitment to a change perceived as desirable. Although motives are complex, Huberman and Miles (1984) report that 'improved classroom instruction' dominates the motive set for administrators (p. 49). This leader commitment is combined with modest levels of adaption and 'tutoring and tenderness', resulting in user commitment (p. 279).

Our view of power or influence in the change literature is that mutual influence is essential, but that again it is constrained by the accountability motif, in this instance defined as strong leaders demanding change on behalf of clients.

Alternate Approaches to Leadership in Educational Organizations

The right-side viewpoint we favor, the 'mutual influence' school of thought, has corollaries within general leadership studies (Yukl, 1989). At one time leadership was defined as mutual influence; consequently, the relations between leaders and followers (Campbell, 1977, p. 223) were central to such studies. But reviews spoke of 'the generally disappointing results obtained in much of the research on leader-subordinated relationships' (Greene, 1977, p. 66). Some theoretical perspectives on educational organizations seemed to challenge the possibility of leadership by emphasizing the 'anarchy' within (Firestone and Herriott, 1982).

Renewed interest in leadership was both illustrated and further stimulated by Burns' *Leadership* (1982) and Peters and Waterman's *In Search of Excellence* (1979). These works, which enjoyed a more than scholarly audience, were innovative because they demonstrated that certain kinds of political or organizational culture were extremely important to effectiveness, and that some interest has rapidly become focussed on the manipulable aspects of the culture or organization, that is, the significance of culture as a leadership tool (Barley, Meyer and Gash, 1988).

Leadership and control in educational organizations is said to consist, at least in part, of creating a common vision, a set of norms which indirectly influence the behavior of members (McPherson, Crowson, and Pitner, 1986). We will use 'transformational leadership', in which a leader 'recognizes and exploits an existing need or demand' and creates 'a relationship of mutual stimulation and elevation' (Burns, 1978, p. 4), to describe such culturally-focussed leadership behavior. Organizational norms are often linked to performance via the assertion of organizational goals, and effort to create commitment to these goals (Rosenholtz, 1989; LaRocque and Coleman, 1986).

In education, revived interest in leadership and its contributions derive at least in part from the effective schools movement. Early studies of school quality tended not to focus on the important of leadership, but often noted it as a somewhat unexpected finding. Discussing a group of studies conducted during the 1970s, Shoemaker and Fraser (1981, p. 178) comment: 'although none of the studies set out to study the role of principals, most concluded that principals were clearly important in determining the effectiveness of schools'.

More recent work on effective schools, following the lead of Little (1982), tends to emphasize the contribution of teacher beliefs and attitudes to school quality; these are thought to be shaped by the workplace generally (Rosenholtz, 1989), and particularly by administrators (Blase, 1987). Articles by Deal and Sergiovanni in the 1987 *Yearbook of the Association for Supervision and Curriculum Development* provide a useful illustration of this trend in reconsiderations of the educational leadership issue.

Leadership research in general, however, still seems to focus on issues other than organizational ethos, the norms and resulting practices of organization members. Yukl's authoritative and recently updated review (1989) finds little room in the 'integrating conceptual framework' (p. 269) for transformational leadership. However, some management scholars are describing a new emphasis in leadership research which has been labelled 'functional leadership' (Hackman and Walton, 1986). Such leaders work in organizations characterized by a focus on commitment, within which one of the functions of the task group is to help in generating and enforcing norms (Walton and Hackman, p. 192).

For us, the notion of transformational leadership, with its focus on organizational culture, which we call ethos (Coleman and LaRocque, 1989), and its combination of strong convictions and openness to influence, is vital to an understanding of differential effectiveness in educational organizations.

Transformational Leaders and the Master Contract

Smircich (1983) has argued that the notion of the culture (or ethos) of an organization can be given more activist connotations by describing it as a 'master contract'. The master contract fits within that broader understanding of control in educational organizations often retitled 'coordination' by scholars in education administration (McPherson, Crowson and Pitner, 1986).

Within the schooling context, then, the transformational leader tries to influence others with respect to norms and values, and associated practices ('what we do here'), by negotiating a master contract. If he or she is a superintendent, the most immediate and significant others to be influenced are school principals. At the same time and because of his or her belief in mutual influence, these other groups can, and do, modify the opinions and actions of the superintendent. Thus in large measure we see transformational leadership in educational contexts as essentially shared leadership, in which strong executive leadership is a necessary but not sufficient element. Our data describe such shared leadership.

There are already descriptions in the literature of the process of negotiating the master contract at school level. Within effective or improving schools, principals strengthen collaborative work and the professional culture:

> Broadly speaking, effective school principals appeared to contribute to school cultures viewed as associative; such cultures were described as cohesive. Interactions between principals and teachers and between teachers and others were viewed as co-operative, empathetic, supportive, respectful, equitable, and productive. In contrast ineffective principals tended to create cultures viewed as dissociative; these cultures were seen as fragmented. (Blase, 1987, p. 609)

To us this constitutes a description of the process of negotiating the master contract at school level.

The element of mutual respect evident here is common in descriptions of the ethos of effective schools (Little, 1982). But Rosenholtz (1989) uses the term 'negotiated beliefs' (p. 174) to describe the shared goals of principals and teachers with respect to instructional practices and outcomes. These descriptions reveal some of the elements — associative professional culture, mutual respect, shared goals, negotiated beliefs — involved in the administrative process of developing the 'master contract'.

Descriptions of the kinds of rewards and inducements exchanged in the negotiation are provided by the teacher efficacy literature (Fuller, Wood, Rapoport and Dornbusch, 1982). In exchange for probable increments in performance efficacy, that is, in the psychic rewards obtained from improving student achievement, teachers provide commitment (Rosenholtz, 1989, p. 144). They also commit themselves to collective values. In so doing they experience increased organizational efficacy (defined as 'feeling efficacious in gaining valued outcomes by influencing another person in a different level of the organization'; Fuller, Wood, Rapoport and Dornbusch, 1982, p. 9) since 'higher levels of convergence between subordinate and superordinated actors' beliefs in and commitment to priority goals and implementation means (tasks) are associated with high levels of performance efficacy and organizational efficacy of both actors' (*ibid*, p. 22).

Attempts to assert shared goals and collaborative approaches within schools and districts based on mutual influence are often, perhaps always, resisted. The teacher 'freedom' which comes with isolation is well entrenched (Feiman-Nemser and Floden, 1986, p. 517). The leadership efforts of change agents can be diluted to futility (Huberman and Miles, 1984, p. 273). Leadership efforts of the superintendent can be constrained, diluted, even sabotaged, by school principals. The effective superintendents we will be describing struggled long and hard to break down independent fiefdoms and to establish collective norms and practices. With respect to school accountability for performance, for example, we have traced a history of the development of accountability norms and practices in a group of districts with effective leadership (LaRocque and Coleman, 1988) which details the persistent efforts of the superintendents over a period of years in the face of resistance, the provincial government financial restraint program, and the ensuing political strife between the Teachers Association and the government.

Transformational leaders are impelled by strong convictions regarding service to clients, and collaborative action. They negotiate a shared ethos, a set of norms and practices, which reflects both these convictions and the influence of colleagues. This ethos is organization-specific and tends to permeate the organization, having a powerful effect on the actions of individuals. Our data provide us with a picture of the superintendency as transformational leadership.

In the three remaining sections of this paper we summarize and re-examine our findings on the leadership of the superintendency presented elsewhere (Coleman and LaRocque, in press) to highlight its transformational nature; to examine the extent to which the superintendency as transformational leadership is shared leadership; and consider the work of the transformational superintendency as negotiation of the master contract.

The Superintendency as Transformational Leadership

In order to capture the salient features of superintendent leadership as it emerged in our data, we developed three linked notions. 'Reach' conveys the ability of the superintendent to influence the norms and practices of subordinates, and encompasses both 'vision' — the professional norms which shape and guide activities towards a desired future state, and 'range' — the scope and diversity of activities to which the superintendent devotes his or her time and energy. While we were working on this analysis we became convinced by the data of the link between the leadership of the superintendency and district ethos (Coleman and LaRocque, in press). It is only subsequently, however, that we began to view the superintendency as transformational leadership. From this perspective, there is a correspondence between 'vision' and 'strong convictions', between 'range' and 'mutual influence', and between 'reach' and 'focus on productive district ethos', all important elements of transformational leadership.

In the descriptions which follow we emphasize the norms and practices of those superintendents in our sample who most clearly exemplified transformational leadership. In each summary we provide some contrasting data to allow some sense of what other kinds of superintendents believe and do. These descriptions are based largely on the interview transcripts of the district administrators in nine of the ten districts in our sample (District C was excluded from this analysis because it did not have a full-time superintendent.) Details of the analysis can be found in Coleman and LaRocque (in press).

Vision-Strong Convictions

It was clear from our data that some district administrators held strong convictions which influenced their approach to their job. This we referred to as the vision of the superintendency,[1] the professional norms which shape and guide the activities of the members of the superintendent's office. There were two, a norm of professional consensuality and a norm of accountability, both of which incorporated sub-norms (see table 5.1).

Consensuality had several faces:

> We are in the process right now of going through exercises with the principals as to how to come up with a growth plan. How to

Table 5.1 Norms Encompassed by the Vision of the Superintendent's Office

Norms	Defining Characteristics
Professional Consensuality	
(a) collaboration — district	concern for collaborative planning between professionals of different status, with emphasis on reaching consensus, at the district level
(b) collaboration — school	concern for collaborative planning between professionals of different status, with emphasis on reaching consensus, at the school level
(c) collegiality	concern for mutual assistance, for professionals of the same status helping one another
(d) care/nurturance	concern for the needs of professionals other than academic or technical
	concern for their opinion with respect to general climate
Accountability	
(a) to community at large	general sense of responsibility to the community for the performance of students, schools, and teachers, with emphasis on goals, supervision, and professional quality
(b) to parents/students	specific sense of responsibility to parents and students
(c) to school board as representatives	specific sense of responsibility to the school board as representatives of the community
Sub-norm High Expectations	
(d) comparative standards	concern for performance standards, with particular emphasis on core subjects; academic orientation
(e) continuous improvement	concern for performance improvement, emphasizing: changes in policies/practices/programs; development of teaching skills; and development of working knowledge

> come up with decision-making models that involve the whole staff. (B1.02)[2]

> In my 12 years as a principal I don't ever remember having a conversation about educational matters with the Superintendent, Supervisor, or Director. Now when I go into the schools it's simply routine we sit down and talk about this school improvement, that school improvement. (J1.03)

> There is much more consultation than there was previously (i.e., than with the previous superintendent), with principals as a group and with individual principals — going to the principals and saying 'what do you think about this?' (R1.03)

> I go in every class in the place . . . I'll often come back after these school visits and dictate little notes to the teacher saying: 'I like what was happening in your room' or 'keep up the good work'. (J1.01)

For the district administrators in our study, the norm of consensuality was exemplified by professionals interacting with professionals, on matters fundamental to the purposes of schooling such as instructional effectiveness and program improvement. It involved collaboration between professionals working at different levels within the organization and collegiality between peers; it involved working together to solve common problems and providing feedback on performance. It created numerous opportunities for expectations to be shared and for understanding of the implications for practice of these to be developed. It conveyed the message that all professionals in the district, teachers as well as administrators, were both capable of as well as responsible for contributing to shared working knowledge, especially as part of a school staff. The care/nurturance subnorm complemented the other subnorms by (i) providing the normative foundation for the provision of feedback to principals and teachers on their efforts to actuate district expectations; by (ii) ensuring that their contributions were recognized; and (iii) by encouraging them to continue striving toward district goals.

Accountability, too, presented different faces:

> We have a six-year cycle of school assessment. Each school internally conducts an assessment. They prepare a report. We externally take one principal from another school and two people from district staff and the three of them will spend time reviewing the whole thing. (V1.01)

> I have told the principals that failure to write an unsatisfactory report on a teacher who deserves it shows up on my report on them (i.e., the principals). The firing process starts with the initiation of the first unsatisfactory report — the principal is expected to write that report. (J1.01)

> We run a public school system. And the public pays us to do that in a particular way. And in that area I have a very strong feeling. We cannot decide what to teach; it is the public's choice. We can decide how to teach.... If you for your convenience decide not to teach this particular program, I think it is a good enough reason for firing the person for neglect of duty. (V1.01)

Accountability was seen by these superintendents as being: a collegial responsibility; a relatively new emphasis; and a moral imperative. These superintendents believed strongly that the school system must be responsive to the public in terms of its broad goals and responsible to the public for district performance with respect to these goals.

Important sub-norms of accountability were a special sense of accountability to parents, and a concern with improvement.

> Traditionally, parents have been viewed as fund-raisers. This is definitely changing. There is more consultation with parents and more direct involvement of parents as aides in most of the schools. . . . There is a greater sensitivity to the potential role of parents and a greater awareness of the benefits among the principals. (J1.03)

> Performance data in relation to the teacher effectiveness program lead the Board to maintain a comparatively high level of support simply because of the very good information that came back from those of us who saw changes in teachers. (B1.01)

The norm of accountability subsumed a concern form high expectations: It was not enough to try to meet community demands; continual efforts to improve and to achieve (and preferably exceed) certain standards of performance were clearly called for.

The norms constituting vision clearly were differentially present in the interview data (see table 5.2). Within each district they tended to be common property within the central office administrative group, although there was some evidence that the superintendent personally set the tone (see, for example, quotations by R1.03 and V1.01). Nevertheless, it cannot be coincidental that the values most strongly expressed by the district administrators in our study centered on consensuality and accountability, with the former, for the most part, serving the interests of the latter.

Range — Mutual Influence

Not only did some of the district administrators espouse strong beliefs, they acted on these beliefs, in such a way as to influence other professionals in the district and to be open to influence by them. This we referred to as the range of the superintendency, the set of activities to which attention is paid. There were three broad categories of range — scope and diversity, intensity, and congruence — which again were differentially present in the interview data (see tables 5.3 and 5.4).

The superintendencies engaged in a number of different activities that were related to the norm of accountability. Such activities included principal and teacher evaluation; school assessment; program evaluation; reporting to the community and responding to public concerns; analyzing test data with respect to means or norms, longitudinal trends, and inter-school comparisons, either with the principals as a group or with principals individually; and supporting teacher learning opportunities (Rosenholtz, 1989) by offering a series of workshops in identified areas of need.

Table 5.2 Mean Frequency of Reference, by District, to Norms Encompassed by the Vision of the Superintendent's Office

Norms	Districts									
	R	V	J	B	P	W	Q	M	H	Mean
	2	3	3	3	2	2	1	2	2	
Professional Consensus										
(a) collaboration-district	16	7	6	7	9	8	0	3	2	6
(b) collaboration-school	3	3	6	6	2	0	5	3	0	3
(c) collegiality	2	0	3	3	1	0	0	0	0	1
(d) care of teachers	6	5	3	8	5	2	5	1	1	4
Consensuality Total	27	15	18	24	17	10	10	7	3	15
Accountability										
(a) to community	16	13	17	13	12	9	9	6	6	11
(b) to parents	16	17	14	20	15	8	14	6	5	13
(c) to school board	2	11	4	7	7	6	9	2	2	6
(d) standards	9	9	5	6	4	2	4	3	3	5
(e) improvement	10	14	11	16	15	13	14	3	2	11
Accountability Total	53	64	51	62	53	38	50	20	18	45

Note: The numbers in parentheses refer to the number of district administrators interviewed in each district. District C was excluded from this analysis because it did not have a full-time superintendent.

Table 5.3 Elements Comprising the Range of the Superintendent's Office

Elements of Range	Defining Characteristics
Activity Scope and Diversity	
(a) Varied Nature	district administrators engage in variety of different activities
1 collaboration	instance of planning between professionals of different status instance of attempts to reach consensus district and school levels
2 collegiality	instance of mutual assistance between professionals (same status)
3 care/nurturance	instance of meeting non-academic professional needs instance of soliciting/responding to their opinion
4 accountability	instance of responsibility to the community/parents/students/school board for performance of students, schools, and teachers, with emphasis on goals, supervision, quality instance of soliciting/responding to public concerns
5 standards	instance of collecting, analyzing, and reporting performance data, with particular emphasis on core subjects instance of demonstrating an academic orientation
6 improvement	specific instance of attempting to improve performance, through: relevant changes in policies/practices/programs development of teaching skills or working knowledge
(b) Varied Location	
1 principal's office	reference to or inference of meeting with the principal at his/her school
2 school generally	reference to or inference of meeting with teachers at schools
3 classroom	reference to or inference of being in classrooms
4 community	reference to or inference of meeting with community members at the school or some other community centre
Activity Congruence	
(a) interdependence	reference to connection or linkage between issues
(b) theoretical basis	reference to theory, research/professional literature

Notes

1 PLATO — Programmed Logic for Automatic Teaching Operations.
2 Note: The teacher's name, the school name and all student names are psuedonyms.
3 Students working at their own pace can, of course, mean trouble, especially if some students allow themselves to fall far behind. To guard against such problems, PLATO reported to teachers whenever a student seemed to be making unsatisfactory progress.
4 The description of lessons in the three Mathematics Strands are in the publications *Description of Graphing Strand Lessons* by Donald Cohen and Gerald Glynn, Computer-Based Education Research Laboratory, University of Illinois, Urbana, Illinois, June, 1974; *Description of PLATO Whole Number Arithmetic Lessons* by Bonnie Anderson Seiler and Charles S. Weaver, Computer-Based Education Research Laboratory, University of Illinois, Urbana, Illinois, June, 1976; *The Fractions Curriculum — PLATO Elementary School Mathematics Project* by David Kibby and Sharon Dugdale, Computer-Based Education Research Laboratory, University of Illinois, Urbana, Illinois, March, 1975.
5 SRA — DeVolt, M.V., Frehmeyer, H., Greenberg, H.J., Venuzks, S.J. (1974) *Mathematics Learning System Texts*. Chicago, IL: Science Research Associates, 974 IBM Subsidiary.
6 MIA — Denhalm, R.A., Hankins, D.D., Herrick, M.C., Vojtka, G.R. (1974) *Mathematics for Individual Achievement*. Boston, MA: Houghton Mifflin, ISBM 0-395-14796-4.
7 Ms. Hamilton individualized much of the instruction in the room, which made it easy to fit PLATO into the day's schedule. For whole group activities, she frequently turned the terminals off.
8 Graphing Linear Equation's workbooks were prepared by the authors at CERL to accompany the PLATO lessons.
9 Comprehensive Tests of Basic Skills, published by CTB/McGraw-Hill, Del Monte Research Park, Monterey, California 93940.
10 REVIEW AND PRACTICE was the lesson a child was routed to at the beginning of a session. When the child had finished two or three lessons to a mastery criterion, two or three tasks similar to those in the lessons were presented for review.

References

Case, R. (1975) 'Gearing the demands of instruction to the developmental capacities of the learner', *Review of Educational Research, 45*, 1, pp. 59–87.

Easley, J.A., Jr. and Zwoyer, R.E. (1975) 'Teaching by listening – toward a new day in math classes'. *Contemporary Education, 47*, 1, pp. 19–25.

Guba, E. and Lincoln, Y. (1981) *Effective evaluation*. San Francisco: Jossey–Bass.

Hicks, B. and Hoke, G. (1974) 'Instructional Applications of Computers (IAC) in the College of Education.' Working Paper 2, University of Illinois, May 18.

Scribner, S. (1976) 'Situating the experiment in cross cultural research'. In Riegel, K. F. and Meacham, J.A. (Eds). *The developing individual in a changing world, Vol. I.* The Hauge: Manton, pp. 310–321.

Smith, L.M. and Pohland, P.A. (1974) 'Education, technology, and the rural highlands,' in this volume.

Stake, B.E. (1977) 'PLATO and Fourth Grade Mathematics'. Unpublished manuscript, University of Illinois, CIRCE. A report for the Educational Testing Service. ERIC DOCUMENT ED228–040.

Superintendents in our study, as elsewhere (Murphy, Hallinger and Peterson, 1985; Rosenholtz, 1989), often modelled the behaviors they expected of others.

It should already be apparent that the superintendents engaged in a number of different activities that were related to the norm of consensuality:

> We have had some workshops [for principals], where we've discussed models of supervision, the full implications of supervision, things like that. Then I think there is the modelling we do, how we handle supervision. We share our process with them, the documentation we use. (P1.02)

> Invariably we require that the principals, in planning their annual performance objectives, must include a report prepared by the principal and the staff where they go through and have a look at test results in relation to district and provincial/national norms . . . and either express satisfaction with these as they are or put forward a plan of action in terms of some possible changes if there seems to be some anomaly. (B1.01)

> Peer observation things are really supposed to be the teachers who say 'I want to do this' rather than the district saying 'You are going to do this.' So what we have done is offer to facilitate arrangements for peer observations, to provide money, and all that kind of stuff if you want to do it. (R1.02)

The superintendencies actively collaborated with other professionals in the district, especially principals, thereby both behaving consistently with their espoused consensuality value and modelling appropriate behavior for others to practice. Such exchanges provided opportunities for superintendencies to influence other professionals in the district while at the same time to be influenced by them. The superintendencies also tried in a variety of ways to help other professionals behave collaboratively and collegially. Furthermore, note how frequently the substance of consensuality activities involved accountability issues — analyzing test data, planning improvement, and so on. While consensuality was valued in its own right, it was clearly a means of enhancing accountability.

Not only did some superintendencies engage in a greater variety of activities than others, they performed each activity with more energy and effort, that is, with more intensity.

> We have identified certain major topics which we keep in the fore. For example, since the beginning of the year we have placed

> that item (district performance on the provincial exams) on the Principal's Meeting agenda twice. It's more or less a technique of reminding: Are you on top of things? Is there anything further we ought to be doing? and so on. (When the Directors visit the principals), they might say: What is the status of your school assessment program? What is happening with the provincial exam results? (V1.02)

Intensity refers to the degree of personal involvement, the amount of energy and effort expended. It is an obvious form of 'paying attention', a signal to the other professionals in the district of the concerns of the superintendency.

Where district administrators carried out their activities was also significant.

> E. (Assistant Superintendent) and I spend a hell of a lot of time out in the schools, and (Supervisor of Instruction) is constantly circulating in the schools. (J1.01)

By meeting in principals' offices, observing in classrooms, and talking with teachers in staffrooms, district administrators acquired first-hand information about what was happening throughout the district; they conveyed that the schools were being held accountable for their performance; they expressed respect for their subordinates (Murphy, Hallinger and Peterson, 1985); and they gave principals and teachers an opportunity to influence them.

The consequences of the way in which the effective superintendents carried out their work were far-reaching. The work environment was being structured so that the professionals had to take collaborative action on a wide range of matters that clearly fell within the accountability domain. Furthermore, the district administrators were in frequent contact with other professionals in the district, and their interactions centered on such issues as school performance, instructional effectiveness, program improvement, and the like. These were truly open exchanges; while the district administrators were guided by their basic values, they collaborated with other professionals (most often principals) to find and implement solutions to problems and encouraged staff collaboration on school-specific problems. Not only were the district administrators open to mutual influence, they engaged in activities that made mutual influence possible and likely.

The superintendencies were open to influence by the broader professional community as well as their immediate one.

Table 5.5 Rating on Performance and Ethos, by District

	Districts R	J	V	W	B	P	Q	H	M
Performance Rank[1]									
(a) Achievement	1	21	13	11	36	24	6	51	6
(b) Costs	17	19	13	8	36	21	5	56	65
Performance Level	high	high	high	high	medium	high	high	low	low
Ethos Ratings[2]									
(a) Focus 1	3	3	3	2	2	2	1	0	0
(b) Focus 2	3	3	3	2	2	2	1	0	0
(c) Focus 3	3	3	3	3	3	1	1	0	0
(d) Focus 4	3	3	2	2	3	1	1	0	0
(e) Focus 5	2	3	2	2	3	3	1	0	0
(f) Focus 6	3	2	2	2	2	3	1	0	0
Leadership[3]	I	I	I	I	I	I	I	II	II

1 I indicates high scores for achievement and low scores for costs.
2 The higher the score the stronger the evidence of norms and practices associated with a productive district ethos.
3 I and II refer to Group I and Group II leadership.

> The teacher reports are more detailed now, they're more related to current knowledge on effective instruction. (W1.02)

This connection between activities and a theoretical or research base was one aspect of what we called congruence. The notion of congruence helps to explain the link between vision and range. The connections provided by 'theory', by which we mean simply anything read in the professional literature, provide a kind of mental map of supposed causal connections. The mental map gave superintendents both a basis on which to select activities likely to result in accomplishment of desired goals, and the ability to undertake a large number of quite different activities without major inconsistencies in direction. In reading the transcripts from the successful districts (defined below) we were impressed by the fact that virtually any question we asked was immediately put into a kind of personal frame of reference by the respondents.

Reach — Focus on Productive District Ethos

Together vision and range constitute the 'reach' of the superintendency — the ability of the superintendency to influence the norms and practices of subordinates, that is, to develop and sustain a productive district ethos. Table 5.5 shows the relationship between district leadership, district performance and district ethos for the nine districts in our study of school district administrative practices which had a full-time superintendent.

District performance level was determined by consideration of both student achievement data and per pupil costs (see Ehrenberg Chaykowski and Ehrenberg, 1988 for a similar approach.) Our procedure with achievement data was to standardize and aggregate student test scores on Provincial Learning Assessments in Math, Science and Reading between 1981 and 1984, and calculate a residual using Community Education Level as a predictor. Similarly, we standardized and aggregated the 1982 per pupil costs, and residualized them with District Mean Grade Size, an important predictor of costs. A high-performing district was one with a high residual achievement score and a low residual cost score (i.e., higher than predicted achievement scores and lower than predicted costs); conversely, a low-performing district was one with a low residual achievement score and a high residual cost score. Table 1 gives the ranking of each district in the sample (out of seventy-three districts) on both the achievement score and the cost score, and also its assigned performance level. (We have provided a more detailed description of these procedures elsewhere — Coleman, 1986a and 1986b; Coleman, Walsh and LaRocque, 1988.)

The district ethos ratings arose from the analysis of the interview data. All line administrators in each district, including the superintendent, assistant superintendents, directors, and supervisors, were interviewed; in addition, all the principals in the smaller districts and about one-third of the principals in the larger districts were interviewed. The interview questions were derived from our conceptual framework. We suggest that a productive district ethos consists of a high degree of interest in and concern about six activity and attitude 'focuses' to which school administrators are encouraged to pay attention. These focuses may affect the ways in which districts cope with a series of common administrative tasks (derived from Coleman, 1972; and Berman and McLaughlin, 1979). The tasks and focuses can be combined to yield a conceptual framework, illustrated in table 5.6, in which the cells represent a series of research questions about district ethos. The most important linkage between elements is leadership, which links the various activities and levels, and operates by influencing principals and teachers to narrow their attention to a limited set of issues.

The focuses together constitute productive district ethos. We have used the term 'productive district ethos' (see Coleman and LaRocque, 1989, for an elaboration of this notion) in order to convey the purposeful nature of the organization's 'shared understandings, norms, and values' (Jelinek, Smircich and Hirsh, 1983). It contributes to two distinct purposes or goals, generally accepted by professionals: the academic success of students, and by extension the effectiveness of professionals; and nurturance or care for students' academic welfare, and by extension the

Table 5.6 District Ethos and District Tasks

Six Focuses (District Ethos)	District Tasks Be Accountable	Improve/Adapt	Set Expectations
Learning Focus 1 focus on instruction	program effectiveness assessed?	changes to improve instruction?	instructional goals most important?
Accountability Focus 2 school accountability	schools held accountable for performance? for practices?	changes to improve accountability	monitoring and instructional goals linked?
Change Focus 3 organizational change	changes as response to performance data?	changes as response to environment	changes in goals/goal-setting processes?
Commitment Focus 4 commitment to effort	commitment to accountability created?	commitment to change efforts created?	commitment to school/district goals created?
Caring Focus 5 consideration	concern for community opinion on performance?	decisions reflect concerns of community?	emphasis on affective goals?
Community Focus 6 community integration	schools/district involve community in monitoring?	community involvement in change efforts?	community involvement in setting goals?

commitment of professionals. Table 5.6 gives the rating of the districts on the six focuses: a '3' indicates that all the practices associated with a productive district ethos for this focus were found in the district; a '2' indicates that the district was moving towards a productive ethos with respect to this focus; a '1' indicates that only a few of the practices associated with a productive ethos for this focus were found in the district; and a '0' indicates a virtual absence in the district of the norms and practices associated with a productive ethos for this focus.

The accountability norm is clearly dominant in the more successful districts. This may be practitioner recognition of the 'paradigm shift' described by Boyd and Crowson (1981). The norm of consensuality which is found with it must be understood at least in part as a set of opportunities for influencing others towards acceptance of the accountability norm. In practice, it seems to be largely instrumental. This is not to imply that the norm is inauthentic; it is, however, a subordinate value (see Guttman, 1989).

Two groupings of districts emerge from the distributions shown in tables 5.2 and 5.4. Group I (Districts R, V, J, B, P, W, and Q) are those in which the norms were frequently expressed, and the pattern of activities illustrated the power of the norms in shaping the use of time by the superintendency. The data on location showed that in these districts, by comparison with Districts H and M, the superintendents were a presence in the schools and in the community. They modelled effort and energy for other professionals, and embodied accountability for community members.

The districts within Group I differed with respect to frequency of expression of norms, reports of activities and district administrator presence in the schools and community; they were at different stages in the transition from 'fiefdoms', in which schools enjoy autonomy without accountability to superordinates, towards a consensual and accountable system; but they can be labelled the 'achievers'. Their student achievement levels were generally quite high, costs were low, the norms were strongly stated and resulted in a wide variety of interdependent activities, pursued in varied locations. Moreover, their ethos ratings were high — they either were characterized by the norms and practices associated with a productive district ethos or were well along in establishing these norms and practices.

In Group II (Districts H and M) the statements regarding norms occurred much less frequently. Similarly there was a noticeably low level of activity: they intended to do things, but for a variety of reasons do not actually accomplish them.

Group II districts can be labelled the 'drifters'. The conflict often referred to in Group I, which arose from superintendent attempts to influence, was absent in Group II districts. In this respect they were similar in many ways to the implementation sites reported by Huberman and Miles (1984), in which conflict is low because little is attempted (p. 273). These districts are still largely fiefdoms, in which principals were neither accountable nor consensual. They were also noticeably more dissatisfied and critical than in the other districts. Their performance level was low, and there was little evidence of the norms and practices associated with a productive district ethos.

These two districts represented the condition from which districts in Group I were emerging. This historical shift was most clearly exemplified in our portrait of school accountability changes (LaRocque and Coleman, 1988). Provincial conditions help to account for this change: Local appointment of superintendents who are responsible to the elected school board rather than the Ministry is relatively new in British Columbia. All the superintendents in this study were the first to be locally appointed in their districts. The superintendents in the Group I districts appeared to be responding to local appointment by strongly advocating norms of accountability and consensuality and acting in ways consistent with these norms. Those in Group II seemed to share the norms, although they expressed them less strongly, but the level of activities was quite different from that of Group I superintendencies.

Our general impression of the Group I superintendencies was of an astonishing level of energy and activity, based on a high degree of conviction and commitment to district improvement. They were initiators, eagerly seeking new ideas, and persistent in their attempts to make changes. They seemed full of confidence about their ability to make a different to students, teachers, and schools. On the other hand, the Group II superintendencies seemed passive, feeling that the important work and decisions were in other hands. In this realm at least it is the best (by our standards) who are filled with 'passionate intensity'; the worst 'lack of conviction'. The ethos of the district seemed to reflect the leadership of the superintendency. Rosenholtz (1989), describing schools in Tennessee, makes a similar point about superintendent leadership in 'moving' and 'stuck' districts: 'Schools seem to be a microcosm for what happens in their districts' (p. 168).

Shared Leadership

Principal involvement in decision-making was an issue in all the districts in our study. At stake was whether power was to be centralized in the superintendency or to be shared by the superintendency and principals. Superintendency leadership was important with respect to this issue. In Group I districts there was a movement towards decentralization; in Group II districts there was a movement towards centralization.

Decentralization was generally attempted by increasing principal involvement in district decision-making. In some districts principals were very actively involved in all phases of decision-making:

> The role of the principal depends on the problem. For example, with 'Let's Talk About Schools', when all districts had to get involved, the principals were told 'This is the format by which we are all going to be involved. Do you wish to see it modified?' But there are other situations where one says to the principals 'Do you think we have a problem here? Do you think we ought to work on it? O.K., then, how do you think we ought to work on it?' Our approach really will vary with the issue. (R1.02)

> The Administrators Association meetings are business meetings with formal agendas. We make policy where we can. Where we're given a mandate, we're fairly confident the policy we draw up will go, once we've got our act together. But we must do our homework, we must be prepared for our meetings, or the superintendent won't accept what we suggest. The guidelines for dispensing funds for administrator professional development and the policy on the supervision and evaluation of school administrators are just two examples of policies developed by principals. But the superintendent doesn't just automatically go along with our proposals. For example, he's concerned about the amount of money being spent on substitutes for special events. He couldn't accept our first proposal, so we've got an ad hoc committee looking at the issue. Right now the superintendent is working on an overall three-year plan to set the goals and direction of the district. A committee of three principals in working on moving that under the effective schools umbrella. (J2.01)

In many of the other Group I districts administrators discussed important issues openly and frequently with principals, but the district officials actually wrote the policy or made the decision. The principals certainly contributed to the decision-making process and influenced the final outcome, even if they were not as actively involved as those in Districts R and J. They spoke very positively of their increased involvement in district decision-making.

> I think things are getting better every year. I think there's more recognition of a school's autonomy. I think there is a greater desire to be involved, to involve field and office in decision-making. I think there is a genuine desire to reestablish the trust environment. (B2.04)

Increasing principal participation in district decision-making was not only professionally rewarding, it contributed to the development of a sense of 'district-ness'.

> I certainly feel that when I first came here schools were seen more as independent operating units. Now I think we see ourselves as part of a district in which we all have fairly common goals. (V2.05)

Interestingly, higher principal involvement in district decision-making was accompanied by increased principal autonomy at the school level. Schools were encouraged to adapt, extend, and supplement district intiatives, and were given funds and other assistance to support these school initiatives as well as school-based staff development activities (see LaRocque and Coleman, 1986 and 1988). One district was even experimenting with school-based budgeting (Coleman, 1986c).

These links between principal involvement in decision-making, a shared sense of direction, and school autonomy within a district framework recurred throughout the interview data of principals in those districts moving towards decentralization. The linking of these themes at first appears paradoxical, but upon consideration the logic is evident. Principal-principal and principal-district administrator collaborations were necessary for a sense of team membership and common purpose. With common purpose, school autonomy to allow responsiveness to local needs and circumstances was possible without a return to fiefdoms.

District administrators in Districts H and M were also concerned with establishing district directions. They were trying to accomplish this through formal policy making procedures which involve seeking feedback from those affected by the policy during the development stage. They frequently cited problems with this approach, however:

> We try to involve those who will be affected by the decision. We are having some difficulty with that. The process is there but I am not sure how comfortable people are with the process.... The fact is that it is very time-consuming. The other problem is that we are so shorted-staffed. (H1.01)

Consequently, although the central administrators intended to discuss issues with the principals, it did not always happen. Even when the discussion occurred and principal feedback was provided, the outcome is often not what district administrators wished.

> District adminsitration is frequently disappointed in that feedback on change is solicited but reaction is always negative. (M2.01)

The process in District M generally resulted in the voicing of negative reactions rather than problem-solving or consensus-building. The principals were very dissatisfied with this approach to decision-making. They felt like a rather weak lobby group vying with others, especially the Teachers' Association (the teacher union local in British Columbia), for the ear of the Board. The district administrators viewed the district's meta-policy on policy-making as a means of opening up the policy process, but the principals saw it as a means of centralizing decision-making power. They did not consider providing feedback on a draft of a policy as meaningful participation in decision-making.

The decentralization approach to principal involvement was based on concern for common goals, collaborative problem-solving, and the development of shared working knowledge. As the principals move from reacting to district initiatives to identifying common problems, working out common solutions, and accepting joint responsibility for district performance, they are sharing in the leadership of the district. This is highly consistent with, and perhaps even an inevitable outcome of, the superintendency as transformational leadership. It should be clear from our data that Group I superintendencies were strong leaders; it should be equally clear that Group I principals were strong leaders. To these administrators, district and school level alike, shared leadership strengthens rather than weakens everyone's influence: 'the total amount of control exercised in a group or organization can increase, and the various participants can acquire a share of this augmented power' just as Tannenbaum (1962, p. 247) suggested.

Group II superintendencies were concerned about principal fiefdoms; their efforts to establish a common purpose centered on the policy process, in which the principals were only one of many groups whose feedback was sought. Principals became increasingly resistant; district initiatives became increasingly ineffective. In sum, both district and school level administrators experienced an increasing sense of powerlessness, although each thought the power was held elsewhere: 'Conversely, the total amount of control can decrease, and all may share the loss' (*Ibid*).

Thus, rather unexpectedly, the issue of principal involvement in the school districts we studied became a control issue. The more successful districts in our group had clearly adopted a coordination rather than a control orientation (McPherson, Crowson and Pitner, 1986), particularly with regard to instructional decisions which related most directly to students and teachers. Historically, they had moved rapidly from fiefdoms, to centralized systems with principal rotation to control empire-building, and then to administrative team approaches in which there was reliance on shared norms to ensure that the district continued to adapt to demands for change arising within the district (often from the formal leaders) or from the social environment. They had succeeded in negotiating the appropriate master contract.

Negotiating the Master Contract

Our thesis is that the productive ethos as we have described it has intrinsic value for educational professionals in the school system. For teachers it reduces anxiety and raises professional expectations for and commitment to success. For teachers the productive ethos is an important aspect of their professional environment, one which largely determines the quality of their workplace (Goodlad, 1983), and thus contributes to teacher commitment and student achievement (Rosenholtz, 1989).

For administrators it is important in a very different way. The creation and maintenance of a productive professional ethos in schools or districts is both the most significant product of their professional activities, and their particular responsibility. Sergiovanni (1984) has suggested that good principals create an atmosphere in which students and teachers 'work much harder than can ordinarily be expected' (p. 5); this contributes to student achievement levels. But productive ethos is of intrinsic value to other professionals in the organization, whether or not it is a condition contributing to the production of other important outcomes.

We have suggested that the notion of productive professional ethos provides a useful metaphoric way of thinking about the work of administrators. Such ethos requires two essential components, first that of effort, and second that of normative purpose. Both are captured by the notion of a continuous negotiation of the terms of the master contract, consisting both of the self-image of the organization and the 'constitutive and regulative rules that organize beliefs and actions in light of the image' (Smircich, 1983, p. 348).

The metaphor which for us best conveys the negotiation process by which the productive professional ethos is created and sustained by good administrators is that of the skillful gardener, in harmony with the natural (social) world, but also modifying its innate patterns of development to her purposes. The gardener uses time well, encourages the industry of others, and produces both intrinsically and instrumentally valuable products. It is this metaphor which we associate with the word 'productive', rather than that of the factory or refinery.

The administrator/gardener continually struggles against a kind of social entropy, exemplified by teacher isolation and stagnation in learning-impoverished 'stuck' schools (Rosenholtz, 1989, p. 81), and by schools as independent fiefdoms in districts lacking a productive ethos. Further, if they are not being tended, the districts/schools/gardens grow wild, with important values and products getting choked out by weeds, that is competing elements such as basketball, fund-raising, PTAs, playing politics and strikes.

The levels within a school district are to a large extent autonomous, but as we have shown there is in high-performing districts a monitored aspect to this autonomy, and we would argue that the professional freedom to operate schools and classrooms is bounded by the prevailing norms and practices of the district which are summarized in the notion of productive ethos. Productive ethos at the district level both constrains and facilitates; that is, it provides a kind of 'Supported-Enforcement' (Huberman and Miles, 1984) element to the work of principals and teachers. As Rosenholtz (1989) suggests, 'schools seem to be a microcosm for what happens in their districts' (p. 168).

The elaboration of the metaphor of productive ethos through further empirical work will constitute a response of the field of Bossert's (1988) challenge:

> The task for future research on school effectiveness, then, is to begin to elaborate the linkages between administrative organization and decisions and those productive instructional processes that occur within schools. (p. 351)

Furthermore, if administrative practitioners are encouraged by this study to pay less attention to resource questions and more attention to ethos, those norms and values and associated practices, which they communicate to colleagues both in discussion and by modelling, we believe that the educators with whom they work will benefit immensely, as eventually will the students and parents to whom they are ultimately accountable.

Notes

1 By 'superintendency' we mean the group of administrators who staff the superintendent's office and share executive responsibilities. In general school superintendents in British Columbia seem similar to their US analogues in training, in the issues which concern them, and in being overwhelmingly male (Crowson, 1987; Brown, n.d.).

2 The quotations identify district and speaker: e.g., V1.01 = District V; 1 = central office speaker, .01 = superintendent.

References

Barley, S.R., Meyer, G.W. and Gash, D.C. (1988) 'Cultures of culture: Academics, practitioners and the pragmatics of normative control', *Administrative Science Quarterly*, 33, 1, pp. 24–61.

Berman, P. and McLaughlin, M.W. (1979) *An Exploratory Study of School District Adaptations*, Santa Monica, CA, Rand Corporation.

Blase, J.J. (1987) 'Dimensions of effective school leadership: The teacher's perspective', *American Educational Research Journal*, 24, 4, pp. 589–610.

Bossert, S.T. (1988) 'School effects'in Boyan, N. (Ed.) *Handbook of Research on Educational Administration*, New York, NY, Longman.

BOYD, W.L. (1975) 'School board-administrative staff relationships' in CISTONE, P.J. (Ed.) *Understanding School Boards*, Lexington, MA, D.C. Heath.

BOYD, W.L. and CROWSON, R.L. (1981) 'The changing conception and practice of public school administration', *Review of Research in Education*, 9, pp. 311–76.

BROWN, D.J. (n.d.). '*A Survey of the Greater Superintendency*', unpublished paper, Vancouver, B.C. Department of Administative, Adult, and Higher Education, Faculty of Education, University of British Columbia.

BURNS, J.M. (1978) *Leadership*, New York, Harper and Row.

CAMPBELL, J.P. (1977) 'The cutting edge: An overview' in HUNT, J.G. and LARSEN, L.J. (Eds) *Leadership: The Cutting Edge*, Carbondale, IL., Sourthern Illinois University.

COLEMAN, P. (1972) 'Organizational effectiveness in education: Its measurement and enhancement', *Interchange*, 3, 1, pp. 42–52.

COLEMAN, P. (1977) 'Power diffusion in educational governance' in WALLIN, J. (Ed.) *The Politics of Canadian Education*, Edmonton, AB, Canadian Society for Studies in Education.

COLEMAN, P. (1986a) 'The good school district', *Journal of Educational Finance*, 12, 1, pp. 71–96.

COLEMAN, P. (1986b) 'School districts and student achievement in British Columbia: A preliminary analysis', *Canadian Journal of Education*, 11, 4, pp. 509–21.

COLEMAN, P. (1986c) '*Finally, a change that makes a difference: An assessment of a pilot project in School-Based Decision-Making in a British Columbia school district*', paper presented at the World Congress on Education and Technology, Vancouver.

COLEMAN, P. and LAROCQUE, L. (1987) 'Educational policies and change in Canadian education: An interpretive discussion' in GHOSH, R. and RAY, D. (Eds) *Social Change and Education in Canada*, Toronto, Ontario, Harcourt, Brace, Jovanovich.

COLEMAN, P. and LAROCQUE, L. (1989) '*Loose coupling revisited*', paper presented at the annual meeting of the American Educational Research Association, San Francisco.

COLEMAN, P. and LAROCQUE, L. (in press) 'Reaching out: Instructional leadership in school districts', *The Peabody Journal of Education.*

COLEMAN, P., WALSH, J. and LAROCQUE, L. (1988) 'School district achievement and unit costs', *Canadian Journal of Education*, 13, 1, pp. 231–7.

CROWSON, R.L. (1987) 'The local school district superintendency', *Educational Administration Quarterly*, 23, 3, pp. 49–69.

DEAL, T.E. (1987) 'The culture of schools', in SHIEVE, L.T. and SCHOENHEIT, M.V. (Eds) *Leadership: Examining the Elusive*, (1987 Yearbook of the Association for Supervision and Curriculum Development) Washington, DC, ASCD.

EHRENBERG, R.G., CHAYKOWSKI, R.P. and EHRENBERG, R. (1988) 'Are school superintendents rewarded for "performance"?, in MONK, D.H. and UNDERWOOD, J. (Eds), *Microlevel School Finance: Issues and Implications for Policy* (Ninth Annual Yearbook's of the American Education Finance Association), Cambridge, MA, Balinger.

FEIMAN-NEMSER, S., and FLODEN, R.E. (1986) 'The cultures of teaching' in

WITTROCK, M.C. (Ed.) *Handbook of Research on Teaching*, New York, NY, Macmillan.

FIRESTONE, W.A. and HERRIOTT, R.E. (1982) 'Two images of schools as organizations: An explication and illustrative empirical text', *Educational Administration Quarterly*, 18, 2, pp. 35–9.

FULLER, B., WOOD, K., RAPOPORT, T. and DORNBUSCH, S.M. (1982) 'The organizational context of individual efficacy', *Review of Educational Research*, 52, 1, pp. 7–30.

GOODLAD, J.I. (1983) 'The school as workplace' in GRIFFIN, G.A. (Ed.) *Staff Development* (Eighty-second Yearbook of the National Society for Studies in Education) Chicago, IL, National Society for Studies in Education.

GREENE, C.N. (1977) 'Disenchantment with leadership research: Some causes, recommendations, and alternative directions' in HUNT, J.G. and LARSEN, L.J. (Eds), *Leadership: The Cutting Edge*, Carbondale, IL, Southern Illinois University.

GUTTMAN, A. (1989) 'Democratic theory and the role of teachers in democratic education' HANNAWAY, J. and CROWSON, R. (Eds) *The Politics of Reforming School Administration* (1988 Yearbook of the Politics of Education Association), Lewes, Falmer Press.

HACKMAN, J.R. and WALTON, R.E. (1986) 'Leading groups in organizations' in GOODMAN, P. and associates (Eds) *Designing Effective Work Groups*, San Francisco, CA, Jossey-Bass.

HANSON, M. (1976) 'Beyond the bureaucratic mode: A study of power and autonomy in educational decision-making', *Interchange*, 7, 2, pp. 27–38.

HARGROVE E.C., GRAHAM, S.G., WARD, L., ABERNETHY, V., CUNNINGHAM, J. and VAUGHN, W.K. (1981) 'School systems and regulatory mandates: A case study of the implementation of the Education for All Handicapped Children Act' in BACHARACH, S. (Ed.) *Organizational Behavior in Schools and School Districts*, New York, Praeger.

HUBERMAN, A.M. and MILES, M.B. (1984) *Innovation Up Close: How School Improvement Works*, New York, Plenum.

JELINEK, M., SMIRCICH, L. and Hirsch, P. (1983) 'Introduction: A code of many colors', *Administrative Science Quarterly*, 28, 3, pp. 331–8.

KAUFMAN, H. (1963) *Politics and Policies in State and Local Governments*, Englewood Cliffs, NJ, Prentice-Hall.

LAROCQUE, L. and COLEMAN, P. (1986) '*School district effectiveness and district ethos: Creating commitment to district monitoring practices*', *paper presented at the annual meeting of the Society for Studies in Education, Winnipeg*.

LAROCQUE, L. and COLEMAN, P. (1988) 'Quality control: School accountability and district ethos' in HOLMES, M., LEITHWOOD, K.A. and MUSELLA, D. (Eds) *Educational Policy for Effective Schools*, Ontario, Canada, OISE Press.

LAROCQUE, L. and COLEMAN, P. (1989) '*The politics of excellence: Trustee leadership and school district ethos*', paper presented at the annual meeting of the American Educational Research Association, San Francisco.

LAWTON, S. (Ed.) (1987) 'Teachers' salaries: An international perspective' in ALEXANDER, K. and MONK, D.H. *Attracting and Compensating America's Teachers* (Eight Annual Yearbook of the American Educational Finance Association) Cambridge, MA, Ballinger.

LIGHTFOOT, S. (1983) *The Good High School*, New York, Basic Books.

LIPHAM, J.M. (1964) 'Leadership and administration' in GRIFFITHS, D.E. (Ed.) *Behavioral Science and Educational Administration*, Chicago, IL, The National Society for the Study of Education.

LITTLE, J.W. (1982) 'Norms of collegiality and experimentation', *American Educational Research Journal*, 19, 3, pp. 325–40.

MCPHERSON, R.B., CROWSON, R.L. and PITNER, N.J. (1986) *Managing Uncertainty: Administrative Theory and Practice in Education*, Columbus, OH, Charles E. Merrill.

MINTZBERG, H. (1979) *The Structuring of Organizations*, New Jersey, Prentice-Hall.

MURPHY, J., HALLINGER, P. and PETERSON, K.D. (1985) 'Supervising and evaluating principals', *Educational Leadership*, 43, 2, pp. 79–82.

PETERS, T.J., and WATERMAN, R.H. (1982) *In Search of Excellence: Lessons from America's Best Run Companies*, New York, Harper and Row.

ROSENHOLTZ, S.J. (1989) *Teachers' Workplace: The Social Organizations of Schools*, New York, NY, Longman.

SERGIOVANNI, T.J. (1984) 'Leadership and excellence in schooling', *Educational Leadership* 41, 7, pp. 4–13.

SERGIOVANNI, T.J. (1987) 'The theoretical basis for cultural leadership' in SHEIVE, L.T. and SCHOENHEIT, M.B. (Eds), *Leadership: Examining the Elusive* (1987 Yearbook of the Association for Supervision and Curriculum Development). Washington, DC, ASCD.

SHOEMAKER, J. and FRASER, H.W. (1981) 'What principals can do', *Phi Delta Kappan*, 64, 3, pp. 178–82.

SMIRCICH, L. (1983) 'Concepts of culture and organizational analysis', *Administrative Science Quarterly*, 28, 3, pp. 339–58.

TANNENBAUM, A.S. (1962) 'Control in organizations: Individual adjustment and organizational performance', *Administrative Science Quarterly*, 7, 2, pp. 236–57.

WALTON, R.E. and HACKMAN, J.R. (1986) 'Groups under contrasting management strategies' in GOODMAN, P. and associates (Eds) *Designing Effective Work Groups*, San Francisco, CA, Jossey-Bass.

WILDAVSKY, A. (1979) 'Implementation as evolution' in PRESSMAN, J.L. and WILDAVSKY, A. (Eds) *Implementation* (2nd edn). Berkeley, CA, University of California Press.

YUKL, G.A. (1989) *Leadership in Organizations (2nd edn)*. Englewood Cliffs, NJ, Prentice-Hall.

Section B

Why Chief Education Officers Act As They Do

Chapter 6

Components of Chief Education Officers' Problem Solving Processes

Kenneth Leithwood and Rosanne Steinbach

This study examined aspects of the problem-solving processes of eight chief education officers (for example, superintendents, directors). Information processing theory and the results of related research carried out with principals provided a framework for the study. Simulated problem-solving interviews were audiotaped, transcribed and content analyzed. Results identify processes used by CEOs in relation to five aspects of their problem solving: how problems are interpreted; goals to be met through problem solving; the nature and role of values in problem solving; perceived constraints; and the nature of CEOs' solution processes. Comparisons are made between CEOs and principals and between CEOs and senior executives in non-school organizations in respect to the five aspects of problem solving.

> . . . administration is the profession of leadership, the art of intelligent coping with an arbitrary fate. It is a minor matter; but our prospects for human control over events are built on collections of minor matters. (March, 1974, p. 17)

Both Bridges (1982) and Crowson (1987) recently have pointed to the lack of knowledge about the effects chief education officers (CEOs) have on their school systems and about the nature of their practices. Nevertheless, there are signs of growing attention to this vacuum; this is evident, for example, in the work of Coleman and La Rocque (1987), Rosenholtz (1989), Peterson, Murphy and Halliday (1987) and Louis (1987). Given the considerable payoff from efforts over the past decade to better appreciate the nature, causes and consequences of what principals do (for a review, see Leithwood, Begley and Cousins, in press), turning attention to the CEO's role seems timely and potentially productive in continuing efforts to foster educational improvement through administrative practices.

It also seems timely and productive to ask what has been learned in the study of school principals that might enhance subsequent study of CEOs. As related to principals' practices, we believe one relevant 'learning' is that descriptions of overt behavior have proven to be of little practical or theoretical value. Studies of the overt behavior of effective principals, for example, were frequently intended to provide models of exemplary practices which others might emulate. Such studies, often conducted within one type of school (urban, elementary, students with low SES), failed to acknowledge the contingent nature of administrative practice, however. Specific overt behaviors attributed to principals in one school or one type of school were more or less 'effective' depending on a host of at least partially unique conditions related to the school's history, parental expectations, school district characteristics, staff competencies and the like. Descriptions of categories of overt behaviors common among principals across schools were sufficiently abstract as to be largely meaningless guides to action.

Of much more value than research resulting in descriptions of overt behavior have been studies aimed at understanding the roots of such behavior. Through such work, we have come to appreciate the importance of the covert mental processes that are part of principals' solutions to whatever administrative problems they encounter wherever they happen to be working. Such processes demonstrate, for example, an important role for the principals' vision of what their school could be (for example, Stevens, 1986), their own professional goals (Leithwood and Montgomery, 1986), the quality of their reasoning processes (for example, Leithwood and Stager, 1989) and the values they use as standards for evaluating both the actions they take and the ends they are trying to accomplish (for example, Begley, 1987, Campbell, 1988).

In an attempt to benefit from these experiences with research on principals, the study reported in this chapter sought to better understand the nature of what CEOs do through an examination of their problem-solving processes. Our initial study (Leithwood, 1988) of such processes focused on how CEOs classify, manage and give priority to their problems, as well as on factors which influence these processes. The purpose of the present study was to describe, more comprehensively, CEOs' problem solving from the early stages of noticing the existence of a problem through the steps taken to solve it.

Framework

The study was guided by a general orientation to research on problem solving and the specific outcomes of applying that orientation to the study of school administration.

General Orientation[1]

The adoption of a problem-solving perspective on educational administration, while rare, is not new. Hemphill (1958) saw value in such a perspective thirty years ago. At that time, however, theories of problem solving were extremely primitive, avoided direct attention to basic cognitive processes involved in problem solving, and were grounded in very little empirical evidence. All of these limitations are evident in Hemphill's (1958) formulation, which appears to have stimulated little subsequent research. But theories of problem solving are no longer so limited, largely due to advances in cognitive science over the past decade. Consequently, an information processing conception of problem solving was adopted as a general orientation for this study and its predecessor (Leithwood, 1988).

Until recently, information processing-oriented research on problem solving has concentrated on characteristics of the problem itself (particularly its 'structure') and studied problems that were 'well-structured' (i.e., clearly presented, with all of the information needed at hand, and with an appropriate 'algorithm' guaranteeing a correct solution; (Frederiksen, 1984) and/or 'knowledge lean' (i.e., involving novel situations, where specialized knowledge and skill are not required — see for example, Glaser, 1984; Simon, 1973 and 1975). However, several new directions are emerging in the field. First, there is increasing awareness that the solution process that is used has more to do with the solver's knowledge of a particular problem than with problem type or chracteristics per se (Frederiksen, 1984). Second, because of the importance of knowledge, studies of problem solving increasingly have been conducted within specific knowledge domains rather than in 'knowledge-lean' ones. Baird (1983) and Glaser (1984) provide substantial evidence for the appropriateness of this direction for research. Finally, there is evidence of more interest in 'ill-structured' problems (i.e., those with indefinite goals and/or incomplete materials provided (Greeno, 1976), along with an awareness of the limitations of generalizing results from research using well-structured problems to processes involved in solving ill-structured problems.

The treatment of problem structure and solver's knowledge in recent information processing literature demonstrates the importance of domain-specific knowledge in accounting for problem-solving processes and hence has strengthened our belief that there is a need for a detailed study of problem solving by CEOs; little in the existing literature can be safely generalized to this role. Indeed, only two empirical studies could be located (Hayes-Roth and Hayes-Roth, 1979; Voss, Greene, Post and Penner, 1983) which provided accounts of ill-structured problems and/or problems concerned with everyday life. One of these studies (Voss *et al.*,

1983) considered problem solving in the domain of the social sciences. This study's application of the general information processing model to ill-structured problems and its approach to the characterization of social science problems (considering more than 'structure') influenced the direction of the present study significantly.

In addition to type of problem and its relationship to solver's knowledge, the context in which administrators' problems were solved (i.e., whether alone or not) is an important determinant of the process involved. Clark and Peterson (1986), in a review of teachers' thought processes, indicate that there appeared to be an important distinction between the kind of thinking that teachers do during classroom interaction and that done before and after such interaction. Presumably, there is an analogous distinction to be made for administrators. Shulman and Carey (1984) reviewed evidence concerning the number of people involved in problem solving and provided a theoretical argument for the importance of this dimension based on Simon's (1957) conception of bounded rationality; the limits on an individual's problem-solving ability, imposed by the boundaries of his/her information processing capabilities, can potentially be extended through group problem-solving processes.

The Problem Solving of School Principals

The amount of empirical research on administrative problem solving, in an educational context, is extremely modest. However, our research team has been engaged in such research with school principals for the past three years (Leithwood and Stager, 1986; Stager and Leithwood, 1988; Leithwood and Stager, 1989). Results of this research provided tentative directions for inquiry into CEOs' problem-solving processes. Further, direct comparisons of processes used by principals and CEOs seemed likely to help understand the nature and extent of influence on administrative problem solving of role and organizational context.

Our research on problem solving of school principals has used the variety of process tracing methods common to studies of problem solving in many contexts, viewed from an information-processing orientation (Hayes and Flower, 1983). These methods include retrospective reports about naturally occurring problems, 'think aloud' interviews in response to simulated problems, stimulated recall techniques and variants of shadowing principals (behavior protocols) in their schools. At each stage of the research, the problem solving of 'expert' principals has been compared with the problem solving of more 'typical' principals — these designations being the product of two independent procedures for identifying the extent of principals' expertise.

One focus for our inquiry with principals concerned components of their problem-solving processes (Leithwood and Stager, 1989). In that study we developed a 'grounded' set of components or categories within which to describe principals' problem solving. Processes used by 'expert' and 'typical' principals were compared within each of these components.

The five components and their abbreviated definitions are as follows:

- Interpretation: a principal's understanding of specifically what was the nature of the problem, often in situations where multiple problems could be identified;
- Goals: the relatively immediate purposes that the principal was attempting to achieve in response to his or her interpretation of the problem;
- Principles: the relatively long-term purposes, operating principles, fundamental laws, doctrines and assumptions guiding the principal's thinking;
- Constraints: 'immovable' barriers, obstacles or factors severely narrowing the range of possible solutions the principal believed to be available;
- Solution processes: what the principal did to solve a problem (in light of his or her interpretation of the problem, principles and goals to be achieved and constraints to be accommodated).

Table 6.1 summarizes the results of comparing the processes used by expert and typical principals within each of these five components, in response to unstructured problems (few differences were apparent in the responses of the two groups of principals to structured problems).

This study of CEOs used the five component model of problem solving developed with principals as the basis for data coding but with two refinements. One modest refinement was to reconceptualize 'constraints' as obstacles to be overcome in problem solving — not necessarily insurmountable. Viewed this way, the ability to anticipate difficulties seems likely to be an attribute of an effective problem solver.

A second, more fundamental refinement of the original problem solving model for this study was to narrow the conception of 'principles' to values. After Rokeach and Hofstede (cited in Hambrick and Brandon: 1988), a value was defined as 'a broad and relatively enduring preference for some state of affairs' (p. 5). Based on recent research with principals (Begley and Leithwood, 1989; Campbell, 1988) and a review of values literature, a classification of values potentially relevant to administrators was used as the basis for analyzing data related to values in the present study. This classification system includes four major categories of values and some sixteen specific values within these categories, as outlined in table 6.2 (a detailed outline of this classification system can be found in Leithwood, Begley and Campbell, 1989).

Table 6.1 Solving Unstructured Problems: Differences Between Expert and Typical Principals (from Leithwood and Stager, 1989)

Component	Expert	Typical
Problem Interpretation		
Basis for priority	• consequences for school and academic growth of large numbers of students	• more concerned about consequences for themselves
Perceived difficulty	• difficult problems are manageable if one used careful thinking	• difficult problems are frightening and stressful
Ways to understand	• collect information • provides clear, comprehensive interpretation of problems	• makes assumptions in lieu of collecting information • irrelevant issues tend to cloud interpretation
Use of anecdotes	• directly relevant to problem	• recounts difficult experiences rather than highly successful ones
Goals for Problem Solving	• concerned with implications for students and program quality • concerned with providing parents with knowledge • more concerned with knowledge	• more often mentions staff-oriented goals • concerned with making sure that parents are happy • more concerned with feelings
Principles	• considers slightly more principles • used as basis for determining long term goals	• not mentioned • not mentioned
Constraints	• indicates few, if any, constraints • finds ways to deal with constraints	• indicates more constraints • sees constraints as obstacles
Solution Processes	• detailed prior planning • consultation used extensively to get specific information • identify detailed steps in solution process • stress importance of information collection • follow-up planned for	• little attention to planning • consult less frequently with fewer specific purposes

Table 6.2 A Classification of Values Potentially Relevant in Administrative Problem Solving

1 Basic Human Values
- 1.1 Freedom
- 1.2 Happiness
- 1.3 Knowledge
- 1.4 Respect for others
- 1.5 Survival

2 General Moral Values
- 2.1 Carefulness
- 2.2 Fairness (or justice)
- 2.3 Courage

3 Professional Values
- 3.1 General responsibility as educator
- 3.2 Specific role responsibility
- 3.3 Consequences for immediate clients (students, parents, staff)
- 3.4 Consequences for others (community, society-at-large)

4 Social and Political Values
- 4.1 Participation
- 4.2 Sharing
- 4.3 Loyalty, solidarity and commitment
- 4.4 Helping others

Building on this prior conceptual work from research with principals, this study addressed five specific questions:

- How do CEOs interpret the problems which they encounter?
- What type and how many goals do CEOs pursue in their problem solving?
- What is the nature and role of values in CEOs' problem solving?
- What constraints to problem solving are perceived by CEOs and how are they dealt with?
- What are the main features of CEOs' solution processes?

Method

Sample

Eight CEOs were selected for the study so as to ensure variation in length of time as CEOs (from 2 to 13 years, average = 6 years), size of school systems administered (10,000 students to one of the largest in Canada), and gender (two were women); these three variables were viewed as potential influences on problem solving although the sample was too small to permit an analysis of the relationship between these variables and CEOs' problem solving. Biographical information collected at the beginning of a previous interview indicated that five CEOs had prior in-school experience at the elementary level, two at the secondary level, and one at both levels. All but one CEO had entered the role from the superintendent's position (Ontario's equivalent to an Assistant Superintendent); one had entered from an assistant deputy minister's position in the Ministry of Education. Three CEOs had worked in faculties of education at an earlier point in their careers and at least two had been CEOs in other school systems prior to their current posts.

Data Collection Procedures

Data were collected through two interviews, each lasting forty-five minutes to about three hours. In the first interview, CEOs were asked: to perform a problem sorting task; to reflect on their own problem solving and the factors influencing it; and to indicate how they selected which problems, of the many they faced, deserved priority. Results of this interview are reported elsewhere (Leithwood, 1988).

In the second interview, CEOs were asked: to rank a set of six brief problems (see table 6.3) in terms of how clear, at the outset, the course of

Table 6.3 Problems Presented to CEOs

Violence in the schools	Evidence mounts daily of a dramatic increase in violence in the high schools in your board. There are reports, from principals and police, of incidents involving youth gangs who have attacking or threatened students in at least half the high schools in the system. These gangs, it is reported, belong primarily to one ethnic group.
Problem principal	One of the principals in your board has been charged by the police with possession of marijuana for the purpose of trafficking. When his case comes up, the judge discharges him for lack of evidence. What should you do in this situation?
New policy	Although you have personally been aware of the need for a policy regarding race relations for some time, your board as a whole has not felt the need to have one. However, in response to a Ministry initiative, the board does vote to have you develop and implement such a policy. How would you proceed with this task?
Trustee disagreement	As a new Director, you discover that there appears to be considerable disagreement, among the members of your board, concerning the board's budget. A number of trustees appear to want you to take action on trimming the budget, because both educational taxes and teachers' salaries are relatively high in the board. However, a smaller but significant group of trustees do not want change. They are strongly committed to the existing policies and practices of the board, even though they are costly. What would you do in this situation?
Staff morality	You have been aware that there has been some concern from some trustees regarding the morals and behavior of some board employees. However, you are unprepared when, late at night, they suddenly move, second and pass the motion that the Director be requested to develop a code of behavior for all board staff. At least some of the trustees support the notion of developing some sort of checklist, so that employees would lose demerit points for various infractions. What could you do?
Walkouts	Negotiations in your school district have been going slowly and morale has deteriorated. The union has been increasingly militant, threatening work stoppages and resorting to various kinds of harassment. Teachers have called in sick and withheld the usual kinds of cooperation found in schools. Suddenly things take a turn for the worse: two principals call to say that all their teachers have walked out in mid-morning. At these two schools, the union representative gave the principal a half-hour's warning of the walkout. What would you do?

action to be taken was; to present, in as much detail as possible, their thinking regarding solutions to the clearest and least clear problems; and to describe from their own experience problems similar in degree of clarity to each of these. The solutions to the two problems, from the set of six presented, chosen by each CEO as least and most clear, constituted the data on which this paper is based (the terms 'clear' and 'unclear' were judged to be the closest synonyms in ordinary discourse to the terms 'structured' and 'unstructured' and hence were used in the interview). Each interview was tape recorded and verbatim transcripts were made.

Data Analysis Procedures

A coding system, originally developed for research with principals was adapted and applied to the CEO transcripts, initially by one analyst. Statements which could not be coded with confidence by the initial analyst were given to a second analyst and a consensus was reached on their coding. Subsequently, the reliability of this coding was tested by having two independent analysts code a sample of twenty-five statements. There was 92 per cent agreement between these two rates.

Results and Discussion

Results of analyzing protocol data from the eight CEOs are described in five sections corresponding to the specific research questions.

How CEOs Interpret Problems

Statements classified as 'interpretation' were those which indicated how CEOs were attempting to clarify the nature of the problem. Specifically defined as interpretation were statements concerning (a) the reasons for awarding priority to a problem; (b) the reasons why a problem was considered difficult or easy, complex or simple; and, (c) ways of understanding the problem. Anecdotes used by CEOs to explain their understanding of problems (d) were also coded as interpretation.

CEOs demonstrated a reasonably high level of consistency in the choices of problems which they considered most and least difficult and complex. As the most structured problems, four CEOs chose the New Policy On Race Relations, three chose Trustee Disagreement and one chose The Problem Principal. As the least clear problems, four CEOs chose Walkouts, three chose Violence In Schools and one CEO chose Staff Morality. No problem identified as most clear was identified as least clear by anyone and vice versa (this is in contrast with results from our studies of principals, (for example, Leithwood and Stager, 1989) in which there was no such uniformity in the labelling of problems).

In reference to the most structured problems, none of the CEOs provided data about the conditions that would make such a problem a high priority. For least structured problems, the need for immediate action (two CEOs) and the need to prevent the problem from getting any worse (one CEO) were identified as conditions that would increase the priority of such problem.

Table 6.4 identifies the criteria on which the CEOs' definition of problem structure (difficulty, complexity) was based. Structured (easy,

Table 6.4 Bases on which CEOs Determined Problem Difficulty and Complexity (Structure)

No. of CEOs	Basis for Defining 'Structured' Problems	No. of CEOs	Basis for Defining 'Unstructured' Problems
8	frequent occurrence, familiar topic	6	unfamiliar, lots of unknowns, complexity of decision
1	'factual' problem	2	lack of background information
1	CEO's responsibility is clear	3	no immediate solution is likely
2	not a crisis or emergency	1	involves peoples' feelings
5	'mechanism' or procedure 'in place'	1	philosophically 'uncomfortable'
		3	number of people/groups involved
		2	affects parents and other non-staff
		2	dire or unpredictable consequences
		1	problem encountered at advanced stage

simple, clear) problems, were, in CEOs' terms, 'straightforward'; this seemed to mean that the CEO was familiar with at least some aspect of the problem already — the general topic, or the background of the problem. In response to the Trustee Disagreement problem, one CEO noted:

> ... this is a familiar kind of scenario. And it often comes up in boards where you've got an old guard component and some newer trustees who are gung-ho and want to move and the old guard is sort of reflecting what they think is the community standard and don't like these renegades ... spending all their money.

Clarity was also a function of a problem involving primarily matters of 'fact' as opposed to feelings (for example, 'I never have any more difficulty than with the human problems') and the CEO's role in relation to the problem being evident. Problems which did not require immediate solution and for which a routine solution procedure was in place were seen as structured, also.

Problems were defined as unstructured (difficult, complex, unclear) when important aspects of the problem reduced the CEOs' perceived ability to control the problem-solving process. Such a perception was partly a function of lack of information of various sorts. For example, in response to the Staff Morality problem, a CEO noted: '... the thing that's completely unclear here is what is being defined as staff morality. Are we talking about after hours activity, are we talking about one teacher...'. Lack of control was also a function of high levels of complexity in decisions that might be required as part of the problem solving, large numbers of people involved (especially non-staff) and low probability of finding a solution perhaps because the problem had become greatly exacerbated prior to the CEO encountering it. In response to the Walkout problem, for example, one CEO commented: '... you're facing a *fait accompli* now. And they are out of school and the decision has to be made'. Problems also were viewed as unstructured when peoples' feelings were a central part of the problem; when the likely outcome of the problem was unpredictable or 'dire', or when the problem involved values and beliefs in conflict with those of the CEO ('philosophically uncomfortable').

CEOs used two strategies for understanding the problem better, whether they viewed the problem as structured or unstructured. The most frequently used strategy was to relate the problem to experiences with similar problems encountered in the past; this strategy was used by six of the eight CEOs in response to clear problems and two CEOs in response to unclear problems. One CEO said, for example:

> ... the walkout [problem] is a very difficult one because it's very complex and the problem I have answering it is one that I have actually lived through. It didn't have to do with negotiations but it had to do with the reported closure of a school and in this case the staff walked out of their classes ...

Three CEOs also decomposed or unpacked problems (for example '... you have to approach this problem from two standpoints ...') or rephrased problems in their own terms in order to better understand them.

For unclear problems, in addition to the two strategies already mentioned, CEOs (1) examined immediate effects. In response to the walkout problem, one CEO pointed out 'the public has a keen interest in this, so, right away, when you are talking about what principals and teachers do you directly affect the students and the parents, ... there will not be enough telephone lines just to satisfy the communication process ... and I'm not even touching what the solution is. I'm just talking to you about the immediate effect'. CEOs (1) also identified alternative possible causes and assured themselves that all the necessary facts were available (for example, ... you 'have to find the information first'). One CEO also considered carefully who 'owned' the problem.

One CEO sought to better understand the clearest problem by searching for an existing problem-solving procedure.

CEOs' use of anecdotes was extremely limited in relation to the interpretation of either structured or unstructured problems: three CEOs used examples or analogies or comparisons with relevant existing policies as a way of clarifying clear problems. No use was made of anecdotes in relation to unclear problems.

In rationalizing the value of a problem-solving orientation to research about administrative practice, Kolb (1983) asserts that:

> The vitality and success of organizations are determined, in this view, by 'doing the right thing' (problem finding) and by 'doing things right' (problem solving). (p. 109)

Our study of how CEOs interpret problems was an attempt to better understand how Kolb's 'problem finding' activity occurs. Data from the present study concerning this component of problem solving are closely related to our earlier attempt (Leithwood, 1988) to understand how CEOs classify and manage their problems. In that study, CEOs awarded high priority to unclear problems when the problem: could only be handled by the CEO, was novel, affected a large proportion of the school system, was highly visible and had significant political content. High priority problems, in addition, had a long time frame for finding a solution, were directly related to board policy and clearly fit within the CEOs' view of their role responsibilities. The present study introduced contradictory — although easy to understand considering the nature of the case problems used in the research — evidence concerning time lines (the need for immediate action increased a problem's priority): an additional basis for awarding priority, identified in the present study, was the need to prevent the problem from getting worse.

Our studies of effective elementary principals (Leithwood and Stager, 1986 and 1989) suggest several similarities in priority setting. Like CEOs, time lines and the number of people affected by a problem influenced its priority for them. But the people, in the case of principals, tended to be students and others in the school, whereas CEOs did not explictly mention students but did focus on trustees.

The previous study, like the present, inquired about the basis on which CEOs judge the difficulty of a problem. Both sets of data suggested that problems are perceived as difficult when: many people are involved in the solution; no immediate solution is evident; and the problem has significant emotional content. The earlier study also identified value conflicts as an element in CEOs' perception of problem difficulty.

Data from our studies of elementary principals suggest principals, like CEOs, judged problem difficulty in terms of numbers of people, availability of a solution and emotional content. Expert principals, as well, saw problems as difficult when they required careful thought and planning. CEOs did not show much evidence of requiring such thought and planning; indeed their problem-solving processes overall seemed less sensitive to problem clarity than did the processes used by principals.

Like expert and typical principals, CEOs attempted to better understand the nature of problems by drawing on past, relevant experiences and by ensuring all necessary information was available. CEOs identified a number of additional procedures, however: rephrasing the problem, searching for existing procedures, examining probable immediate effects, and identifying alternative causes. Whereas expert principals made frequent use of relevant anecdotes (or analogies) to understand the problem, this tactic appeared not to be used by CEOs.

In sum, available evidence suggests that CEOs possess a relatively extensive array of strategies for interpreting their problems. Many of these strategies are similar to those used by expert principals but the number of strategies used by CEOs appears to be somewhat greater. In this respect, CEOs appeared similar to Isenberg's (1987) general managers who devoted more of their mental resources, than a less experienced control group, to initially defining and framing their problems. In addition, CEOs' interpretation strategies, as compared with expert principals, were applied in a more automatized fashion and were more closely attuned to the larger school system and political environment which constitutes their work environment.

Nature and Number of Goals for Problem Solving

Statements classified as 'goals' were those which indicated the relatively immediate ends to be served by the CEOs' problem solving, either the overall problem solution or some significant stage in the solution process. Of interest were both the nature and number of CEOs' goals.

Evident in the nature of CEOs' goals was the distinction between those primarily concerned with aspects of the problem-solving process and those concerned with the outcome (process vs. product goals). Process goals were usually of two types. One type was aimed at ensuring that members of the organization played appropriate roles in the problem solving process. In response to the Violence in the Schools problem, for example, one CEO's goal was: '[to mobilize principals] to look clearly at the problem and decide upon their own methods of dealing with it'. The Trustee Disagreement problem was viewed by several CEOs as an opportunity for educating trustees in their role: '... make sure the trustees all recognize that at any particular time they are not all going to think alike ...'; '.. set up a series of in-services for the trustees ...'. This concern for playing appropriate roles in problem solving might be seen as part of a more fundamental, second goal of CEOs — to control the problem-solving process. As one CEO said when confronted with the New Policy problem, '... [don't leave it open ended] so we're managing it to some extent and we have fewer surprises'. This control theme is evident, as well, in such other comments as:

- '... the very best thing is the communication. You have to have very central control of every aspect of your operation' (Walkouts)
- '... Let the politicians fight amongst themselves, once all the work has been done' (Trustee Disagreement)

- '. . . make sure both the minority and majority [of trustees] understood that the process is sound' (Trustee Disagreement)

Problems directly involving trustees elicited more expression of control-oriented goals than did other sorts of problems.

Product goals also appeared to be of two sorts. One sort, usually implicit in the CEOs' talk, was to solve the problem as stated; in the case of the New Policy problem, for example, to comply with the trustees' request. A second type of product goal, explicit in CEOs' remarks, was to ensure that certain key sub-goals, critical to a successful overall solution, were achieved. For example:

- 'I think that we have to give a lot of concentration to finding out the diffused frustrations that exist at that level' (Violence in the Schools)
- 'I would have to deal with the immediate [situation] of the school and the children' (Walkouts)
- 'Have those reports or items on a special list — in order of priority, or in any order, to help the trustees rank order' (Trustee Disagreement)

Twenty-four goal statements were generated by the eight CEOs in response to the total set of six hypothetical problems. This amounts to about four goals per problem with a range of two to five. Although there were many sub-goals not counted, it seems clear that CEOs did not generate very many explicit goals and they never used the term goal or reasonable facsimile in talking about their problem solving.

Problem clarity or structure did not appear to make any difference in the number of goals generated. Each set of three least clear and three most clear problems elicited twelve goal statements.

Number of goals elicited from CEOs did vary when the nature of the goals (process vs. product) was considered in relation to problem structure or clarity. The set of three least clear problems generated twice as many process as product goals (8 vs. 4). In contrast, the set of three most clear problems produced twice as many product as process goals (8 vs. 4). This suggests that CEOs responded to lack of problem clarity by attending to what they considered to be crucial aspects of the problem-solving process in order to ensure a satisfactory resolution. Problem clarity meant the CEO could envision a satisfactory outcome, perhaps, as well as the process for arriving at it.

Isenberg (1987) claims that, by definition, unstructured problems are likely to have multiple goals; such goals may be conflicting with inherent trade-offs. Data from our study of expert principals (Leithwood and Stager, 1989) suggested that they responded to such multiplicity and conflict by focusing on people and groups. Expert principals' goals acknowledged the various stakeholders in the problem and espoused a relatively large number of product goals balanced among these stakeholders, with special attention to students.

Data from the present study imply that CEOs' responses to unclear problems were more like the responses of other senior managers than expert principals, in this component of their problem solving. They set relatively fewer goals and these goals were dominated by a concern for process. Such practice is consistent with Isenberg's (1987) finding that senior managers appeared to think and act in close tandem. For them '... the process of thinking through a problem involved attempting to solve it, and only through its solution could anything approximating true understanding emerge' (p. 180).

Nature and Role of Values in Problem Solving

Statements classified as values reflected, as we noted above, a broad and relatively enduring preference for some state of affairs. Our system for coding such statements was keyed to the four categories of values described earlier: basic human values, general moral values, professional values and social and political values. Data analysis aimed to clarify both the nature and function of CEOs' values in problem solving.

Table 6.5 reports the frequency of occurrence in the protocols of statements coded according to the four categories of values. As a means of clarifying the nature of values 'used' by CEOs in their problem solving we considered first, the broad categories then specific values within each category. Finally, the overall ranking of specific values was examined.

More than 50 per cent of all value statements (forty-one of eighty-one) were coded as Professional Values and about a quarter (twenty-one of eighty-one) were coded as Social and Political Values. General Moral Values and Basic Human Values accounted for the remaining value statements (14 per cent and 10 per cent respectively). CEOs showed relatively extensive use of some specific values within each category and little or no use of others. Within the category Basic Human Values, Knowledge and Respect for Others received modest use; there was virtually no evidence of use of Freedom, Happiness or Survival. Fairness was the only frequently (9) used General Moral Value, although Carefulness was mentioned twice. The category Professional Values, was dominated by CEOs' sense of their Specific Role Responsibility (mentioned thirty-one times). Consequences for Immediate Clients was mentioned eight times. Use was made of all the specific values associated with Social and Political Values: Participation and Loyalty, Solidarity and Commitment were most frequently used, however (mentioned eight times each).

The right hand column of table 6.5 ranks specific values without

Table 6.5 Frequency of Differenct Types of Value Statements made by CEOs in Response to Most and Least Clear Problems

Categories of Values	Frequency Most Clear	Frequency Least Clear	Total	Rank
1 Basic Human Values				
1.1 Freedom	1	0	1	7
1.2 Happiness	0	0	0	8
1.3 Knowledge	0	4	4	4
1.4 Respect for others	2	1	3	5
1.5 Survival	0	0	0	8
2 General Moral Values				
2.1 Carefulness	2	0	2	6
2.2 Fairness (or justice)	5	4	9	2
2.3 Courage	0	0	0	8
3 Professional Values				
3.1 General responsibility as educator	1	1	2	6
3.2 Specific role responsibility	16	15	31	1
3.3 Consequences for others (students, parents, staff)	2	6	8	3
3.4 Consequences for others (community, society-at-large)	0	0	0	8
4 Social and Political Values				
4.1 Participation	4	4	8	3
4.2 Sharing	0	2	2	6
4.3 Loyalty, solidarity and commitment	2	6	8	3
4.4 Helping others	2	1	3	5
Total	37	44	81	

reference to their broader classification. The frequencies suggest that the CEOs' sense of their Specific Role Responsibility was mentioned at least three times more often than any other specific value. The form this value took is evident in these statements:

- 'I wouldn't even be involved with it. I have two superintendents that are the resources to that committee' (New Policy problem)
- '... and I was sitting there as what we call a principle resource person' (Trustee Disagreement problem)
- '... [I would probably be] involved initially but [would be] making a determination of some kind of role that I would play as you get more information' (Violence in the Schools problem)

A cluster of specific values from three different value categories were ranked second and third and appeared about equally as frequently. These include:

- Fairness (for example, '. . . once a decision . . . is made, that we recognize that the process was fair and that somebody didn't get their own way');
- Consequences for Immediate Clients (for example '. . . if these were generally known [i.e., violence in schools] . . . and parents were afraid to send their children to school because of this, then the director would make a statement to the press . . .)
- Participation (for example, 'I would have that meeting right away . . . and try to work with [the principals] and the superintendents on what we feel can be done . . .)
- Loyalty, Solidarity and Commitment (for example, '. . . the nature of the talk [with staff] would be positive and constructive and as forward looking as possible . . . and try to get people back together again . . .').

Responses by CEOs demonstrated the generally acknowledged role of values as broad guidelines for action and as standards against which the goodness of a solution or solution process is judged. Our data, however, provided only modest support for the more frequent use of values in response to unstructured or least clear problems: thirty-seven value statements in response to most clear problems and forty-four value statements in response to least clear problems.

Finally, there were no statements made that could not be accommodated within the a priori categories of values.

As compared with principals (Begley, 1987; Campbell, 1988), CEOs in the present study demonstrated a similar, strong commitment to most of the specific values in the category Social and Political Values. CEOs differed from principals, however, in a number of ways: they showed a more uniform use of values whether problems were defined as most or least clear; they identified 'consequences' less frequently as a value guiding their problem solving; and they used as a value much more frequently, their own understanding of their specific role responsibilities.

While the values framework used in this study appeared to capture CEOs' values satisfactorily, it has several significant differences in comparison with an alternative framework developed by Hambrick and Brandon (1988) to guide the study of executive behavior. The Hambrick and Brandon framework consists of 6 broad categories of values, four of which also appear in our framework. Their fifth category, 'materialism' (to value wealth and pleasing possessions), does not appear in our framework because our earlier data from principals found no evidence of this value. The present study of CEOs provides no support for its inclusion, either. More support can be found for the Hambrick and

Brandon category 'power' (to value control of situations and people). Control was a strong theme in the CEO data, which we coded as Goals, However, its pervasiveness probably warrants reconceptualizing the theme as an expression of a value and expanding our values framework accordingly.

Perception of and Responses to Constraints

Statements classified as 'constraints' indicated the CEOs' awareness or anticipation of an obstacle that might be encountered in working out a solution. Data were summarized to indicate the number and nature of constraints identified by CEOs as well as the CEOs' general orientation to constraints.

The eight CEOs identified a relatively small number of constraints — eleven in response to the most clear problems (Trustee Disagreement, Race Relations Policy) and nine in response to the least clear problems (Violence In Schools, Walkouts). For the most clear problems, 3 CEOs did not cite any constraints, one identified one, two cited two and two cited three constraints. In the case of the least clear problems, seven CEOs identified one constraint. Two constraints were identified by one CEO.

Five different types of constraints were included in CEO's responses to the most clear problems. One such constraint, not viewed as serious, was limitations on the CEO's authority. For example, one CEO in response to the Trustee Disagreement problem outlined a long term solution involving educating the trustees in board priority setting prior to entering into budget decisions. He concluded, however, by noting:

> . . . I don't know that there is much more that the [CEO] can do. If you have provided all the information, you've made every reasonable effort to educate them in terms of what needs to be done and their responsibility as a trustee, I think you have to live with the results.

Other types of constraints included lack of information about the background to the problem and possible opposition from other people or groups. An example of the latter type of constraint is evident in one CEO's response to the New Policy problem:

> . . . a typical kind of complication is that some . . . representative of some group, real or otherwise, is likely to phone or in or write and say: 'Listen, I've heard that you're developing this policy. I'm an expert on it and I'd like to be involved'. And that person may indeed by very effective in helping or may be a real problem

> because they've got a single issue that they want to promote and could really complicate the development of the policy.

A final constraint identified (by three CEOs) in response to most clear problems was organizational policies and practices and the limitations they created in how flexibly one could approach a problem.

In response to least clear problems, CEOs identified two of the five constraints already discussed — lack of information (three CEOs) and opposition from other people or groups (two CEOs). Other types of constraints included the personalities of specific people involved in problem solving and lack of existing guidelines for helping manage the problem (for example, the Staff Morality problem: '. . . the parameters of the problem would have to be far more clearly set out before I even begin to tackle the problem').

Constraints identified by CEOs ranged in nature from those they considered relatively minor (for example, limitations on their own authority) to those that were potentially quite disruptive (for example, opposition of others). Nevertheless, virtually all CEOs viewed constraints as an inevitable part of problem solving — things to anticipate but not to prevent one from getting on with the job. Therefore, for each constraint, they also generated an approach to dealing with it. In response to the Walkout problem, for example, one CEO readily generated contingency plans in case the teachers refused to go back to their classes (as he had directed the principal to request), in case they wanted to meet with him during school hours, in case they wanted more information about negotiations, and the like.

Because constraints were conceptualized differently in the present study than in our previous studies of principals, it is possible to compare CEOs' responses with those of principals in only a limited way. Both expert principals and CEOs were similar in viewing constraints as sub-problems to be solved, not insurmountable hurdles. We are unaware of data about constraints from other types of senior managers which would permit a comparison with the CEO data.

Main Features of CEOs' Solution Processes

Statements about the relatively specific actions or sequences of actions CEOs would take once the problem was interpreted were labeled 'solution processes'. By way of example, one CEO's response to the unclear Violence in the Schools problem included eight actions:

- Check the facts with several sources including the principals
- Discuss the problem with police and other social agencies

- Check for relevant information in the media
- Arrange a meeting with police, social agencies and responsible members of ethnic groups
- Elicit the support of these groups in finding a solution
- Try to develop a common understanding of the problem
- Determine the school's role in solving the problem
- Search out key players to take an active role in solving the problem.

The mean number of actions identified by all CEOs in response to the set of three unclear problems was 8.5.

In response to a clear problem, Trustee Disagreement, another CEO outlined five actions:

- Provide trustees with information about the meaning of a high quality education;
- Discuss with trustees the setting of budget priorities based on educational goals;
- Provide information to assist trustees in setting priorities
- 'Educate' trustees regarding their responsibilities
- Accept the results of whatever decisions are made by trustees after these actions.

CEOs identified, on average, 6.9 actions in response to the set of three clear problems.

Table 6.6 summarizes the number of CEOs who responded in particular ways to five additional aspects of solution processes. These data indicate a strong propensity for forward planning in response to either clear or unclear problems with some circular, non-linear or iterative planning activity among three CEOs. Only one CEO decomposed a problem into sub-problems as part of his or her planning. The sources of their solution processes depended a good deal on problem clarity. In the case of clear problems, there was usually an existing procedure that could be used, at least in adapted form (seven CEOs). Least clear problems demanded more invention for at least three CEOs.

Least clear problems also led to either extensive or modest information collection by the majority of CEOs (six) and extensive consultation with others as part of the solution process (six). Irrespective of problem clarity, however, there was little evidence of planning for follow-up; that is, monitoring the solution and evaluating its success.

Table 6.6 Elements of CEOs' Solution Processes

Elements of Solution Process	Most Clear Problems	Least Clear Problems
1 Direction of solution process planning[1]		
1.1 forward planning	8	7
1.2 backward planning	—	—
1.3 iterative	3	3
1.4 decomposes problem	—	1
2 Source of solution process plan		
2.1 existing institutionalized procedures	4	1
2.2 adaptation of procedures	3	1
2.3 novel process	—	3
2.4 can't tell	1	3
3 Evidence of attention to information collection as part of solution process		
3.1 extensive	1	3
3.2 modest	3	3
3.3 none	4	2
4 Consultation with others as part of solution process		
4.1 extensive	2	6
4.2 modest	5	1
4.3 none	1	1
5 Evidence of planning for follow-up		
5.1 yes	2	1
5.2 no	6	7

1 For this element some CEOs' solution processes fall into two categories.

CEOs' solution processes were similar, in a number of ways, to those of expert principals (Leithwood and Stager, 1989). Both groups attempted to consult all those with a stake in the problem and saw information collection as an important action. Although more visible among expert principals, neither group gave much attention to monitoring and following up the consequences of their solutions. For the most part, expert principals generated a larger number of more detailed actions as part of their solution processes than did CEOs; they appeared to plan more extensively.

In the context of studying the thinking of senior managers, Isenberg (1987) depicts the solution processes for unclear administrative problems as involving multiple paths toward solutions which are not initially identifiable. Further, attempted solutions often changed the originally perceived causes of the problem and feedback about success or progress was slow and often ambiguous. In the face of such problems, Isenberg claims that senior managers typically reject a hierarchical model of action planning, a model others have labelled 'backward planning'. This model begins with general goals and systematically refines the related sub-goals until specific actions have been identified; actions are then implemented. Such backward planning was not strongly evident in our data from either expert principals or CEOs. However, the more detailed action steps and greater number of goals suggests that principals were more inclined in that direction than were CEOs.

The solution processes of CEOs, like other senior managers in Isenberg's (1987) study, more closely approximated an opportunistic model. This model assumes that:

> . . . the plan develops incrementally, there is jumping around within the planning space, several unrelated specific sequences are planned without linking them together, . . . priorities may be ignored at any one point, and each new decision produces a new situation. (p. 190)

Opportunistic planning requires an active, flexible memory, the ability to make new connections among previously unrelated phenomena and a positive attitude toward exploiting possibilities, some of them surprising. Such planning also requires the ability to simulate action-result sequences during implementation because they cannot all be planned in advance. This pattern seems similar to the one advocated by Hayes (1981) as a way to solve ill-defined problems. '[It may be necessary] to jump into the problem before we fully understand it. Very often the real nature of a problem is hidden from us until we actually try to solve it' (p. 22).

Acknowledging that, from time to time, some senior managers do engage in planning more like the hierarchical model, Isenberg (1987) describes a third model that seems to take advantage of the strengths of the other two (clear direction, flexible action), while avoiding their weaknesses. Labelled 'strategic opportunism', this model combines a clear understanding of one's general or long term purposes and the taking advantage of opportunities that arise to move toward them. Senior managers show signs of using this model, claims Isenberg, as they move back and forth between relatively abstract strategies, goals and policies and quite specific thinking about specific people and organizational processes. CEOs' extensive use of values, as distinct from short term goals, in solving both clear and unclear problems may be evidence of clear long term general directions; their consideration of a small number of specific action sequences may suggest that they are sensitive to the unanticipated issues that will arise as they begin the solution process and the futility of excessive prior planning.

Conclusion

It would be tempting, but inadvisable, to overinterpret the results of this study. Because the collection and analysis of protocol data is time consuming, expensive and effortful, the study only provided data about the thinking of a small number of CEOs. Furthermore, as Ericsson and Simon

(1984) have pointed out so well, protocol data varies widely in its ability to capture thought processes depending on how it is collected. Additional types and amounts of such data are needed to bolster confidence in results of the current study. With this in mind, we sum up the study, offer several additional interpretive observations and point to areas for future research.

At the outset, the need for this study was rationalized on the grounds that descriptions of overt administrative behavior by themselves contribute little to either understanding administrative practice or improving it. Such understanding and improvement, it was argued, depended on a better appreciation of how administrators think about the wide variety of problems they face in the wide variety of contexts they encounter. An information processing orientation to problem solving was adopted as a general framework for the research. This orientation had been used in our previous and ongoing research with principals and Schwenk (1988) has recently argued for the value of such a perspective in understanding the strategic decision making of senior executives.

The specific framework used to generate research questions for the study was a model of problem-solving components which emerged from a recent study with principals (Leithwood and Stager, 1989; Leithwood and Stager, 1986). The components of the model included interpretation, goals, values, constraints and solution processes. Results of the present study appeared to be interpretable within this overall model with one addition, not yet discussed. Throughout their simulated problem solving, CEOs exuded an unmistakable air of self-confidence. This was more evident in what they did not say than what they did say. For example, none of the CEOs, in spite of identifying certain problems as complex, difficult, unclear or messy, expressed any doubt about being able to manage their problems, nor did they show any signs of anxiety or tension. The same air of assurance was evident among expert (but not typical) principals in our previous studies as well. We are not the first to notice this quality; Kemp and McClelland (1986) identify it as a 'generic competence' for senior managers indicated by the manager who: 'sees self as prime-mover, leader, or energizer of the organization; mentions being stimulated by crises and other difficult problems; sees self as the most capable person to get the job done' (p. 41). As well as adding self-confidence (or Affect) as a component to the general model, further theoretical and empirical work needs to be devoted to clarifying the relationships among components of the model. So far, these relationships have not been explored in detail.

Data related to specific components of the model indicated similarities as well as differences between expert principals and CEOs. Some of these differences appear to be a function of work context. For example, because CEOs have considerable resources for problem solving, they can assume the routine availability of adequate information which principals have to more self-consciously seek out. Furthermore, since there appears to be much that is similar in the problem solving of CEOs and senior managers in other fields, this lends support to the idea that one's position in the organization (work context) may be a significant factor accounting for variation in problem-solving processes.

Other differences may be a function of experience. CEOs, for example, show more signs of 'opportunistic planning' if not 'strategic opportunism' than do principals. Perhaps they have better learned the importance of fundamental directions (as their use of values suggests) and the capricious nature of their environment (which makes backward planning frequently a waste of time).

Another observed difference between CEOs and principals might also be due to experience. While expert and typical principals solved well-structured problems similarly, there were significant differences between them in the solutions to ill-structured problems. In contrast, the CEOs in our sample showed no such distinction between well and ill-structured problems for several components in the problem-solving model. Even for the problems they called 'very complex', there was very little evidence of grappling with dilemmas. (This might also be a manifestation of their observed self-confidence.) It's as if the CEOs are able to translate difficult problems into familiar scenarios which can then be treated as routine problems. In fact, at the end of their solutions to the least clear problems, two CEOs stated that the problems weren't so hard after all.

On the whole, the results of this research indicate that senior school administrators appear to operate more like senior managers in other fields than like principals. In contrast to principals, CEOs spend more time interpreting the problem, use more values or principles to direct their problem solving, have fewer explicit 'product' goals, and plan fewer steps in the solution process.

One interpretation of these differences is that CEOs are more concerned with the process of problem solving than with the actual details of the solution. Whether this is a function of work context, experience, or personality (the game is more fascinating) remains to be seen. Nevertheless, it seems that CEOs behave as if they believe that, if the process is right (and they work hard to ensure that it is), whatever the outcome is will be fine. One CEO captured this sentiment well:

> And that's a key role for the director, is finding things, just looking at things with this broad look, that nobody else has in the system. Nobody else can have the broad look that the director has, and that's one of the most important parts of the director's role, is to have a finger in every pie. You've got to know what's going on.... So you don't look at the detail, but you can see the gestalt, and you can try to find things that will not fit.

In terms of future research directions, two have already been identified. One direction is simply to increase sample sizes and the variety of data used. A second direction involves exploring, more explicitly, relations among components in the problem solving model. This is likely to involve developing a series of lower order models, an example of which is provided by Hambrick and Brandon (1988). They conceptualized the relationship between values and solution processes by initially hypothesizing both direct ('behavior channeling') and indirect relationships (values affect solution processes through their influence on whether and how 'stimuli' are perceived). Finally, this study assumed that all CEOs in the sample had comparable expertise. In fact, this is not any more likely than it would be in relation to any role and we developed our own opinions about the relative levels of problem-solving expertise possessed by the eight CEOs in the sample. If the aim of improving CEO problem solving is to be taken seriously, it will be necessary to undertake future research with CEOs who are known to be exceptionally expert at what they do.

Note

1 This section is modestly adapted from Leithwood (1988).

References

Baird, L.L. (1983) *Review of Problem-solving Skills* (Research Report). Princeton, NJ: Educational Testing Service.

Begley, P. (1987) '*The influence of values on principals' problem-solving processes*', paper presented at the annual meeting of the American Educational Research Association, New Orleans.

Begley, P. and Leithwood, K.A. (1989) *The Nature and Influence of Values on Principals' Problem Solving*. Toronto, OISE, mimeo.

Bridges, E.M. (1982) 'Research on the school administrator: The state of art, 1967–1980', *Educational Administration Quarterly*, 18, pp. 12–33.

Campbell, G. (1988) '*The relationship between principals' values and their decision making processes*', unpublished doctoral dissertation, Toronto, OISE.

Clark, C.M. and Peterson, P.L. (1986) 'Teacher thought processes' in Wittrock, M.C. (Ed.) *Handbook of Research on Teaching* (3rd edn) New York, Macmillan.

Coleman, P. and LaRocque, L. (1987) *Reaching Out: Instructional Leadership in School Districts*. Vancouver, Simon Fraser University, mimeo.

Crowson, R.L. (1987) 'The local school district superintendency: A puzzling administrative role', *Educational Administration Quarterly*, 23, 3, pp. 49–69.

Ericsson, K.A. and Simon, H.A. (1984) *Protocol Analyses: Verbal Reports as Data*. Cambridge, MA, MIT Press.

FREDERIKSEN, N. (1984) 'Implications of cognitive theory for instruction in problem solving', *Review of Educational Research*, 54, 3, pp. 363–407.

GLASER, R. (1984) 'Education and thinking: The role of knowledge', *American Psychologist*, 39, pp. 93–104.

GREENO, J.G. (1976) 'Indefinite goals in well-structured problems', *Psychological Review*, 83, pp. 479–91.

HAMBRICK, D.C. and BRANDON, G.L. (1988) 'Executive values' in HAMBRICK, D. (Ed.) *The Executive Effect: Concepts and Methods for Studying Top Managers*, London, JAI Press.

HAYES, J.R. (1981) *The Complete Problem Solver*. Philadelphia, PA, The Franklin Institute Press.

HAYES, J.R. and FLOWER, L.S. (1983) 'Uncovering cognitive processes in writing: An introduction to protocol analysis' in MOSENTHAL, P., TAMOR, L. and WALMSLEY, S. (Eds) *Research on Writing: Principals and Methods*, New York, Longmans.

HAYES-ROTH, B. and HAYES-ROTH, F. (1979) 'A cognitive model of planning', *Cognitive Science*, 3, pp. 275–310.

HEMPHILL, J.K. (1958) Administration as problem solving' in HALPIN, A.W. (Ed.) *Administrative Theory in Education*, New York, Macmillan.

ISENBERG, D.J. (1987) 'Inside the mind of the senior manager' in PERKINS, D.N., LOCHHEAD, J. and BISHOP, J.C. (Eds) *Thinking*, Hillsdale, NJ, Lawrence Erlbaum.

KELMP, G.O. and MCCLELLAND, D.C. (1986) 'What characterizes intelligent functioning among senior managers' in STERNBERG, R.J. and WAGNER, R.K. (Eds) *Practical Intelligence*, Cambridge, Cambridge University Press.

KOLB, D.A. (1983) 'Problem management: Learning from experience' in SRIVASTVA, S. (Ed.) *The Executive Mind*, San Francisco, CA, Jossey-Bass.

LEITHWOOD, K.A. (1988) *How Chief School Officers Classify and Manage Their Problems*, Toronto, OISE, mimeo.

LEITHWOOD, K.A., BEGLEY, P. and CAMPBELL, G.L. (1989) '*The nature and role of values in school administrators' problem solving*', paper presented at the annual meeting of CSSE, Quebec City, June.

LEITHWOOD, K.A. and MONTGOMERY, D.J. (1986) *Improving Principal Effectiveness: The Principal Profile*, Toronto, OISE Press (chapters 8 and 9).

LEITHWOOD, K.A. and STAGER, M. (1986) '*Differences in problem-solving processes used by moderately and highly effective principals*', paper presented at the Annual Meeting of the American Educational Research Association, San Francisco.

LEITHWOOD, K.A. and STAGER, M. (1989) 'Expertise in principals' problem solving', *Educational Administration Quarterly*.

LOUIS, K. (1987) '*The role of school districts in school innovations*', paper prepared for the conference on Organizational Policy for School Improvement, OISE, Toronto.

MARCH, J.G. (1974) 'Analytic skills and the university training of educational administrators', *Journal of Educational Administration*, 12, 1, pp. 17–43

PETERSON, K.D., MURPHY, J. and HALLIDAY, P. (1987) 'Superintendents' perceptions of the control and coordination of the technical care in effective school districts', *Educational Administration Quarterly*, 23, 1, pp. 79–95.

ROSENHOLTZ, S. (1989) *Teachers' Workplace*, New York, Longman.

Schwenk, C.R. (1988) 'The cognitive perspective on strategic decision-making', *Journal of Management Studies*, 25, 1, pp. 41–56.

Shulman, L.S. and Carey, N.B. (1984) 'Psychology and the limitations of individual rationality: Implication for the study of reasoning and civility', *Review of Educational Research*, 54, 4, pp. 501–24.

Simon, H. (1957) *Administrative Behavior: A Study of Decision-making Process in Administrative Organization* (2nd edn) New York, The Free Press.

Simon, H.A. (1973) 'The structure of ill-structured problems', *Artificial Intelligence*, 4, pp. 181–201.

Simon, H.A. (1975) 'The functional equivalence of problem-solving skills', *Cognitive Psychology*, 7, pp. 268–88.

Stager, M. and Leithwood, K.A. (1988) '*Cognitive flexibility and inflexibility in principals' problem solving*', paper presented at the annual meeting of the American Educational Research Association, New Orleans.

Stevens, W. (1986) '*The role of vision in the life of elementary school principals*', unpublished doctoral dissertation, University of Southern California, Los Angeles.

Voss, J.F., Greene, R.R., Post, T.A. and Penner, B.C. (1983) 'Problem-solving skill in the social sciences' in Bower, G.H. (Ed.) *The Psychology of Learning and Motivation* New York, Academic Press, pp. 165–213.

Chapter 7

The Values and Beliefs of Ontario's Chief Education Officers

Mark Holmes

CEOs are generally seen to represent a consensual program of education to be delivered within the school system they lead. This idea implies both that there is public consensus and that local school boards choose CEOs to represent it. The idea also raises questions about those not represented by the central consensus.

Ontario's CEOs, of public and separate (Roman Catholic) systems, were asked to complete questionnaires pertaining to their educational philosophies, demographic characteristics, personal beliefs and affiliations as well as to their administrative practices and policies. A reduced questionnaire was administered to a similarly educated sample of about the same age as the CEOs. The comparison group consisted of graduates of the University of Toronto employed full-time in activities other than education.

It was found that CEOs were quite similar in terms of their demographic characteristics, personal beliefs and educational philosophies, but that they differed in some important ways from the comparison group (and from, as far as it can be determined, the Ontario population). The most important findings concerned differences between the CEOs' educational philosophies and those of the comparison group and similar differences in preferred educational policies. Ontario's CEOs are strongly Progressive in educational philosophy and have little sympathy for the Technocratic philosophy. In contrast, the comparison group ranked the Progressive philosophy fifth out of six options, preferring the Cultural and Technocratic philosophies. The comparison group is also more Traditional than are public CEOs, but not more so than separate CEOs. CEOs are more accepting of increased public spending particularly on elementary and secondary education, while the comparison group would prefer deficit reduction and a lowering of taxes. The comparison group chooses more rigorous policies with respect to testing, program and discipline, as compared with CEOs.

The beliefs and values of senior administrators have not been a major focus of educational research. When they have been examined, it has usually been in the context of investigation into decision making and problem solving; the central focus of interest has been the influence of personal beliefs and values on the effective and efficient administration of the organization. In research carried out as a part of this project, Leithwood and Steinbach (chapter 6) adopt this perspective and provide a summary of previous research.

The central purpose of this study was not to consider the immediate practice of CEOs, although it was considered; rather was it to place administrators' values within the larger context of educational policy. Thus while other chapters in this book have focused on behavior, beliefs, values and norms as they emerge in the local school system, the focus here is on the implications of CEOs' values, beliefs and behavior, insofar as they are expressed in the delivery of publicly funded education, for educational policy.

I am not suggesting that the relationship between educational administrators' background, social class and belief systems and the policies they espouse, support and implement has been systematically ignored. Tyack and Hansot's fine history of the American superintendent (1982) traces the change in role of the senior administrator. From being a semi-secular priest overseeing the inculcation (and modeling) of virtue in the nineteenth century, the superintendent became a more clearly secular administrator responsible for the delivery of a wide range of programs, all within a consensual system of values and ideology, in the early 20th century. But during the last two or three decades, the superintendent is increasingly a political broker, more a manager of resources than a model of educational value. Analogously, Marxist critics have seen in the chief education officer the embodiment of middle class, capitalist, bourgeois, patriarchal hegemony (for example, Katz 1973).

My perspective is neither historical nor Marxist. My first purpose is to develop some large scale, descriptive, empirical data to provide a picture of the Ontario CEO. Secondly, I seek to show examples of the way the beliefs and values are expressed and modified in the context of local policies, practices and expectations. Thirdly, I examine CEOs' beliefs and values in the larger context of ideas concerning the delivery of education in a contemporary pluralist, liberal democracy.

More specifically, the questions being addressed are:

1 What are the educational philosophies of Ontario CEOs?
2 What are the political, religious and demographic characteristics of CEOs?

3 How do the CEOs see their working lives?
4 What are the favored educational policies of CEOs?
5 How do CEOs compare, in terms of the above respects, with similarly educated professionals in areas other than education?
6 How are CEOs' philosophies and values reflected in their daily working lives?
7 What are the implications of the findings of the empirical research for educational policy and program in a liberal democracy characterized by multiculturalism and respect for individual rights?

The first five questions are addressed in this chapter, the last two in chapter 10.

Methodology

An eighteen page questionnaire was developed, reviewed by faculty colleagues and mailed to all CEOs in Ontario (N = 116), in April 1988. Overall seventy-five (64.7 per cent) were returned. As one was received many months after the statistical analyses were completed, the findings are based on a sample of seventy-four (63.6 per cent). Although there is no apparent empirical pattern separating respondents from non-respondents, it is possible that there may be a qualitative pattern. Responses were, it seemed, received from most if not all of the most prominent CEOs in the province. Anonymity was optional. The majority did not choose anonymity (83 per cent). I intended, as stated in the questionnaire, to follow up a small sample of CEOs for the second part of the research (to address research questions 6 and 7). Further, I chose to select the sample on the basis of answers to questions concerning educational changes introduced by the CEOs and the relationship of those changes to the CEOs' chosen philosophies. Such follow up was incompatible with anonymity — hence its optional status.

As the central focus of this enquiry was one of educational policy, it was important not to view the values and beliefs of the CEOs in isolation. It is a matter of interest, possibly concern, when CEOs deliver policies closely identified with their own beliefs and values, if it transpires that those beliefs and values are not shared consensually by most others. Similarly, if CEOs find themselves delivering policies in which they do not believe, that too is problematic. Finally, if CEOs are delivering policies representing a public consensus, which they individually share, questions arise as to the appropriateness of the delivery of a public, consensually shared education to the children of parents who are not represented by the consensus.

For these reasons, it was felt important to poll a comparison group as well as the CEOs. Such polling posed both academic and practical problems. A questionnaire designed for both CEOs and the general public would have necessarily been superficial. Further, mailed questionnaires to the public often have quite low response rates (below 30 per cent). Extensive interviews with a representative sample of the public would have been prohibitively expensive, as would the interview of a large sample of the CEOs. Even though interviews with the public might have attained a high response rate, the problem of the sophistication of the nature of the questions would have remained. For both academic and practical reasons, it was decided to use graduates of the University of Toronto in the year 1960 as a comparison group. It was believed that the group would be similar to the CEOs in terms of age and education. Names and addresses of the over 1300 graduates (those with graduate degrees and degrees in education were excluded from the population) were obtained. A random sample of 367 was selected with mailed questionnaires being sent in July 1988. The later date of mailing is attributable to practical problems in obtaining permission to use the University of Toronto sample. The length of the delay was not anticipated when the CEO questionnaires were mailed and, in any case, spring was seen as a better time than summer to mail questionnaires to CEOs. The result is that most CEO responses were received in May and June, most comparison group responses in July and August. Responses were received from 161 of the 367 members of the sample control group (44 per cent).

Unfortunately, there is no reason to believe that those who respond to a mailed questionnaire are a random sample of the original random sample. Indeed, it seems likely that those with an interest in education are more likely to respond than those without. That suspicion was reinforced by the finding that forty-four of the 161 respondents were full time workers in education. As the interest was in comparing CEOs with the educated lay public it was decided to exclude educators from the main analysis. In addition, thirty-eight respondents stated they did not work full time. As it was felt desirable that the comparison group should be as similar to the CEOs as possible except for occupation, they too were excluded. Separate analyses of the entire set of respondents, the actual comparison group (full time workers not in education) and of the educator (sub-sample) were published in an interim report (Holmes, 1988). The comparison sample used here comprises eighty-three respondents.

The comparison group questionnaire consisted of questions taken from the CEO questionnaire together with a few questions devised to determine the kind of occupation in which the respondents were employed. The questions chosen for inclusion were those of a general nature requiring little specific knowledge of current characteristics of elementary and secondary schools. The decision to use selected questions without changing the wording from the CEO questionnaire led to one unfortunate anomaly: a semantic differential question refers to 'life as a CEO' — potentially confusing for the members of the comparison group, who are not in fact CEOs. If this anomaly had been spotted in advance, the wording would have been slightly changed.

Findings

Personal, Political and Religious Beliefs

As shown in table 7.1, CEOs in Ontario are almost entirely male, even more so than the comparison group of similarly educated full time workers. They are a little younger than the comparison group and are strong family people. The vast majority are married to their first spouse; the median number of children is three, compared with two for the comparison group. While both groups are predominantly British or Irish in origin and almost entirely European, the comparison group is slightly more likely to come from a non-English or non-French speaking background, the CEOs slightly more likely to come from a Francophone background. While about half of both groups has a wife not employed full time or part time, the employment pattern of the two groups of spouses differs, with CEOs' working wives very likely to be involved in education (table 7.2).

As might be expected among a highly educated population, fundamentalist religions (for example, Pentecostal, Seventh Day Adventist, Jehovah's Witness, Islam) are not highly represented (table 7.3). However, the exclusiveness of the CEOs is particularly marked, with 95.9 per cent being Roman Catholic, United, Anglican or Presbyterian, compared with 68.3 per cent in the comparison group and 74.7 per cent in the Ontario population. If Catholics are excluded (table 7.4), on the grounds that one would expect a separate school board to have a Catholic CEO, the pattern remains equally strong. Of CEOs, fully 58.5 per cent of non-Catholics describe themselves as United, compared with 38.8 per cent of the comparison group and 30.1 per cent of the (non-Catholic) Ontario population. As the Ontario statistics were seven years old in 1988, the difference between the CEOs and the Ontario population is probably understated. The fundamentalist Christian population of 12.6 per cent is unrepresented among CEOs, as are the eastern religions. Those members of the Ontario population who do not state any formal commitment to religion are also, but only slightly, underrepresented among CEOs.

Table 7.5 shows that both the CEOs and the comparison group are much less likely to support Ontario's New Democratic Party (NDP) than is the general population. CEOs are more likely than either the comparison group or the general population to be Liberal.

Tables 7.6 and 7.7 show that comparable differences emerge when specific questions of public policy are addressed. Over recent years,

Table 7.1 Personal Characteristics of CEOs and Comparison Group in Percentages: Sex, Age, Marital Status, Children, Grandchildren, Parental Ethnic Origin, Language (N in brackets)

	CEOs	Comparison Group
Sex		
Male	98.6 (73)	86.4 (81)
Age		
under 50	28.8 (73)	17.1 (81)
60 or over	1.4	2.4
Marital Status		
Never married	1.4 (73)	4.9 (82)
Married to first spouse	78.1	84.1
Permanently separated	5.5	3.7
Widow/widower	1.4	1.2
Other (including married to spouse other than first; common-law separated from second spouse)	13.7	6.1
Children		
None	2.7 (73)	11.0 (82)
1–2	27.4	42.7
More than 2	69.9	46.3
Grandchildren		
None	76.4 (72)	93.8 (80)
1–2	15.3	5.0
More than 2	8.4	1.3
Ethnic origin, Father		
British or Irish	69.9 (73)	61.0 (82)
Other European	27.4	32.9
Non-European	2.7 6.1	
Ethnic origin, mother	65.8 (73)	65.8 (82)
British or Irish	28.6	30.5
Other European	5.5	3.7
Non-European		
Language		
spoken at home today		
English	93.1 (72)	95.2 (83)
French	6.9	0.0
Other	0.0	4.8
first spoken at home		
English	79.2 (72)	79.3 (82)
French	9.7	0.0
Other	11.1	20.7

Note: Tests of statistical significance should be applied with care to data such as these as the CEO sample is not random; it more closely represents a population. However, 15 percentage points approximate the 95 per cent confidence level for samples of this size (a little more between the two samples where the percentages are close to 50; less when an Ontario sample is used and when the percentages are close to 20 or 80). Generally, a difference of 15% is considered worthy of note in this research.

Table 7.2 Spousal Occupation of CEOs and Comparison Group in Percentages (N in brackets)

	CEOs	Comparison Group
At home	52.9 (70)	46.7 (75)
Full-time employment	31.4	20.0
Part-time employment	15.7	33.3
Spousal employment (full-time)		
Education	68.0 (25)	23.5 (17)
Other professional	8.0	29.4
Manager	4.0	5.9
Salesperson	8.0	0.0
Secretarial/Clerical	8.0	11.8
Other	4.0	29.4

Table 7.3 Religious Affiliation of CEOs, Comparison Groups and Ontario in Percentages: Stated Religion (N in brackets)

	CEOs (73)	Comparison Group (81)	Ontario (8 534 265)
Religion			
United	32.9	31.7	19.4
Anglican	11.0	16.1	13.6
Presbyterian	8.2	2.4	6.1
Sub-total	52.1	51.2	39.1
Baptist	0.0	1.2	3.4
Pentecostal/fundamentalist	0.0	0.0	4.8
Sub-Total	0.0	1.2	8.2
Roman Catholic	43.8	17.1	35.6
Jewish	0.0	7.3	1.7
Other Protestant	—	—	3.4
Eastern	—	—	1.6
Eastern Orthodox	—	—	2.0
No religion	4.1	11.0	7.4
Other	0.0	12.2	—

Note: Ontario statistics are for 1981 (*The Canadian World Almanac and Book of Facts 1989*, 1988). The *no religion* statistic for Ontario is an estimate. Most likely, the mainstream Protestant denominations have lost ground since 1981. The *no religion* and *fundamentalist* percentages have probably increased since 1981.

public opinion in Canada has consistently run in favor of capital punishment (generally around 60 per cent are in favor, but there is variation depending on the precise wording of the question). The comparison group reflects public opinion, but the CEOs diverge markedly (table 7.6).

There are no precisely comparable data available with respect to public opinion on spending priorities (table 7.7). However, OISE surveys have shown that health care and education are the two highest priorities for provincial spending among the Ontario public (Livingstone and Hart, 1981). Most likely, public opinion would (at least in 1988) have placed a lower priority on deficit reduction than does the comparison group.

Table 7.4 Religious Commitment of CEOs, the Comparison Group and Ontario (excluding Roman Catholics) in Percentages: Stated Religion (N in brackets)

	CEOs (41)	Comparison Group (67)	Ontario (5 498 020)
Religion			
United	58.5	38.8	30.1
Anglican	19.5	20.9	21.2
Presbyterian	14.6	3.0	9.4
Sub-total	92.6	62.7	60.7
Baptist	0.0	1.5	5.2
Pentecostal	0.0	0.0	7.4
Sub-Total	0.0	1.5	12.6
Jewish	0.0	9.0	2.7
Other Protestant	—	—	5.2
Eastern	—	—	2.5
Eastern Orthodox	—	—	3.0
No religion	7.3	13.4	13.3
Other	0.0	13.4	—

Note: Ontario statistics are for 1981 (*The Canadian World Almanac and Book of Facts 1989*, 1988).

Table 7.5 Political Commitment of CEOs, Comparison Group and Ontario in Percentages: Federal and Provincial Voting Intentions (Decided Voters Only) (N in Brackets)

	CEOs	Comparison Group	Ontario
Federal election			
Liberal	50.9 (57)	36.9 (63)	39 (680)
NDP	1.8	13.8	31
PC	47.4	49.2	30
Other	0.0	0.0	0
Provincial election:			
Liberal	64.5 (62)	42.6 (68)	45 (1001)
NDP	0.0	11.8	25
PC	32.3	45.6	28
Other	3.2	0.0	0

Note: The Ontario statistics are taken from *Globe-Environic* polls. The federal poll was conducted between 9 June and 27 June 1988 and published in *The Globe and Mail* on June 29. There was some volatility in the electorate during the April-July period but no overall trend. The Liberals were a little higher, the NDP a little lower, both before and after the June polls.

The provincial statistics are taken from the *Globe-Environic* poll conducted between 19 May and 4 June 1988 and published in *The Globe and Mail* on June 16. The trend at the time was upward for the Progressive Conservatives, downward for the NDP. The federal sample size of 680 is an estimate from the national sample of 1992 eligible voters.

Table 7.6 Attitude to Capital Punishment of CEOs and Comparison Group in Percentages (N in Brackets)

	CEOs (69)	Comparison Group (82)
Approve capital punishment	31.9	65.9

Table 7.7 Rank Order of First Priorities for a Larger Share of Provincial Revenue, CEOs and Comparison Group in Percentages (N in Brackets)

Ranked	CEOs (72)		Comparison Group (82)	
1	Elementary/Secondary Education	48.6	Deficit Reduction	35.4
2	Health Care	21.4	Health Care	17.1
3	Support for low income families	10.0	Tax reduction	14.6
4	Deficit reduction	8.6	Elementary/Secondary Education	11.0
5	Low income housing	5.7		
	Tax reduction	5.7	Low income housing	7.3

Note: Not included among the first five ranks are: post-secondary education; judicial system; retirement homes.

Clearly, the CEOs favor government spending, particularly on elementary and secondary education, much more than does the comparison group, of whom 50.1 per cent would give priority to deficit or tax reduction, compared with 14.3 per cent of CEOs.

Commentary. The implications of these findings are further addressed in Chapter 10, including the problem of the delivery of educational public policy in times when consensus is lacking. At this point three important generalizations will be made. First, CEOs in Ontario are clearly not demographically representative of the public. One would, of course, expect CEOs to be of a certain age and education. But those characteristics either lead to, result from or are associated with such characteristics as social class and political ideology. Beyond that, CEOs are almost entirely male. Although race was not directly addressed, one may infer that CEOs are generally white and we know they are mainly of European origin. Second, CEOs are generally drawn from the centre of any political, religious or ideological map. Dissenting religious views, for example, are not represented. Third, CEOs tend to be more liberal than the general public; although they are neither left wing nor right wing they are to the left of centre. The capital punishment issue illustrates this most directly. The predominance of adherents of the United Church supports this generalization. Political party affiliation is more difficult to interpret (as I shall illustrate later). Clearly, there is no support for the NDP among CEOs. The CEOs are more collectivist liberal than their educated peers in the sense that they are more willing to spend additional money on elementary and secondary education and health and less keen on deficit and tax reduction.

Educational Philosophy and Policy

Both the CEOs and the comparison group were asked to rank order up to six different *philosophies of education*. For simplicity's sake, the philosophies are referred to here as: Progressive (*the Child at the Centre*); Technocratic (*Success in Future Life*); Cultural (*Intellectual and Cultural Development*); Traditional (*Development of Good Character and Personal Responsibility*), Individualistic (*the Development of Individual Freedom*); and Egalitarian (*the Search for Social Equality*). The short labels were not used in the questionnaires. It was intended that CEOs would respond to the more extensive content of the description provided in the questionnaire rather than to a superficially attractive label (see appendix) The follow-up interviews suggest that CEOs did not find the set frustrating or confusing. Typically they did say, however, that aspects of all or most of the philosophies appealed. No one felt that a single descriptor could capture one's entire philosophy adequately. When a variety of ways of measuring the prevailing ideologies of the CEOs was used (Holmes, 1988, p. 3), the results were very similar. Tables 7.8 and 7.9 illustrate two ways of assessing the choices of the CEOs and of the control group; the two patterns are virtually identical. The CEOs adhere strongly to the Progressive philosophy with 57.2 per cent ranking it first or second and only 27.8 per cent not ranking it in the first three (out of six) choices. In contrast, the comparison group ranks it as a poor fifth, 22.8 per cent ranking it first or second, compared with 34.2 per cent for the Individualistic philosophy. The comparison group ranks the Cultural and, particularly, the Technocratic philosophy much higher than do the CEOs.

There is, it can be seen, a marked divergence in educational purpose between the two groups. The CEOs consensually believe the purpose of education is to permit healthy growth, to provide for individual self expression, to develop tolerance and to develop a good self concept. The school is a 'field of opportunity' and should not be 'imposing a preconceived set of desired outcomes'. In stark contrast, the comparison group consensually believes that education should cultivate the intellectual, aesthetic and social senses, develop an appreciation of our culture and environment as well as develop the skills, habits and attitudes required for 'future success and good citizenship'.

As we shall see, the preference on the part of the comparison group for the latter Technocratic purpose is particularly robust. This greater Technocratic concern on the part of the comparison group almost certainly underestimates the interest of the general public. Gallup Polls in

Table 7.8 First and Second Ranked Philosophies by CEOs and Comparison Group: Percentage Ranking each Philosophy First or Second (N in Brackets)

Philosophies	CEOs (72)			Comparison Group (81)		
	Ranked First	Ranked Second	Total	Ranked First	Ranked Second	Total
Progressive	37.5	19.7	57.2	11.1	11.7	22.8
Technocratic	13.9	12.7	26.6	27.2	22.1	49.3
Cultural	16.7	22.5	39.2	27.2	24.7	52.0
Traditional	15.3	23.9	39.2	18.5	19.5	38.0
Individualistic	16.7	16.9	33.6	16.0	18.2	34.2
Egalitarian	0.0	4.2	4.2	0.0	3.9	3.9

Table 7.9 Philosophies Not Appearing Among First Three Ranked Choices, in Percentages for CEOs and Comparison Group (N in Brackets)

	CEOs not ranking in first three (72)	Comparison Group not ranking in first three (81)
Progressive	27.8	61.7
Technocratic	55.6	33.3
Cultural	38.9	30.9
Traditional	44.4	46.9
Individualistic	55.6	56.8
Egalitarian	77.8	92.6

Ontario in 1978, 1979 and 1980 asked respondents to rank order secondary school objectives. In all years, *job training and career preparation* exceeded all other priorities put together; combined with *every day life skills* it received 75 per cent or greater first choice support in all three years (Livingstone and Hart, 1981, p. 16).

Some of the differences between the CEOs and the comparison group are reflected in what might be called 'folk wisdom' (table 7.10) and views on policy (table 7.11 a, b, c and d). For example, the CEOs' belief that education should be individualized is reflected in the small proportion (5.6 per cent) which strongly agrees with fewer special programs (and therefore smaller classes), compared with 25 per cent of the comparison group (table 7.10). Only 4.1 per cent of CEOs strongly believe it is too difficult to suspend students from high school, compared with 25.3 per cent of the comparison group, consistent with a higher level of tolerance on the part of CEOs for deviant behavior and dress (table 7.10). The stronger support among the comparison group for Technocratic (utilitarian) purposes is reflected in the much greater dissatisfaction with the status quo of secondary education (only 27.5 per cent support it, compared with 54.8 per cent of the CEOs). Almost half of the comparison group would support the abolition of streaming in grades 9 and 10 and the development of separate programs designed to prepare young people

Table 7.10 Educational Folk Wisdom: Beliefs of CEOs and Comparison Group, in Percentages (N in Brackets)

	CEOs strongly agree	Comparison Group strongly agree
1 Principal key to school quality	69.9 (73)	24.7 (81)
2 Elementary schools better with fewer special programs and smaller classes	5.6 (72)	25.0 (80)
3 Too difficult to suspend and expel students from high school	4.1 (73)	25.3 (83)

Table 7.11a Educational Policy Issues, Percentage of CEOs and Comparison Group in Agreement: (a) Reforming Secondary Education (N in Brackets)

	CEOs (73)	Comparison Group (80)
(i) Abolish streams in grade 9 and 10; separate programs depending on future in grades 11 and 12	30.1	47.5
(ii) Provide common core without streaming and with few options	2.7	13.8
(iii) Status quo	54.8	27.5

Table 7.11b Educational Policy Issues, Percentage of CEOs and Comparison Group in Agreement: (b) Achievement Testing and Basic Skills (N in Brackets)

	CEOs (70)	Comparison Group (82)
(i) Annual testing in elementary grades	11.4	58.5
(ii) Once or twice in elementary grades	65.7	31.7
(iii) No regular testing; only for special purposes	12.9	7.3
(iv) Other	10.0	2.4

for their post-high school lives in grades 11 and 12 (in comparison, 30.1 per cent of CEOs support that option). Interestingly, although the comparison group slightly prefers the Cultural philosophy to the Technocratic philosophy the most obviously Cultural option for the secondary school, a common program for all as advocated by Mortimer Adler in the USA and George Radwanski in Ontario, gained only 13.8 per cent support from the comparison group, and only 2.7 per cent from CEOs (table 7.11a)

As one would expect from other opinion polls (for example, Canadian Gallup Poll, 1985), the sharpest divide is on the issue of student evaluation. Whereas only 11.4 per cent of CEOs support annual testing of students in the basic skills, 58.5 per cent of the comparison group would like to see such a policy in place (table 7.11b). The comparison group may even understate public opinion here — as reflected in polls from

Table 7.11c Educational Policy Issues, Percentage of CEOs and Comparison Group in Agreement: (c) Funding Independent Schools (N in Brackets)

	CEOs (74)	Comparison Group (70)
Christian Schools	8.1	4.3
Jewish Schools	6.8	4.3
Ethnic Schools	2.7	4.3
Independent schools with own philosophy	13.5	7.1
Not fund any other schools	75.7	92.9

Table 7.11d Educational Policy Issues, Percentage of CEOs and Comparison Group in Agreement: (d) Approach to Sexual Equality (N in Brackets)

	CEOs (70)	Comparison Group (82)
School should move gradually to reflect society	23.6	17.1
School should reflect will of individual parents and respect the home culture	6.9	8.5
Total sexual equality with almost no distinctions	59.7	54.9
Recognize male and female differences and provide different experiences, but with same outcomes	5.6	13.4
Other	4.2	6.1

British Columbia and Ontario. In 1984, 66 per cent of Ontario adults agreed with province-wide testing of individual performance in high school with only 20 per cent disagreeing (Livingstone, Hart and Davie, 1985).

On some policy issues, there is little difference between the two groups. Neither group supports the funding of independent schools — with the comparison group being even less favorable than the CEOs (table 7.11c). And both groups want schools to impose a policy of total sexual equality (table 7.11d). CEOs were asked their opinions about two matters to which educational research has made important contributions. Most of this chapter is concerned centrally with values, beliefs, ideologies and attitudes — always central but not always recognized in education. Table 7.12 shows the different ways CEOs acknowledge research findings in education depending on its consistency with their values. (I am not here simply asserting cause and effect. Quite possibly, research findings contrary to generally accepted ideas are not generally disseminated to CEOs.) There is some research support for the value of very small classes (of fifteen or fewer pupils) in the primary grades, while at other grade levels achievement and class size are generally unrelated. It is arguable that small classes are particularly advantageous to teachers in the progressive, activity centred classrooms advocated by progressive educators. CEOs agree (78.4 per cent) that small classes are particularly valuable for the primary grades. The research evidence is even stronger that

Table 7.12 Educational Research: Consistency of CEOs' Opinions with Established Research Findings: Percentage in Agreement with the Research Findings (N in Brackets)

	agree
1 Small classes are particularly important in the primary grades	78.4 (73)
2 Individualization:	disagree
(i) Generally to be preferred to grouping, and grouping to whole class instruction at all grade levels	11.1 (73)

whole class instruction is generally more effective than individualization in the teaching of the basic skills. Although the research is less clear cut, there is also some support for whole class instruction as compared to grouping. Only 11.1 per cent of CEOs disagree with the empirically incorrect proposition that individualization is generally to be preferred to grouping, and grouping to whole class instruction.

Commentary. It is evident that the personal and ideological differences between the CEOs and the comparison group are carried over to education. It will be recalled that the prototypical CEO in a public system is male, adheres to the United Church, is married to his first wife who is either a housewife or an educator, has three children, is of British background, votes Liberal or Progressive Conservative, is opposed to capital punishment and believes that more provincial revenue should go to elementary and secondary education rather than to a reduction of either the deficit or taxes.

It is not surprising if this fictional composite: is a Progressive in education, believes in learning experiences rather than predetermined outcomes; does not see discipline as being a major problem in the school; supports individualization whether or not it leads to higher achievement; is opposed to making the secondary school either more academic or more related to young people's futures; and is opposed to annual testing by means of external standardized tests.

In these respects he is quite different from his fictional counterpart not employed in education. This person's personal background is quite similar, but he or she supports capital punishment and believes that additional provincial revenue should be used to reduce the deficit or lower taxes. Unlike the CEO, this person expects schools to provide results — in the basic skills, in academics and the arts and most certainly in terms of skills required either for access to post secondary education or for employment. This person favors rigorous testing.

The reader should be cautioned against seeing the CEO as being simply left wing and the comparison prototype as being conservative. The traditional conservative philosophy (Traditional) was ranked the same by both (fourth out of six). The socialist option was rejected equally by both (a distant sixth). The options favored by both, the Progressive, the Cultural and the Technocratic, could all be seen as falling generally within an elastic definition of the term *liberal*. Bowles and Gintis (1976) characterized the liberal mainstream as having two parts — a technocratic and a progressive. It could be argued then (perhaps Bowles and Gintis would agree) that the Cultural tradition is the respectable ghost to which both sides lay claim but to which neither is completely faithful. The CEOs are not prepared, it would seem, to sacrifice experience, process and learning centres for rigorous academic work in the disciplines; and the comparison group is no more prepared to sacrifice the earning of credentials in the name of a broad open cultural education for all.

So, the two prototypes have much in common. Both favor the expression of a central consensus in education. Neither is willing to accept dissenting views in education, although both, the CEO particularly, believe in tolerance as an important central value. But they sharply disagree on what the central consensus to be imposed should be. They agree only one type of education should be imposed — their own; or so it would appear. This question is again raised in chapter 10.

Public and Separate CEOs

The empirical findings concerning the values and beliefs of CEOs and the comparison group are followed up in chapter 10 in a general discussion of the policy for the delivery of public education. I address there the issue of the CEO as a model and public representation of a consensual view of education. One possibility, not discussed so far, is that there are important differences between the values and beliefs of Roman Catholic separate CEOs and those of public CEOs. If this were the case, it could then be argued that public CEOs may in fact be quite similar to the comparison group. Therefore, a separate analysis of the responses of separate and public CEOs was run. The most important matters which differentiated the CEOs from the comparison group will be discussed in the context of the separated data.

Before commenting on this issue directly, I should point out that the problem is more complex than simply having a Catholic system run by and for Catholics and a public system run by and for non-Catholics (or as would once have almost been the case, Protestants). While all separate CEOs are Catholics, so are a few public CEOs. Some non-Catholics attend separate schools and some Catholics attend public schools. Most important, public and separate schools are both fully funded by government, and differences in the level of funding are being rapidly reduced. Although the extension of funding of separate schools in Ontario from tenth grade to the end of high school led to bitter and divisive debate, many observers, including many Catholic educators, have informally indicated to me that they believe the two systems are gradually becoming more and more alike — and that full funding is hastening that process. For example, teachers in newly funded secondary schools are seeking collective agreements like those of their public counterparts.

For these reasons, the simplest and most straightforward approach is to compare the values and beliefs of all (or a representative sample of) CEOs of publicly funded systems with the values and beliefs of a representative sample of the public (or a sample comparable in some respects with the CEOs). The central policy question being addressed is the extent to which CEOs represent the ideals, beliefs, values and philosophies of the public.

From a practical point of view, immediate policy questions include the desirability of public boards providing a variety of types of education, as distinct from a single model. Therefore, there is some immediate relevance in seeing whether or not public CEOs are more or less representative of the public than are separate CEOs. In this more specific sense then it could be argued that there is more legitimate public interest in comparing the beliefs and ideologies of public CEOs with the public-at-large than would be the case for separate CEOs.

Overall, results of the survey suggest that although there are some important differences between public and separate CEOs, the differences between them both and the comparison group generally remain. On the crucially important question of educational philosophy, the Progressive option is ranked first by both groups of CEOs (and fifth by the comparison group). The Technocratic philosophy, ranked first tied with the Cultural philosophy by the comparison group is ranked fourth by public CEOs and third by separate CEOs. In the case of one philosophy, the difference between the CEOs and the comparison group is substantially reduced by the exclusion of separate CEOs. The Cultural philosophy is favored by 27.2 per cent of the comparison group, 23.9 per cent of the public CEOs but by only 3.8 per cent of the separate CEOs. In one case, a new difference emerges. The Traditional philosophy is favored by 18.5 per cent of the comparison group, 30.8 per cent of separate CEOs but by only 6.5 per cent of public CEOs. Overall, the differences between public CEOs and the comparison group are as great as between CEOs as a whole and the comparison group; but the nature of the differences varies, except in the case of the central Progressive philosophy.

In terms of political commitment, the difference in support for the NDP remains; neither separate nor public CEOs support the NDP. However, the strong adherence of separate CEOs to the Liberal party does explain the overall preference among CEOs as a whole; support for Progressive Conservatives is actually a little greater among public CEOs than in the comparison group (or the public as a whole).

The strong antipathy of separate CEOs explains some of the difference between CEOs and the comparison group on the question of capital punishment. Even so, only 42.9 per cent of public CEOs support capital punishment compared with 65.9 per cent of the comparison group (and 16 per cent of separate CEOs).

Although there are very slight differences between public and separate CEOs on the question of spending priorities, the major patterns remain unaltered. A clear majority of public (65.9 per cent) and separate (76.9 per cent) CEOs support more government spending on elementary/secondary education and health, compared with 28.1 per cent of the comparison group. In contrast, 50 per cent of the comparison group favor deficit and tax reduction compared with 18.1 per cent of public CEOs and 7.7 per cent of separate CEOs.

Thus, whether one chooses public CEOs or all CEOs as the more important sample for study the implications for representativeness and delivery are not very different. Both groups of CEOs are more liberal and less socialist than the comparison group and the general public (although public CEOs are not more Liberal). Public CEOs are much more Progressive in educational philosophy than the comparison group, much less Technocratic and much less Traditional; unlike CEOs as a whole, they are not much less Cultural. On the crucial litmus test of achievement testing, 58.5 per cent of the comparison group favors annual testing of the basic skills in the elementary school, compared with only 15.9 per cent of public and 3.8 per cent of separate CEOs. Certainly, although both groups of CEOs are centrist, both also lie to the left of centre in terms of educational policy and public spending; in that sense they can be described as being more liberal (i.e., collectivist liberal as distinct from individualist liberal) than the comparison group. One may infer that separate CEOs are just as likely to be left of centre in terms of their population as the public CEOs are in terms of theirs; the alternative explanation is that the Roman Catholic portion of the population is much more liberal on educational issues than is the non-Catholic population — a proposition which runs quite contrary to most general supposition.

The CEOs' Working Life

This study is concerned with CEOs' beliefs and values and their relationship with educational practice. That enquiry and discussion will lead to a more general examination of the delivery of public education in societies characterized by pluralism and dissent. The major part of the questionnaires dealt with personal, political and religious beliefs and educational philosophy and policy. In addition, it was thought valuable to obtain a picture of what CEOs do, or at least think they do.

My purpose here is not really to make a new contribution to the research. There have been more detailed studies of the life of the CEO

Table 7.13 Working Life: Characteristics of One's Working Life as Seen by CEOs and Comparison Group: Very High, High or Neutral Assessment of Pairs of Adjectives (N in Brackets)

	CEOs (69)	Comparison Group (75–79)
hectic-serene	very high hectic	very high hectic
exciting-calm	very high exciting	high exciting
predictable-surprising	high predictable	high surprising
demanding-easy	very high demanding	very high demanding
political-pedagogical	very high political	high political
technical-humanistic	high humanistic	neutral
professional-administrative	high professional	high professional
collegial-independent	high collegial	high independent
authoritative-subordinate	high authoritative	high authoritative
isolated-sharing	neutral	high sharing
leading-following	very high leading	very high leading
frustrating-fulfilling	high fulfilling	high fulfilling
well rewarded-poorly rewarded	very high well-rewarded	high well-rewarded
satisfying-stressful	high satisfying	high satisfying
managerial-educational	neutral	high managerial
hierarchical-collaborative	high hierarchical	high collaborative
proactive-reactive	high proactive	high proactive
idiosyncratic-bureaucratic	neutral	neutral
legalistic-traditional	high legalistic	neutral
calculated-spontaneous	high calculated	high calculated
transparent-subtle	high subtle	neutral

Note: The N of the comparison group varied slightly with the item concerned.
Key: Very high (first adjective) > 70; high (first adjective) 55–69; neutral 45–54; high (second adjective) 30–44; very high (second adjective) < 30. The scale is from 0 to 100.

(for example, McLeod, 1984). However, a brief examination of the working lives of this population of CEOs (through their eyes) serves as a bridge to the more detailed discussion of a sample of CEOs in chapter 10. In addition, it is possible to assess what they say they value in the light of what they say they do.

Table 7.13 provides a summary of responses by CEOs and the comparison group to a semantic differential question concerning their feelings about their working lives. CEOs see their lives as being notably hectic, exciting, demanding, political (rather than pedagogical), leading and well rewarded. Members of the comparison group see their lives in a similar way. Some differences are that the comparison group members see their lives as being more independent than collegial and more collaborative than hierarchical.

These findings are consistent with table 7.14a, which shows that CEOs claim to give 75 per cent of their time to political (external and public relations) and managerial (including financial management) issues and general communication within the system. Only 20 per cent of their time, they say, is devoted to substantive issues of program-broadly

Table 7.14a CEOs' Time: How They Spend It (N 73)

	Median Percentage Stated
Political (trustees, Ministry, external groups, public relations)	25
Management (supervisory, day-to-day problems, transportation)	20
Communication (internal-committees, in-service, school visits)	20
Program (curriculum, extracurricular activities, schedules, school closing)	10
Personnel (hiring, firing, contracts)	10
Financial management (budget, revenue, expenses)	10
Other	6

Table 7.14b CEOs' Time: First Ranked Priorities in Percentages (N = x)

Ranked	
1 Political	30.8
2 Communication	26.9
3 Management	17.9
4 Program	14.1
5 Other	5.1
6 Personnel	3.8
7 Financial Management	1.3

defined to include curriculum, extra curricular activities, scheduling and school closing and personnel. Table 7.14b confirms this picture, with only 17.9 per cent giving program or personnel as the first priority.

Commentary. When I began this research, saying I was looking for a link between CEOs' philosophies and their working lives, some of my colleagues said, semi-seriously, that it would be a short piece of research — implying there is no link between educational philosophy and the work of the CEO.

One of the questions not appearing on the CEO questionnaire is: 'How important is your educational philosophy during your working life?' An examination of how time is spent and the CEOs' priorities could lead to the conclusion that the philosophy of the CEO is essentially irrelevant. The CEO is busy with external problems, management, day to day affairs and has little time to think about education — or even about hiring, firing and promoting. After all, one might argue, who cares what a butcher's, a lawyer's or a doctor's philosophy is? What matters is the meat, the contract and the recovery. If the buses run on time, the teachers are in the classroom, does the CEO in fact matter? Is the CEO a manager, to use Hodgkinson's distinction, concerned with day to day efficiency, or an administrator concerned with policy and values?

Chapter 10 will address those questions. Directly, I shall be looking at six CEOs in action in an attempt to tease out the kind of influence they and their values have on the system. Indirectly, I shall try to infer the degree to which CEOs, intentionally or unintentionally, broadcast and legitimate a set of values and beliefs about education which become embodied as material with which other administrators and educators can work. The influence of the CEO may stem from personal philosophy and values, which are conveyed informally, or the influence may be hierarchical and bureaucratic. In the latter case, the influence may be more managerial (i.e., not strongly related to educational philosophy) rather than adminstrative. This discussion leads to a consideration of public policy and educational delivery.

Appendix

Educational Philosophies

(i) **The Child at the Centre**
The prime purpose of education is to allow children to grow healthily, to express themselves as individuals, to be tolerant of others and to feel at one with themselves. The school then should be seen as providing the field of opportunity rather than imposing a prescribed set of desired outcomes.

(ii) **Success in Future Life**
The prime purpose of education is to prepare children for their future lives as citizens and workers. The school's responsibility therefore is to provide them all with the basic skills, habits and attitudes required for future success and good citizenship in Canada.

(iii) **Intellectual and Cultural Development**
The prime purpose of education is to cultivate the intellect, together with the aesthetic and social senses. The school's responsibility is therefore to develop children's ability to think clearly, to express themselves and to appreciate our culture and environment.

(iv) **Development of Good Character and Personal Responsibility**
The prime purpose of educaiton is to help children grow into good adults who will help the development of our society and culture through their work and through family and community activities. The purpose of the school, therefore, is to provide instruction in the skills, disciplines and other attributes of our culture, within a clear moral framework.

(v) **The Development of Individual Freedom**
The prime purpose of education is to educate every individual child to the limits of his or her abilities and interests, within a framework of parental wishes. The purpose of the school is to challenge every child with the possibility of excellence and to encourage reasonable competition, particularly in the academic and vocational fields.

(vi) **The Search for Social Equality**
The prime purpose of education is the development of a better society characterized by much reduced social and economic divisions. The purpose of the school is to promote the harmonious development of all children, without regard for social background, ability, gender or race, so they may learn to participate in an equal and cooperative manner.

References

BINFORD, LEWIS (1962) 'Archeology as anthropology', *American Antiquity*, **28**, 2, October, pp. 217–26.

BOWLES, S. and GINTIS, H. (1976) *Schooling in Capitalist America*, New York, Basic Books.

THE CANADIAN GALLUP POLL (1985) 3. *Let's Talk About Schools — Gallup Survey*, Victoria, Ministry of Education, British Columbia.

The Canadian World Almanac and Book of Facts 1989 (1988) Toronto, Global Press.

EWEN, S. (1976) *Captains of Consciousness: Advertising and the Social Roots of the Consumer Culture*, New York, McGraw Hill.

HOLMES, M. (1988) *Ontario's CEOs: Their Values, Beliefs and Actions: An Interim Report*, Toronto, OISE.

HOLMES, M. (in press) 'Bringing about change in teachers: Rationalistic technology and therapeutic human relations in the subversion of education', *Curriculum Inquiry*.

KATZ, M.B. (Ed.) (1973) *Education in American History*, New York, Praeger.

LIVINGSTONE, D.W. and HART, D.J. (1981) *Public Attitudes Toward Education in Ontario 1980*, Toronto, OISE Press.

LIVINGSTONE, D.W., HART, D.J. and DAVIE, L.E. (1985) *Public Attitudes Toward Education in Ontario 1984*, Toronto, OISE Press.

MCLEOD, G.T. (1984) 'The work of school board chief executive officers', *Canadian Journal of Education*, 9, 2, pp. 171–90.

TYACK, D. and HANSOT, E. (1982) *Manager of Virtue: Public School Leadership, 1820–1980*, New York, Basic Books.

Chapter 8

Administrative Artifacts: Inferring Values from the Physical Culture of the CEO's Office

Stephen B. Lawton and Joyce Scane

The study reported in this chapter looked for evidence of the values underlying CEO practices in the physical space of CEOs' offices and the material objects occupying that space. Adopting an anthropological frame of reference, the method used for the study assumed that 'material culture makes culture material ... palpable, present and ubiquitous.' Data about CEOs' offices, the objects in them and their symbolic meaning were collected by on-site visits and interviews with nine CEOs. These data suggested that CEOs' offices were civic and, in some cases, religious symbols conveying a strong commitment to children and their educaiton. Through their offices, CEOs expressed conserving values, as well as a desire for change. While their offices acknowledged the desirability of integrating personal and professional lives, the collective values of CEOs' school systems were far more extensively symbolized in the physical attributes of CEOs' offices.

On their deathbed, nobody ever says, 'I wish I'd spent more time at the office.' (anon)

This study is about administrators' offices: what is in them, how they are arranged, and how they reflect their occupants' personalities, values, objectives, and administrative styles. The topic, at first glance, may seem of peripheral interest. However, changes we observed in the executive office when a new chief was appointed at an institution of higher education suggested these questions might be of considerable significance. Over a twelve-year period, we saw the following changes transpire.

When a new administrator, a noted connoisseur of the visual arts and a spiffy dresser, was appointed to replace the institution's founder, the office was redecorated in grand fashion. Plain walls were recovered in dramatic cloth with brown, black and white swirls reminiscent of the inside covers of Victorian-era books. New furniture was purchased to replace the utilitarian desk and a brilliant magenta and blue wall hanging installed. The office was a pleasure to visit, if a bit flamboyant.

One era passed into another, and a new administrator was appointed upon his predecessor's retirement. The cloth covered panels were removed and relocated to the foyer of a suite of offices occupied by a major research project managed by an assistant chief, the furniture banished, the wall-hanging returned to its owners, and a new identity was installed. A tall, monk's copy-table, a computer terminal hooked up to an electronic mail system, and a large, modern oval table for meetings were installed. The plain walls were hung with delicately coloured seventeenth and eighteenth century prints in narrow black and gold frames. Visits to this office were always an ascetic experience.

One December, this administrator moved on and the current official moved in. A noted 'people-person', for months his office was piled high with the boxes of a man who was seemingly too busy about important matters to worry about physical things, things whose care would take time that could be put to better use. Eventually, the room was rearranged, focussing on a circle of chairs surrounding a low table — a pleasant conversation place for listening to concerns.

No doubt we could all tell similar, anecdotal tales that may be interesting local history but little more.[1] On the other hand, the objects and decorations people use may have an important story to tell. Anthropologists, for example, commonly focus on the physical culture or artifacts associated with various groups (Deetz, 1977) and, in the past decade, increasing numbers of social scientists have accepted the idea that everyday objects have important meanings and are worthy of study. Evidence suggests that people, in their selection of clothes, furniture, decoration, books, and their arrangement of objects, are sending messages about who they are, who they would like to be, and what is important to them (McCracken, 1988). Certain objects possess special meaning to individuals who, as a result, commit considerable energy and time to their care. What these objects are and the meanings they hold may be idiosyncratic or may reflect the social and demographic traits — for example, ethnicity, gender and age — of their owners (Czikszentmihalyi and Rochberg-Halton, 1981).

A number of schemes for analysing the function and meaning of objects have been developed. Deetz finds Binford's (1962) typology useful for categorizing objects in a way which links them to people's behaviour:

> Technomic function is strictly utilitarian and relates directly to the technology of culture. A candle used for lighting serves a technomic purpose, since it solves a problem directly imposed by

> the environment. The socio-technic function of an artifact involves its use in a social rather than a technological way. Our use of candles at formal dinner parties is a good example of social-technic function. We certainly do not need candles to supply light in our modern, electrical world, but they do contribute to the social aspect of our lives at birthday parties, in investiture ceremonies, and on Christmas trees. Ideo-technic function sees the use of artifacts in religious and ideological contexts. Votive candles in the Catholic Church, and the candles of the Jewish menorah serve an ideo-technic function. Obviously, the same artifacts can function at all three levels much of the time. (p. 51)

Much of Deetz's work is concerned with the diffusion of objects and the ideational system that accompanied their spread. He makes a particularly interesting distinction between 'folk culture' and 'popular culture': 'Folk culture is traditional and conservative; it exhibits great variation in space and relatively little change over time. Popular culture changes rapidly in time and shows great similarity over large areas' (p. 41). Clearly, popular culture is analogous to modern consumer culture, which has served and is serving to displace traditional cultures everywhere (McCracken, 1988; Ewen, 1976).

As McCracken notes, it is somewhat ironic that little attention has been paid to the objects in people's worlds, given that modern society is driven as no society before it by the consumption of goods. The anthropologist concerned with pre-historic cultures generally has little choice but to examine physical objects or artifacts, since these alone remain of the cultures being studied. Deetz's work, especially in its initial phases, was unusual in that it was concerned with historical archeology — the archeology of New England for which many written records, statements, and so forth existed. His work revealed, and subsequent studies have demonstrated, that investigation of the physical culture often provides insights and understandings not immediately apparent from written records. Especially through aggregating data and linking the results to broad patterns and trends, one is able to place an individual's world — physical and psychological — in a broader context.

For example, the trail of physical objects — installed, removed, and passed on — tell of status and status relationships. In the institution described above, only one panel remains of the striking wall cloth (the other panels were removed when the special project ended and the foyer was sacrificed for a meeting room). It is an artifact that reflects the power of a second tier administrator to acquire a cast-off from the first tier. The situation is analogous to that described by Deetz in his study of a eighteenth and nineteenth century village of black New Englanders. Among the artifacts were some hand-painted cream ware of very high quality found in the cellar of a dwelling occupied by one family. 'Types such as hand-painted creamware are not often encountered on New England sites representing people of average means. We might guess that not only was the pottery given to the people of Parting Ways by the townspeople of Plymouth, but it was given by the wealthier ones. Might it not be that the ceramics were provided the men by their former masters? After all, ownership of slaves and the more elegant kinds of dishes are both characteristic of the more elite members of the community' (pp. 146–7).

While the primary motivation for this study was to explore the meaning attached by the executive to the executive's office, our investigation has an implicit link to scientific management and even ergonomics (or biotechnology). That is, if the Chief Executive Officer (CEO) is viewed as an information and knowledge worker who makes key decisions, one can enquire as to the most efficient and effective manner for setting up the 'command post' from which he or she works. In the end, then, the study may have some very practical implications for office design.

Study Design

The present study is concerned with a particular type of location and a particular population — the personal offices of CEOs of school systems. The study is exploratory and involves the study of a small number of offices. It is primarily intended to develop a methodology, pose questions, suggest a mode of analysis, and offer interpretations.

The sample for this study includes the same school systems described in chapter 11: nine school systems in all, eight of which were 'matched pairs' of public school boards and coterminous Roman Catholic separate school boards. All were in southern Ontario within a two-hour drive of Toronto.

The interview and observation guide for the study was based not only upon the notions of archeology which would require an exhaustive 'dig' in each office to reveal the type and locations of artifacts present, but also the cultural anthropological and sociological emphasis on 'the meaning of things' (Czikszentmihalyi and Rochberg-Halton, 1981). We relied heavily upon the latter authors (although they looked at objects in homes rather than offices) in the design of the interview guide (appendix A), asking first for a description of the executive's office, including both its physical and social character and its relationship to the central office of the school system. Information was sought on various work areas within the office, how they related to the individual's work, how much time was spent at the various locations, and whether an attempt had been made to achieve a particular 'style' in the office. Subsequent questions focused on 'special' objects in the office, where they were located, why they were special, and when and how they were obtained. Attention was also given to the objects that were used most frequently and for what they were used. Specific questions were asked about books or reports that the CEO had in the office or at home that were of current interest and about the use of an office area at home. Finally, they were asked about the changes they had made on assuming the office and changes they would like to make were the office to be redesigned.

Complementing the interview data were observations made during the interviews: sketches of office layout and guesses as to their size — we were too embarrassed to be good archaeologists and string a metre-square grid over the office to make precise measurements. As well, still photographs and videotapes were made of the personal offices and CEOs were invited to provide a guided tour of the central office area.[2] All but one, who had to meet his wife at a prearranged time, acceded to the request. The chief custodian was appointed the guide in the remaining case.

For purposes of analysis, the data were arrayed on a grid (table 8.1) displaying each question and the response in each board. Summary tables were prepared for descriptive purposes; key tables are reported here.

The School Board Offices

The central offices of the nine school boards offered striking contrasts, ranging from Victorian to post-modern architecture.[3] We were surprised to note that seven of the nine were recycled or renovated buildings. The two 'recycled' buildings were former corporate head offices in industrial areas that had been assumed by the school systems; in each case relatively minor renovations had been done (for example, constructing meeting rooms for the school board), although in one a major industrial-type structure was added for ancillary services. The two Victorian renovations were a study in contrasts: in one case the brutal gutting of an elegant Italianate home that included stripping out seven of its eight fireplaces and in the other case a sensitive restoration of a fine, Romanesque-style brick and stone school that has since become the school system's symbol. The restoration of the latter had become a cause for the CEO and his retired head of maintenance. They spent three years in acquiring grants, developing plans, and overseeing the project.

The two 'new' central offices were built when the respective school boards were formed in 1969; both are in the 'international style' — one-storey square boxes with large windows and horizontal brick lines. One of the two includes skylights in open atria; the other is attached to an unrenovated Victorian-era school that is used as is for ancillary services. The character of these is rather similar to a third central office where a massive renovation and addition gave an anonymous front to a 1920s neo-Elizabethan brick school. However, a gracious skylit atrium and

Table 8.1 Characteristics of School Systems and their CEO's Offices

Characteristic	School System Identification Number 1	2	3	4	5	6	7	8	9
Board									
Type	Public	RC Separate	Public	RC Separate	Public	RC Separate	Public	RC Separate	Public
Location	Small city/ Rural	Small city/ Rural	Small city	Small city	City	City	Rural	Rural	Large city
Enrolment (000's)	15	10	25	10	40	15	14	5	50
Central office structure	New- 20 years	Gutted century house	Recycled- 30 years old	Recycled- 30 years old	Renovated school	Restored school	New- 20 years	Renovated industrial	Renovated school
CEO's Office									
Size (m^2)	35	20	30	25	40	30	20	25	50
Adj. meeting room	no	no	yes	no	yes	no	yes	yes	yes
Washroom	yes	yes	yes	yes	yes	no	no	no	yes (shared)
Shower	no	no	yes	no	no	no	no	no	yes (shared)
Pantry	yes	no	yes	no	no	no	no	no	yes (shared)
Character	Utilitarian	Intolerably small	Corporate presidents'	Small/ unsuitable	Functional renovation	Gracious	Warm	Modern	Pleasant and quiet

Work Areas									
Number	4	4	4	4	3	4	4	4 or 5	3
Desk	yes	yes	yes	yes	yes	yes	yes	no (tables)	yes
Credenza	yes	yes	yes	yes	yes	yes	no	yes (sort of)	yes
Conversation area	yes	yes	yes	yes	yes	yes	yes	yes	yes
Meeting table	yes (pull out)	no	no (mr)	no	no (mr)	no	no (mr)	no (mr)	no (mr)
Writing area	no	yes	no	no	no	no	yes	yes	no
Files	no	no	yes	yes	no	yes	yes	yes	no
Equipment & Location									
Phone	Desk	Credenza	Desk-auto dial	Desk	Credenza	Desk	Desk	Credenza	Credenza
Calculator	Table	Desk	Desk	Desk	no	Desk	yes	Table (desk)	Desk
Computer	no	no	Desk	no	no	no	no	Credenza	Beside desk
TV/VCR	no	no	yes	no	in m.r.	no	yes (?)	no	yes
Radio	no	no	no	yes	Credenza	Sideboard	yes	no	yes
Tape recorder	no	no	yes	yes	no	no	yes	no	no
Chair's Office	yes	no	no	no	yes	yes	no	no	yes

mr = meeting room adjacent

p. 107
Table 8.1

restoration of the murals in the large auditorium has made the building's interior considerably more engaging.

The two post-modern structures were major redesign/reconstruction projects in very contrasting school systems. In one, a rural school board, an industrial plant was converted into an bright and engaging complex whose origins are, to say the least, not evident. The other, in a major metropolitan centre, is an entertaining adaption of a 1920s bungalow-style, red-brick school. Carefully matched bricks were used to extend the exterior while pastel-shaded columns turned the rear of the building into front and strike a theme carried throughout the structure. The residential setting on a ravine required close work with neighboring residents to ensure the conversion from school to administrative use did not create significant disturbances.

The predominance of renovations over new space is explicable. The province of Ontario does not pay grants on funds used to construct central offices for school systems; the full cost is out of the local rate-payers' pockets. Economical solutions are, therefore, in order. And, economical solutions they are. Even in the last case, where a major redesign was undertaken, the converted space was provided, as the CEO pointed out to us, at a cost per square foot that was one-third the rate for new urban office space.

The CEOs' Offices

'How', we asked the CEOs, 'would you describe your personal office?' This Rorschach test of interior design elicited three types of responses, one concerned with the practicality of the office, one with its mood, and one with style. Those four concerned with *utility* either identified their office as 'functional' (two cases) or commented on how it failed to serve them: 'small' or 'intolerably small'. Those emphasizing *mood* described their offices as 'gracious', 'pleasant and quiet', or 'warm'. *Style* dominated in two cases; in one the richly panelled office was that of a 'corporate president' and the other the office was 'modern' — we might even say avant garde.

Both of the small offices were inherited, one in a recycled corporate office where the facilities did not accommodate the physical handicap the CEO had to deal with, and the other in the Italianate house where every square inch of the building's 6000 square feet was fully utilized. One utilitarian or functional office was found in both a 'new' structure, where the perception of rural conservative values meant a show of extravagance should be avoided. The other office given this label was hardly modest, given its oak panelling, but was quite institutional in feel.

Each of the CEOs who focussed on the mood of their office had played a major role in their office's creation; in two cases, they had worked with designers in developing the building's restoration or redesign. In the restored Romanesque school, all wood panelling in the building had been stripped, bleached, and stained, replacing near-black shellac with a honey coloured natural appearance. The tin ceiling was removed, fire sprinklers installed, and the ceiling panels carefully replaced on a lowered ceiling that was still twelve feet high. The CEO personally bought and donated period-style furniture for the halls and office. In the neo-modern school conversion overseen by the other CEO, an expansive office overlooking a ravine, with a bird-feeder he personally hung and filled, made the office an enviable quiet retreat in a busy metropolitan centre. The third CEO, not given a chance to renovate or design, personalized his office with posters reflecting his heritage, incandescent lighting, a scholastic writing table for his creative moments, and soft (and not so soft) classical music playing from his portable sound system. Quite clearly, style can create a mood, but in all three of these cases, the personal offices did not draw excessive attention to themselves as stylistic tour de forces.

Of the two offices where style dominated, one was inherited and one was personally designed. The first was assumed from a corporate president who, clearly, had taken his status seriously. The floor-to-ceiling teak panelling, adjacent pantry, three-piece washroom, and meeting room, provided an executive suite without peer. Of course, its inherited status means that no hint of ostentation can be attached to the school board or the CEO. In contrast, the avant garde design in the final CEO's office is both unexpected and breathtaking. A pedestal table replaces a desk, that, along with mauve partitions with hanging cabinets, a stand-up writing/correspondence table, and the like, almost give the office the appearance of something out of Stat Trek. It is the latest style from Toronto's office designers, but located in rural setting where one — or at least we — would least expect it.[4]

The executive office cannot be viewed in isolation from the remaining offices and working areas in the school board office. Other rooms, facilities, or areas attached to them may include one or more of the following: an adjacent meeting room, a washroom (with or without shower), a pantry, a secretarial station, a file storage area, and an office for the chair of the school board. Of the nine, five had adjoining meeting rooms; the remaining four wished they did, in all cases feeling that they would sacrifice space in their own office in order to have a convenient location for meeting with board members, lawyers, architects, negotiators, and the like. They wanted a room that was separate from their own inner sanctum to which they could withdraw for private caucuses or phone calls during meetings.

Six had washrooms. (The avant garde designers let their CEO down or recognized that pervasive rural values may have seen such a facility as a 'frill' — the coterminous school system's CEO did not have one, either).

Of these six, two had showers although one of these was inherited and the other was designed to be shared with the school board chairperson. The latter arrangement worked well when the chairperson was a chairman; now that it is a chairwoman, a certain reserve has arisen that has disturbed the arrangement. While a shower may, in any case, be viewed as excessive, it was noted that with school board meetings and collective negotiations sometimes running into the wee hours of the morning, the ability to freshen up for public appearances is not the luxury it might appear to be.

Three offices had pantries, usually a small fridge, hot plate and storage area. One board added a jerry-rigged facility in the adjacent meeting room to fill the need. Again, the prevalence of late night meetings made the facility a matter of convenience, although one of the CEOs reported little use for it since his office was too small for meetings in the 1980s; meetings that used to involve two or three people now seem to require six or eight.

Four of the nine central offices had a special room set aside for the chair of the school board; the others had a room set aside for all trustees. The four chairs' offices were close by their CEOs' offices; in three cases, they were separated by a secretarial station and in one case attached via a corridor to the shared bathroom and meeting room. In two cases the CEOs' secretary served the chair; in the other two, a separate individual within the executive suite provided these services. In one case, it had been 'noticed' that the chair's office was smaller than that of the CEO, a fact that held true in all four cases.

CEOs' Work Areas

The CEO's office is not, as one might expect, simply a room with a desk. Each office, in fact, was divided into three to five zones or work areas. Different types of activities were carried out in each area. A typical office is shown in figure 8.1. On average, the office is about 30 square metres — 300 square feet or 15 feet by 20 feet. In it are located a large desk, usually facing the main entrance, backed by a credenza against the wall behind the desk. On the credenza is a telephone and perhaps a computer terminal and radio (or cassette player). Facing the desk or to the side of the desk is a conversation area: two chairs, perhaps a small couch, a low table, and a table lamp. Against a wall is likely to be a sideboard, bookcase, or filing cabinets, and perhaps a writing area. Perhaps a television and VCR are present. As noted above, an adjacent meeting room may be available for times when a meeting needs more space. Two exits are typical: one opening into the secretarial area and the other to the conference room or to a main hall. The latter, we were told, occasionally served as the 'escape hatch'.

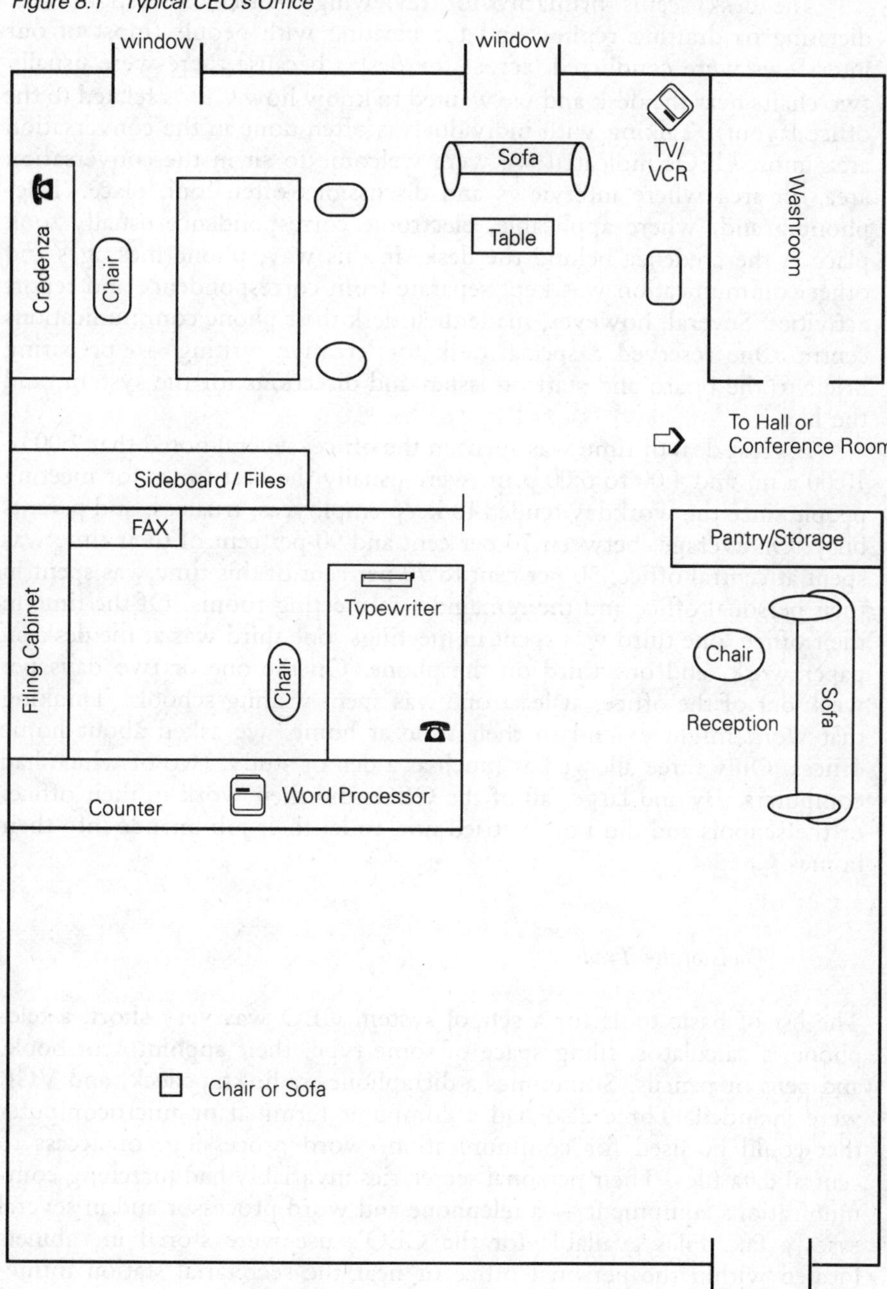

Figure 8.1 Typical CEO's Office

The desk seems primarily for reviewing written correspondence, dictating or drafting replies, and for meeting with people (most of our interviews were conducted 'across the desk', because there were usually two chairs near the desk and we wanted to know how CEOs related to the office layout). Talking with individuals is often done in the conversation area; most CEOs indicated we were welcome to sit in the conversation area, an area where interviews and discussions often took place. Telephoning and, where applicable, electronic correspondence usually took place at the credenza behind the desk. In this way, phone messages and other communication was kept separate from correspondence and report activities. Several, however, made their desk their phone communications centre. One reserved a special desk for 'creative writing' — preparing briefs to the board and staff on issues and directions for the system, and the like.

A great deal of time was spent in the office; several noted that 7:00 to 10:00 a.m. and 4:00 to 6:00 p.m. were usually the best times for meeting people since the workday tended to keep employees, trustees, and parents busy. On average, between 70 per cent and 90 per cent of their time was spent at central office; 50 per cent to 70 per cent of this time was spent in their personal office and the remainder in meeting rooms. Of the time in their office, one third was spent in meetings, one third was at the desk on paper work, and one third on the phone. On the one or two days per week out of the office, at least one was spent visiting schools. Thinking that work might extend to their time at home, we asked about home offices. Only three allowed as much as a den or study, two of which had computers. By and large, all of the CEOs did their work in their offices or the schools and did not, or tried not, to let their job intrude into their homes.

Tools of the Trade

The list of basic tools for a school system CEO was very short: a telephone, a calculator, filing space of some type, their appointment book, and pens or pencils. Sometimes a dictaphone, radio, tapedeck, and VCR were included. Three also had a computer terminal or microcomputer that could be used for communication, word processing, or access to central data files. Their personal secretaries invariably had matching communications equipment — a telephone and word processor and in several cases a fax. Files available for the CEO's use were stored in cabinets located within the personal office or near the secretarial station immediately outside. In either case, key files (board minutes, board committees, negotiations, acts and regulations, ministry of education memoranda, grievances, and the like) were close at hand.

Other than face-to-face conversations the telephone seemed to be the primary means of communication. Their telephones varied in sophistication. One had an auto-dialer that provided memory for scores of numbers which could be called up on a screen. Several others had a 'speed dialing' feature that allowed up to twenty or so numbers to be dialed with just two digits. Invariably, trustees' numbers, their home number, and key superintendents' numbers were given this special status. Several also reported an 'unlisted' number, usually known only to their spouse, so that they could be reached at any time by family members. None of the phone systems were state-of-the-art 'voice messaging' systems and, as far as we determined, none of the CEOs had a car phone.

Hand calculators, while almost uniformly available, were reportedly used in varying degrees. Several CEOs indicated that they regularly used them during negotiations to verify financial details and to develop rough estimates for themselves. Others indicated that they never did such a task and made rare use of it. Computer terminals, though quite evident in two of the cases, were apparently little used. In the third, it was used for drafting memos subsequently retyped by a secretary. None used computers on a regular basis for 'massaging' mainframe data, spreadsheet analysis, and the like. As one indicated, if he needed such information, he would call the appropriate person and would have the data on his desk in ten minutes.

The electronic equipment — radio, tapedeck, and VCR — were present primarily for professional reasons. Several in rural areas indicated that they monitored the winter weather, school closing, announcements and so forth when the situation called for it. The VCR would be used for screening controversial school materials (for example, a video on sex education) and for viewing school produced tapes. The TV was used to monitor developments such as news reports during a teachers' strike. The tapedecks and radio were also used for personal purposes; three of the CEOs liked background music when alone in their offices.

The Personal Touch

Many of the CEOs had personal objects in their office; as well, a number had objects which were personally meaningful but which had strong professional linkages. We asked, quite simply, what five things in their office were most special to them, why they were special, and how and when they were acquired. Table 8.2 presents a tally of their responses grouped according to the categories devised by Czikszentmihalyi and Rochberg-Halton (1981). Not all categories mentioned by these authors, who studied objects in the home, were mentioned by the CEOs. This process made it possible to compare objects in CEOs' offices with those found in typical homes.

In terms of relative frequency, visual art was the object most often mentioned, followed by photographs, books, furniture, sculptures,

Table 8.2 Special objects in the CEOs offices (n = 9)[1]

No.	Category	Object	Board	Percentage
1	Furniture	Rocking chair	2	7.7
		Metal wastebasket	3	
		Oval table	8	
		Custom coordinated furniture	9	
3	Visual art	Children's art	1	21.1
		Valuable paintings		3
		Kids' paintings	4	
		Don Quixote print		4
		Posters of Ireland	7	
		Painting of child with Christ	8	
		Pictures by Native artist	5	
		Board mission statement	5	
		Pictures by former teacher	6	
		Pictures of Canadian scenes	9	
		Political cartoons on education	9	
4	Sculpture	Carving	1	5.7
		Inuit carving	3	
		Carved goose	9	
		Don Quixote sculpture	7	
5	Collectibles	Japanese fan	1	7.7
		Affirmative action button	3	
		Old ornamental sword	8	
8	Stereo	Tape recorder	7	3.8
		Stereo	5	
10	Books	Books, board minutes, etc.	4	9.7
		Books on leadership	7	
		Binders with boards' minutes	7	
		Bible	8	
		Professional magazines	5	
11	Photographs	Photos of grandchildren	2	11.5
		Family pictures	1	
		Family pictures		7
		Photo of children	8	
		Photos by students	5	
		Pictures of children	6	
12	Plants	Plants	5	3.8
		Plants	9	
13	Plates	Teapot	2	3.8
		Coffee mug with board's name	3	
15	Glass	Red apple	3	5.7
		Demijohn	6	
		Antique green bottle	6	
22	Tools	Calculator	2	5.7
		Computer	8	
		Weights used in drug trade	9	
23	Sport equipment	Chess set	1	1.9
24	Trophies	Framed certificates	2	3.8
		Hole-in-one golf ball	9	
33	Washroom	Private washroom	2	1.9
35	Telephone	Speaker phone	4	1.9
37	Personal papers	Desk blotter with graph paper	4	3.8
		Folders on board issues	7	
40	Yard	Window overlooking lawn	8	1.9

1 The full category scheme appears in table D.1 of Czikszentmihalyi and Rochberg-Halton (1981).Rules for classification are given in appendix D. Although five items were requested, several gave fewer than five and some more than five, so a total of fifty-two objects were mentioned.

collectibles, glass, tools, and personal papers. The classification of some objects was difficult. Is a chess set, given to the CEO by a daughter and displayed in the office, a sculpture, a collectible, or sports equipment? Perhaps whimsically, we have classified it as the last since its functional purpose is for use in a game.

The visual art mentioned by the CEOs was varied, from paintings by children that had been awarded prizes at local art shows to attractive tourist posters of Ireland. One set of paintings had been restored and reframed — and hung in the CEO's office — when a routine inventory and evaluation process revealed them took be worth over $10,000. One CEO prized a small sculpture of Don Quixote; another, an oil of Christ with a young child that had been done for a cover of a record of religious music. Not in the tally here, because it was not in an office, was another religious work of Christ with children. This was a large wood carving done by the former head of maintenance who had been involved in the work to restore the nineteenth century Romanesque school to become the school board's home.

One object, classed as visual art because of its presentation in gold gilt on a walnut plaque, was the mission statement of a school system. This articulation of board goals had been the outcome of an extensive process of development led by the CEO. The plaque's presence on his wall reflected not only a pride in the achievement the statement represented, but, it appeared, a symbol of the great importance he placed upon the mission statement.

The photographs were quite different in nature from the visual art. In only one case did they represent photography as an art form. For the most part, they were family photographs, especially of children and grandchildren.

Books mentioned were of a professional variety directly related to the CEOs' work — board minutes, books on leadership, and so forth. Even a Bible, it was noted, was used in school board meetings for the taking of oaths.

Interesting stories tended to relate to objects that were unique to individuals: the brass weights used in the drug trade which a son (who had been posted to southeast Asia) gave his father, a metal wastebasket another son made for his father in a shop class, a chess set acquired by a daughter while abroad and passed on to Dad, a golf ball that was sunk on one stroke in a school board golf tournament, a rather radiant red apple that had appeared on the CEO's desk one day — its origins never discovered.

Czikszentmihalyi and Rochberg-Halton group objects into two fundamental categories: action objects and contemplation objects. In this study, the action objects mentioned were furniture, stereos, plants, tools, sports equipment, washrooms, and telephones; these comprised a total of fourteen objects — 27 per cent of all objects mentioned. Most special

Table 8.3 Percentage of School CEOs (n = 9) Mentioning a Category Compared with Respondents from Households (n = 315) in Czikszentmihalyi and Rochberg-Halton

No.	Category	Percentage CEOs Mentioning	Percentage in Households
1	Furniture	44.4	35.9
3	Visual art	88.9	25.7
4	Sculpture	33.3	19.0
5	Collectibles	33.3	13.3
8	Stereo	22.2	21.6
10	Books	44.4	22.2
11	Photographs	66.7	23.2
12	Plants	22.2	14.9
13	Plates	22.2	14.6
15	Glass	11.1	8.3
22	Tools	33.3	2.8
23	Sports equipment	11.1	8.3
24	Trophies	22.2	4.8
33	Washroom	11.1	3.5
35	Telephone	11.1	2.9
37	Personal papers	22.2	5.4
40	Yard	11.1	3.5

objects, then, were objects whose 'use' involved mental processes rather than physical interaction.

According to the analysis of domestic objects by Czikszentmihalyi and Rochberg-Halton men tend to favour action objects. TVs and stereos appear high on the men's list (ranks 2 and 3) compared to women's lists (ranks 10 and 12). Among the top fifteen objects in the home, men mentioned four categories that women did not mention: sports equipment, pets, vehicles and trophies; women cited plants, plates, glass and textiles, which men did not. The references to trophies and tools by male CEOs could reflect gender preferences; otherwise, the list of objects they noted does not reflect the gender differences noted in the study of special objects in the home.

Table 8.3 compares the percentage of CEOs who mentioned each category of object with those given by the respondents in the households studied by Czikszentmihalyi and Rochberg-Halton. The small sample in our study makes it impossible to infer differences in patterns with a high degree of confidence; nevertheless we chose to infer that a distinctive difference between office and home existed when at least two CEOs referred to an object in a given class and when one percentage exceeded the other by a ratio of two to one. Following this rule, furniture, sculpture, collectibles, stereos, plants and plates were of similar importance to these CEOs as to persons in the previous study, while visual art, collectibles, books, photographs, tools, trophies, and personal papers were relatively more important. Part of these differences, as noted, might spring from gender differences. Otherwise, the differences might be attributed to the nature of the CEOs' profession, education, and to the difference between offices and homes.

The preference for visual art in the office may simply reflect the need to hang something on the wall and easy portability of paintings, prints, and so on. At the same time, the preference for work-related artwork — the paintings of pupils, for example, may reflect a desire to demonstrate in a public way the accomplishments of the school system. Similarly, the prevalence of family photographs and collectibles may simply reflect a desire to link one's home and personal interests with work. Bringing in one's favorite piece of furniture would not be nearly as convenient. The mention of tools and personal papers by the CEOs, on the other hand, seems to reflect a primacy of work.

A minister in a provincial government, in discussing the question of family photographs, described his own debate on the issue. At first, he had no such photos in his office because he wanted to separate the public arena from the privacy of his home. Recently, he had changed his views, to a degree, by bringing family photographs to the office, but arranging them so that only he could see them. Home was brought into the office, but family privacy was preserved.

The meaning of objects, so important to the minister that the arrangement of photos symbolically separated the domains in his life, can be classed as person-related or non-person related. Czikszentmihalyi and Rochberg-Halton classify person-related meanings according to whom the objects relate: the self, the immediate family, kin, and nonfamily members. They code non-person related meanings into seven categories: memories, associations, experiences, intrinsic qualities, style, utilitarian, and personal values.

An ideal object for illustrating the multiple meanings that may accrue to an object was the portrait of Christ and a child mentioned earlier. The painting related to one of the CEO's immediate family — his wife who had seen him admire a record cover on which it was reproduced and had searched out the artist and purchased the painting. For the CEO, the picture involved memories of his wife and the music, and gave the CEO a pleasurable experience in viewing it. As well, it had intrinsic qualities as an original work of art and, finally, symbolized his personal values as the CEO of a Roman Catholic school system in that it reflected his commitment to his religion and to children.

While Czikszentmihalyi and Rochberg-Halton indicated that objects in the home had an average of four meanings, CEOs ascribed an average of only 2.3 meanings, suggesting that offices may not be a 'meaning saturated' as are homes, a finding that might not be surprising as far as an administrative office is concerned. Only one CEO ascribed an average of four meanings: the CEO with the painting described above and who had overseen the conversion an industrial building into a post-modern office with state-of-the-art furnishings. He would appear to be an individual

Table 8.4 Proportion of Respondents Mentioning Various Kinds of Meaning for Special Objects in Office (n = 9) Compared With in Home (n = 315)[1]

A. Person-related reasons	Percentage of people mentioning	B. Non-person related reasons	Percentage of people mentioning
1 Self	89 (87)	1 Memories	89 (74)
2 Immediate Family	78 (82)	2 Associations	67 (52)
3 Kin	22 (23)	3 Experiences	78 (86)
4 Nonfamily	56 (40)	4 Intrinsic Qualities	67 (62)
		5 Style	33 (60)
		6 Utilitarian	56 (49)
		7 Personal Values	78 (53)

1 Percentages for the meanings of objects in home taken from table 3.2 of Czikszentmihalyi and Rochberg-Halton (1981).

who placed a great emphasis on the embodiment of his values in physical objects.

As can be seen in table 8.4, person-related meanings most often involved the CEO himself or his immediate family, a finding consistent with that reported for objects in the home. Kin were mentioned only 22 per cent of the time, again quite similar to the home context. However, non-family associations were more common; usually, other members of the school system or profession were identified as the link — a former student, teacher or whatever (see appendix B for detailed coding of objects).

Non-person related meanings usually involved memories, associations (usually gifts, as the Japanese fan from a group of visiting Japanese educators), experiences (as enjoying music on the stereo), or intrinsic qualities (as the antique, hand-blown glass jar). The prevalence of meanings in these categories were similar to those in homes. Style (as the modern pedestal desk/table in a post-modern office) was less important than in homes, while utilitarian purposes and personal values were more important. Books, personal papers, and the speaker phone were cited for their utilitarian meaning. The computer, however, seemed more appreciated for its style — the technological qualities it offered in conjunction with a counter-top linked to a stand-up desk. The expression of personal values through specific objects — the plaque with the mission statement, the prize-winning paintings by students, the Bible, the red 'apple for teacher', and even that hole-in-one golf ball reflected the activities and commitments that they valued.

The Impact of Succession

In one case, the CEO first interviewed left his position to take another over the summer of 1989 and, on 1 September, a new CEO took office.

The individuals, and their offices, were a study in contrast. The former CEO was an older man whose administration and office reflected the small city and rural conservativism long dominating the county. His office was one where some of the furniture, reflecting the parsimonious values of the community, included a table build by school board staff from a tree blown down on school property. The new CEO is a woman, one of the first from the 'baby boom' generation to be appointed to the head of a school system in the province. On taking office, a planned reconstruction of the school board offices discussed by the previous CEO in our interviews, was converted — in part due to costs — into a partial refurnishing and redecoration of the school system's central offices.

While the CEO described her office as 'comfortable' and 'restful' — which it is — it is also dramatic. The room spoke for itself: rich, violet or eggshell walls, a deep purple ceiling, and mauve carpeting; indirect lighting that produced little ambient light reflected from the walls, but spotlighted the art and work areas; and, as the centrepiece, a Chippendale partners' desk with cabriole legs, provided a setting that is breathtaking. At the fringes of the room, in darker areas, are a glass-door bookcase behind the desk and a conference table (originally intended, with its Queen Anne's lines, to be a dining room table). The small windows, hardly noticed behind the drapes that had served the office before, were like portholes, admitting diffuse light through sheers and rimmed with floral flounces. Only when seated in a Queen Anne style chair with floral covering did one notice the spotlighted bouquet on the side-table and, through the floor into the pantry, an unframed portrait of her son that was not quite ready to be installed in an appropriate location.

How did this change come to take place? Were the individuals as different as their offices? Did they have something in common? What did this dramatic change mean?

The process by which the changes took place were straightforward. The board, upon appointing the new CEO, approved the redecoration of the office, which had been essentially unchanged since it was first built. An interior designer, recommended by the purchasing unit of the school system, met with the CEO and asked her what she desired in terms of atmosphere and if she had any favorite items she wished included in the design. The atmosphere that she wanted was one that would be comfortable and restful; the only items she selected were the painting — by children who had won arts awards in the system and which hung on the walls of her previous office — and the portrait of her son. From there, the colour scheme was developed, indirect light plan sketched, and furniture selected.

Ironically, the new CEO was not entirely at ease with the stylish result. She noted that she had stored files in the glass book case, and was told that did not look good. As a result, a new, low, and modernistic wooden file cabinet was added in a corner. As well, the portrait of her

Table 8.5 Types and Meanings of Objects in Prior and Current CEO's Office

No.	Category	Prior CEO	Current CEO
3	Visual art	Children's art	Children's art
4	Sculpture	Carving	
5	Collectibles	Japanese fan	
6	Photographs	Family	Family
12	Plants		Large and small plants Floral arrangements
22	Tools		Automatic pencil
23	Sports	Chess set	

son could not be added to the decor without a proper frame. She did praise the chair she used, however. It is a modern, black, swivel rocking chair that, covered with the same mauve and pink print used elsewhere, blended with the decor while providing the lumbar support she wished.

The redecoration of the school board's chambers, using a mauve rug and dusty blue walls, revealed a similar sensitivity to fashionable colours, replacing the dominate orange and brown used previously. The change reflected, no doubt, the taste of new members of the board who had much in common with the new CEO — women of professional and business backgrounds. Indeed, the CEO herself was as much a symbol of the changes that had occurred on the school board as was the physical change to the CEO's office.

A comparison of items in the new and former CEOs offices, however, reveals commonalities that are not at first evident. Table 8.5 indicates the classes of items present and why they were valued. Two commonalities are immediately in evidence: children's artwork and family photographs. The artwork, although different in the two cases, were all selected from the winners of the school system's annual competition in the visual arts. The key difference is the new CEO's love of plants, although even here the meanings of the objects shared a commonality: the floral arrangement was a gift from a secondary school staff, reflecting the same type of professional association that several of the items displayed by the former CEO had held. In both cases, the majority of objects was associated with students, members of the education profession, or family. Memories seemed to be the key set of meanings except in the case of the visual arts and plants (where appreciation was also an important factor).

Discussion

Various perspectives can be used to 'make sense' out of the patterns of objects found in the CEOs' offices. Czikszentmihalyi and Rochberg-Halton, in their 1981 study of homes, chose to emphasize the development of the the self — the individual's identity and its links to physical objects. Deetz's concerns focus on the manner in which physical objects and their arrangement express world views, including world views that may not be recorded in the written records a society leaves. McCracken (1988) posits the communicative properties of objects (telling others who we are or wish to be) critical to the commitment that Western society has made to constant change. The three perspectives are complementary and overlapping.

The ten offices studied (counting the one studied twice as a separate office) reflect the actions of different individuals making public statements about themselves through the medium of their offices, but one common feature is probably salient: the extent to which the office reflects the 'whole' person. It seems that by collecting in their offices artifacts that reflect the multiple dimensions of their lives individual CEOs are portraying an integration of their lives and the integration they perceive between worklife and homelife. This is not to say that the individuals necessarily live such integrated lives — it could be that those who most demonstrate their wholeness are the very individuals having most difficulty in living integrated lives. Perhaps some use their offices more to express ideals rather than reality.

Czikszentmihalyi and Rochberg-Halton found that the distinction of objects in happy and unhappy homes differed in the numbers of objects rich in family associations. If we use the above finding as an analogy, it may be that CEOs' offices reflect differences in school system morale, social climate, or culture. Some offices seemed rich in objects associated with school system personnel and programs, with the CEO's family and personal tastes, and with the over-riding values of education and the community. Others seemed more restricted in their palette, although none excessively so. Some of the 'bachelor pads' of recently divorced men described by Czikszentmihalyi and Rochberg-Halton suggested that their inhabitants were just passing through, living out of a suitcase. That was not the case of any of the CEOs' offices. Each one reflected the personal occupant.

Expressing the same idea underlying Deetz's work, McCracken comments:

> Material culture makes culture material. It makes it palpable, present, and ubiquitous. To borrow the phrasing of the poet Hass, when culture is insinuated into our physical landscape, our housing, and its furnishing, the premises of our existence are also the existence of our premises. Ideology and the material world are one. (p. 132)

To what extent did this notion apply to our CEOs? To test this notion, applying Binford's typology of the technomic, socio-technic, and ideo-technic is useful. One contrast is found in the ideo-technic domain between the public school system CEOs and the Roman Catholic school system CEOs. Only one of the former had so much as a Bible in the office. This represented the inclusion of a religious school in the system, and that many in the community maintained a commitment to religion. In contrast, all of the Roman Catholic CEOs had some religious symbolism in their offices and it included, in two cases, the special objects they mentioned.

Most ideotechnic objects (including the two mentioned above) were classified as visual art. Aside from the religious objects, most prominent were paintings by children or of children, reflecting the commitment to the education of young people. The gilt plaque of the school system's mission statement was probably the most explicit secular statement of this notion.

While purely technomic items were present in offices (telephones, VCRs, and so forth), these tended not to be included among the special objects. When they were mentioned they either related explicitly to the individuals personal pleasure in them (for example, the stereo sets) or they might better be considered socio-technic in function. Computer terminals, in particular, seemed more for display — for style — than for day-to-day use. If so, the question arises as to what their public meaning may be.

One of the themes developed by Deetz is the replacement of 'folk' culture, which is traditional, conservative, and localized, with modern 'popular' culture, which changes rapidly, is widespread over large areas, and often disseminated by powerful central institutions. We looked for evidence of a folk tradition in CEOs' offices that was being displaced by a powerful new set of ideas. Although the evidence was mixed, one could argue something of the sort was occurring.

Older offices, built twenty years ago, particularly in the rural and small town school board, tended not to call attention to themselves. The classic example was the office in which school board personnel had made the furniture out of a tree blown down on school property. Local personnel, local materials, and thrift were all reflected in this office, even though the building itself might be characterized as then-contemporary 'international style' (a 'popular' style now becoming unpopular). The CEO reported his plan to renovate in line with the values of new trustees, but indicated cost was still a factor. An urban CEO, knowing that the small city board's officials had contacted the design firm that had executed his system's post-modern renovation of an old school, noted that the other board was still too 'small town' to pay what was necessary for a proper job.

Given this expected contrast, it was unexpected to find that a rural Roman Catholic board had successfully executed such a renovation, one that was more avant garde than the big-city reconstruction that had retained very traditional (albeit custom) furniture in the CEO's office. The contrasting, but equally fashionable, decision of another Roman Catholic CEO to conduct a massive restoration and renovation to an historic school against the initial opposition of his trustees (who wanted a 'new' building) was also a surprise. Both CEOs seemed to emphasize the school system headquarters as a symbol of the school system, and wished to convey a particular set a values through their buildings and, in the first case, personal offices. In the second case, although the CEO admitted a desire to refurnish his office with nineteenth century furniture, he felt he could not justify that expense to the board. He made do with a few pieces of antique glass. In these systems, recycling and renovation symbolized a concern with cost, while the restoration and post-modern choices, in their own ways, implied conservation of the past and dedication to the future.

Our second visit to the school system in which a new CEO had been appointed, provided affirmation of both conservatism and a desire for change. A major renovation of the central office was rejected by the school board's conservative finance committee, but funds were allotted to employ a professional interior decorator to redecorate the school board's meeting room and CEO's office. At the same time, new office furnishings of contemporary design were provided for staff in the older section of the office. Designing for a female rather than male CEO, the designer chose furniture and colours that would be comfortable in many homes, not traditional or high-tech office furniture. The design scheme, with its use of strong colours and striking furniture, is associated with high fashion promoted by professional designers rather than traditional rural and small community values. The former CEO's furniture was placed in storage.

All of these choices were quite unlike those being made in one small city planning a new board office. Its planned office building — a cool blue glass cube — reflects the current version of the international style which emphasized the future as a break from the past. It seems that the new popular (some would already say passé) post-modern style — which links past and future — had not replaced the old. In other words, traditional values of cost efficiency may still dominate in this board; a routine, business-park office building is being purchased, not a corporate symbol. The proposed addition of a daycare centre and atrium may help make it a more active, living building.

If one change was being disseminated among these school systems, it was the change from a large CEO's office with a conversation area to that of a smaller office with an adjacent conference room for a dozen people. Although some reported that this desire resulted from an increase in the numbers in attendance at most small meetings, office consultants in Toronto[4] indicated that the cost per square foot of office space had forced corporate headquarters to look toward more efficient space utilization, and the separation of office from meeting room functions is a popular solution. Perhaps, the desire to remove the meeting room function from personal offices has economic roots; however, it is also possible that a more directive, less collegial form of administrative decision-making underlies this structural change.

Another trend evidenced in comments was a desire for office space for school trustees, who in the past have often had an office-in-common attached to the school board chambers. The symbolism of the office space for trustees is one which recently made headlines in one Ontario community where the new chair of the school board tried to evict the CEO from his office in order to make it her own. In another case, a former chair described how, when she first asked for office space, she was given a former storage closet; a year later she moved down the hall to a former administrative assistant's office; and still later, when an assistant superintendent left, was given an office adjacent to the CEO. In all, four of the school system offices we visited had offices for the chair; in all cases these were close by the CEOs; three of the four were created recently when renovations or restorations were carried out. According to Davis (1989), the expanding role of school trustees, some of whom are full-time trustees, is one of the important shifts in the governance of education in Ontario.

The jostling for office space for trustees, for superintendents, and others, is part of a continuous process of bargaining over a scarce resource. Who wins or loses these 'space wars', as they are sometimes called, may reflect the advance (or retreat) of different groups or individuals. Space close to CEO, close to his or her ear, is particularly valued for both its political and symbolic value. The size and location of one's office is perhaps invariably linked to one's status in the hierarchy.

For the CEO who restored a building as his system's home, space was not an issue, nor were washrooms or meeting rooms. He was disappointed because his office furniture 'clashed' with the building's style. For the most part, his furniture was non-descriptive 1950s' modern while the building was nineteenth century Romanesque (or Richardsonian, for the architecture buffs). In McCracken's language, there was an example of the Diderot effect — the failure of objects to coalesce into a consistent style:

> 'Diderot unities' are highly consistent complements of consumer goods. The 'Diderot effect' is a coercive force that maintains them. The unity and the effect, named here for the French Enlightenment philosopher Denis Diderot, are key instruments with which culture controls consumptions. The Diderot effect is especially interesting because it can operate in two quite different ways. It can constrain the consumer to stay within his or her existing patterns of consumption. But, in a second mode, it can

force the consumer to transfer these patterns of consumption beyond all recognition.

McCracken names his concept after Diderot because the notion is implicit in an essay Diderot wrote entitled, 'Regrets on Parting with My Old Dressing Gown'. As McCracken explains,

> The essay begins with Diderot sitting in his study bemused and melancholic. Somehow this study has undergone a transformation. It was once crowded, humble, chaotic, and happy. It is now elegant, organized, beautifully appointed, and a little grim. Diderot suspects the cause of the transformation is his new dressing gown.
>
> This transformation, Diderot tells us, took place gradually and by stages. First, the dressing gown arrived, a gift from a friend. Delighted with the new possession, Diderot allowed it to displace his 'ragged, humble, comfortable old wrapper'. This proved the first step in a complicated and ultimately distressing process. A week or two after the arrival of the dressing gown, Diderot began to think that his desk was not quite up to standard and he replaced it. Then the tapestry on the study wall seemed a little threadbare, and a new one had to be found. Gradually, the entire study, including its chairs, engravings, bookshelf and clock were judge, found wanting, and replaced.
>
> All of this, Diderot concludes, is the work of an 'imperious scarlet robe [which] forced everything else to conform with its own elegant tone'.... Diderot looks back with fondness and regret to his old dressing gown, and its 'perfect accord with the rest of the poor bric-a-brac that filled my room' ... (pp. 118–9)

McCracken concludes that,

> ... [We] are captives of the Diderot effect.... It insists that there is no such thing as a sufficiency of goods, a complement of possessions which once obtained can be considered complete. Sometimes it is dressing gowns, sometimes a new car, sometimes a new pipe, but continually we admit objects into our lives that will radically change the whole of our product complements and force us to new levels of expenditure. Sometimes we will achieve in the process a level of expenditure that brings us happiness. But just as often we are likely to end, as Diderot did, surrounded by a new complement of goods that bears no necessary relationship to our concepts of self and the world. The Diderot effect ... can alienate us from ourselves. (p. 128)

The CEOs who oversaw the recycling and restorations of buildings clearly felt the Diderot effect at work. Two completed the work, acquiring fashionable, post-modern buildings and complementary (but strikingly different) personal offices. Both seemed satisfied with their accomplishments. The CEO who oversaw an historic restoration largely with special funds allocatd for heritage structures, lacked the means (or chose not to incur the political costs) that were necessary to complete the project by furnishing a stylistically consistent office. The new woman CEO, present in a school system hesitant about change, has found herself in a situation virtually identical to that Diderot described: the office too formal for her personal style and she cannot, she is told, hang the portrait of her son until it is 'properly' framed. The unity of the office's design has become a tyrant.

This largely cultural analysis has emphasized symbolic function above technical function. While we did not conduct a time-motion study to determine if more efficient ways exist to arrange the administrator's office, the data also suggest some things that function well, and some that do not. Three of the CEOs without adjacent meeting rooms indicated that they would like them. Two CEOs whose administrative staff had offices scattered in several buildings desired an office arrangement that would place their key superintendents in close proximity. One CEO without a washroom said he did not want one and commented, too, that he preferred having meeting rooms away from his office — he believe that the current arrangement forced him to get out of his personal office to wander the halls and meet people for informal chats.

Readily available storage for board minutes, policies, provincial guidelines and the like were almost uniformly available on credenzas behind desks. A few CEOs lacked adequate convenient storage space in their personal offices and relied on crowded filing cabinets in a corner or passing the problem on to their secretary. In one case, a spacious, bright CEO's office was complemented by a shaded, crowded secretarial station where inadequate cabinets went unseen by the CEO. As well, jerry-built stands for TVs, VCRs, and, on occasion, refreshments bespoke a need to think through the full range of functions played by a CEO before offices are designed. Arguments for efficiency may succeed in defending an improvement to administrative offices in a world dominated by the view that money not spent on children is money wasted.

The extent to which offices were divided into different work areas surprised us. Perhaps too used to our own cluttered desktops where everything from our lunches to a novel sits, we noted the rational allocation of one area to the phone, another to administrative paper, another for creative writing, and so forth, even in relatively small offices. As soon as we clear two square feet of our own desks we intend to do the same. Perhaps the arrangement does reflects an administrator's world view that is distinct from our own. Deetz (1977) indicated that as the rationalism of the enlightenment replaced the mystical views of the medieval mind, trash pits were dug at a decent distance from the back door to contain the refuse that formerly was tossed out the front door. He suggests the saying, 'a place for everything, and everything in its place' could have been coined in this period of change (p. 126). We take comfort in the adage a colleague has posted above his desk, 'If a cluttered desk is the sign of a cluttered mind, what is an empty desk a sign of?'

Conclusion

We set out to document the artifacts found in the offices of chief executive offices in a selection of school systems and to determine how these reflect their occupants' personalities, values, objectives, and administrative styles. In some ways, we found more than we expected, in that in a number of cases the CEO's offices were but one room in administrative buildings that the CEOs had been instrumental in acquiring, designing (by selection of the building or influence in selecting the architectural firms responsible), and overseeing the construction. To these individuals, the buildings and their styles were, in McCracken's language, part of a dialogue about the place of these educational systems in the community.

For their school systems' offices, these officials did not create administrative boxes, they created civic and, in the case of Roman Catholic school systems, religious symbols. The selection of former schools, in most cases, as sites to renovate or recycle may have been as much economic as intentional, but the ability to transfer the emotions most individuals attach to individual schools to the political and administrative centre could work only to their advantage. Transfer of positive meanings from one object to another is one way to fix the value of a new object in the community's collective mind. In these cases, the educational dimension of the corporate image was reinforced.

Not all CEOs seemed to embrace the notion that the school system's offices should convey educational or religious connotations. One recycled school had been made so anonymous in its international-style modern coat that its origins as a school could only be discerned by the buildings' auditorium and gymnasium (the only school board office with its own athletic club, so to speak). Another school system, planning its new office, was opting for a standard office building. Administrative efficiency, not schooling, seemed to be its dominant message. We would dismiss their intent to communicate anything, except for their decision to place the building adjacent to a heavily travelled freeway so that it would be visible.

We can surmise, therefore, a dialectic on the centrality and the meaning of central offices being carried out in architectural language. Is the school the site of primary importance with the political and administrative centre but a shadowy service to those who educate young people? Or is the core of contemporary education located in the political and administrative centre where power is wielded?

CEOs were more united in the imagery of items displayed in their personal offices. The primary message was a commitment to students — pictures by and of students hung on their walls — and to their professional associates — modest gifts with organizational and professional meanings conveyed their link to the broader world. For most, personal artifacts, things made by or given by their children, family photos, and the like also were displayed as if to say 'there's more to life than just work.'

The non-materialistic values of these officers is something that may be worthy of praise. Czikszentmihalyi and Rochberg-Halton (1981) end their work decrying the excessive consumerism — they call it 'terminal materialism' (p. 231). They see it a threat to the environment when it is manifested in terms of more automobiles, larger houses, and so forth. Their work shows, quite clearly, that an object's value to the individual may be quite different from the objective value placed on it by the economy. Most of our CEOs, at least in their offices, display a lack of concern about materialistic values. Those whose offices display, in brilliant manifestation of the Diderot unities, a contemporary splash of materialistic office design, are saved by the integrated design of their recycled post-modern buildings and strong educational and religious symbolism. We can argue (perhaps a bit generously) that their collective civic consumption is to be praised in its manifestation of collective values over individualistic pride of possession. The redesign of the new female CEO's office in a distinctive fashion may be seen as an assertion of women's arrival in the administrative hierarchy. Perhaps women no longer need to suggest power by adopting styles associated with male styles, as McCracken (1988) suggests; they have acquired the right to purvey their own styles when occupying the executive suite.[5]

The typical CEO's office is not a display case for evidence of the occupant's personal status and accomplishments. One might even claim that the latter are downplayed — in only one office is a certificate of any kind displayed and in only one is there a display of special accomplishment in private life (the hole-in-one golf ball). In terms of the artistic pursuits, considerable indication is evident of the CEO's appreciation of visual and performing arts. Only one office includes valuable art, and this was already in the possession of the school system. Literary interests and accomplishments are less obvious; relatively few books are present (this in striking contrast, say, to academics' offices in the university). The relative absence of books in the offices (we did not visit the homes) may reflect an administrative dependence on condensed, pre-digested information and on a valuing of oral sources known for the currency of information. Instead, their offices convey a commitment to students and their learning, to the school system and its accomplishments. Perhaps this is not a surprising conclusion given that education is a pursuit whose primary end, education, is itself non-materialistic.[6] That this is the case is reassuring.

Notes

1 The 'local history' of an organization is probably an important part of the 'myth-making' that can be central to an organization's identity and vision. It is worth noting that articles about influential people in the popular press invariably describe these individuals' surroundings. Here are some recent examples.

Karen Howlett's (1989) review of Ian Brown's *Freewheeling,* the story of Canadian Tire's Billes family, comments that Brown 'pokes the most fun at Fred and his wife Barbara Billes and the store dealers he presents as a collective of 348 rather than as individuals. With merciless wit, he writes about the way they look, act and decorate their homes and offices.... The dealers furnished their offices in a total look known as Rec Room Plus. The color scheme: "vegetable stew brown"'.

Kelly Campbell, in 'Desk tops tell all' (1987), writes, 'A man's work space isn't just about his job. It is a kind of Rorschach test, psychologists say, communicating everything from a love of power to a desire to create an impression or simply feel at home.' Photographs accompanying the article show, among others, Malcolm Forbes, Henry Kissinger and Ronald Reagan at work at their desks.

2 A 16 minute videotape based on the findings of the study has been prepared.

3 For a perceptive and entertaining look at central office structures, see Hickcox (1986).

4 The Interior Designers of Canada and the Association of Registered Interior Designers of Ontario (ARIDO) were contacted about trends in office design. It was indicated that offices are becoming smaller because of the escalating cost of office space and because storage is taking up less space as more electronic media are used. Gone are the massive wood desks, which are the wrong height for computers, and chesterfields. The modern CEOs office has two 'dedicated workspaces': (a) a work wall with computers (including necessary wiring which, incidentally, means that this equipment must be near a wall rather than on a centre desk), telephone, any other equipment, bookcases, space for charts, and storage bins (which are now frequently hung from the ceiling); and (b) a conference section with chairs around a table that people can write on (i.e., not a coffee table). Most CEOs, we were told, have their own computers for two reasons: convenience and appearance — keeping up with the world.

Special rugs are also gone. The CEO will now have the same rug as the rest of the staff to give a democratic face to the corporation. Colours in offices are becoming 'more visual' — brighter with more primary colours on a neutral background. Referenced were *Canadian Interiors* and *Contract Interiors*.

5 The choice of purple (and shades of purple) as the dominant hue in this CEO's office was drawn from the students' artwork she favoured. Nevertheless, the colour has regal associations. As Webster notes, 'purple: 2. a cloth dyed purple; esp., a purple robe emblematic of rank or authority, specif. that worn by Roman emperors. 3. Imperial or regal rank or power; also, *Colloq.*, exalted station.' We did not determine whether the designer was aware of this connotation, but suggest it could be a choice open to misinterpretation.

6 The lack of adult student art perhaps has a negative connotation: these educational systems and their CEOs may not have fully embraced the education of adults as part of their role in society.

Appendix A: Interview Guide

Our study is concerned with administrative practices. We are focussing on two areas. The first of these is concerned with the physical facilities that you have available at your disposal and the second with administrative organization. We have a consent form indicating the nature of the study and your willingness to participate in it. If you wish to withdraw at any time, you may do so. Also, we would like to tape the interview so that we have a complete record to complement our notes. We'd like to begin, now, with the first set of questions that focus on the office.

1 Could you describe your office to me, as if I were someone who had never seen it?

Interviewer:

1 If the respondent describes social atmosphere, feeling or mood but not physical description, then probe for physical description. If physical description is given, then vice versa.

2 If the respondent describes just the personal office, then probe for description of central office; if a description is given of the central office, then probe for description of 'personal office').

2 (a) What are the primary work areas associated with the director's office — your office — in this board?

(b) Where, exactly, are these situated and how do they relate to your work?

(c) How much time do you spend in or at each of them on a typical day?

3 (a) What are the primary work areas within your personal office?
(b) How do you use these areas?
(c) How much time do you spend at each of them on a typical day?

4 Are you trying to have a certain style or atmosphere in your personal office? Please describe it.

5 (a) What are the things in your personal office that are special for you? Could you indicate where they are located in the office and why they are special?

Interviewer: Remember (b), (c) and (d) will be asked sequentially. Also, use additional sheets for any section if necessary.

Area	Object	Why Special

5 (b) What would it mean to you not to have this thing?

Interviewer: List the objects the person has named in 5(a).

Object	Without Object

5 (c) When did you acquire these things?

(d) How did you acquire these objects?

Interviewer: (d) should be asked only for those objects for which the circumstances of acquisition have not already been described.

Object	Without Acquired	How Acquired

6 (a) What are the things in your personal office that you use frequently? Could you indicate where they are located in the office, and what they are used for?

Area	Object	What Used For

7 If you had a fire in your personal office, what things would you save? Why?

8 What books or reports on education you have read or become intrigued with? Do you have copies? Where do you keep them?

9 Do you have an office at home? How would you compare it with your office here?

10 When you were first appointed as director, how did you go about arranging your personal office?

Interviewer: If necessary, ask probes such as, 'What changes did you make?'

11 If you were designing a new central office for your school board, how would you change the layout of the executive offices? Your own personal office?

References

BROWN, I. (1989) *Freewheeling: The Feuds, Broods, and Outrageous Fortunes of the Billes Family and Canada's Favorite Company*, Toronto, Harper and Collins.

CAMPBELL, K. (1987) 'Desk tops tell all', *The New York Times Magazine*, 13 September, pp. 66–7.

CZIKSZENTMIHALYI, M. and E. ROCHBERG-HALTON (1981) *The Meanings of Things: Domestic Symbols and the Self*, Cambridge, Cambridge University Press.

DAVIS, J. (1989) 'Trends in the Trusteeship', *Education Today*, 1, November/December, pp. 14–15.

DEETZ, J. (1977) *In Small Things Remembered*, Garden City, NY, Anchor Books.

EWAN, STUART (1976) *Captains of Consciousness: Advertising and the Social Roots of Consumer Culture*, New York: McGraw-Hill.

HICKCOX, E.S. (1986) 'Outward symbols of inner meaning', *Orbit*, 17, 2, pp. 12–13.

HOWLETT, K. (1989) 'Billes saga tells a tale of Canada', *The Globe and Mail*, 13 November, p. B2.

MCCRACKEN, G. (1988) *Culture and Consumption*, Bloomington, IN, Indiana University Press.

Appendix B: Five Special Objects by Category and Meaning for Nine Respondents

No.	Category	Board	Object	Percentage	Meaning[1] Personal	Non-Personal
1	Furniture	2	Rocking chair	7.7	1, 2	1, 3
		3	Metal wastebasket		2	4
		8	Oval table			5
		9	Custom coordinated furniture			5
3	Visual art	1	Children's art	21.1	4	4, 1, 3
		3	Valuable paintings		1	4, 7
		4	Kids' paintings		4	7, 1
		7	Posters of Ireland		3	1, 2
		8	Painting of child with Christ		2	2, 3, 4, 7
		5	Pictures by native artist		4	1, 2
		5	Board mission statement		1, 4	7, 3
		6	Pictures by former teacher			1, 3
		9	Pictures of Canadian scenes			2
		9	Political cartoons on education		1, 4	1, 4
4	Sculpture	1	Carving	7.7	3	4
		3	Inuit carving			2
		9	Carved goose			2
		4	Don Quixote sculpture		1	7
5	Collectibles	1	Japanese fan	5.7		2
		3	Affirmative action button		1	
		8	Old ornamental sword		2	
8	Stereo	7	Tape recorder	3.8	1	3
		5	Stereo		1	3, 6
10	Books	4	Books, board minutes, etc.	9.6	4	
		7	Books on leadership		1	6, 7, 3
		7	Binders with board's minutes			6
		8	Bible		1	2, 6, 7
		5	Professional magazines		1	6

Appendix B: Five Special Objects by Category and Meaning for Nine Respondents

No.	Category	Board	Object	Percentage	Meaning[1] Personal	Non-Personal
11	Photographs	2	Photos of grandchildren	11.5	2	1, 7
		1	Family pictures		2	1
		7	Family pictures		2	1
		8	Photo by his children		2	1
		5	Photos by students		4	1, 4
		6	Pictures of his children		2	1
12	Plants	5	Plants	3.8	5	
		9	Plants		4.5	
13	Plates	2	Teapot	3.8	1	3, 6
		3	Coffee mug with board's name		4	2
15	Glass	3	Red plastic apple	3.8		2, 7
		6	Demijohn		2	1, 2, 4
		6	Antique green bottle		1	4
22	Tools	2	Calculator	5.7	1	6
		8	Computer		1	4, 5
		9	Weights used in drug trade		2	2
23	Sports equipment	1	Chess set	1.9	2	2
24	Trophies	2	Framed certificates	3.8	1	7
		9	Hole-in-one golf ball		1	7
33	Washroom	2	Private washroom	1.9	1	7
35	Telephone	4	Speaker phone	1.9	1	6
37	Personal papers	4	Desk blotter with graph paper	5.7	1	3, 6
		7	Folders on board issues		1	6
40	Yard	8	Window overlooking lawn	1.9	1	1, 3, 4, 5, 7

1 Codes are as follows: For personal-related, 1 = self, 2 = immediate family, 3 = kin, 4 = non-family. For non-personal related, 1 = memories, 2 = associations, 3 = experiences, 4 = intrinsic qualities, 5 = style, 6 = utilitarian, 7 = personal values. See Cziksentmihalyi and Rochberg-Halton (1981) appendix C for full coding system.

Chapter 9

Pride and Privilege: The Development of the Position and Role of Chief Education Officers in the United States and Canada

Derek J. Allison

After a brief description of commonalities in the position of Chief Education Officer in the United States and Canada as it exists today, this chapter sketches the evolution of the position in each country. The formative influence of the Prussian school system on the development of educational policies in both the United States and Canada is noted, and key differences in the ways in which this influenced the development of administrative structures and positions in the two countries are explored. In the US, the attainment of efficiency in education was linked to the appointment of superintendents to assist elected boards in technical aspects of school administration. Over time and in response to a variety of factors the superintendency acquired increasing executive powers, culminating in the position as it exists today. The early tensions between board and executive rule over schools also became institutionalized, giving rise to the endemic tensions and conflicts often used to characterize the position in contemporary literature. Canadian concerns for efficiency in the nineteenth century encouraged the development of much more highly centralized, Prussian-like, state regulated educational bureaucracies in which school administration was supervised by provincially appointed and regulated inspectors and superintendents. Increasing complexity and diversity in educational policy — together, particularly in the Western Provinces, with the influence of US practices — subsequently led to increased powers for locally elected school boards, including the local appointment of superintendents. The position of contemporary Canadian CEOs, therefore, is the result of devolution of centralized authority and expertise. In the US situation, the current role is the product of executive centralization at the local level. Important common differences between the evolution of the superintendency in urban and rural settings are also discussed.

History is more than just a static backdrop to the present. Past events and decisions structure social and organizational settings, while shared memories and inherited traditions weave webs of mutual understanding between people, influencing how they interpret and construct the roles they are called to play in the pageant of life. An inquiry into the role, work, and practices of chief education officers should thus take stock of historical factors that moulded the position into its present form. This is the task undertaken here. More specifically, the chapter seeks to trace and contrast the development of the school superintendency in Canada and the United States.

This will be done in broad strokes, with many details necessarily being ignored. My main aim is to sketch the emergence of two quite different traditions of school supervision. On one level these traditions can be interpreted as reflecting key values enshrined in the constitutional charters of each country. In the United States, the principle of 'government by the people, for the people and of the people', together with the constitutional guarantees of 'life, liberty and the pursuit of happiness', has undergirded a long established preference for local control of schools. On the other hand, the Canadian constitutional guarantee of 'peace, order and good government', exemplifies a quite different set of political and administrative values, but one which is altogether consistent with the pattern of centralized regulation and inspection which characterized school supervision in the Canadian provinces until the middle decades of this century.[1]

The Canadian provinces have now replaced their traditional systems of school administration with arrangements similar to those in the United States. Despite some variation in official titles, virtually all chief superintendents in both countries are now employed by local boards of education and — although not specifically authorized in some jurisdictions — virtually all act as chief executives for their boards. In this context the divergent history of school supervision in Canada may seem little more than a curiosity — a somewhat irrelevant backdrop to modern conditions. Yet in various ways and to different degrees inherited elements of Canada's educational history continue to influence how school administration is constituted and understood in the different provinces. The main point, nonetheless, is that despite current structural and functional similarities between school system administration in the two countries, the modern Canadian superintendency was not formed by the same traditions and historical forces that moulded the office in the United States.

Even so, historical developments in each country were conditioned by a number of common forces and features. The federal structure of both countries ensured that characteristic differences at the national level were a product of polices adopted within constituent states and provinces.

Consequently, the features which will be described as characteristic of each country were not necessarily manifest to the same degree or at the same time in particular states or provinces. Further, the administrative structures which evolved in both states and provinces all incorporated the three generic offices of: (i) chief state (provincial) school officer; (ii) regional (county) superintendent/inspector; and (iii) local, board employed, superintendent. Yet despite structural similarities, key differences developed between the functions, authority and status which attached to the offices associated with these generic positions in each country. To better illustrate and contrast these differences the chapter is organized around the characteristic ways in which each of these three generic positions developed in, first the United States and, second, Canada. The chapter begins, however, with a brief overview of other common conditions which influenced the early development of school supervision in North America.

Background

In both the United States and the British colonies and territories which were to become Canada government provisions for schooling were generally rudimentary until the mid-nineteenth century. Government supported schools which were available often competed with the many voluntary and private schools which were characteristic of the times. Government grants in support of local schools were usually conditional on the election of a trustee board authorized to manage financial affairs, hire a teacher and supervise the teaching, this last function representing a tradition which can be traced back to 1721 when the Boston selectmen appointed their first permanent school visiting committee. Some states and colonies experimented with central or regional administrative boards — and in some cases county or township superintendents — but these were generally ad hoc, part-time appointments, and the duties and powers of incumbents were often unclear. Moves toward enhanced official control were typically viewed with suspicion by parents and political opponents with the result that early steps in this direction were often abandoned in the face of opposition or indifference. Thus, while the first state superintendencies in the United States were established in New York in 1812 and Maryland in 1826, they were subsequently discontinued before being re-established in 1854 and 1864 respectively. Similarly, the General Board of Education created in 1823 to exercise control over government funded schools in Upper Canada was disbanded ten years later, a process which was paralleled in Vermont, where the state board of education which was initially established in 1827 was temporarily dissolved in 1835.

Even so, the patchworks of voluntary and semi-public schools which were common to both countries in the early nineteenth century were regarded as less than satisfactory by some leading citizens, and as the century progressed pressure built for more comprehensive approaches to public schooling which would provide opportunities for all children to be educated in high quality common schools financed out of the public purse and operated according to more uniform standards. Some voluntary agencies had developed complex organizational structures which provided early advocates of such reforms with examples of how schooling might be better coordinated and controlled. The American Sunday School Union (ASSU) was one. Founded in 1824, this non-denominational enterprise was administered from a central office in Philadelphia from which a president and specialized managers coordinated travelling field agents who promoted the idea and ideals of Sunday schooling — together with ASSU teaching materials and organizational principles — across the length and breadth of the then United States. The ASSU was remarkably effective. As early as 1828 it had 'enrolled about one-seventh of all children aged five to fifteen', and by 1854 it had 322 field agents (Tyack and Hansot, 1982, pp. 35–36). As Tyack and Hansot note, 'long before (American) public-school systems acquired their superintendents, the Sunday school superintendent was a familiar male authority figure organizing the work of his unpaid, mostly female teachers' (p. 36).

Yet by far the most impressive examples of systematized, standardized and supervised schooling were to be found in Europe. The New World was not, of course, isolated from the Old. Immigrants brought their experiences, observations and prejudices with them, while influential school promoters toured Europe to inspect and report on educational arrangements there. North American visitors were generally impressed with what they found, and many, including Horace Mann from Massachusetts and Egerton Ryerson from Upper Canada (Ontario), were especially fascinated with Prussian schooling. Prussia had instituted a form of compulsory education as early as 1717, and by the nineteenth century a diversified system of compulsory, centrally regulated and free schooling was in operation complete with a standardized curriculum, graduation examinations, well-trained teachers, and a corps of superintendents and inspectors.

Such centralization and compulsion was anathema to many Americans, and Horace Mann's report of his visit concentrated on extolling the virtues of Prussian pedagogy. Nonetheless, the comparatively modest reforms proposed by Mann and other public school promoters were vilified by some opponents as attempts to introduce a 'Prussian system', while the Massachusetts state board of education of which Mann was the secretary was attacked as a 'Prussian-inspired "system of centralization"' (*ibid*, p. 60). In Canada, Ryerson's proposals attracted similar condemnation from some quarters, but with better reason. Although Ryerson's 1846 report acknowledged that compulsory attendance legislation would be inappropriate, he strongly advocated a centralized system of public instruction, laying particular stress on the importance of 'an efficient System of Inspection', and the careful selection of 'the class of officers' charged with this task (p. 206).

It was against this background that the crucial battles for publicly financed, more uniform, systems of common schooling in North America were fought and won. The outcomes of early political struggles ensured that key legislative frameworks were in place by the mid-nineteenth century, but the actual creation of the common schooling systems envisaged by Mann, Ryerson and their compatriot school promoters was a project which absorbed them and their spiritual successors until the twilight of the century, and beyond. Yet while the stage was set in both countries by the mid-nineteenth century the dramas which unfolded over the next century followed two quite different scripts, each producing a distinctly different system and tradition of school administration.

The American Superintendency

Throughout the balance of the nineteenth century the work of building the American school system devolved largely on the shoulders of local trustees, community notables and enthusiastic officials who preached, promoted and directly implemented reforms within increasingly supportive legislative frameworks. Consistent with tradition local boards continued to directly administer and supervise their schools, although they were increasingly required to observe minimum curriculum, attendance and operational standards prescribed by the state. For the most part such standards were intended to increase the quality of one-room rural schools and they often lagged behind those already attained in the cities where the boards often enjoyed a remarkable degree of independence, even to the extent of certificating their own teachers and establishing their own curriculum in some instances.

State Superintendents

By the turn of the century the structural patterns and arrangements which were to constrain and characterize school administration in the United States were beginning to emerge. Provisions were made for centralized control, but the deep rooted aversion to 'Prussian inspired' systems of schooling ensured that these were generally weak. By 1900, thirty-four of the forty-four states then admitted to the Union had established a state board of education, and all had state superintendents of schools, the great majority of whom were elected to their office. But while chief state school officers (CSSOs) were in a position to influence state policy and public opinion, most exercised little effective authority. On average, the state departments of education which they headed boasted fewer than three employees, while five CSSOs discharged their duties in solitary splendour, lacking even a secretary to assist them (Beach and Gibbs, 1952).

At this time state departments were primarily concerned with the collection and dissemination of statistical information regarding the provision of schooling. Concerns over compliance with minimum curriculum, operational and building standards, particularly in rural areas, encouraged more direct monitoring over the next three decades or so, including in some instances the deployment of state inspectors. Nonetheless, the median number of state department employees had only risen to a modest thirty-eight by 1930 when many departments began to abandon their inspection policy in favour of a more consultative and developmental relationship with school systems (Knezevich, 1984, pp. 215–7). Thus, while acknowledging that some state departments enjoyed considerable authority over curriculum and more exerted substantial indirect influence through teacher training and state funding, Newlon could declare in 1934 that 'in most states the central administrative authority . . . exercises only nominal control' (p. 80). Since then increasing diversification and complexity of federal as well as state educational policies has considerably expanded the administrative role and activities of state departments, ensuring that they now exercise more than purely nominal — if still largely indirect — control over schooling. Even so, eighteen states still elected their CSSOs by popular vote in the early 1980s (Campbell, Cunningham, Nystrand and Usdan, 1985, p. 61).

Regional Superintendents

Although state departments engaged in an inspectorial role in the early decades of the twentieth century, and although some still maintain an inspection bureau, the direct supervision of rural schools in the United States has generally been the responsibility of intermediate units of school governance and administration. From the mid-nineteenth century on, the relevant office has typically been known as the county superintendency, but use of this title as a generic term runs the risk of confusing intermediate supervisory positions with the school system superintendency in the thirteen states where the county constitutes the basic operating unit. Consequently, the term 'regional superintendent' is used here as a generic title for county and other intermediate level officials responsible for supervising schools operated by a number of independent boards within a homogenous geographic area.

In the type-case these regional superintendents were responsible for overseeing the operation of one-room schools in a host of small rural school districts. This was a crucial role in the development of public schooling in the late nineteenth and early twentieth century. Dedicated regional supervisors acted as travelling missionaries as well as official functionaries, encouraging, cajoling and advising residents, trustees and teachers on desirable practices and state requirements. The position was typically an elective and, in the beginning, often a part-time office, with no qualifications required beyond popularity at the polls. Even when formal qualifications began to be specified, they were initially less than demanding. As late as 1930 only four states required incumbents to be college or normal school graduates, while in fourteen possession of a teaching certificate was the only formal qualification required (Knezevich, 1984, p. 192). In the thirties, moreover, most regional superintendents were still being elected by popular vote (Newlon, 1934, p. 81), a practice which continues in some areas today.

Throughout the first half of the twentieth century the regional superintendency was a low status position; 'the salary was typically below that paid to high school principals and well below that of superintendents in small cities' (Tyack and Hansot, 1982, p. 189). It was nonetheless an important and perhaps surprisingly numerous office, with some 3000 regional superintendents pursuing their appointed rounds to provide an administrative backbone for the 150,000 one-room school districts which quilted rural America in the mid-thirties (Newlon, 1934, p. 79; Tyack, 1976, p. 272). Subsequent amalgamation of rural districts into larger administrative units enabled the new consolidated boards to employ their own administrators, although some small one or two room districts continue to operate in some states. Rural consolidation also brought about a redefinition of the position, role and status of regional superintendents. The current situation is complex, but in general most are now primarily involved in providing and coordinating a wealth of services to boards and schools within their regions, a development which can be seen as a reemphasis of the traditional missionary and leadership functions of the office, dressed in modern clothes.

Board Superintendents

If conscientious, poorly-paid, travel-weary, regional superintendents touring dusty or muddy rural roads to visit isolated teachers in one-room schools were the unsung administrative heroes of American public schooling in the first half of the twentieth century, superintendents employed by urban boards were without doubt the administrative champions. From the turn of the century on, the urban superintendency dominated school administration in the United States: it became the most prestigious position within the administrative structures in each state, with superintendents of large city boards often enjoying higher status, larger salaries, and often greater influence than state superintendents; it became the focus for the professionalization of school administration, and the structural referent for the imagery of executive responsibility and heroic leadership which both rationalized and symbolized the professionalization project; it became the pivotal position in the control of public schooling around which revolved key — and continuing — conflicts between traditional political values and emergent notions of administrative efficiency; it became, in short, the leitmotif around which the American culture of school administration was orchestrated. Indeed, the position of board employed superintendent became so dominant that by the middle of the twentieth century it had emerged as *the* superintendency, and become accepted as constituting a necessary and proper office in the operation of local school systems.

Beginnings

The Superintendent as Factotum

Such was not the case in earlier times. The first board employed superintendents were appointed in the cities of Buffalo and Louisville as early as 1837, but the practice spread slowly at first, with only forty or so large city boards engaging superintendents during the next fifty years, and in five cases the position was discontinued before being re-established (Reller, 1935; Knezevich, 1984, p. 293). In the minds of trustees and the eyes of the community, the principles of lay governance and elective accountability remained paramount and most boards continued to directly administer their schools, typically treating their superintendent as a hired hand who helped with the administrivia and attended to some technical details, such as organizing students into graded classes and inspecting teachers. Thus, in its public report of 1841, the school committee of Providence took pains to declare that their recent appointment of a superintendent should not be construed by the voters as evidence of 'lukewarmness or supineness in the execution of the task committed to their hands', explaining that the new employee would not 'relieve the committee from their own peculiar duties' (Newlon, 1934, p. 83). The 'peculiar duties' which most boards reserved for themselves typically included hiring and assigning teachers, organizing and revising the curriculum, selecting textbooks and instructional equipment, and managing monies and property. City boards normally dealt with such matters by organizing themselves in standing committees, each committee attending to a major function. This was the situation which faced Ellwood P. Cubberley in 1896 when he began his two-year stint as superintendent of San Diego schools. The board exercised firm control over staffing, curriculum and finance through its committees, and Cubberley — who was later to become the great architect of professional, executive, educational administration — was only partially successful in persuading the trustees to delegate greater control to him (Tyack and Hansot, 1982, p. 123).

Rise of the Corporate Model

Yet as Cubberley's partial success suggests, conditions were changing in the twilight of the nineteenth century. Some large city systems, Boston and New York in particular, were pioneering more bureaucratic forms of organization (Katz, 1971; Tyack, 1974), while social conditions, the spirit of the times, and the evangelism of an increasingly influential band of administrative reformers encouraged the spread of modern ideas as the new age dawned. Rapid industrialization and commercialization together with increased immigration placed the city schools under great strain. At the same time a new social ethos was becoming established in which business was the new theology, machines the new metaphor, efficiency the new watchword, and 'Captains of Industry' the new heroes. To reformers fired with enthusiasm for these new principles, lay management through trustee committees appeared as an embarrassingly archaic and sublimely inefficient way to run modern city school systems enrolling thousands of children. More tellingly, traditional modes and methods of school administration appeared incapable of dealing with the very real and pressing problems confronting the city systems. What was needed, urged reformers, was for school system administration to be remodelled along modern business lines. Large, inefficient boards dominated by petty politicians more interested in playing to the public gallery and meddling with managerial matters should be replaced with small, streamlined governing bodies modeled on the corporate directorate and composed, ideally, of apolitical men of business who could deal rationally with important decisions and policy matters, while delegating management matters to a responsible executive. The force of this argument was significantly enhanced by blatant weaknesses in the organization and operation of some city boards. Corruption was by no means uncommon, particularly where trustees were elected by wards. In some cases smoothly running political machines were in place to deliver votes and divide the spoils of office, which could be substantial: city boards hired numerous janitors and clerks as well as teachers, they let many profitable construction and maintenance contracts, while there were potential fortunes to be made in the textbook and school supply businesses. Teachers, and most certainly superintendents, had good reason to fear for their jobs when old scores were settled and new promises kept in the aftermath of trustee elections. The critics also had a valid point with regard to the unwieldy size of some city boards. Indeed, some had grown grotesquely large as a result of amalgamating pre-existing boards as their districts were absorbed within expanding city boundaries. Philadelphia was an oft-cited example, with a city board of 559 members in 1905, which was a composite of trustees elected to forty-three district boards. Similarly, Pittsburgh schools were governed by a board of some 400 trustees as late as 1911 (Newlon, 1934, p. 80).

In retrospect, given the educational problems of the cities, the spirit of the times, and the reality of 'crochety (sic) or corrupt school boards' (Tyack, 1976, p. 261), the rapid adoption of the more business-like structures and procedures advocated by the administrative reformers appears virtually preordained. But this transformation did not proceed without opposition. Blumberg (1985) quotes an editorial from a 1895 issue of the *American School Board Journal* which vigorously attacked what was described as the movement 'to arrogate powers to superintendents which do not belong to them, and to relegate the school board to the function of a mere clerk' (p. 24). Those who shared this view — and they included some superintendents — saw the reform agenda as a direct threat to the deeply rooted principle of lay control through elective accountability. Yet during the first decades of the new century the tables were thoroughly turned. The once clerkish position of superintendent became increasingly invested with the functions and aura of the chief executive, while old, ponderous, ward based, big-city boards were replaced with small, often five to nine member, boards elected at large, or, in some cases, even appointed (Newlon, 1934, p. 80). Indeed, the key notion of apolitical, expert, executive administration was so much in tune with the spirit of the times and so vigorously and assiduously promoted by business men and educational reformers that it quickly cascaded down from big to small cities and from large to small towns. Of the 3333 superintendents employed by boards in 1931, no less than 2353 administered school systems in cities and towns with populations between 2500 and 10,000 (Tyack, 1976, p. 274).

Organizational Contrasts

There were sharp differences, however, between the big-city and small-town superintendencies. From the beginning superintendents in big cities had to deal with large, complex organizations that became increasingly diversified and bureaucratized as enrolments mushroomed and new programs were introduced. Before the turn of the century, some city superintendents had staffs to assist them, and as the century matured they were increasingly working with and through more complex hierarchies of subordinate and specialist administrators. As such city superintendents were indeed in the position of chief executives, and their colleagues in other urban settings increasingly found themselves in a similar position as school systems grew and diversified.

Circumstances in small towns were quite different. Although the spread of secondary schooling and the new administrative ethos encouraged town boards, and later consolidated rural systems, to appoint superintendents, incumbents were often more of a glorified principal than a corporate executive. Indeed, in 1931 the *School Executives Magazine* asked 'Is the small town superintendency a glorified janitorship?'

> The answer, not surprisingly, was yes.... He teaches a class; visits all classrooms regularly; monitors pupils at recess; is the final court of appeal in all disciplinary matters; handles all business from the hiring of teachers to the purchase of stamps; keeps office hours for parents who are frank to question the soundness of his educational principles; arranges extracurricular activities, out-of-town contests, and ad infinitum. (Tyack and Hansot, 1982, p. 177)

A survey of superintendents enrolled in graduate programs in 1927, most of whom were in small town superintendencies, adds some empirical flesh to this image. No less than 71 per cent reported that they taught high school classes, 86 per cent made a daily trip to the post office, 93 per cent inspected toilets weekly and 18 per cent wrote literary gems on blackboards (Tyack and Cummings, 1977, p. 61; Tyack and Hansot, 1982, pp. 176–7).

This was clearly a very different situation from the big-city superintendency which gave substance to both the reality and imagery of executive educational administration. Nonetheless, single-superintendent school systems were in an overwhelming majority in mid-century, small town America. Further, the small system superintendency has continued to dominate the American scene with no less than three-quarters of the 14,260 superintendents employed by local boards in 1982 administering systems enroling less than 3000 students (Cunningham and Hentges, 1982, p. 13).

Professionalization

While the practice of employing board superintendents in an executive capacity and then holding them responsible for results spread rapidly, it was not immediately clear how these new responsibilities might best be handled, or indeed what they should be. The new doctrine called for expert administrators, but a well developed body of professional knowledge was not immediately at hand. Administrative reformers such as Samuel Dutton, Ellwood Cubberley and George Strayer diligently set about remedying this deficiency through the creation of a new academic field to train and certificate professional school administrators. The early foundations were laid at the beginning of the century, the first doctorates in the field being earned by Cubberley and Strayer in 1905 in the pioneering program established at Teachers College Columbia, which was destined to become the first temple of academic educational administration (Cremin, Shannon and Townsend, 1954). The new field quickly spread across the country, so that by 1933 at least 290 doctorates had been completed at thirty-three different universities, more than half of which had been earned at Columbia (Newlon, 1934). Doctoral programs, of course, represented the pinnacle of professional study in the new field, a pinnacle which was supported by an increasingly broad base of masters' degree programs, specialized literature, professional associations, conferences, research and consultancy work.

Although the knowledge and values which were created, validated, and disseminated through the academic study and teaching of educational administration may have had a more marginal effect on the work of superintendents than its champions believed, the formal effects of the professionalization project were impressive. By 1922, 32 per cent of board employed superintendents had completed masters' degrees, and over the next decade this proportion rose to almost 60 per cent (Knezevich, 1971, p. 43). Thus, even though he was less than satisfied with the content and quality of some academic programs, Newlon had reasonable grounds for declaring in 1934 that the academic study of educational administration 'is giving to this country the only administrative service staffed by executives who bring to their work extensive professional training and professional ideals' (p. 101). State legislatures also began to provide formal support for the professionalization project by mandating certification requirements for board employed superintendents which were typically based on the completion of graduate training. By 1950 almost all states had established such requirements, although the academic qualifications of superintendents continued to exceed basic certification requirements. By 1960, 95 per cent of board employed superintendents had completed at least a masters' degree, while some 20 per cent held doctorates. (Tyack, 1976, p. 279). This trend has continued until modern times, with 50 per cent of the superintendents surveyed in 1982 having undertaken studies beyond the masters' level, and a third having completed doctorates (Cunningham and Hentges, 1982, p. 39).

Local Accountability

The rise of the board superintendency was at heart inconsistent with the traditional principles of popular democracy and elective accountability which had long dominated school governance and administration in the United States. Yet removing the schools from the vagaries of political influence was a key objective of the administrative reformers. The political corruption which had characterized some big-city boards helped them carry their point, but they were more interested in 'taking the schools out of politics' rather than simply cleaning-up corruption, which was seen as more of a symptom of what was wrong with the old approach rather than the fundamental problem. Education, the argument went, was too important a matter to be left entirely to the political process; schools needed to be protected from, rather than ruled by, politics, while the complex problems of educational administration demanded that attention of professional experts rather than untrained lay-folk, however well-intentioned they might be. Furthermore, the corporate organizational model underlying their vision of politically neutral expert management allowed for the preservation of local control through the principle of accountability to shareholders, for school superintendents would be held accountable to the public — who were clearly the 'shareholders' in the enterprise of public schooling — through their elected representatives on the board of education.

Such reasoning was compatible with early employment practices. Few of the early board superintendents had been popularly elected to their office — although such was the practice in Buffalo until 1917, and San Francisco as late as 1920 (Newlon, 1934, p. 82). Most had been hired directly by their boards on annual contracts and, if it appeared necessary or politically expedient, they could be easily let go. Under the new corporate model this approach became institutionalized through the ritual of 're-election' whereby the trustees, as the representatives of the people, would vote on whether or not to retain their superintendent. Consequently the superintendency quickly gained a reputation as a less than secure position from which incumbents might expect to be dismissed — or forced to resign — at the unpredictable whim of their board. A 1916 article written by a 'Veteran Fighter' observed that while 'Lloyds will insure the English clerk against rain on his weekend vacation, no gambling house would be sufficiently reckless to bet on the chances of re-election for school superintendents three or even two years ahead' (Callahan, 1962, p. 205). According to the Veteran Fighter, reasons for dismissal included:

> . . . he couldn't make a speech; he talked too much; he was unmarried; he was married to the wrong kind of woman; he was too active for local opinion; he was not active enough; . . . he was too much occupied with his own affairs; he was too much interested in church work; he was not enough interested etc., etc., ad nauseum. (p. 207)

Whether this was an accurate account or not, fragile tenure and fickle boards readily became an accepted part of the mythology of the local superintendency. The past and present reality of the situation is difficult to ascertain, but while job security appears to have increased, and while

American superintendents do not appear to be as mobile as popularly believed, the mythology is not without foundation (Blumberg, 1985; Carlson, 1972; Cunningham and Hentges, 1982; Knezevich, 1971).

Developments in recent decades have forcefully propelled American schools back into the political arena with the result that board superintendents have found themselves implementing new legislative and court mandated initiatives while confronting increasingly demanding boards and militant community groups. As a consequence the image of the 'beleaguered', 'browbeaten', and 'embattled' school superintendent has become increasingly common in the literature (Boyd, 1975, and 1976; Blumberg, 1985; Maeroff, 1975). Again, the reality of the situation appears elusive (Tucker and Zeigler, 1980; Zeigler, Kehoe and Reisman, 1985), but these developments appear to have heightened the endemic tensions and uncertainties discussed above, prompting Blumberg (1985, p. 207) to conclude that '"Living with Conflict" is the "axial principle" ... by which the superintendency may be most fruitfully understood'.

Summary

Of the three generic positions of chief state school officer, regional superintendent and board superintendent, it was the latter that came to dominate the culture of school administration in the United States. Until relatively recently, chief state school officers were primarily elected to their positions and exercised little direct control over the schools. Similarly, while regional superintendencies in rural areas played an important role in the development of American public schooling, these have traditionally been low status, often elective offices. The board superintendency, however, developed in the big-city systems from originally humble origins to an executive position of considerable responsibility and prestige. Aided by a supportive social and business climate and subsequently bolstered by the spread and success of the professionalization project, the practice of employing an expert, executive chief administrator was adopted by both large and small school boards across the nation. But while the employment of the expert, professional, superintendent has become an established — indeed now usually a mandated — practice for local boards, the role and position continue to be characterized by ambiguities and uncertainties.

The Canadian Inspectorate

From the mid-nineteenth century until the 1960s a quite different system of school administration and supervision prevailed in Canada. The division of responsibilities between provincial education authorities and local boards followed a once more commonly drawn distinction between the *interna* and *externa* of school administration. As discussed by Kandel (1933), *interna* are the strategic factors at the heart of the schooling process, particularly curriculum, textbooks, examinations, and teacher training, certification, and supervision: *externa* are the surrounding elements which condition and support the provision of schooling, such as buildings and personnel policies. The Canadian pattern of school administration placed *interna* under the direct control of provincial authorities and delegated defined responsibility for specified *externa* to local school boards. Specific duties and powers assigned to the local level varied between provinces and over time, but in general boards were required to build, maintain and operate schools, employ, pay and if necessary dismiss teachers, raise or requisition local school taxes, and manage the financial accounts. Local management of such matters was indirectly controlled by the central authorities through standardized management procedures and operating regulations. The central authorities, however, directly controlled curriculum, textbooks, teacher training and certification and, most important for our purposes, school inspection and supervision.

The Central Authorities

Nine of the ten provinces[2] which comprise modern Canada were in existence by 1905, and by that year a strong central educational authority was in place in each and exercising active control over the strategic *interna* of public schooling. The tenth province, Newfoundland, did not join Canada until 1949. But despite the independent evolution of Newfoundland's unique system of denominational schools, early provisions were made for various — if somewhat novel — forms of central inspection, and after its establishment in 1920, the Newfoundland department of education exercised administrative and supervisory powers similar to those enjoyed by its Canadian counterparts.

Newfoundland aside, the historical roots of Canada's strong central educational authorities can be most convieniently traced to events precipitated by the 1841 Common Schools Act. At that time Quebec and Ontario were temporarily amalgamated as the province of United Canada, and the 1841 act authorized the appointment of a superintendent to oversee the development of education in both provinces. As an afterthought, apparently, it was realized that a single appointment would be inadvisable and in 1842 Dr. Jean Baptiste Meilleur and the Reverend Robert Murray were appointed as assistant superintendents for Canada East (Quebec) and Canada West (Ontario) respectively. Notwithstanding their initial official designation as "assistant" superintendents, Meilleur and Murray were, in effect, Canada's first chief provincial school officers and each, in his own way, laid important cornerstones for the different forms of centralized control which were to develop in Quebec and the English-speaking provinces.

Meilleur was an energetic school promoter who vigorously argued the benefits of tax supported schooling to the *habitants*, while also advocating legislative changes to better accommodate the religious realities of his overwhelmingly Roman Catholic province. Among other accomplishments he drafted the act of 1851 which institutionalized the Quebec school inspectorate and led to the appointment of twenty-three inspectors who immediately began to augment his promotion of publicly funded schools. Desaulniers (1958) notes that the efforts of these inspectors in this regard 'saved education in Quebec' (p. 59). Following a ten year hiatus from 1867–1875 during which the functions of the provincial superintendency were assumed by a Minister of Public Instruction, control over public schools was vested in the Council of Public Instruction. The Council was organized into Roman Catholic and Protestant committees which, in effect, independently controlled the *interna* of two separate school systems until the Parent reforms of the 1960s. Responsibility for administration and supervision, however, was retained under the provincial superintendent who, with the assistance of the secretaries of the two confessional committees, coordinated and implemented the policies of each committee through the Department of Public Instruction.

Murray was also less than satisfied with the provisions of the 1841 act, especially with the lack of authority accorded to his office. He nonetheless set about laying the foundations for a small but efficient central administrative bureau which Egerton Ryerson, who succeeded Murray in 1844, was to transform into a powerful educational bureaucracy. Once installed in office Ryerson drafted and promoted the passage of a revised legislative framework which assigned offical control over the regulation of school operations, the selection of textbooks, and the certification of teachers to an appointed Council of Public Instruction. 'In theory the Council made policy and the Education Office, under the chief superintendent, administered it. In fact, . . . there is no evidence, for the 1850s at least, to suggest that it ever initiated any policies except those recommended by Ryerson' (Gidney and Lawr, 1978, p. 175).

Ryerson did not create Ontario's system of public schooling. As Gidney and Lawr (1978) point out, many of the key ingredients were already in place. But by arrogating to his office control over the organization, staffing, operation and curriculum of Ontario public schools he was able to transform a variegated collection of locally run semi-public schools into a province-wide system of uniform, efficient and standardized schooling which was remarkably effective. In the process he created a powerful and efficient administrative structure and set of traditions which, by conscious imitation or cultural diffusion, served as a model for centralized control in other provinces. Murray had already established official communication with local boards and begun to collect and collate statistical information. Under Ryerson a flood of instructions, circulars, memoranda, standardized forms, requests for information and replies to inquiries flowed from the department and a counter flood of replies, inquiries, pleas and complaints flowed in. During 1858 alone the department distributed 27,150 copies of printed circulars, attendance registers, forms and other official documents while also attending to a staggering 11,717 items of correspondence (Prentice, 1978, p. 137). True to British administrative tradition, Ryerson attended to much of the official correspondence himself, but as early as 1858 the department already had thirty full-time employees, counting the staff of the normal and model schools, teacher training also falling under the direct control of the central authority in Ryerson's design.

Ryerson retired in 1876, at which time the administrative organization he had created came under the formal direction of a Minister of Education, although the position of chief superintendent was retained. Under the Canadian political system Ministers are elected members of the political party which forms the government. They are not, however, elected directly to their positions, but are assigned to head permanent administrative departments of government by the leader of their party who becomes the 'Premier' or Prime Minister, and as such is head of the government. This development, therefore, brought Ontario schools under more direct political control. Nonetheless, the tradition and practice of centralized, apolitical administration had become so well established that the department continued to exercise dominion over the strategic stuff of Ontario schooling essentially free from political influence.

With the exception of Quebec, where the confessional system of centralized schooling held sway, all other Canadian provinces developed systems of centralized control similar to that which became established in Ontario during Ryerson's rule. The degree to which this is attributable to Ryerson or the evident success of his system is moot. Even though key educational legislation in some other provinces was directly copied from the Ontario statute books and some early chief provincial school officers were disciples of Ryerson, other factors and forces encouraged centralization. There was a shared need, for example, to define and preserve a distinct identity in the shadow of the United States, and centralized schooling was a powerful instrument to this end. Further, political institutions and values in Victorian Canada — which was, one must remember, a proud part of Victoria's Empire — were more accepting of properly constituted centralized authority than was the case in the 'older colonies' to the south. Even so, if Ontario had opted for a decentralized system similar to the American model — as many of Ryerson's critics had urged — then developments in at least some other provinces may have followed a different path. But be that as it may, all of the other English-speaking provinces adopted centrally administered systems of schooling similar to the Ryerson model. Indeed, the administrative structures which became established in some other provinces — particularly British Columbia, New Brunswick and Nova Scotia — were markedly more centralized.

Between 1870 and the turn of the century, each province (or territorial area in the case of Saskatchewan and Alberta), assigned formal control over the *interna* of schooling to an appointed committee which was either directly responsible to (or was, in some cases) the provincial cabinet. Each province also appointed chief provincial school officers and accorded them extensive authority and influence over the development and operation of public schools. Particularly noteworthy figures included T.H. Rand (New Brunswick), David Allison and A.H. Mackay (Nova Scotia), William Cyprian Pinkham (Manitoba), David Goggin (Saskatchewan/Alberta) and John Jessop (British Columbia). Under the leadership of these and other officials central administrative departments were established to disburse government grants, regulate the content and operation of schooling and teacher training, collect and collate operational statistics, and deploy and coordinate the inspectors who supervised school boards and teachers throughout each province. As had already happened in Ontario, each of these administrative departments was eventually brought under more direct political control, although this transition was sometimes not accomplished until well into the twentieth century. The first Minister of Education was not appointed in British Columbia, for example, until 1920; in New Brunswick until 1936; and in Nova Scotia until 1949.

Throughout the first half of the twentieth century provincial education departments continued to wield extensive and primarily apolitical control over the *interna* of Canadian schooling. They were typically the largest provincial government bureaucracies and often administered budgets which exceeded those of many federal ministries (Stamp 1970, p. 451). The reconstruction of Canadian education which took place in the 1960s assigned greater control over the content and supervision of education to local school boards, but the central authorities have retained strategic control, although this is now exercised more indirectly. Education policy has also come under more direct political control in recent decades. Currently the functions of chief provincial school officer are, in effect, shared jointly between the Minister and an appointed Deputy Minister. The Minister is formally responsible for his department and for the development and administration of provincial education policy, but specific tasks and responsibilities are necessarily delegated to department officials under the supervision of the Deputy Minister who is the senior administrative officer and who, by virtue of experience and status, is in a position to exercise considerable influence over provincial educational policy.

Summary

Beginning in the mid-nineteenth century, schooling in the Canadian provinces came increasingly under centralized control and throughout the first half of the twentieth century the content and operation of Canadian schools was directly regulated by strong provincial departments of education. Regardless of the precise effect of his influence, Ryerson's (1846, p. 205) dictum that 'to be a State system of Public Instruction, there must be State contoul (sic) as well as State law', was implemented across the country. Moreover, the early practice of appointing chief provincial superintendents and making them directly responsible to the cabinet ensured that Canadian education was 'taken out of politics' long before this became a major objective of twentieth century administrative reformers in the United States. This crucial element of the Canadian approach to school administration was deliberately at variance with the elective system which characterized the selection of chief state school officers and other key officials in the United States. As Ryerson had also observed, Americans did not appear to grasp that 'the *administration* of the law should be free from the influences of popular passion' (Ryerson, 1868, p. 178, as quoted by Prentice 1978, p. 141).

Inspectors

While Canadian systems of public schooling were centrally designed and regulated, the systems themselves were created, school by school, in and by local communities. The central authorities provided the blueprints, as it were, but local boards and teachers had to translate them into reality. They were not, of course, allowed a free hand in doing so. Provincial legislation specified how trustees were to be elected, stipulated their duties and limited their powers, while a steady flow of regulations, memoranda and propaganda specifying or recommending how schools were to be built, furnished, equipped, organized and operated issued from the central authorities. Even so, there was an evident need for a cadre of field officials to provide expert advice and counsel to boards and to ensure that the laws and regulations were being properly interpreted and correctly applied. Furthermore, the success or failure of the provincial schools hinged ultimately on what happened in classrooms, and thus it was clearly necessary to provide a means of supervising teachers and ensuring that the centrally prescribed curriculum was being taught properly. In all of the Canadian provinces these and other important tasks were performed by a centrally regulated corps of inspectors.

Functionally the work of Canadian inspectors was similar to that of the regional superintendents who were their structural equivalents in the United States. Like their American counterparts, Canadian inspectors were typically responsible for providing supervisory services to a 100 or so of the small rural school sections, most with but a single, usually one-teacher, school that dominated the Canadian educational landscape throughout the latter half of the nineteenth and well into the twentieth century.[3] Unlike their American counterparts, however, Canadian inspectors held positions of considerable power and prestige. All were appointed to their office and, with one temporary exception, appointments were all made at the provincial level. As appointed officers of their provincial educational authories, they were accountable only to the department and their professional conscience, rather than local opinion and the ballot box. This did not mean, of course, that they could afford to disregard local sentiment. To the contrary, the effective promotion and implementation of departmental policy and the smooth operation of the schools under their supervision demanded sensitivity to local opinion and, where possible and prudent, accommodation of local concerns. Nonetheless, inspectors were agents of the central authorities. To borrow Fleming's (1986) description of the British Columbia inspectorate, they were, from the perspective of their provincial departments, 'our boys in the field'. As such they were expected and empowered to enforce official policy even in the face of local opposition, and should serious political or other repercussions ensue, the department would normally support and protect its 'boys'.[4]

The exception, somewhat ironically given its status as the Ryersonian exemplar, was Ontario. When Ryerson assumed office he inherited a recently created system of regional superintendencies under which appointments were made by county councils. He was able to circumvent the potential threat which this represented to his centralization project through subsequent legislation bringing local superintendents under the authority of his office. He would have preferred, nonetheless, to have followed Meilleur's lead and instituted a provincial inspectorate along the lines of those he had admired in Holland and Prussia during his European tour. But while a centrally appointed and regulated inspectorate quickly became the norm in other provinces, Ontario did not achieve fully centralized control over all its regional supervisors until 1930. Even so, Ontario's county superintendents acted in fact, if not entirely in law, as Ryerson's 'boys in the field', especially after the passage of his 1871 school act which formally redesignated them as inspectors and instituted qualifications for appointment. Henceforth prospective elementary school inspectors were required to pass a stringent set of provincial examinations before being eligible for appointment and the department exercised veto power over appointments made by the county councils (Allison and Wells, 1989).

Quebec also instituted qualifying examinations for its inspectors, but other provinces relied on less formalized selection methods. In all provinces successful teaching experience was a prerequisite for appointment as was possession of the highest teaching certificate issued by the province concerned. By the beginning of the twentieth century the great majority of inspectors had a Bachelor's degree (Miller, 1913) and by mid-century Master's degrees were generally either formally required or demanded in practice (Phillips, 1958). But while Canadian inspectors generally held high academic qualifications relative to the teachers they supervised, their graduate degrees were typically in the traditional liberal arts disciplines. Educational administration did not become established as a field of academic study in Canada until the 1960s, the first Canadian doctorate in the field being awarded in 1958. A few inspectors treked to American universities for graduate work in educational administration, but while this became more common after mid-century — especially in the western provinces — the Canadian inspectorate was largely unaffected by the values and content disseminated by the many graduate programs in educational administration which proliferated in the United States.[5]

Universalistic threshhold qualifications notwithstanding, recruitment and final selection methods ensured that only the 'right kind' of teachers were admitted to the provincial inspectorates. Prospective candidates were often identified by incumbent inspectors and encouraged to prepare themselves appropriately or apply for upcoming vacancies. Character and values (and, it would seem, appearance) were typically given great weight in the final selection process, inspectors naturally being expected to embody and exemplify both the values and the full authority and majesty of the department. Moreover, while they were primarily required to supervise elementary teachers, formal and informal recruitment criteria conspired to ensure that most inspectors came from secondary school backgrounds. McNally's (1958, pp. 4–6) recollections are revealing in this regard. He was recruited to the Alberta inspectorate in 1909 and assigned to supervise all of the schools in 'an area roughly the size of Wales', although he had 'never taught any pupils below Grade 8 and had never so much as seen the inside of a primary room'. He naturally sought advice from a seasoned inspector who, with the certainty and aplomb that can only come from the weight of well-established tradition, declared: 'You've seen inspectors in action all your life haven't you? Well, do what they did.'

What McNally and the hundreds of other Canadian inspectors who went before and came after him actually did was evaluate the progress of pupils, counsel and assist trustees, speak to community meetings, advise, encourage, and support teachers and, of course, formally appraise the quality of their work. In Nova Scotia, Quebec, Ontario and Manitoba, they also performed important administrative functions for their provincial departments, including the collation of statistics and apportionment of government grants. 'Of writing reports', McNally (1958) recalled, 'there was no end: one for the Department, one for the school board (much softened, since the mildest criticism gave the habitual teacherbaiters a vantage point for attack), and a third for one's own files' (p. 7). The sensitivity toward the plight of teachers displayed by McNally's parenthetical comment seems by no means atypical. Although, in Stamp's (1970, p. 326) words, the inspector was in the nature of things 'an awesome figure.... descending on a school unannounced with the full authority of the provincial agency behind him', and thus was likely to be 'viewed as an enemy agent sent from the provincial capital to expose the weaknesses of local teachers', inspectors appear to have been well aware of the professional and social difficulties faced by their teachers and the desirability of rendering as much assistance and encouragement as possible. Miller's (1913) survey of the supervisory practices of rural inspectors offers many illustrative examples of such attitudes of which the following is broadly representative:

> First get to know the teacher by observing her work, noting mentally any excellencies or defects in manner, method or management. Sometimes ask permission to teach a class so that I can illustrate the more excellent way, and towards the end of my visit discuss the principles underlying my suggestions in a quiet talk with the teacher.... I am in my office every Saturday and am regularly consulted by teachers on difficulties — on reading, on methods, on selecting books for school libraries or supplementary reading etc. (p. 163)

Few teachers, however, had easy access to their inspectors for in most cases their schools were scattered over large geographical areas. Typically inspectors were required to visit each of the schools under their charge once or twice a year and this almost inevitably meant that they would spend much of their time travelling. The heroic mythology of the Canadian inspectorate dwells lovingly on the difficulties and hardships encountered in journeying to solitary schools over bald, muddy and snow-gripped prairies, along rugged coasts and mountain trails, through silent forests and scattered farms. Such indeed was the lot of many inspectors, those surveyed by Miller (1913) reporting that on average they travelled 2550 miles a year in the course of their supervisory duties. All modes of transportation appropriate to the times and circumstances were pressed into use including horses (buggies and cutters), trains, steamships, automobiles, bush planes and, more prosaically, bicycles.

Many provinces abandoned the title of inspector with its harsh Victorian overtones before or around mid-century in favour of variants on the title of superintendent. Increased urbanization and school district consolidation also produced a shift toward more locally employed administrators after the second world war. But regardless of changing titles and organizational structures, the 'honoured and powerful post of inspector' (Wilson, 1984, p. 5) continued to dominate school supervision in

Canada until well after the middle of this century. As Flower and Stewart (1958, p. 83) observed, 86 per cent of the 750 'superintendents of schools' in Canada in 1956 were employed by provincial departments of education and as such were representative of the traditional inspectorate in spirit if not in name. Developments in British Columbia, Alberta and Saskatchewan offer interesting insights into the tenacity of the assumptions and values underlying the inspectorate. Each of these provinces instituted programs of school district consolidation which resulted in the creation of large area units of school administration in the 1940s. But rather than authorizing these large districts to employ superintendents of their choice, the central authorities appointed or assigned provincial superintendents as they saw fit, a practice which continued until after 1970. In other provinces small districts and schools persisted beyond mid-century, thus perpetuating a structural need for centrally coordinated supervisory services. As late as 1950, for example, 64 per cent of all Ontario schools were one-room elementary schools (Report of the Minister, 1951, p. 63). Ontario did not embark on a serious program of school consolidation until the 1960s with the result that the Ontario inspectorate was not formally dismantled until 1969.

One other factor which contributed to the longevity of the inspectorate was the organization and availability of secondary schooling. A much smaller proportion of Canadian youth attended secondary schools in the first half of the twentieth century than was the case in United States. Further, many Canadian secondary schools were governed by boards which were organizationally distinct from those operating elementary schools, and in some provinces the high schools were also supervised by a separate inspectorate. The key consequence, however, was that the development of integrated local school systems in which one or more high schools were organically linked to a network of elementary feeder schools was delayed far longer in Canada than it was in the United States. The emergence of such systems provided the key structural base for the rapid spread of the local superintendency in small town America during the 1930s. Despite early movements in this direction in the western provinces and many of the larger cities, fully integrated local systems of elementary and secondary schools did not become widely established in Canada until the 1960s, thus delaying the development of administrative units of a size and complexity sufficient to justify internal supervision.

Board Employed Superintendents

Fraternities of provincially employed and deployed 'distinguished looking gentlemen' (McCordic, 1984, p. 44) travelling by buggy, bicycle and automobile across varied landscapes to advise and monitor small boards, inspect small schools, and observe, counsel and write official reports on teachers formed the administrative and supervisory backbone for Canadian public education for a century or so, and in doing so created webs of tradition, myth, and heroic imagery quite different and distinct from those spun by the cult of the professionalized, locally employed educational executive which flourished concomitantly in the United States. But locally employed board superintendents were also an integral part of Canadian school administration over the past hundred years. They were proportionately far fewer than their American counterparts, however, and much of the prestige and influence associated with their office derived from the same centralized font of authority which sanctified provincial inspectors, rather than the management ethos and academic credentials which empowered American superintendents.

As in the United States, the first locally employed superintendents in Canada were appointed in the big cities, first in Toronto as early as 1844, then Halifax in 1869, Montreal in 1873, Winnipeg in 1885 and Vancouver in 1901. Unlike in the United States, however, the practice did not spread to smaller urban centres and consolidated rural districts until the provincial inspectorates were disbanded in the 1960s. The central authorities quite simply declined to authorize the independent employment of supervisory officials by smaller boards. As noted above, the organizational base necessary for a viable system of executive administration at the local level just did not exist outside of the larger urban centres, where elementary and secondary schools were more easily and thus more frequently integrated. Moreover, there was no obvious or necessary reason for boards in other than the largest urban areas to employ administrative or supervisory officials. Principals could look after the multi-room schools in small towns — that was their job; they could also attend to or assist with routine administrative matters that were not handled by secretary-treasurers, while the provincial inspector, who likely lived in town, would provide assistance in more weighty matters and handle official supervisory functions — that was his job.

Consequently, the major practical limitation on the numbers of locally employed superintendents in Canada prior to the 1960s was provided by the number of large urban centres. But urbanization proceeded at a much slower pace in Canada than the United States. In 1921 there were only fifteen urban centres in Canada with populations in excess of 25,000, and 70 per cent of the total Canadian population resided outside those centres. Even so, not all these cities had a locally employed superintendent.[6] There were still only 48 towns and cities of that size in 1961, and although they accounted for 53 per cent of the total Canadian population, only fifteen of these urban centres were in provinces other than Quebec or Ontario (Weir, 1968, p. 152).

Yet even in those cities where local superintendents were employed, neither Canadian boards nor their superintendents enjoyed the same autonomous powers as their American counterparts. Generally boards were required to satisfy provincially specified criteria before being allowed to employ their own supervisory officials, and even then they could only appoint individuals who were properly qualified under provincial regulations and who met the specific approval of the central authorities. This normally ensured that city administrators were experienced provincial inspectors who were well socialized to official values and expectations. Further, board superintendents were legally bound to perform the same duties as provincial inspectors, the first and greatest of which was to enforce the acts and regulations administered by the provincial department of education. As such, board superintendents in Canada owed fealty to the central authority as well as their employer: they were, in essence, the department's 'boys in the cities'. This was clearly signalled in Ontario and British Columbia where locally employed superintendents were officially designated as 'municipal inspectors' by the provincial authorities. One important corollary of central control over the appointment and authority of board superintendents was that Canadian school boards were not able to dismiss their superintendents as cavalierly as did American boards. Consequently, a tradition of secure and prolonged tenure developed in the Canadian superintendency, contrary to that which developed in the United States.

Nor did Canadian city superintendents, initially at least, act as the chief executives of their boards. Specific arrangements varied over time, between boards and within provinces but many urban boards often employed a secretary-treasurer or some similar business official to manage fiscal affairs, building maintenance and other *externa*. In cases where a board did not also employ a superintendent, then the business manager would typically perform executive functions for the board, although he was normally prohibited from meddling with the sacred *interna* of the schools, authority over which was reserved to the provincial department and its properly accredited representatives, namely inspectors, principals and teachers. Where boards did employ their own superintendent, then he naturally, as a properly authorized representative of the central authority, exercised dominion over instructional affairs. It did not necessarily follow, however, that the superintendent would exercise authority over the business affairs or the official placed in charge of such matters. In some instances the secretary treasurer was designated or acted as the chief executive; in others the superintendent and business official reported independently to the board; in yet others the superintendent was the chief executive officer.

Such arrangements were roundly condemned by Richardson (1921) in his survey of school administration in forty-five Canadian cities. From his vantage point as professor of education at Butler College in Indiana and an evident disciple of the doctrine of executive educational administration as preached by Cubberley and other stalwarts of the American professionalization project, Richardson would appear to have had some difficulty in comprehending both the philosophy and some of the details of the Canadian approach to school administration. Nonetheless, after reporting and proffering more than a few didactic asides on the facts uncovered by his survey (which in many respects is a model of its kind) he concluded with these remarks:

> In many Canadian cities, several of the following officers — the secretary, treasurer, inspectors, superintendents, supervisors, medical health officer, senior high school principal, and others are directly responsible to the board for the work of their respective departments.... Canadian city school boards must put an end to this unbusinesslike practice.... Every Canadian city school board desirous of having an efficient central organization must eventually subscribe to the principle of one general manager over the whole system. He should be known as the 'Superintendent of Schools'. (p. 290)

Richardson's prescription was eventually put into effect, although not for fifty years or so. In the interim Canadian city boards began of their own accord to move toward administrative structures in which their chief education official increasingly assumed the role and functions of chief executive. The complete implementation of Richardson's presciption, however, had to await the massive restructuring of Canadian education which began, and was largely completed, in the 1960s. These changes swept away the provincial inspectorates, amalgamated small rural and town boards, integrated elementary and secondary schooling and installed board appointed and employed superintendents as local educational executives. Not that all provinces authorized the appointment of superintendents as chief executive officers, this Cubberlian ideal still remaining at least formally unachieved in some Canadian jurisdictions (Boich, Farquhar and Leithwood, 1989), as, indeed, it is in some of the United States.

Conclusion

Contemporary school superintendents in Canada and America share much in common: they are appointed and employed by local boards; they act in practice if not in name as the chief executives of their boards; they direct the educational affairs of complex systems of schooling and bear responsibility for the educational outcomes of this important endeavour. Yet the positions which they occupy have different histories, and the weight of the hand of history should not be understimated. Ontario superintendents, for example, must still qualify for their position by an examination process initiated in 1871 when Egerton Ryerson consolidated his hold over the Ontario inspectorate. In other, less obvious ways, legacies of the Canadian inspectorate condition the role and position of current superintendents. The tradition of centrally specified duties which is continued in current legislation serves to reduce the ambiguities, uncertainties and endemic conflicts that have long characterized the American superintendency. Similarly, whereas American traditions stress the insecure tenure associated with the ritual of re-election, and even celebrate the heroism attendant on the likely prospect of being sacrificed on the altar of political expediency, Canadian traditions stress security of tenure that flows from being associated with superior authority. Nor do the traditions, teachings and faddishness associated with the American professionalization project have as tight a hold in Canada as they do in the United States on the qualifications necessary for appointment, or the way in which the position is understood by either incumbents or aspirants. The force of such differences may well be eroded with the further passage of time. But even if this should be the case, the distinct histories themselves will remain: the history of proud professionalism associated with the pioneering of executive educational administration on the one hand, and that of privileged selection and service in the interests of high ideals on the other.

Notes

1 I am indebted to Michael Murphy for this point, who drew my attention to W.L. Morton's (1972) discussion of the historical implications of these constitutional differences.

2 Independent schooling systems also developed in the Yukon and the present North West Territories, but these will not be considered here.

3 Miller's (1913) survey of 102 inspectors found the median number of schools supervised in various provinces to be (in ascending order): Ontario (75), Manitoba (83), Alberta (117), Nova Scotia (139), Quebec (152), Prince Edward Island [n = 2] (162–174), New Brunswick [n = 4] (181–239). The median number of teachers supervised per inspector was (in the same order as before): Ontario (108), Manitoba (100), Alberta (129), Nova Scotia (186), Quebec (192), Prince Edward Island (196–213), New Brunswick (259–260) (p. 153). The excess of teachers over schools stems from inspectors having responsibility for the multi-room schools found in towns and other urban centres in their territory.

4 Inspectors were, of courses, virtually all men, which provides another point of contrast with the American regional superintendency for Tyack and Hansot point out that in and around the 1930s local voters, especially in the western states, were prepared to elect an appreciable number of women to the office. They speculate that given the conventions of the day it would have been most unlikely for similar numbers of women to have achieved office if those positions had been filled by appointment.

5 But this is not to say that the administration of Canadian schools was unaffected by the management fads and fashions from the United States. The

early twentieth century obsession with quantified management practices certainly made its mark on Canadian school administration (Fleming, 1986) although Canadian schools appear to have been immune from many of the scientific management excesses documented by Callahan (1962) in the United States. Nonetheless, the degree to which Canadian educational administration was infected by Taylorism is by no means clear and much interesting work remains to be done in this regard.

6 Let alone all of the boards in these cities. In Ontario, Saskatchewan, and Alberta there were separate boards for the public and Roman Catholic schools (and separate city boards under the Protestant and Roman Catholic confessional committees in Quebec) and also separate high school boards in some cases.

References

ALLISON, D.J. and WELLS, A. (1989) 'School supervision in Ontario' in BOICH, J.W., FARQUAHAR, R.H. and LEITHWOOD, K.A. (Eds) *The Canadian School Superintendent*, Toronto, OISE Press, pp. 69–114.

Beach, F.F. and GIBBS, A.H. (1952) *Personnel of State Departments of Education*, US Office of Education, Washington, DC, GPO.

BLUMBERG, A. (1985) *The School Superintendent: Living With Conflict*, New York, Teacher's College Press.

BOICH, J.W., FARQUAHAR, R.H. and LEITHWOOD, K.A. (Eds) *The Canadian School Superintendent*, Toronto, Oise Press.

BOYD, W.L. (1976) 'The public, the professionals, and educational policy making: Who governs?', *Teachers College Record*, 77, pp. 539–77.

BOYD, W.L. (1975) 'School board — administrative staff relationships' in CISTONE, P. (Ed.) *Understanding School Boards*, Lexington, MA, Lexington Books.

CALLAHAN, R.E. (1962) *Education and the Cult of Efficiency*, Chicago, IL, University of Chicago Press.

CAMPBELL, R.F., CUNNINGHAM, L.L., NYSTRAND, R.O. and USDAN, M.D. (1985) *The Organization and Control of American Schools* (5th edn) Columbus, OH, Charles E, Merrill.

CARLSON, R.O. (1972) *School Superintendents: Careers and Performance*, Columbus, OH, Charles E, Merrill.

CREMIN, L.A., SHANNON, D.A. and TOWNSEND, M.E. (1954) *A History of Teachers College, Columbia University*, New York, Columbia University Press.

CUNNINGHAM, L.L., and HENTGES. (1982) *The American School Superintendency, 1982, A Summary Report*, Washington, D.C., American Association of School Administrators.

DESAULNIERS, O.J. (1958) 'Public education in Quebec' in FLOWER, G.E. and STEWART, F.K. (Eds) *Leadership in Action: The Superintendent of Schools in Canada*, Toronto, W.J. Gage.

FLEMING, T. (1986) '"Our boys in the field": School inspectors, superintendents, and the changing character of school leadership in British Columbia' in

Sheehan, N.M., Wilson, J.D. and Jones, D.C. (Eds) *Schools in the West: Essays in Canadian Educational History*, Calgary, Alberta, Detselig Enterprises.

Flower, G.E. and Stewart, F.K. (Eds) (1958) *Leadership in Action: The Superintendent of Schools in Canada*, Toronto, W.J. Gage.

Gidney, R.D. and Lawr, D.A. (1978) 'The development of an administrative system for the public schools: The first stage, 1841–50' in McDonald, N. and Chaiton, A. (Eds) *Egerton Ryerson and His Times*, Toronto, Macmillan.

Government of Ontario (1950) *Report of the Minister of Education*, Toronto, King's Printer.

Kandel, I.L. (1933) *Comparative Education*, Cambridge, MA, Houghton Mifflin.

Katz, M.B. (1971) *Class, Bureaucracy and Schools: The Illusion of Educational Change in America*, New York, Praeger.

Knezevich, S.J. (Ed.) (1971) *The Administration School Superintendent*, Washington, D.C. American Association of School Administrators.

Knezevich, S.J. (1984) *Administration of Public Education*. (4th edn). New York, Harper and Row.

Maeroff, G.I. (1975) 'Harried school leaders see their role waning', *New York Times*, 9 March, pp. 1 and 29.

McCordic, W.J. (1984) *The Supervision of Public Education in Ontario*, Toronto, Ontario Association of Education Administrative Officials.

McNally, G.F. (1958) 'Memories — grave and gay', in Flower, G.E. and Stewart, F.K. (Eds) *Leadership in Action: The Superintendent of Schools in Canada*, Toronto, W.J. Gage.

Miller, J.C. (1913) *Rural Schools in Canada: Their Organization, Administration and Supervision*, New York, Teachers' College, Columbia University.

Morton, W.L. (1972) *The Canadian Identity* (2nd edn) Toronto, University of Toronto Press.

Newlon, J.H. (1934) *Educational Administration as Social Policy* (Report of the Commission on the Social Studies, Part VIII) New York, Scribner.

Phillips, C.E. (1958) 'An historical perspective' in Flower, G.E. and Stewart, F.K. (Eds) *Leadership in Action: The superintendent of Schools in Canada*, Toronto, W.J. Gage.

Prentice, A. (1978) 'The public instructor: Ryerson and the role of public school 'administrator' in McDonald, N. and Chaiton, A. (Eds) *Egerton Ryerson and His Times*, Toronto, Macmillan.

Reller, T.L. (1935) *The Development of the City Superintendency of Schools in the United States*, Philadelphia, P.A. published by the author.

Richardson, W.L. (1921) *The Administration of Schools in the Cities of the Dominion of Canada*, Toronto, J.M. Dent and Sons.

Ryerson, E. (1846) 'Commission of the Reverend Egerton Ryerson, D.D. as superintendent of schools in Upper Canada' in J.G. Hodgins, (Ed.) *Documentary History of Education in Upper Canada*, Volume VI; 1846 (1899), Toronto, Warwick Bro's and Rutter.

Stamp, R.M. (1970) 'Government and education in post war Canada' in Wilson, J.D., Stamp, R.M., and Audet L.P. (Eds) *Canadian Education: A History*, Scarborough, Ontario, Prentice-Hall.

Tucker, H.J. and Zeigler, H. (1980) *Professionals Versus the Public: Attitudes, Communication and Response in Local School Districts*, New York, Longman.

TYACK, D.B., (1974) *The One Best System*, Cambridge, MA, Harvard University Press.

TYACK, D.B. (1976) 'Pilgrim's progress: Toward a social history of the school superintendency, 1860–1960', *History of Education Quarterly*, 16, pp. 257–99.

TYACK, D.B. and CUMMINGS, R. (1977) 'Leadership in American public schools before 1954: Historical configurations and conjectures' in CUNNINGHAM, L.L., HACK, W.G. and NYSTRAND, R.O. (Eds) *Educational Administration: The Developing Decades*, Berkeley, CA, McCutchan Publishing.

TYACK, D. and HANSOT, E. (1982) *Managers of Virtue: Public school Leadership in America, 1820–1980*, New York, Basic Books.

WEIR, T.R. (1968) 'The people' in WARKENTIN, J. (Ed.) *Canada: A geographical interpretation*, Toronto, Methuen.

WILSON, J.D. (Ed.) (1984) *An Imperfect Past: Education and Society in Canadian History*, Vancouver, BC, Centre for the Study of Curriculum and Instruction.

ZEIGLER, H., KEHOE, E. and REISMAN, J. (1985) *City Managers and School Superintendents: Response to Community Conflict*, New York, Praeger.

Section C

Fundamental Challenges for Chief Education Officers

Chapter 10

A Delicate Balance: Leadership or Stewardship

Mark Holmes

Six Ontario CEOs were selected in order to examine the relationship between their educational philosophies and their educational practices. They were not randomly selected. Instead they represent Ontario's varied school systems and variations in personal educational philosophy. In all six cases, there appeared, from answers to questions in a questionnaire discussed more fully in chapter 7, to be a good connection between philosophy and practice. A second purpose of the research was to consider implications of CEOs philosophies and practices for the delivery of public education in a pluralist, liberal democracy.

The CEOs, and two administrative associates suggested by them were interviewed about the relationship between the personal philosophy of the CEO and educational action and about the implications of personal philosophies for the service of a wide, dissenting public. The six CEOs all managed to carry out their chosen priorities consistently with their philosophies. In three cases, there is some conflict between their personal philosophy and that of important interest groups. Two suppressed their dissent from the dominant Progressive philosophy of Ontario educators. A third, a supporter of the dominant philosophy, is the only CEO of the six not to impose it in all schools, as a result of intense local dissent.

Two problems are identified: How can the CEO deal with differences between the educators' consensus and the public consensus? How can the CEO deal with increasing dissent (and therefore decreasing support for any central consensus)?

Four models for the delivery of public education are considered, two of which are identified as satisfying the criteria required for education in a pluralist, liberal democratic state. The role of the CEO, with particular respect for the CEO's personal philosophy, is discussed in these contexts.

This chapter examines the ways in which six Chief Education Officers in Ontario attempt to combine their own educational philosophies and values with the wishes of the important groups involved in educational policy making and delivery. On the one hand, educational leaders are normally expected to have integrity and a clear sense of direction. On the other, they are expected to be sensitive to the interests of the people with whom and for whom they work.

Two major conclusions arise from chapter 7. One is that Ontario's CEOs are middle-of-the-road people in a number of important respects. Politically, CEOs are neither socialist nor right wing; they are generally liberal. Generally they may be more centrist than is the case of most other professions. For example, there would probably be few other professions in Ontario without a single Jewish member. Not a single CEO is a member of Baptist, Pentecostal or fundamentalist Christian congregations. The other important conclusion from chapter 7 is that Ontario's CEOs, although centrist, differ in some systematic ways from either the average Ontario adult or the average Ontario educated adult of their age. CEO's are more liberal — in the sense that they are more accepting of government spending, notably on education, and less concerned about budgetary deficits; they are opposed to capital punishment. They also differ in a peculiarly educational sense — they are educationally Progressive as distinct from being Technocratic or Cultural; i.e., they favor greater emphasis on educational process than on outcomes and they are more interested in children's general development than in their being prepared for work or their being intellectually challenged. In sum, they can be described as being centrist but somewhat left-of-centre, providing one bears in mind that they are not at all inclined to be Marxist or socialist or egalitarian. Consistently, Marxists see progressivism in education as being the antithesis of egalitarianism (see, for example, Bowles and Gintis, 1976; and Sharp and Green, 1975).

These findings raise important questions about educational policy. Is it appropriate in pluralist jurisdictions for public education to be heavily centrist in character? If the answer is affirmative, then the question arises: Should not CEOs represent, as Durkheim would have put it, society's ideal sense of itself, as distinct from a vision identified with the professional group delivering education, but not shared by the general public? If it is argued that administrative values are irrelevant as CEOs' role is purely to carry out rather than develop policy, it should be recalled from chapter 7 that most CEOs do claim that they have clear philosophies and values and that they are reflected in changes that are brought about in the school system.

Specifically, the questions addressed in this chapter are: How are CEOs' philosophies and values reflected in their daily working lives? What are the implications of the empirical research on the Ontario CEO for educational policy and program in a liberal democracy characterized by pluralist multiculturalism and respect for individual rights?

Choosing the Sample and Arranging the Interviews

As part of the CEO questionnaire described in chapter 7, CEOs were asked to list up to three 'changes, programs, policies and innovations' for which they had 'major responsibility'. They were further asked how these changes reflected their own 'educational values or philosophy'. They were finally asked to consider foregoing complete confidentiality by providing their name for a possible follow up interview. Sixty-one of the seventy-five respondents (81.3 per cent) agreed to be interviewed. I examined the sixty-one sets of changes described and chose those which met two criteria:

(i) they appeared to be clear and value laden;
(ii) the associated values were compatible with the first three ranked philosophies selected by the CEO concerned.

Thus, the planned introduction of 'active learning' would be perfectly compatible with the Progressive philosophy, not very compatible with an Egalitarian or a Technocratic philosophy. Many CEOs named managerial changes which were excluded because they were not directly related to education. Nineteen of the sixty-one were selected as members of a possible short list for interview. The nineteen appeared to me to include many of the best known CEOs in the province. (Names and geography were not considered in the selection of the short list.) Neither the short list of nineteen nor the final group of six actually interviewed is in any way a random sample. These CEOs are not statistically representative, but, as table 10.1 shows, they are reasonably representative of the variety of beliefs and demographic environments.

The intent was to choose a sample that would be reasonably representative of those CEOs who make claims with some face validity that they act educationally in ways consistent with their educational philosophy. As will become evident later, I believe that the claims of all six are valid; I infer that the claims of most or all of the thirteen CEOs not interviewed would be equally valid. With less certitude, I infer that there would be less obvious consistency between clear philosophy and administrative behavior in the remainder of the set of respondents. It is important to note that I am not assuming that a CEO ought to have a clear personal philosophy of education which should be delivered within the school system. It is arguable that there should be no room for the expression of personal values by the leader of an educational enterprise devoted to the education of children representing extremely varied values.

The sample of six consists of leaders with clear but different values which are supposedly represented in the system. The question arises as to

Table 10.1 Characteristics of Interviewed Sample: By Philosophy and by Board Type, Size and Demography (N in brackets)

	Ontario (118)	Short List (19)	Sample (6)
CEO Philosophy			
Progressive	27	2	1
Technocratic	10	2	1
Cultural	12	5	1
Traditional	11	5	2
Individualistic	12	4	1
Egalitarian	0	0	0
(N = 72)			
Board Type			
Public	72	15	4
Separate	46	4	2
Board Size			
Over 30,000	17	4	1
20,000 to 30,000	6	3	1
10,000 to 20,000	29	7	2
5000 to 10,000	27	1	0
Under 5000	39	4	2
Board Demography			
Urban	29	6	1
Suburban	9	4	1
Suburban/exurban/rural	8	0	0
Town centre and rural	33	8	3
Small town	24	1	1
Rural	15	0	0

the extent that these people represent and accommodate the differing values held by members of the public.

The six CEOs were selected using four formal and two less formal criteria. The formal criteria are shown in table 10.1. In order of importance, they are: first ranked philosophy; type (public and separate); size; and demography. The two informal criteria, low level of involvement in other segments of the research project and representation from northern Ontario were applied before the last two formal criteria. Thus, representation by demography is not perfect. Language was not used as a criterion.

The six selected CEOs agreed to be interviewed. The interviews were scheduled to last one hour. In all cases I was extremely well received and the interviews exceeded the allocated time and were in most cases pursued informally later over coffee or lunch.

There was advance agreement on the basic format of the interview. The CEO was to be interviewed for one hour, the interview to be taped. Two other administrators, nominated by the CEO, would be interviewed for shorter periods of time, separately from the CEO. Notes were made on the later interviews. Transcripts of the tape or notes were subsequently mailed to those interviewed for editing or clarification. Only one important deletion was made — one CEO asked that no mention of references to his family be made, references which actually illustrated the confluence of his personal and professional decision making in education rather nicely. All those concerned recognize that complete anonymity is impossible in an undertaking of this kind. Pseudonyms are, however, used throughout and minor liberties have been taken with Ontario geography to help obscure the identity of the boards and their CEOs. Nevertheless, the subjects concerned and I all realize that any determined detective will be able to identify the subjects, particularly if the detective is a colleague. From a research perspective, it should be noted that the administrators nominated by the CEO for interview understand fully that the CEO knows who they are. As they were nominated by the CEO, one would surmise that they are reasonably positive toward the CEO — and that appears to be the case.

Interviews

Although interviews took their own course, the essential format was the same for all CEOs, and very similar for the administrators. The protocol used with the CEOs was as follows:

- (i) 'Tell me about the innovation you have made.' (The CEO was reminded beforehand and at the beginning of the interview of the particular innovation or innovations he had identified in the questionnaire.)
- (ii) Follow up questions on the innovation. For example, 'What opposition has there been?' 'What happens if a principal decides he or she does not want to go along with it?'
- (iii) 'Tell me about your philosophy and how it ties in with this particular idea.' (At the beginning of the interview, the CEO was reminded of the six philosophies and his ranking of them.)
- (iv) What happens when others, trustees, for example, do not share your philosophy?
- (v) Should the CEO represent the public will? Does that mean that only people in the centre should be eligible to become a CEO? (The CEOs had been mailed a copy of the preliminary report of the project before the interview took place.)
- (vi) How should the wishes of parents who lie outside the central consensus be represented in the schools? (In the case of Catholic separate boards, this question was concerned with 'flaming liberal' Catholics and very traditional Catholics, although separate CEOs were also asked the more general question.)

The protocol used with the administrators paralleled the CEO protocol. The same four strands of thought were emphasized:

(i) the nature of the innovation, its reception, its acceptability;
(ii) perceptions of the CEO's philosophy;
(iii) dealing with conflict in philosophy;
(iv) representing the public will and those who lie outside the central consensus.

Although pseudonyms are used for all persons and places and geography have been altered, an attempt is made to retain a true if not factual picture of the six CEOs and their systems.

The Six CEOs

Grant Wilmot, Director of the Northampton Board of Education

Situated in southwestern Ontario, Northampton lies outside the fertile agricultural belt and much of its farm land is marginal. There is some industry, both traditional and modern, in the largest town in the county, where the school board office is situated. The population is mainly of British origin, being more educated and liberal in the south around Hinton, and more conservative in the 'Bible belt' to the north.

Wilmot's innovation is the development and implementation of a continuing sequence of curriculum development and change. Central to the innovation is the identification of core skills, common in most or all subjects, which should be identified and sequentially developed. Wilmot identified himself with this project at an early stage, when he was a principal. Gradually, he has risen through the ranks to become CEO, always using his various positions to advance this particular idea, which he himself did not originate. The development of a comprehensive writing program, including regular evaluation using impression scoring, is an important example of one part of his program. Writing is no longer carried out in a hit or miss fashion; rather, there is a careful focus of the various skills required in writing for different purposes and audiences. Wilmot is exceptional in that his major focus is on program, on which he is very well informed.

His first ranked philosophies were: Cultural, Progressive and Technocratic, but he argues that he includes all six in his overall philosophy. He approves active learning because it appeals to one strand of a child's thinking; the child becomes involved in his or her own learning. The intellectual skills are vitally important too and there must be strong links to work. Values, such as respect for the environment, must be integrated into the program. He is egalitarian in his wish to open up school for children from all walks of life; and he is a great lover of the arts.

Gary Williams, an elementary principal in the system, says Wilmot is both process and outcomes oriented. He wants to 'empower' principals to do things, but not to do nothing. However, Wilmot would draw the line at letting a principal run a non-active learning school, however good the outcomes and however satisfied the parents. Why? Well, 'active learning is a Ministry goal. And there is research around saying outcomes are better'.

Bill Fulton, a superintendent, sees Wilmot's great strength as being 'inclusive'. Wilmot avoids confrontation. If trustees defeat his project (for example, introducing French immersion into the Bible belt), he does his homework and comes back to fight and win another day. If a group wants a special program, for example a 'back to the land' group of parents wanting a special school, he provides it — but on his terms and conditions. He works with people who come up with a different idea helping them realize it but at the same time ensuring that the idea finally meets his own criteria.

Wilmot's approach to the central policy question in this research can be described as *inclusion*. He expands the central consensus, drawing limits widely so as to embrace as many as possible. He supports both testing and active learning, school-to-work programs and the arts. One advantage for him is that Northampton is a fairly homogeneous county — a traditional area with modern and increasingly dominant urban enclaves. If one were to place him on the map of public opinion and CEO opinion, he would be quite close to the centre — between the two. His first three philosophies, for example, embrace both public and educator opinion. He defines the CEO's job as bringing the schools and the public together. He is admirably prepared for the task.

What happens when a group cannot be included? There is one clear instance of this — the case when a 'back to the land' group of parents demanded their own school. Eventually, the parents were helped by Wilmot to set up their own program, which still survives. The example is instructive. These parents are comparatively educated and politically aware; they live in the Hinton area. In contrast, the more remote, northern Bible belt has no special schools or programs. Although principals are encouraged to modify their programs according to the local community, already noted are the strict limitations of that policy. Essentially, principals may move faster in the desired direction, but not consolidate what they have and certainly not move in an opposing direction. Further, there is regular rotation of principals, a policy which serves the function of providing a common approach in all schools as no principal can become too entrenched in one community. Wilmot is eager to accommodate, to include, to assist, to 'empower'; the groups lacking powerful, educated, forceful leadership are unlikely to modify the direction in which all schools are moving pretty much in tandem.

Sean Costello, Director of the Melton Roman Catholic Separate School Board

Melton is an industrial city and port in northwestern Ontario, predominantly working class. The Roman Catholic population is mainly immigrant, but comparatively few have immigrated within the last fifteen to twenty years. Most students therefore have English as their first language.

Costello's innovation is the introduction of 'trusting and compassionate leadership' at the level of the school. His purpose is to delegate more authority to the principal with the objective of building strong school communities, linking teachers and parents in a joint enterprise.

Costello recognizes that the change will take time and he is not trying to force the pace. He sees some principals as being reluctant to accept the authority and its attendant responsibility; some of them still feel that 'downtown makes all the decisions', but, as was the case in Northampton, the principal's freedom appears to be quite constricted. Dino Tebaldi, a superintendent, asked about the school's freedom to interpret the Catholic program (it is the Catholic community that lies at the heart of Costello's innovation) says, 'The schools must follow the official Roman Catholic program; there's not much room for variation. In Melton, we try to stay dead ahead, middle-of-the-road, following the programs as they are laid down. You might say conservative.' He sees Costello as being very sincere in his attempts to build local communities. Costello starts meetings with a prayer, he imparts his philosophy, he talks of the church and he remembers deaths and serious illness in the family. Tebaldi feels there is no problem of Costello clinging to central authority; rather it is the reverse. Some principals need to be weaned from reliance on central authority.

Jean Lefebvre, a reflective principal in the system, sympathetic towards Sean Costello and his ambitions, generally agrees although he is even more sceptical about the extent to which local autonomy is taking hold, '. . . about one-third of our principals have the confidence to move independently'. But he agreed that some principals still see a hidden hand, particularly when they are dealing with teachers and parents. As for whether principals would have the authority to develop a non-active learning school, he answered that they would be challenged by the superintendents. Costello would be very nervous about it, his response depending on his level of confidence in the particular principal.

It should not come as a surprise that Costello's first ranked philosophy is Traditional. Of the six CEOs interviewed, his seemed to me to be the purest; key words in that statement are character, personal responsibility, good adults, society, culture, family, community and clear moral framework. His second choice, Technocratic, also comes through clearly in the interview as does the third, Cultural. Placing the Progressive philosophy fourth makes him anomalous among CEOs, particularly among separate CEOs.

Ironically, active learning is being imposed in the elementary schools, as already noted, but less rigorously than in Northampton, where Grant Wilmot shares an adaptation of the Progressive philosophy. Whereas in Northampton, Wilmot has integrated Progressive forms in a cultural, intellectual and results-oriented curriculum, Costello is uncomfortable with the sense that there is some discrepancy between his own philosophy and what he sees as the official, provincial direction of progressivism. Interestingly, Lefebvre thinks Costello's first philosophy is Progressive, possibly reflecting his own orientation, seeing his own ideals in a person he sincerely respects.

Ironically too, Costello had at one time to defend the Progressive ideas going into the schools against the wishes of traditional trustees. Costello had not felt any major internal conflict; after all his Traditional views are concerned more with community and relationships, while active learning is more to do with instructional methodology.

Ultimately, of course, there are important inconsistencies between Deweyan pragmatism and a Catholic Thomism based on external authority. Thoughtful educators who become strongly committed to progressive ideas are likely to extend them beyond an activity centre and the use of concrete materials; progressivism is sceptical of authority and tradition, believes in tentative truths rather than Truth and believes in fulfilment and dynamic experiences rather than in a more static virtue.

Lefebvre, despite his Progressive leanings recognizes the importance to a strong community of a single version of Catholicism within the Melton Catholic community. He sees no place for theologically liberal and conservative schools, which would tear the community apart.

Costello's reaction to lack of consensus can be seen as one of *accommodation*. His central focus on Catholicity, community, family, character and practical training for life remain strong; but he is willing to move with the times — to delegate more authority and to permit, even enforce, progressive teaching methodologies.

How does this *accommodation* differ from Wilmot's inclusion? Wilmot builds disparate parts into a single unifying direction. In contrast, Costello has no enthusiasm for elements which he senses may endanger his central focus, but recognizes that changes must be made, perhaps reluctantly, always slowly, to accommodate external pressures and changing circumstances. Wilmot welcomes new ideas, always provided they can be fitted into his flexible, overall scheme; Costello has a clear central focus and is wary of new influences which may threaten it.

Ross O'Brien, Director of the Swansea Roman Catholic Separate School Board

Swansea is an industrial city in southwestern Ontario surrounded by a rural agricultural area. As Swansea's industry is based mainly on the production of auto parts for GM, Ford and Chrysler, it has experienced severe changes in its economic fortune. Similarly, the surrounding rural area has some passable agricultural land but there are few large, rich farms such as can be found further west. The small Catholic community is generally poorer than the Protestant community and is found mainly in the city, although there are a few small rural Catholic schools.

O'Brien's innovation is similar to Costello's, but has a more practical focus. His innovation is to change from a pattern of twinned schools, i.e., two schools served by a single principal, part time in each, to the traditional pattern of a principal in every school. His purpose is similar to Costello's; he wants to make every school a genuine community. He saw the twinned principal as being an 'accountant-type manager' instead of a program and community manager.

However, his idea of community is a little different from Costello's. Whereas Costello appears to see the school as representing the church in the community, O'Brien sees the school, while being Catholic, representing the community. O'Brien sees principals spending too much time in the office. They may talk to parents, but they are not 'listening enough to the community and listening to the parents in a genuine way'. While he acknowledges that the school cannot be responsible to every individual parent, he believes it should represent the community view; for O'Brien that requires conscious action.

O'Brien, like Costello, chose the Traditional philosophy first — character comes before intellect or self-realization. But it seems that his second and third philosophies rank very closely behind — the Individualistic and the Progressive. There would appear to be some tension between the Individualistic and the Progressive philosophies on the one hand, both beginning with self, and the Traditionalist, beginning with societal authority. As a comment on his philosophy, O'Brien wrote on the questionnaire that education starts with fostering 'the natural curiosity of the child', more consistent with his second and third choices than with his first. For Costello, one suspects, education is more likely to start with the love of God and the authority of the church. The tension among O'Brien's philosophies becomes more evident if one imagines the Catholic community demanding traditional instruction, with strong inculcation of basic skills and basic religion. But working-class Swansea, although it might like such a regimen, is unlikely to articulate it.

From one perspective, O'Brien has been more successful than Costello. Twinning, by means of regulatory change, has almost gone, and its elimination is foreseeable. Regulatory change is easier to bring about than change involving teachers' behavior. Unlike Costello, O'Brien is a strong progressive when it comes to instructional methodology. Thus, Roland LeMaitre, a superintendent, explains the new grading and reporting system. The child's progress is expressed in terms of himself or herself, not in comparison with others. This could mean, he agrees, that a sixth grade child working two years below grade level will be given the top grade of G. The policy is that the teacher should povide additional, explanatory oral comments. This type of reporting can be seen as an extreme form of Progressivism, one that would, for example, be unlikely to be prescribed or accepted in Northampton, let alone in Melton Separate.

Asked about this policy, George Greene, a principal in the system, said he was 'insistent' that the level of work be 'written' on the report card although he realized this was not done throughout the system. His own policy seemed to be drawn from his conviction that everyone has to be accountable rather than from any sense that the CEO approves local autonomy. While he recognized that schools do have some autonomy, he also felt there is 'considerable guidance'.

There is no real conflict between O'Brien and either the trustees or the parents on the central issue of the school as an entity reflecting the community, each with its own principal. For many, the twinning issue was economic rather than ideological. O'Brien, unlike Costello, is a somewhat liberal Catholic. There is agreement, as in Melton, all the same, that neither an extreme liberal nor an extreme conservative (in theological terms) would either be appointed in the first place or survive if he/she were appointed.

Consistent with his belief in the primacy of the home and respect for the community, O'Brien would be supportive of varying schools for different communities if he headed a pluralist system. But Swansea Separate is not pluralist — so that is not a problem. He does welcome non-Catholics into the Catholic system providing they will subscribe to the system's culture. This greater tolerance of dissent differentiates O'Brien from Costello and perhaps from Wilmot. Wilmot wants to encompass, *include*, co-opt dissenters. Costello is prepared to *accommodate* them. Wilmot allows an alternative school as a last resort; one senses that less skilled negotiators would simply have been drawn in, co-opted. Costello sees no place for dissent. O'Brien, while seeing no need or demand for it in his own system, *accepts*, even welcomes, the prospect of separate provision. 'One has to recognize the fact' that the minority cannot simply be rejected as not having rights because 'that does some violence to the notion of the parent as educator.'

Peter Brendel, Director of the Caswell Board of Education

Caswell is a small one industry town on the Ottawa river in eastern Ontario. Isolated, it depends on its pulp and paper mill together with logging and a little poor farming to the southeast. While Wilmot, Costello and O'Brien are essentially locals (although, like most CEOs, they have made the necessary moves to rise up the hierarchy), Brendel is a cosmopolitan. Wilmot wants to implement a coherent, cohesive, inclusive curriculum; Costello and O'Brien want to develop community schools. Brendel has a more ambitious agenda — he wants the school system to reach out for, to grasp, the future. He is developing a strategic planning process and procedure which will lead to innovations; he is a 'mover, shaker and visionary'. Society — politics, economics, the workplace — is, he believes, in transition as we move from an industrial to an information age. School systems should look beyond tomorrow, to a future ten or fifteen years away.

As an advocate of broad based change, Brendel accepts, welcomes variety in education. A practical manifestation is an alternative education centre at the high school level for adolescents unsuited to the regular high school, as well as adults. He has also encouraged a broadening of programming in the arts, in French immersion and in Native education. However, his single most important and innovative activity is a strategic planning committee and process whereby he is encouraging educators and the public alike to think about education beginning with fundamental assumptions, and to plan for a very different future.

Sarah Khan, a principal, was selected by Brendel for the planning initiative. She, like Brendel, is bright, imaginative — in some ways an outsider. She observes that the participants in the process were all selected by the CEO. There is no clear impression where the planning initiative is going or is meant to go. In the beginning, she was a bit cynical but was convinced by the quality of the people selected that it was not to be a rubber stamp for already selected plans. She has her own agenda — the future to her means employment equity. Some of the principals, she thinks, believe that this too will pass, remarking that they 'went through all this in the 70s'. Others, however, are believers.

A plan for the future has inherent difficulties not evident in the other more practical innovations. If the plan is already developed in Brendel's mind, then it is his future towards which the schools are to change, and there is a little suspicion to that effect. Fred Holden, superintendent, to the contrary, believes that Brendel sincerely wants to develop a collaborative 'vision' — not something simply of his own creation. But he recognizes, as does Khan, that Brendel has values, preferences, like everybody else. Brendel favors active learning; he would like more options in the programs. And politically, according to Khan, he is seen as being left of centre, a bit 'NDP'.

Brendel ranked the Individualistic, Technocratic and Progressive philosophies first, second and third respectively. But he demurred strongly when I used an earlier label for the Individualistic philosophy — neo-conservative. Possibly, his second and third choices indicate a heavier collective responsibility for individual development while an unadulterated Individualistic philosophy stresses challenge, competition and excellence. Brendel believes in the 'balance of life'; 'I cycle, I sail, I run, I do art; I go to the symphony'. He wants children to be exposed to all aspects of life and culture, to be challenged and to make autonomous choices. Totally distinct from traditionalists like O'Brien and Costello, he is also different, but less so, from Wilmot. Wilmot is developing a clear, coherent, common program for the near future. He too embraces the artistic and the physical — but he has developed a tidy package. The package can be enriched to include other ideas, but it is a package, a recipe, a program. Brendel has no clear framework of this kind; rather he wants to reach out, challenge, activate. I suspect that the cynics in the system who think he has had a private agenda all along mistake his clear values and preferences, which will clearly limit his acceptance of new ideas, for a plan like Wilmot's . Possibly Brendel is more accepting of divergent ideas — ideas that should not be rejected. 'I believe in my vision', it is meaningful, 'in terms of the people', but 'I do not have the right' to impose it on everyone else.

It is fair to say that Caswell's trustees selected Brendel because he seemed bright, energetic and open to new ideas. Although they are sympathetic to his futurist vision, one may infer that they are more centrally concerned with today's bread — the alternative education program and other specific new ideas including the mainstreaming of special education, French immersion, and Native education. I have suggested that Wilmot tries to *include* dissent, Costello *accommodates* it, and O'Brien's *accepts* it. Of the three, O'Brien is the most open. However, O'Brien's acceptance (and speculative welcome) must be put in the context of a fairly homogeneous school system with quiescent parents who do not challenge his values. Brendel *welcomes, converts* and *accepts*. He is hoping for different deviant ideas — yet ideas which will not affront his own values. So, his openness is necessarily limited by those values; I infer he would not be delighted if a school decided to de-emphasize the Arts and focus on academics alone. Probably his superintendent, Holden, would quietly squelch the plan on Brendel's behalf.

While O'Brien is building homogeneous communities (but is willing to accept some diversity among communities), Brendel welcomes diversity but will be persuasive or even regulatory if the new ideas fail to meet his criteria. It is not surprising then if principals are somewhat varied in their reaction; those who favor diverse ideas in the arts are welcomed but those whose ideas are less amenable will be converted or restrained. In that context, it's possible to see why some principals feel that they have been through all this before; in practice, the emphasis on alternative (i.e., more open) schools, child-centred instruction, French immersion and mainstreaming is indeed redolent of the early 70s. In the final analysis, however, Brendel will accept a clear vision different from his own if it seems to represent a genuine educational alternative for a particular group of parents, one that is relevant to his expectations of the future; what that vision would look like and whether it exists are matters of conjecture.

Jim MacKenzie, Director of the Suffolk Board of Education

Suffolk is a rural county adjacent to the Niagara Peninsula with one medium-sized city, increasingly influenced by its proximity to the rapidly expanding Golden Horseshoe (from St Catharines to Oshawa) on whose fringes it lies.

Jim MacKenzie's innovation is twofold: the development of long range planning and a system of performance appraisal for senior administrators. The intent is to get a 'focus on a direction' for the system. The long range planning component comprises committees working on different aspects of the work of the school system, for example, curriculum. The performance appraisal component is management by objectives. Superintendents develop their own thrusts, but these are generally consistent with the overall thrusts of the system. These innovations arose from both the CEO and the trustees.

Two superintendents, Harry Shaw and Bill Leeder, are both sympathetic to the general thrust. Shaw says that 'his' goals are '100 per cent mine' — but 'based on Ministry expectations'. One of Shaw's goals is interestingly the 'development of child-centred' and 'active' learning not only in the junior but also in the intermediate grades, thrust which, it will become apparent, is not entirely consistent with MacKenzie's philosophy. Leeder agrees with Shaw that he chooses his goals — and that they are consistent with the 'mainstream'.

The two superintendents agree that the performance appraisal system does not work quite the way it is supposed to. What is lacking is firm accountability, because MacKenzie dislikes 'confrontation'. The result is that they do not receive the clarity of feedback they would like.

The innovation appears to provide a framework for a highly centralized, bureaucratic system (and MacKenzie worked with the Ministry when it was strongly bureaucratic and centralized). But MacKenzie does not have the appetite, according to the superintendents, to force the thrusts through; from MacKenzie's perspective he must accommodate the unavoidable ambiguity of modern education. He is 'less hierarchical' and more 'broad-based'.

MacKenzie did not rank either the Progressive or the Traditional philosophy, choosing the Technocratic, Cultural and Individualistic philosophies in that respective order. Consistently, another innovation he named was the development of a strong cooperative education program.

The Suffolk Board of education may be seen as being typical of the ideal lying behind the rationale for larger county boards of education twenty years ago. There is emphasis on equal opportunity (MacKenzie did rank the Egalitarian philosophy). The general intent is that all schools offer essentially the same program in the same way. Central planning is quite consistent with a high level of central delivery and a low level of local diversity.

Mentioned earlier was the strong thrust in the system to active learning. While all six systems have this thrust in common, it appears to be particularly strong and uniform in Suffolk, probably because of its uniform, systematic and hierarchical organization. MacKenzie feels that it is is important for the CEO to have a clear philosophy but to some extent it should be held in abeyance, like one's personal religion. He sees his job as being that of a professional, not as one of simply promoting his own ideas. Similarly, the CEO should not become too closely involved with trustees and politics. As for active learning, he sees that as being an approach that makes some sense at the elementary level, but the secondary school is different. With the current emphasis from the Ministry being the evaluation of outcomes rather than the inculcation of child-centred methodologies, he sees his own philosophy becoming more fashionable again.

MacKenzie is not accepting of different directions in the schools. He acknowledges that there are differences among the schools, inevitably, but he sees them as moving in the same direction, if at different rates. In this then, he is close to Wilmot, whose *inclusive* program includes virtually everyone, with the single exception of the 'back to the land' alternative. Costello, too, sees no reason for much philosophical deviation from school to school, but he is attempting to introduce an element of school autonomy. In Costello's case, there is no need for differentiation because the schools all reflect a Catholic community. MacKenzie recognizes the increasing dissent in society but believes that the different perspectives must be subsumed in a common school. 'I have a more moderate view and wouldn't necessarily follow the dictates of the religious group to which I belong'. Neither MacKenzie nor Brendel wants to impose his single personal vision on all parents and students. But there the agreement ends. Brendel wants to proselytize his values, but he's willing to recognize dissenters — at the very least the idea of dissent. MacKenzie, in contrast, believes it would be inappropriate either to act strongly on his own personal values and beliefs or to encourage dissent. He is delivering what he believes to be official policy.

Of the five CEOs discussed, MacKenzie is perhaps the most straightforward, the least ambiguous. He is acting out the role described by Tyack and Hansot as characterizing the early part of the twentieth century in the US. (The three historical, successive roles described were modelling and inculcating character; managerially offering an increasingly varied program equally open to everyone; and acting as a broker among interest groups.)

In contrast to the other CEOs, MacKenzie believes he must deliver the provincial educational plan, whatever it may be. It may or may not reflect his own philosophy, and he must be careful not to impose his own philosophy too indelibly on decisions that are not rightfully his. Parents' ideas should only be followed if 'we can identify that the parents in fact have the appropriate background to make those sorts of decisions'. The schools in Suffolk are not that far apart (educationally) and 'I don't think they should be that far apart'. Generally, he feels comfortable with what he is delivering but recognizes that the official policy cannot always match his private philosophy. 'Those with extreme views look at the position of CEO and say "I couldn't exist in that" so they are not part of the scene. They exclude themselves or maybe the system excludes them', because there are moderate people who can roll with the situation without having to compromise their own views 'too badly'. MacKenzie excludes those whose views cannot be reasonably accommodated by the official school program.

Hank Braun, Director of the Brock Board of Education

Brock is a large urban/suburban centre in the greater Toronto region. Of the six systems, it is the most socially diverse. There are important Jewish, Black and Asian minorities, together with smaller minorities representing a multitude of linguistic and ethnic groups. Not surprisingly, this is the only one of the six systems with a well developed private system within its bounds. In the other five boards, there is some competition between public and separate boards but comparatively little fear of the private system.

Braun's innovation is the introduction and implementation of race relations and affirmative action policies. Race relations policies stemmed from a Ku Klux Klan incident which led to the formation of a committee and to a policy with four components:

- (i) no racial discrimination or racial intolerance;
- (ii) awareness exercises for students;
- (iii) curriculum changes;
- (iv) affirmative action in employment. The affirmative action concerned itself first with gender equality in employment and second with encouraging young women to consider non-stereotypical employment.

Affirmative action in employment has meant an internship program designed to produce a pool of qualified women, as distinct from simply making additional appointments or developing a quota system. This policy has been successfully accomplished with there now being more women than men in the pool of qualified applicants for administrative positions. Female strength is particularly noticeable at the elementary level.

Ken Molson, a central office administrator, feels that the affirmative action program for women has been particularly successful and is generally accepted, although there was initial opposition. In the area of race relations, support is less than solid and less progress has been made in it.

According to Molson and Irene Fielding, a high school principal, the problems in implementing the policies affecting students are much more serious than those involving the implementation of staffing policies. Originally, the idea was that the allocation of administrators to schools would be blind to both race and religion. But increasingly the policy is changing so that there is some commonality of religion and race between the administrator and the dominant school population. Fielding, whose school is mainly Jewish, predicts that, 'my school will likely have a Jewish principal. Our school is over subscribed on open enrolment patterns and a large proportion of those coming in from outside are Jewish. We are looking at twinning with a school from Israel. Andrews is becoming a Chinese school.'

Braun only ranked three philosophies, the Progressive, the Cultural and the Individualistic, in that order. Affirmative action is perhaps most naturally linked to the Egalitarian and Progressive philosophies, least to the Traditional, Technocratic and Individualistic philosophies. However, these policies are supported unanimously by Braun's trustees. They are simply not controversial, at least not today after they have been more or less successfully implemented. The origin of the policies was community concern rather than a thrust from either the CEO or the Board. Although the policies are clearly consistent with Braun's personal philosophy (he feels justifiably proud of their successful implementation and acceptance), their origin was quite pragmatic.

An irony in these six studies is that Brock, the only one of the six systems with a Progressive CEO, is the only one not rigorously enforcing progressive ideas (child-centred and active learning) in all its schools. Costello and MacKenzie are quite consciously unsympathetic to progressive ideas yet the Melton Separate and Suffolk Boards are both imposing them.

In Brock, open enrolment is a vigorously implemented policy at the secondary level. Brock has several academically intensive schools and schools broadly characterized by the students' ethnicity, a characterization emphasized by open enrolment policies. Consideration is being given to offering a formal choice of program at the elementary level to respond to various parental demands.

To Braun the existence of strong, traditional, academic schools is not something 'I particularly like to accept'. Such schools are not consistent with progressive ideas. But Braun has come to welcome the diversity of choice so schools have been encouraged to develop their own identity and specialization. Personally, he prefers the child-centred approach but recognizes that not everyone else does and that it does not work for every child. So he is proud of the Board's choices and is planning a consumer guide that will help parents pick the right school for their son or daughter. His own reservations are reflected in a response by administrators to a question on what Braun's bottom line as CEO would be: 'He would be opposed to a very narrow back-to-basics approach.'

So, Braun who has a clear philosophy of education which he would like to see prominent in Brock schools (spoken ruefully and wistfully perhaps), is implementing instead a plan to represent parental wishes. Molson and Fielding agree that the administration and Board would even be glad to bring in Christian and Jewish independent schools — perhaps the latter are developing *de facto*. Brendel welcomes variety and dissent — but does not in practice face very much. Facing considerable dissent very directly, Braun also welcomes it, although there are aspects of parental choice he does not care for. He incorporates dissent in the system by means of vertical segmentation, i.e., there are schools of very different character within the same system. In contrast, MacKenzie in Suffolk defended a kind of horizontal segmentation, with progressive elementary schools feeding into secondary schools with a more cultural and technocratic orientation.

The Six CEOs — Educational Leaders and Public Servants

Of the six CEOs interviewed four have served over five years in their current position, one less than two years. Five are married to their initial spouse and all have at least one child. Two are Roman Catholic, two are United, one is Anglican and one is a non-believer. They are all over 50, none is 60, all are in sight of retirement should they so choose; one has in fact already retired. Demographically, they are quite typical of the larger group.

Philosophically, they are atypical, as only one is Progressive. Even so, they are more like the CEOs than the comparison group (who ranked the Progressive philosophy fifth). One of the six ranked the Progressive philosophy first, one ranked it second and two ranked it third.

All six find ways to express their philosophy through their working lives, but some find it easier than others. Costello and O'Brien have the easiest task in this regard; both lead fairly homogeneous Roman Catholic communities. Both have Traditional philosophies which serve to support the idea of a school as a living reflection of the local religious community. Progressive educational ideas cause some problems for Costello. He is unsympathetic, but feels he must support loyally what he believes to be a provincial plan, rendering to Caesar what is Caesar's, while retaining control of the spiritual aspects of children's school lives. Costello would only hesitatingly intervene to help a principal wanting to develop an instructional program based on direct instruction desired by parents, but would eagerly intervene to prevent the appointment of a principal whose personal behavior was inappropriate for a Catholic school. O'Brien has less difficulty because he supports Progressive, child-centred instruction. O'Brien is apparently willing to accommodate different ideas, but his willingness has not been tested seriously.

Wilmot cleverly *includes* the opposition, in order to build a broad consensus. Closer to the public consensus than most CEOs, in a not very heterogeneous system, his is not an impossible task. Nevertheless, the centralized program initiatives leave comparatively little room for strong local deviation. Although principals are encouraged to take autonomous initiatives, they must move in the prescribed direction.

Brendel has an Individualistic philosophy — probably the most difficult to blend in a hierarchical, bureaucratic social organization, based on compulsory membership. Despite the general popularity of 'school autonomy' (itself a far cry from individual autonomy), only the Brock system takes it seriously. And as school autonomy is often based on a consensually felt strong direction, individual autonomy may actually be impeded in such a school. If a school stands for something close to value neutrality, then there is room for individual expression. The more a school stands for a clear set of values, for specific ideals, for community, for distinctive perspectives, the less it can permit individual deviance.

MacKenzie expressly excludes deviance. That is not to say, of course, that deviant children and parents are unwelcome. Quite the reverse, the school's job is to give an equal opportunity and to some extent an equal education to all. Individual biases, including the CEO's own, must be tempered so that the official program is delivered.

Is the public represented by these six men? The evidence can be interpreted either way. One can argue that all six CEOs ensure the genuine representation of the public in their different ways. The two separate CEOs help their boards serve Catholic communities. Wilmot in Northampton makes inordinate and genuine efforts to include most people, most interests, even helping outsiders articulate a special program when they cannot accept the consensual program. Brendel welcomes and seeks different ideas. MacKenzie provides a common program to all in the public interest, in the North American tradition. Braun offers a range of programs to meet public demand in his, the most demographically heterogeneous system.

Alternatively, one can use the six cases to illustrate that the public interest, at least as expressed by the comparison group, is systematically overlooked, not so much rejected as not considered. By this account, there is no genuine attempt in any of the six systems to determine precisely how a hypothetical, consensual Ontario program can be modified and adapted to achieve the consent of the population being served. The evidence for this assertion is reasonably strong. The public in Ontario wants a school system that prepares students either for work or for post-secondary education, which provides regular, external evaluations of student achievement, and which emphasizes a school atmosphere of orderly discipline, high expectations and clear values. In all six systems, even when the CEO does more or less share the public viewpoint, these desired characteristics are modified or even ignored when they conflict with progressive principles. Even Brendel, who accepts pluralist views, prefers and advocates the progressive model for teaching. Wilmot, who, like MacKenzie, is himself close to the public consensus, imposes active learning in the elementary schools. O'Brien, who exhorts his principals to 'listen to' the parents, attempts to impose an evaluation system inconsistent with public opinion. Costello and MacKenzie recognize that they are imposing an instructional regime with which they themselves are not sympathetic. The question of public will is scarcely considered; paramount are the opinions of prominent educators in the system and their perception of the position of the Ministry of Education.

The two accounts, although giving opposed interpretations of the delivery of public education in the six systems studied, are not in factual conflict. The six CEOs are sincere, well-respected, hard-working, genuine educators. They are not conspirators attempting to gull the public. They see themselves, not unreasonably, as both educational leaders and public servants. But they are also part of a system — not in the sense that they are figures in bureaucracies with limited power and influence, but more importantly that they are members of the professional educational community — a community with its own shared beliefs, values and myths.

Before turning to examination of the larger issue of the role of the CEO in modern, pluralist times, I shall raise two further issues to provide further context to the accounts already given and the discussion to follow; the problem of public challenge and the problem of public consensus. In none of the six cases described is there divisiveness among the trustees. More specifically, in not one case is there disjunction between the direction and philosophy of the CEO and the directions and philosophy of the trustees — or at least none is perceived by the CEO and the other administrators interviewed. This is not to suggest that all is sweet harmony at board meetings. Nevertheless, there is no divided caucus and no common front against the CEO. In contrast, the Toronto Board of Education has had a quasi-two party system for some years and CEOs in that system attempt to maintain neutrality between the two competing groups.

The Problem of Public Challenge

In December 1988, Evelyn Dodds was elected Chair of the Lakehead Board of Education in Thunder Bay. Formerly a single dissident trustee, she was elected Chair with a majority of supporters on the Board. Her distinctive educational policies were a clear public manifesto chosen by voters in a hard fought election. Her manifesto generally reflected Ontario public opinion as already described in chapter 7. She favors emphasis on the basic skills, preparation of students for work or post-secondary education, regular standardized testing and clear sequential instruction; she does not support progressive education. The result to date has been continuing confrontation between the new majority on the Board and the administrators, teachers and Board minority. Also in December 1988, Ruth Weir was easily elected elected a member of the Etobicoke Board of Education. She advocates an emphasis on the basic skills in the elementary schools and the use of direct, sequential instruction. She strongly opposes progressive education which she believes is being imposed on schools in Etobicoke. Parent groups in two areas of the city have enlisted her help in their fight to make 'instruction' as distinct from 'play' the main characteristic of elementary education. This has led to confrontation between Ruth Weir and senior administrators of the Board as well as with other trustees who support the senior administration. These two examples suggest that it is possible that confrontation and discord may be inevitable if the dominant education ideology in Ontario is frontally challenged. It should be noted too that in these two cases the ideology was challenged from without. I am not aware that any CEO in Ontario has publicly challenged the educational establishment's progressive ideology, certainly none of those interviewed in this study.

If these observations are indicative, they provide a slightly different interpretation of the behavior of the six CEOs. O'Brien and Braun are both quite progressive in orientation — at least at the level of the classroom. Braun has helped provide alternative arrangements — but has certainly not tried to stanch the dominant ideology with which he sympathizes; quite the reverse. Brendel is somewhat sympathetic to progressive ideas — although instruction is not the major focus of his interest. Wilmot combines progressive instruction with a degree of cautiously applied Technocratic accountability, thereby assuring some public support without antagonizing educators unduly. MacKenzie and Costello are in the most difficult positions. Opposed to progressive ideas, they knowingly oversee their imposition arguing that this is Ministry policy. MacKenzie, however, seemed aware that if this ever had been Ministry policy ('unwritten') the situation was certainly changing. Yet in his system, progressive ideas were being expanded into the intermediate grades. Thus, both Costello and MacKenzie apply their philosophy in areas where they will not confront the dominant ideology; Costello develops a caring school community (at the same time maintaining regular standardized testing); MacKenzie develops a coherent systems model governed by management by objectives. Obversely, Braun supports his progressive philosophy as the dominant model in the system but willingly supports alternative models for those who cannot accept it. Thus, both supporters and opponents of the dominant model accommodate themselves to the local environment, not in terms of some sentimental attachment to public will or public opinion but in regard to the Realpolitik of the arrangement of power.

The Problem of Public Consensus

I have discussed the ways in which six CEOs reflect a public consensus — an Ontario consensus — a local consensus. Underlying that discussion is an assumption that publicly funded schools should represent a public consensus. My criticism of that representation by CEOs has essentially been that CEOs tend to represent professional educators' consensual values more than they represent the public's. It is important in this context to attempt to distinguish the question of expertise from values. It is one thing to claim that educators should make technical pedagogical decisions; it is another to claim that they should determine the guiding values and goals of the school. If it is argued that progressive ideas are simply matters of technical pedagogy, then one must question why administrators would assume the right to impose such technical, professional ideas on professional educators; it is presumably ethical for professional educators to make their own professionally technical decisions providing they are accountable for the results. In fact, both sides cross the indeterminate line between pedagogical expertise and philosophical direction. Evelyn Dodds and Ruth Weir, trustees, know very well what kind of instruction they want in the schools of Thunder Bay and Etobicoke, just as administrators typically articulate the Progressive philosophy and its associated active learning methodologies.

The assumption that publicly funded education should be consensual is an important one. An excellent and thorough discussion of the complexities involved can be found in Crittenden (1988). Crittenden's conclusion is that public schools should reflect only the necessary basic values of a democratic, pluralist society. But the state should fund on the same basis, schools representing different religions or educational values in the formative elementary and junior secondary years. As young people become adult and autonomous there is no compelling public interest in providing separate schools based on varying values.

The prevailing view in Ontario, illustrated by CEOs and the comparison group, is that only a single consensual theology or ideology should be represented by publicly funded schools. According to both groups, those who dissent should pay the full price for private education. There are obvious problems in the notion of an avowedly pluralist society demanding that dissenters pay for the right to perpetuate their fundamental values, particularly when the CEOs and the comparison group do not even agree on what the consensus that everyone must have should be.

Canada claims to be more pluralist than Britain or Australia. A federal act of Parliament and our 1982 constitution both support the idea of multiculturalism. Yet both Britain and Australia provide more opportunities for educational choice. As shown elsewhere there is a degree of hypocrisy in the claim that Ontario only supports a single consensual common model of schooling (Holmes, 1988). The reality is that many dissenting ideas are represented and publicly funded in the schools, for example, alternative 'free schools' in Toronto, the alternative 'back-to-the-land' school in Northampton, and the proliferation of French immersion classes and schools, whose enrolment now exceeds the total of elementary private schools. In addition, and most significantly, the Roman Catholic religion has a privileged position, compared with Islam, Judaism, and other Christian denominations. That right is safeguarded in law under the British North American Act of 1867. But it apparently conflicts with the Charter of Rights and Freedoms (which is overridden by the earlier constitution); so it is therefore government choice to extend the privilege. The Ontario Government does not have the right to cease funding Catholic schools; but it does have the right (and, according to the *Charter*, the moral obligation) to grant access to other religious denominations.

In short, policy for the provision of publicly-funded education should take into account two different anomalies: (i) the delivery of public education in Ontario does not reflect a central consensus of the population; (ii) no conceivable central consensus can reasonably reflect the diverse beliefs of Ontario's multicultural and multi-faith society. I turn now to a review of four models of delivering publicly funded education and at the same time examine the role the CEO might play in each of them.

Models of Delivery of Publicly Funded Education

Model 1: The Classic North American Model of Geographic Community

The idea behind this model is that there is a greater or lesser level of local autonomy represented by a local, usually elected school board. This model was epitomized by nineteenth century New England. Fiercely independent Protestant communities supported local community schools. This became an idealized model for the US and, in modified form, for Ontario. In Ontario, there has been traditionally a comparatively high level of centralized provincial control.

Tyack and Hansot show that the nineteenth century CEO represented a mold, a set of consensual values. Although Marxists argue that the values represented those of the capitalist ruling classes, those excluded pressed for inclusion rather than for an entirely new set of values (and schools). During this century, much of that consensus has fallen apart and, to the extent that it remains the consensus, is represented in small isolated and segregated communities — perhaps a rural farming community in Iowa, or a self-contained middle class suburban community in California.

Attempts in the US to break down the walls of segregation (mainly but not only racial) among small contiguous communities have been largely unsuccessful. New Jersey has maintained much of the traditional decentralization characterizing the American model in its purest form. There remain hundreds of small school districts, many with only a few hundred students. A court desegregation order compelled Morris County, a fairly affluent exurban region in western New Jersey, to balance its school attendance by race across school district and municipal boundaries. Thus, local community control and local community schools were in this one exceptional case replaced by a large school system with balanced enrolments across a large region. The result has been successful in decreasing racial segregation (the schools are exactly balanced by race). But social segregation has greatly increased as enrolment in private schools has increased astronomically. More generally in New Jersey, as in the rest of the US, local public school systems and local public schools are increasingly socially segregated in response to the growth of socially homogeneous suburbs, cities and even rural municipalities. The CEO may try to represent the values of the community. But this becomes impossible when large school systems comprise a variety of schools representing sharply differentiated populations. I have already noted that Tyack and Hansot point out that in this most recent stage, CEOs become brokers among varying political interest groups.

The local boards in Ontario were combined in large county boards in the late sixties and early seventies. The result has been a considerable reduction in the level of homogeneity within the single school system. Although there remain important differences between counties such as Northamptom and cities such as Brock, the differences within the school systems are equally great or greater. In other words, there are many parents in Brock who could much more readily send their children to schools in Northampton than they could to some of the schools in Brock. Braun and Wilmot espouse somewhat different philosophies, one Progressive, the other Cultural. Yet both are middle-of-the-road in religion and politics and both support child-centred programs in the schools. Northampton has its Bible belt not well represented by Wilmot, and Brock has rich Jewish, poor black and upwardly mobile Chinese communities not personally represented by Braun.

The classic model is generally obsolete. The problems are least in separate and rural public systems. Even there, however, problems have been noted. Neither the Melton nor the Swansea Catholic community, being predominantly urban working class, appears to be characterized by strong educational dissent. In both cases progressive ideas are being imposed. Superficially, these problems appear much more readily solvable than those of Brock, with its deep racial, ethnic and religious divisions. Yet, if these problems are so easily solvable, why have they not been solved? Melton is particularly interesting; Costello it will be remembered, does not even share the Progressive philosophy that is being imposed in Melton schools, (admittedly less rigorously than in many other systems).

In urban, suburban and exurban areas of Canada the idea of a CEO representing a consensual ideology which is to be imposed on all students, while it may make some sense in homogeneous countries like Denmark and Sweden, is incongruous. Some readers of chapter 7 may infer that what is needed is a strong affirmative action program to bring women and racial and ethnic minorities into the ranks of Ontario's CEOs. That conclusion, though possibly justified on entirely different grounds, is peripheral to the data developed in this research. This research is concerned with beliefs, values, ideologies and philosophies, together with their manifestation in educational practice. The appointment of individuals with different physical characteristics does not necessarily lead to any change in values. Indeed, if there is, as I suggest, a strong consensus among educational leaders centering on the Progressive philosophy, it would appear that the fastest route to administrative power for minority groups would include adherence to that philosophy.

In Ontario, with the exception of many separate systems and some rural public systems and some rural public systems, the classic model appears to be anachronistic, both because the dichotomy between professional and lay philosophies is large and because there can be no large consensual centre if philosophical division runs deep and wide. A secular, middle-of-the-road Progressive or Technocratic school cannot represent the values of fundamentalist Moslems, Orthodox Jews and Seventh Day Adventists. Tyack and Hansot show that social diversity tends to turn the CEO into a power broker, who attempts to assuage and appease various interest groups. None of our six cases clearly illustrates this trend, which is probably less strong in Canada than in the US. The nature of our sample, chosen on the basis of consistency between philosophy and action, also served to exclude the brokers. Even so, the pressures towards brokerage administration are evident in the more urbanized public boards. The interviews do not reveal exactly why Braun has endorsed a pluralist system, i.e., why he has departed from the classic model. One may guess that the pressures in Brock were irresistible; by endorsing rather than fighting the move to pluralism, Braun was able to maintain his own philosophy intact and ensure its continued mainstream representation. Thus, he can avoid becoming a broker by publicly accepting and endorsing differences.

MacKenzie has strongly resisted differentiation, with the support of a school board which is resistant to local pressure and local autonomy. The pluralist forces are much less powerful in Suffolk, on the fringes of the metropolitan region and still partly rural, than in Brock. But the price of centralization is its embodiment of the alien Progressive philosophy, which is likely a continuing factor in the growing dissatisfaction with public education in Ontario. It is unlikely that the educational leadership in Suffolk, excluding the CEO, would gladly accede to the centralized imposition of a Technocratic or Cultural philosophy, as the case of Thunder Bay illustrates.

It may be said that I am exaggerating the problem of the difference in philosophy between CEOs and the public. After all, although a plurality of CEOs ranked the Progressive philosophy first, a majority did not. The cases of Etobicoke and Thunder Bay, it may be argued, merely show that the confrontational approach adopted by two particular individuals is counter-productive; and in any case those are just two cases. For that counter-argument to be sustained, one would have to be able to show that different methods have proved successful; that there are, in Ontario, public school systems where the senior administration is successfully imposing the public consensus, as distinct from the educational consensus, on all schools.

It may further be said that Ontario is a unique case, the classic model has worked imperfectly in Ontario as a result of local factors leading temporarily to some conflict between public and professional values. This study is an Ontario study. Certainly, one cannot generalize simply from Ontario to other provinces and other countries. The classic model is very likely under much less stress in rural Canada — in New Brunswick, Prince Edward Island and Saskatchewan. There are undoubtedly important local circumstances which have exacerbated the problem in Ontario. On the other hand, Ontario lacks the economic and class divisions found in England, the class division of Australia and the racial, economic and social divisions of the US. To that extent, Ontario is a highly favored place, where the educational system should be under minimal stress.

If the thesis being developed here is generally valid, that there are important differences in interest between educators and the public and that the endorsement of pluralism has important implications for the delivery of publicly funded education, then one would expect to find analogous stresses in other jurisdictions attempting to maintain or install the classic system of school administration.

Model 2: The Classic Model Decentralized

The most obvious response to pluralist pressure is decentralization of authority to the level of the school. It is not surprising then that five of the six systems espoused some measure of school autonomy — Brock, Swansea, Northampton, Melton and Caswell. Brock has moved well beyond decentralization to formal differentiation which will be discussed later. In the case of the other four, autonomy appears principally to consist of freedom to develop initiatives which reflect the system's own established directions and philosophy. Costello in Melton would, however, seriously contemplate an autonomous elementary school representing Technocratic and Cultural ideals, if it represented a consensus among principal, teacher and parents. In that case, Costello's 'tolerance' probably results from his own personal sympathy with such an enterprise. In practice, it is doubtful that other senior administrators would permit the development of such a consensus by a principal.

In fact, to the extent that the CEOs represent educators generally, it seems unlikely that many principals would embark on a plan for such radical and open autonomy. The teachers and principals to whom I speak informally who are unsympathetic to the dominant ideology tell me that they work quietly, as far as possible behind closed doors with limited publicity. To announce their ideas and plans is to invite, they believe, criticism, interference and even direct orders to cease.

There are several fundamental difficulties with this model. It directly addresses neither of the basic issues which I have suggested make the classic model obsolete. If one problem is an ideological gap between educational leaders and the public, decentralizing authority to the school may only serve to decentralize (and dissipate) dissent. If another problem is the lack of consensus within geographical communities, local school accommodation of geographically defined values is of little assistance. Further, insofar as genuine accommodation of local geographical community is feasible (for example, suburban developments and subdivisions), local autonomy may merely encourage parents to identify their interests more in terms of class status, income and material goods (i.e., the most obvious common factors binding the subdivision together) than to encourage them to reflect on their underlying educational values. A strong case can be made that children's education should reflect their parents' thoughtful, reflective, considered values and traditions instead of accommodating their current social and economic standing. One may argue, as the United Nations Charter of Human Rights implies, that equal opportunity means that parents should have an equivalent right to have their own values reflected in their children's education. It is less reasonable to argue that equal opportunity means different education for children according to their parents' material status.

For the CEO, the autonomous school poses additional problems. The classic model, where and if it works, presents a clear role for the CEO. He or she should represent the central consensus and must work to include the excluded. Wilmot, Costello and O'Brien follow that role, even though there may be problems in their definition of the consensus. But if autonomy really means anything, the CEO may have to support and encourage an idea that is personally distasteful, or become distanced from all the autonomous schools. England has traditionally encouraged local autonomy by school. At the same time, the role of the CEO in England has traditionally been more managerial, i.e., less involved in school policy, more involved in school support. That tradition is changing today. On the one hand there is increasing centralization in terms of educational objectives, curricula and evaluation. On the other hand, there is increasing autonomy as individual publicly funded schools are permitted to obtain direct funding from government, instead of through the local school board. One interpretation is that local school autonomy worked in England as long as there were not major differences among the schools.

Overall, local school autonomy is an improbable solution to the problem of pluralism. The policies individual principals might like to embrace may often not be those desired by the parents. Involving the public in school policy making too often means public relations intended to obtain public support for what the school is doing or planning to do. O'Brien asserts, sincerely enough, that educators should listen to parents; but it is not obviously apparent that the school program in Swansea schools is more reflective of the public will than is the program in, say, the Melton schools. As geographical communities are unlikely to be entirely homogeneous in terms of fundamental educational values (even though they are increasingly superficially homogeneous), open enrolment and access to transportation become mandatory. Suppose, for example, that one autonomous elementary school becomes a free school, another an academically intensive school. It is unreasonable to expect parents in either community to move to the other catchment area to obtain access to the school of their choice. As open enrolment becomes necessary, so central planning becomes important and we move from an option of local autonomy to a full pluralist model.

Model 3: The Pluralist Model

The pluralist model acknowledges the legitimacy of different values other than those based on local geographic community. It implies that public education is a compact between individual parents and the larger society, not one between central government and local government. While education remains necessarily a matter of community for most people (the very existence of a school demands some minimal definition of community), community is not necessarily defined in geographic terms.

Brock has moved some way to acknowledge this model. Its policy is to offer a certain choice of secondary programs within each of its different regions. The difference between this and the school autonomy model is crucial. There is no assumption in Brock that its different regions are distinctive and should have different programs based on that distinction; the assumption is that within the city there are different aspirations irrespective of area of residence. The model is imperfectly applied because it is new and because there are difficulties in dealing with religious orientations, some of the most crucial differences in Brock. Further, it is, to date, applied only at the secondary level. Crittenden, it will be recalled, argues forcefully that parental choice is most crucial in the early years, autonomy more important during the later years of adolescence.

There are several ways of interpreting the pluralist model. The most common, the one adopted by Brock and by Edmonton, Alberta (the system with the most developed pluralism in Canada) is to offer a mainstream with alternatives. A weakness in the practice of this interpretation (not in the model itself), is that in Canada, distinct religious alternatives are generally not allowed. (In the case of Edmonton, a de facto Jewish alternative school operates by demanding a knowledge of Hebrew on the part of the teaching staff. But the Edmonton system will not discriminate in its appointments on the basis of religion, thereby excluding comparable Christian schools.) Yet religious differences are precisely the ones around which alternative focuses are likely to develop.

Another interpretation would be to develop an array of options in consultation with the parents being served. A large system might develop two, three or four major options (for example, a progressive option, an independent learning option, a Christian option and an academically-intensive option), together with minor options, consisting of a single school or a program within a school, for smaller groups.

Yet another interpretation, probably the one most suited to most of Ontario, would be to offer two mainstream options, one Progressive/

Individualistic, one Cultural/Technocratic/Traditional, together with minor options. In many systems, the two options, with slight local variations among them, might accommodate virtually every child.

All of these interpretations of pluralism demand a change in the role of the CEO. One possibility is for the CEO to become a manager providing support rather than remain a policy-driven administrator. In the long term, such a change might not be negative. As school personnel become more genuinely autonomous and responsible and as responsibility within systems becomes cooperative and self-perpetuating, bureaucratic hierarchy may wither. In the short term, the removal of an instructional leader from the system would leave the system leaderless and open to invasion by special interest groups, possibly with a single interest agenda to be imposed upon all schools.

Many CEOs, particularly in the transition, would probably want to maintain their philosophical affiliation with some schools. Braun, for example, clearly and openly supports the Progressive school, while acknowledging it is not the best for everyone. In general, school boards might choose CEOs who reflect a model of the dominant program offered. But there would be nothing to prevent an able representative of the minority programs from being a CEO. Indeed, such an appointment would affirm the understanding that the CEO's professional affiliation with one model does not preclude equality among models. Different senior administrators might affiliate formally or informally with different models.

There are other reasons for maintaining an educator as CEO, and therefore other corresponding role responsibilities. Although there is no reason to believe that pluralist schools will be of lower quality than schools that are supposedly identical in quality, it is important that all schools be compelled to provide satisfactory instruction and that parents be made aware of the outcomes of the various schools to which they may choose to send their children. Further, a vibrant school system will keep abreast of educational research and ideas and will make a variety of educational programs available to its professional staff. Thus, the CEO, besides providing a managerial maintenance function and pursuing his or her own educational interests, should supervise program evaluation and the further education of the professionals.

Model 4: Publicly Funded Independent Schools

The fourth model permits the CEO to retain the traditional role of consensual leader of a single public system. Those who feel they lie outside the consensus are eligible in this model, for partial or full public funding. This is the Australian and Netherlands model. Alberta and British Columbia are moving strongly in this direction and Quebec has adopted aspects of the model. With this model, a decision would have to be made as to whether the public school would be generally value-neutral (as Crittenden suggests), or whether it would try to build a strong if limited consensus. The former approach might lower the level of commitment within public schools. The latter approach might effectively force out large numbers of people from the public school system.

Either way, the CEO would remain a conscious representative of the middle consensus, without divided loyalties.

Eventually, this model could be extended to combine aspects of Model 3. A CEO and a school board might be given some overall responsibility for the basic program, evaluation and professional development of all schools both public and independent. At the same time, individual schools and school systems within the larger unit would operate with autonomy except in terms of the provision of minimum satisfactory instruction, fair access, accountability for results and professional opportunities for teaching staff.

Conclusion

Chapter 7 shows that CEOs are quite unrepresentative of the Ontario public. Quite apart from necessary attributes such as age and education, CEOs differ from the rest of the population in terms of their personal values, beliefs and educational philosophies. Even when, as in this chapter, CEOs with quite varying philosophies are interviewed, it is evident that the education they represent to the public is systematically different from the public will.

To propose affirmative action as a cure is to misinterpret the thrust of the research findings; the major differences identified are not related to physical attributes of gender, race or ethnicity but are differences of value and philosophy. To provide training and preparation for members of minority groups would merely mean the perpetuation of the dominant ideology; one must assume that CEOs are either selected on the basis of their ideology, or gain the ideology through their experience on the job or are representative of the pool of applicants. Affirmative action may be desirable, but it is not directly relevant to the ideas developed here.

What is required to address the imbalance is a careful study of the role of contemporary CEOs and of the school systems they serve. I have suggested that the lack of identity between the educational consensus and the public consensus, together with the increasing pluralism characterizing modern Ontario, requires a change in public policy with respect to the delivery of public education.

The current classic model, based on the rather absurd assumption that a single consensus represents such conglomerates as the Peel or Etobicoke or Durham school systems, is outmoded. Feeble thrusts towards ill-defined school autonomy are weak palliatives, as it is unlikely that school staffs will be either willing or able to reflect a community consensus, even if one exists. Even when they are, new inequalities will arise for those parents not represented by the local consensus.

Pluralist societies require some recognition of pluralist education. Pluralism can be recognized either within the public system or by publicly funding both public and independent alternatives. In either case, the role of the CEO must be carefully developed. Clear educational purposes remain for a CEO in a pluralist society at least in the foreseeable future. Indeed, if pluralism is not to decay into centrifugal disintegration, then the need for clear public accountability for the schools, publicly funded or not, public or private, becomes even more paramount; and the role of the CEO becomes more crucial.

Note

1 These two cases are based on personal communication with Evelyn Dodds and Ruth Weir, together with newspaper accounts. Pseudonyms are not used as the details are in the public domain.

Concerning Etobicoke, articles appeared in the *Etobicoke Life*, 31 May 1989, *The Etobicoke Guardian*, 31 May 1989 and the *Toronto Star*, 25 May 1989.

Concerning Thunder Bay, the *Chronicle–Journal* ran an article on 15 May 1989.

References

BOWLES, S. and GINTIS, H. (1976) *Schooling in Capitalist America*, New York, Basic Books.

CRITTENDEN, B. (1988) *Parents, the State and the Right to Educate*, Melbourne, Melbourne University Press.

HOLMES, M. (1988) 'The fortress monastery: The future of the common core' in WESTBURY, I. and PURVES, A.C. (Eds) *Cultural Literacy and the Idea of General Education*, Eighty-seventh Yearbook of the National Society for the Study of Education, Chicago, IL, University of Chicago Press.

SHARP, M. and GREEN, A. (1975) *Education and Social Control: A Study in Progressive Primary Education*, London, Routledge and Kegan Paul.

TYACK, D. and HANSOT, E. (1982) *Managers of Virtue: Public School Leadership in America, 1820–1980*, New York, Basic Books/Harper.

Chapter 11

Centralize, Decentralize, Control and Liberate: CEO's Views of Restructuring School Systems

Stephen B. Lawton and Joyce Scane

Restructuring is in. The news from all sources is the same: the heavy hand of bureaucracy is dead and managers must be liberated to achieve their potential and their organization's potential. However, someone has forgotten to tell this to the Ministry of Education and to many school system CEOs in Ontario.

In a series of interviews with nine CEOs, the researchers' evidence sought fundamental restructuring in Ontario education of the type reported from Britain, New Zealand, parts of the United States, and other parts of Canada. The authors focused on three terms: school-based budgeting (SBB), school-based management (SBM), and local management of schools (LMS) (a term used in the United Kingdom). Evidence was gathered to determine CEOs' levels of awareness and understanding of these notions, their opinions about them, and initiatives that they had taken along these lines. The authors sought to determine if the CEOs believed that there was a trend toward decentralization to the school level, who they believed was supporting the trend, and what role they believed the Ministry of Education as playing in promoting the trend.

Restructuring Education

Restructuring school systems is a phenomenon of the 1980s. Linked to the general movement toward deregulation and privatization, it is seen as one method of improving the effectiveness and efficiency of schools systems while, at the same time, increasing their accountability. The specific form restructuring has taken differs from locale to locale, but one of the universal elements is an increase in the number and breadth of decisions made by those in schools (Caldwell, 1987). Among the more dramatic reforms are those mandated in England and Wales by the Education Reform Act of 1988, reforms which will require school-level, local management of schools (LMS) and even provide individual schools the right to 'opt out' of local education authorities (LEAs) and receive funding directly from the national government (Coopers and Lybrand, 1988). Equally dramatic reforms are being adopted at the national level in New Zealand, the state level in Australia, and the local level in the United States (for example, Chicago). One widely recognized leader in restructuring at the local level is the public school board in the city of Edmonton, a school system whose reform has been the subject of considerable research (for example, Brown, 1989).

Given these reforms, it is natural to ask what effect they are having on the organizational practices of the chief executive officers (CEOs) in school systems in Ontario. Are they aware of this widespread trend? Do they embrace it? And, if so, how? Guided by these questions, a series of interviews was conducted with CEOs of a sample of Ontario school systems. The results of this exploratory study provide baseline data against which future changes can be measured. At present, the 'winds of change', as far as restructuring Ontario school systems is concerned, seem to be blowing rather softly.

Decentralization to the School Level

In itself, decentralization to the school level is not a new concept. In fact, most modern school boards were formed in order to solve the problem of the traditional arrangement of one school-one school board that was the predominate model in North America until the middle of this century (Lawton, 1989). Even as a response to concerns about ineffective bureaucracies, school-based management (SBM) is not new: there is an extensive, mostly hortatory literature, on the subject dating from the 1960s, when school-based budgeting (SBB) was a focus of attention. Nevertheless, the movement (and some advocates of school-based management refer to it as such) has gained strength in the present decade and is rightfully considered a major structural innovation that is part of the repertory of those who see current structures as a major impediment to the improvement of schools and schooling. Vast central bureaucracies in school systems are accused of being inefficient and ineffective, dedicated only to the furtherance of the careers and welfare of the 'public servants' that staff them. Economist studying such institutions (for example, Niskanen, 1973) suggest that unit managers judge their success by the sizes of their units' budgets and the numbers of individuals supervised.

A manager's operational objective, they suggest, is to increase the budget and the staff, not to improve client satisfaction or student learning.

The loss of legitimacy of education bureaucracies was succinctly recognized in The Report of the Commission on Private Schools in Ontario. Bernard Shapiro, the Commissioner, wrote, 'Expressed criticism of board schools tended to focus on the perceived bureaucratization of these schools and the extent to which they are perceived to have become primarily instruments of the state and the professional experts rather than partnerships between government and professionals on the one hand and both parents and the local communities on the other ... Given the effective near-monopoly of the publicly funded schools, it is not surprising that as institutions ... they exhibit some of the behavioural characteristics of monopolists.' In contrast, 'The development and maintenance of the special character of each private school was seen ... to be largely due to the commitment of the community that supported that particular school.' Therefore, the 'Commission does believe that school board trustees have a responsibility not only for the development and administration of general schools policy but also for both a sensitivity to the needs of local communities and the development of programmes that reflect these needs' and it recommended, 'That ... each board school be required to establish a School Committee including the principal and elected parents and teachers in a mimimum ratio of two to one. The task of the Committee would be to communicate, through the principal, with the school board so that the board is informed as to the community's priority concerns with regard to the school's policies and programmes and the community is similarly informed with regard to the board' (The Report of the Commission, pp. 57–8).

In addition, the Commission indicated that the Ministry of Education should 'identify and initiate strategies and programmes to provide school boards and board schools with greater autonomy in order that they can better respond to the specific needs whether of a particular board and/or the community of an individual school or family of schools....' As well, the Ministry should 'refrain from the development of complex guidelines and concentrate on materials that will encourage programme variation in schools and communities across the province' (p. 60).

Implicitly, the Commission recommended a significant degree of both political and administrative decentralization to the school level. The Commission emphasized both social control through 'voice' (i.e., political action) and 'choice' (i.e., market mechanisms) (Hirschman, 1970). The distinction is an important one, in that studies to date indicate administrative decentralization is far more common than political decentralization (Brown, 1989; Briggs and Lawton, 1989; Lawton, 1989). Judging from the literature, it is an open question as to whether or not political participation is an important part of client (i.e., parent and student) satisfaction, although it is clear that the Commissioner believed it to be. It is possible that real choice on the part of clients frees energies that can force those providing services — such as education — to develop and deliver programs that fulfill clients' needs and desires. Voice, in the form of direct political control, may not be needed.

Sample and Method

In order to explore the current status of decentralization to the school level in Ontario, a small-scale exploratory study seemed in order. To our knowledge, no previous research on the topic has been undertaken in the province and it seemed necessary to learn how current practices reflected the concerns expressed above.

In all, the CEOs of nine schools systems were interviewed. Eight of the systems were composed of matched pairs, one a public school board and the other a coterminous Roman Catholic separate school board; the ninth school system was a large public urban school board. Its 'matched pair', the coterminous separate school board, was not included in this study since it was the subject of other research being carried out by colleagues; its inclusion in this investigation was not practicable.

Of the four pairs of school systems, one pair was composed of large urban school boards; one pair of large suburban school boards; one pair of rural school boards including a moderate sized city; and one pair of rural school boards. All school boards were in central or western Ontario (as defined by Ministry of Education regulations); all had, at most, a very small enrolment of students with French as their first language.

The authors interviewed the CEOs in their offices in spring, 1989, using a four page interview guide; notes were taken, transcribed, and analysed on a question by question basis. The thrust of the interviews was to determine, first, the familiarity of the CEOs with school-based management (and decentralization to the school level) in its various manifestations. Second, we sought their views on its primary objectives, their opinions about it, and the extent to which it was practicable. Finally, we sought their insights into who might gain, who might lose if SBM became widespread, and who was promoting the practice. This last point touches upon the role that various provincial actors, including the Ministry of Education, may be playing in centralizing or decentralizing Ontario school boards.

Given the small sample, it is not possible to make provincial, let alone more general, inferences with a high degree of confidence. Nevertheless, when consensus exists among a group as diverse as those in the sample, it is likely that their view is applicable within the province of Ontario.

Results

Familiarity with Decentralization to Schools

The first stage in implementing any innovation is awareness of the innovation (Rogers and Shoemaker, 1971), so we asked CEOs if they were familiar with the terms 'school-based budgeting' (SBB), 'school-based management' (SBM), and 'local management of schools' (LMS) and, if so, where they had heard these terms, what the terms meant to them, and what school systems used these or other forms of decentralization to the school-level.

All nine CEOs were familiar with the terms 'school-based budgeting' and 'school-based management'; only two were familiar with 'local management of schools' and of these, just one identified with reforms taking place in the United Kingdom. This last CEO planned a trip to the UK to learn more about it and had a staff member (from the business side) who was taking part in an exchange program with a British school system and who was to prepare a report for the school board.

The CEOs varied in the distinction they saw between SBM and SBB. Two saw the terms as essentially synonymous while others saw the former as a more inclusive term. 'SBM', one said, 'means that the principal and staff make decisions about educational processes with accountability; decisions are made at the school level. SBB means that each school has money allocated for day-to-day operation, for professional development, etc.' (Board 7). There was no standard, however; some did not include staff participation as part of the definition, others included the community.

No specific sources were noted for information about decentralization to the school level. Key sources were other CEOs, conferences, and readings in professional magazines such as *Canadian School Executive*, *Phi Delta Kappa* and the like. Six of the nine could name other school boards that were noted for implementing school-based management; Edmonton, Alberta was identified by five, Dade County, Florida by two, and North York and Carleton school boards in Ontario by two. One, as noted, was aware of reforms in Britain, and none expressed knowledge of activities in other nations than Canada, the United Kingdom, and the United States. At the same time, six described practices in their own boards which moved more decisions and responsibility to the school level. Two described programs of flexible staffing at the school level (one referred to as 'units of strength' and one as 'resource allocation formula' or RAF) that they had had in place in their own school boards for almost two decades.

Decentralization to the school level addressed three distinct sets of goals, in the CEO's view: better responsiveness to the needs of the local community (mentioned by seven), wiser or more efficient use of money (mentioned by two), and more meaningful roles for teachers and principals in the running of schools (mentioned by three). Sometimes, these objectives were summarized by a single goal, better decisions. In addition, one indicated 'better education for kids' was an objective; and one suggested that implementing a school board's mission statement and model for education was a key purpose, referring to the strategy of 'tight-loose' management whereby central goals and values are centrally controlled while operational decisions are left to the local level (for example, Peters and Waterman, 1982; Peters, 1988).

All but one CEO endorsed decentralization to the school level, albeit with differing levels of enthusiasm and under varying conditions. Three enthusiastically endorsed the concept, one arguing, 'It must be made to work; we must have integration of the community at every level. The tax burden is too high not to involve the community . . . We must maintain a philosophical direction of a cooperative system'. Two others, in separate school boards, found that fiscal limits placed on them meant that little more than a basic education could be offered; with no discretionary resources, there was little opportunity for decentralization since there were few decisions to be made at the school level. Yet, they supported it in principle. Three from larger public systems were most conditional in their endorsement. One of these preferred what he termed 'distributed authority', allocating some decisions to the school level, some to the family of schools, and some centrally. The need to take account of efficiencies in some areas (planning of new schools), of restrictions in others (especially union contracts), and of a desire to maintain a consistent corporate image in the community, meant that schools were limited in their sphere of influence. Another, in a similar vein, suggested it was inefficient and inappropriate for each school to have to 'sell itself' in the community without reference to the school board. He too emphasized the board's image in the community and the school's need to act in a manner consistent with that image. To paraphrase, a McDonalds' does not serve chicken chow mein.

The skeptic in the group was forthright: 'What's new about it (SBM and LMS)? The parents might not like school-based decisions; decisions are better left to the school board. The trustees would not want to give up being the employer!' In any case, 'I've always operated in a decentralized manner. Schools set their priorities, which must be approved by the board. In one school, the staff decided to spend a lot of money on more comfortable chairs for the staff room even though student desks needed replacing. The board did not approve this expenditure!' Clearly, neither did the CEO.

Table 11.1 CEOs' Opinions as to the Extent to which Functions Can Be Decentralized

	Amount of Responsibility Delegated					Mean	s.d.
	None (1)	Little (2)	Moderate (3)	Substantial (4)	Total (5)		
Teacher staffing	2	0	2	2	3	3.4	1.6
School cleaning	1	2	1	3	2	3.3	1.4
Selection of texts	0	0	0	5	4	4.4	0.5
Psychological testing	3	0	2	2	2	3.0	1.7
Transportation	4	2	2	0	1	2.1	1.3

What Can Be Decentralized to the School-Level?

Decentralization to the school-level is usually a matter of degree: decisions regarding some domains are given to the school and some are not; even those that are given may have conditions upon them. For example, a school may select any textbook — so long as it is one on the school-board approved list. To determine how much decentralization CEOs felt possible they were asked about allocating responsibility on six domains to schools. The six domains included teacher staffing, including salaries and sizes of staffs; school cleaning; selection of textbooks and supplies; psychological testing; building maintenance; and transportation. A scale with five positions was used: 1, no responsibility; 2, a little; 3, a moderate amount; 4, a substantial amount; and 5, total responsibility. CEOs were also asked to comment on why they felt the way they did and to indicate what the delegation of responsibility might entail (for example, selecting a contractor to provide a service). Table 1 reports the frequency and average of their scale responses.

There was a consensus on only two items, selection of textbooks and responsibility for transportation. Textbooks and supplies, they believed, could be selected, for the most part, at the school level (the mean response was 4.4), noting of course that approved texts in Ontario must appear on Circular 14 published by the Ministry of Education. In contrast, they agreed that school-to-home transportation had to be a central responsibility (mean response of 2.1). On being pressed, a few admitted that it could be otherwise, noting that school were often fully responsible for arranging transportation to special events, including trips to Europe. However, negotiated contracts, efficient bus routes, and the like, together with the need for uniform policies from school to school, seemed to point in the direction of centralized services.

The averages for the other items tended to be around 3.0, or moderate responsibility. Yet the frequencies make clear that the average is misleading as responses ranged from none to complete responsibility. How is this range possible, from individuals occupying similar positions?

The key to understanding these responses is in understanding the assumptions brought to the question. Some individuals immediately assumed that the question meant 'possible within the existing context', meaning that provincial laws, union agreements, and trustee expectations had to be maintained. Under these circumstances, some saw the notion of deciding upon the number of teaching staff and their salaries at the school level to be beyond reason. Others thought in terms of a hypothetical environment where 'anything goes'. In this, they pictured an autonomous principal designing a school from the ground up, hiring teachers in accord with his or her vision of the school. Both of the CEOs who had some form of differentiated staffing within their own schools knew school-level staffing decisions were possible, but both noted that government mandates (especially that setting the class size in grades 1 and 2 at 20) and union contracts were making it virtually impossible to maintain the practice.

Delegation of cleaning to the school level was also problematic, albeit for slightly different reasons. Again, union contracts and the need for uniform standards were cited as a limiting factor; several added, however, that many principals were simply disinterested in house-keeping matters: if schools were not cleaned for them, they (the schools) might not be cleaned. The paternalism evident in the latter assessment also applied to psychological test, although again with a new wrinkle. First, some could not conceive of the idea of a principal thumbing through the yellow pages to select a psychologist to assess a student, even though they might admit that their board's psychologists were either overworked or not really all that skilled at specialized assessments. In the backs of their minds was a greater threat, that Jaws of the 1980s, a lawsuit. Without central control and review, they were sure that their school boards would end up in the Supreme Court of Canada because some principal didn't know the difference between a psychiatrist, a psychometrist, a psychologist, and psychogenesis. Of course, they might well be right.

Who Should Be Involved in School-Level Decisions?

If the decisions related to a particular function were devolved to the school level, there would be many choices in how the decisions would actually be made. Brown (1989) stresses a dichotomy between administrative and political decentralization. Administrative decentralization implies that only school personnel are involved in the decision-making process; political decentralization implies the school community participates in an active manner. If decentralization to the school level were to occur, who do these Ontario CEOs believe should be involved in making decisions?

Table 11.2 CEOs' Opinions as to Who Should Participate in Secondary School Staffing

	Extent of Participation[1]					Mean	s.d.
	None (1)	Consulted (2)	Participate (3)	Make (4)	Veto (5)		
1 Principal	0	0	2	6	1	3.9	0.6
2 Department heads	0	2	7	0	0	2.8	0.4
3 Teachers	3	4	2	0	0	1.9	0.8
4 Parents	5	2	2	0	0	1.7	0.9
5 Students	3	4	2	0	0	1.9	0.8
6 Community	6	3	0	0	0	1.3	0.5
7 Area superintendent	0	0	3	0	3	4.1	1.1
8 Supt. of personnel	2	0	0	0	6	4.0	1.9
9 CEO	3	2	0	0	3	2.8	1.9
10 Local trustee(s)	7	2	0	0	0	1.2	0.4
11 Other trustee(s)	8	1	0	0	0	1.1	0.3
12 Teacher union rep.	7	2	0	0	0	1.2	0.4

1 Responses may total less than nine if a particular category (for example, area superintendent) was not applicable in a given school board or if the CEO believed the influence was contextual rather than decision specific.

Only one function was discussed in this context, namely that of teacher staffing at the secondary school level. Although we were primarily concerned with the question of how many staff a school should have (in accord with our focus on school-based budgeting, and the like), almost invariably the question was interpreted as which staff members should be appointed. Attempts to insist on an answer to our question, rather than their interpretation of our question, were usually futile since (i) union contracts and limited resources, in their view, pretty much decided the 'how many' question and (ii) the 'which' question is a live political issue with which they must deal. As well, the respondents tended to respond, first, by describing the current situation in their board rather than how they felt participation ought to take place if responsibility were delegated to the school level. We believe this difficulty we had in obtaining responses about hypothetical situations is itself an interesting phenomenon, one which we shall comment on later.

CEOs were asked to indicate how extensively twelve different parties should be involved in a school-level decision concerning the staffing of a secondary school. The scale had five responses: responses were 1, none; 2, consulted; 3, participate in decision; 4, make the decision; and 5, veto power. The frequency of their responses are reported in table 11.2.

According to the CEOs interviewed, the process by which staffing decisions should be made at the secondary level — if this responsibility were lodged at the school level — should involve principals, who make decisions (mean response 3.9), department heads who participate in the decision-making process (mean response 2.8), and teachers and students who are consulted (mean responses both 1.9). In school systems with area superintendents (and perhaps families of schools), these officers might be called upon to participate in the decision or might, like superintendents of personnel and the CEO, have veto power by virtue of having approved the list from which candidates are selected. Only in two smaller, separate school boards did the CEO expect to be consulted. Parents and other community members, they felt, should at most be consulted (mean reponses 1.7 and 1.3, respectively). Specifically excluded from the process would be trustees, including the trustee in whose area the school might be located, and teacher union representatives (mean responses 1.1, 1.2 and 1.2, respectively). CEOs were adamant that the role of the trustees and union representative (and to a significant extent themselves) was one of establishing the rules and criteria by which a decision would be made.

Given the lack of consensus among CEOs about what functions could be delegated to the school level and the difficulty we had in conveying the question about staffing decisions, the responses are surprisingly consistent: if there were to be a delegation of authority to the school level, these CEOs believe it should entail administrative, not political, authority. They may believe the school should be responsive to the local community and, perhaps, that the community should lead the school, but they do not believe this situation should be brought about by giving the community and its members — local trustees, parents, and others — the political power to make authoritative decisions. Their approach would be one of preserving professional and organization prerogatives to organize and administer programs according to their interpretation of community needs and tastes, within the framework of relevant laws, regulations, and agreements.

The preferences of these CEOs parallels the nature of actual programs initiated in western Canada and studied by Brown (1989). He found, 'decentralization observed is organizational and not political, which means that it exists at the pleasure of the board and schools are accountable to the boards. There are no parent advisory committees which act as neighbourhood school boards and make school personnel decisions . . .' (p. 207).

Is School-Based Management a Good Idea?

In assessing any organizational change, a sort of calculus may be carried out to determine who the winners — and who the losers — may be. Often, identifying the sponsors of an innovation may be a clue as to whose interests may be served. CEOs were asked if they perceive a trend toward decentralization to the school level and, if so, what its limits were, who was behind it, who would gain by it, and who might lose by it.

Three of the nine perceived a definite trend, one noting its international character and describing it as 'weak'; three suggested that there was some talk in the province, but no action; and two saw no trend. One frankly admitted he did not know.

Two identified what, in their view, were critical limitations to the application of school-based management. One spoke of the problem curriculum diversity would create in even a single school board where student mobility is prevalent; of conflict in collective bargaining as various groups tried to protect their interests; and of possibility of breaking provincial laws. The other spoke more generally of the need for a system of philosophy to provide glue to hold the system together and of the disruption maverick schools might create. 'It won't do', he suggested, 'to have every tub on its own bottom' (Board 9). Six others spoke not of limitations of school-based management but of systemic limitations that would prevent its implementation: a lack of funds, provincial legislation concerning school board responsibility, negotiated agreements, and adequate business systems.

There were several views as to who might be supporting a trend toward decentralization to the school level. Four mentioned practitioners, including senior administrators and principals. In this context, two commented upon its 'trendy' nature and referred to the bandwagon effect. One, perhaps saying the same thing, indicated, 'I don't know and I don't care' (Board 8). Five suggested teachers' federations and special interest groups were supporting the trend, seeing it as a route to power at the school level that they could not achieve at the school board level. Two believed parents groups supported the idea, although one specifically indicated that parents and trustees were not championing the idea. Finally, one suggested that educational researchers going around asking questions on the topic were the main proponents.

Who they saw as possible winners and losers paralleled, to some extent, who they believed supported the idea. Eight of the nine suggested students and the local community would benefit most if school-based management were implemented in a moderate and careful manner. In an extreme form, excessive diversity might undermine the entire system. Several suggested that principals, too, might gain; one suggested that teachers' federations would win, implying that others might lose as a result.

Losers, two suggested, would be the middle-level supervisory officers whose positions might become redundant; one suggested that teachers' federations would lose; and two suggested that children might come out short if special interest groups took control of education at the school level.

And what role is the Ministry of Education playing in any trends to decentralize school systems? There was a consensus the Ministry had no visible activity in this area and, in fact, its actions were seen as directly contrary to the notion. Numerous examples were given of mandates sent out for implementation, often without adequate funds. Most often mentioned was the requirement that the average class size in Grades 1 and 2 be reduced to 20 within several years. One CEO derisively asked, 'Do they really think we can operate kindergartens or Grade 3 classes with more than twenty students, once the expectation has been created for small primary classes? And where is the money for that?' (Board 1). Others pointed to a general lack of funds that virtually eliminated all local discretion. Two, with some apparent wisdom, indicated that the Ministry was not to blame: 'Politicians, not the MOE, make policy!' Another reported the apocryphal rumor that implied the same thing: 'The policy to extend kindergarten was made for the Premier's nanny. She wanted another day off.'

Underlying these frustrated comments was a more fundamental critique advanced by two CEOs. In essence,they argued that there was a philosophical vacuum at the provincial level. Without a picture of where the provincial system of education is headed and without a rationale for its direction, each school board was forced to develop its own image of itself. In a sense, each tub is 'on its own bottom'. Unilateral mandates, they suggested, whether appropriate or not, are not a substitute for leadership.

In conclusion, one CEO suggested that reforms in management are difficult to 'sell' to trustees because they are conceptual and procedural rather than materialistic. He believed that appropriate research that attended to the capabilities of teachers and principals and the desires of communities for consultation and communication was needed. It might prove useful for suggesting ways to improve the communities' sense of control and to ensure parents' satisfaction with schools.

Discussion

Radical restructuring of Ontario's school system, it must be said, appears to be one of the farthest ideas from the minds of the nine CEOs interviewed for this study. Only one was aware of the dramatic initiatives that have occurred in Britain. When asked of the degree to which a number of functions could be decentralized to the school level, most chose a conservative approach that assumed the continuation of present parameters — legislation, contracts and the like. Even within this restricted framework, some did not conceive as possible even of the flexibility that some of those interviewed already had practiced for almost two decades.

Radical restructuring, as we use the term here, refers in effect to a type of privatization of the local school, giving it over to its local community to be governed and managed. Critics refer to it as 'franchising' education, but the metaphor is not altogether inapt. If anything, it is too modest. Franchises must follow standard routines, purchase from approved sources, and meet standards policed by the franchiser. A radical restructuring of education could provide far more autonomy, allowing the purchasing on the open market of virtually all services — psychological testing, maintenance, cleaning, and so forth. The model, so to speak, is that of the independent private school which does, in fact, take care of its own business.

Quite clearly, in Ontario such flights of fancy are more the whim of academics who enjoy letting their minds wander than they are of CEOs of complex organizations delicately balanced between powerful unions, a skeptical electorate, local politicians, and a somewhat mandate-prone government ministry. The difficulty is that CEOs in Britain, in New Zealand, in Australia, and in Chicago did not conceive that political forces would conspire to overturn — or try to overturn — their organizational structures and processes with radical reforms. Which is not to say that Ontario will do so, but one should not ignore the fact that a problem of legitimacy continues to plague Ontario school boards. Why else would the government decide to run the schools from Toronto? School boards are not trusted to spend money appropriately, just as the CEO described earlier did not trust his schools to do so.

Based on the sample interviews, it appears that neither Ontario CEOs nor the government's ministry are on the 'restructuring' bandwagon. Instead, the CEOs are trying to play the ministerial role of providing a guiding philosophy to their systems, even though their work is constantly betrayed by mandates from above. They have no other choice, it appears, if their systems are to continue to operate. Any structural reform of the nature of those adopted elsewhere would require, first, an assumption of leadership at the provincial level that would link schools to a provincial rather than local vision. Such provincial leadership, ironically, would reduce the need for reliance upon provincial mandates, regulations, and targeted funding.

Whether such a change would improve education in Ontario is another matter. Certainly it warrants the attention of CEOs and others concerned with effective management of vast resources committed to education in Ontario. Careful analysis, not jumping on a bandwagon, is called for; the data reported in this paper provides an initial statement of where we are. It does not indicate where we should be going.

References

Briggs, G. and Lawton, S. (1989) 'Decentralization in local school systems: A review of the literature', paper presented at the annual conference of the American Education Finance Association, San Antonio, Texas.

Brown, D.J. (1989) 'A preliminary inquiry into school-based management' in

Lawton, S.B. and Wignall, R. (Eds) *Scrimping or Squandering? Financing Schooling in Canada*, Toronto, OISE press, pp. 191–221.

Caldwell, B.J. (1987) 'Educational reform through school-site management: An international perspective on the decentralization of budgeting', paper presented at the annual conference of the American Education Finance Association, Arlington, Virginia.

Coopers and Lybrand. (1988) *Local Management of Schools*, London, Coopers and Lybrand.

The Commission on Private Schools in Ontario (Shapiro Commission). (1985) *The Report of The Commission on Private Schools in Ontario*; Toronto, The Commission.

Hirschman, A.O. (1970) *Exit, Voice and Liberty: Responses to Decline in Firms, Organizations and States*. Cambridge, MA, Harvard University Press.

Lawton, B. (1989) 'Political values in educational finance in Canada and the United States', Lawton, S.B. and Wignall, R. (Eds) *Scrimping or Squandering? Financing Schooling in Canada*, Toronto, OISE Press, pp. 29–40.

Niskanen, W.A. (1973) *Bureaucracy — Servant or Master*?, London, London Institute of Economic Affairs.

Peters, T.J. (1988) *Thriving on Chaos*, New York, Alfred A. Knopf.

Peters, T.J. and Waterman, R.H. (1982) *In Search of Excellence*. New York, Harper and Row.

Rogers, E.M. and Shoemaker, F.F. (1971) *Communication of Innovations: A Cross-cultural Approach* (2nd edn) New York, Free Press.

Chapter 12

Assessing Organizational Culture: Implications for Leaders of Organizational Change

Donald Musella and John Davis

The problem for this study arises out of the lack of understanding of the organizational culture as it applies to school systems (see Chapter 13). One of the solutions identified by the authors was the development of a means for assessing the culture of all or part of the school system. The results of this study include a forty-seven item questionnaire and a fifteen item interview guide which can be used to obtain judgmental perceptions of system norms, values and practices. The questionnaire yields eleven sets of norms: success, planning, orientation, support, satisfaction, quality, involvement, change, communication, cooperation and effectiveness. The interview guide yields fifteen evaluation descriptors of organizational practice: success, failure, communication, satisfaction, promotion, school system, CEO role, orientation of staff, allocation of resources, professional development, organizational structure, relationships, desired role model, unsupported behaviors, and desired changes. Either of these instruments yield information useful to the CEO who wants to understand the culture of the school system and/or who is considering making changes directed at improvement in some aspects of the system.

In recent times, the concept of organizational culture has been given increasing attention by scholars, researchers, trainers, and managers. Several reasons can account for its popularity. One reason is that it introduces a major new metaphor for thinking about organizations (Jelinek *el al.*, 1983). The periodic creation of new metaphors provides a refreshing and useful approach in the constant search for greater understanding of organizations and life in organizations. Another reason is that it provides a paradigm (Smircich, 1985) for collecting like ideas intended to improved our insight into how organizations work. A third reason is that culture is seen as the means for introducing changes in organizations

(Wilkins, 1983; Peters and Waterman, 1982; Martin, 1982; Sproull, 1979). Hence, once the determination has been made, that changes are required to arrive at certain specified outcomes, the need for understanding and changing the culture of an organization is seen as the critical means for realizing the desired changes. By far the major impetus for the increasing attention to organizational culture has been the assumption that it can be managed and adapted to increase the organization's effectiveness.

What is Organizational Culture?

In spite of the contemporary importance placed on organizational culture by researchers and developers, the concept is neither fully understood nor agreed upon (Lundberg, 1985). A review of the literature produces a wide variety of definitions: 'the way we do things around here' (Deal and Kennedy, 1982); 'a general constellation of beliefs, mores, value systems, behavioral norms and ways of doing business that are unique to each corporation' (Turnstall, 1983); 'a set of common understandings for organizing actions and language and other symbolic vehicles for expressing common understandings' (Louis, 1980); 'a cognitive frame of reference and a pattern of behavior transmitted to members of a group from the previous generations of the group' (Beres and Porterwood, 1979); 'essentially a construct that describes the total body of belief, behavior, knowledge, sanctions, values and goals that make the way of life of a people' (Herskovitz, 1948); 'the transmitted and created content and pattern of values, ideas, and other symbolic-meaningful systems as factors in shaping human behavior' (Kroeber and Parsons, 1958).

The meaning of culture has been debated extensively (Geertz, 1973). Several are offered which have some major elements in common. Smith and Peterson (1988) provide a concise summary definition, which captures major elements expressed by others: 'agreed ways of interpreting signs, symbols, artifacts, and actions' (p. 101).

More specifically, Van Maanen and Barley (1985) see organizational culture as a product of four attributes: ecological context, differential interaction, collective understandings, and reproductive and adaptive capacity. The first two are structural prerequisites, that is, cultures can only develop where people are in proximity to one another and interacting. The third attribute is central: 'Only when members of a group assign similar meanings to facets of their situation can collectives devise, through interactions, ritual and value' (p. 34). The natural fallout of this conceptualization is that it is rare that an organization would have a unified culture. Hence, the concept of sub-cultures becomes essential. The fourth attribute, reproductive and adaptive capacity, implies that organizational cultures are neither fixed or immutable.

Another point of view is that one learns about the culture by uncovering the underlying assumptions that direct behavior in organizations. Schein (1985) defines organizational culture as the 'pattern of basic assumptions that a given group has invented, discovered, or developed in learning to cope with its problems of external adaptation and internal integration' (p. 3). The assumptions that he identifies (taken from Kluckhohn and Strodtbeck, 1961) include: (i) the organization's relationship to its environment, (ii) the nature of reality and truth, (iii) the nature of human nature, (iv) the nature of human activity, and (v) the nature of human relationships.

Others (Smircich, 1985; Trice and Beyer, 1984; Evered, 1983; and Hirsch and Andrews, 1983) do not accept culture as a separable quality which organizations possess; they assert that organizations are cultures. Hence, cultural analysis of organizational life, which is essentially ascertaining the meaning given to events, is all that is required.

Although some differences exist in meaning and the uses of the concept, there is enough commonality among researchers and writers to conclude that the concept of organizational culture is a viable one. It can further our sense of organizational life and therefore assist in directing changes, leading ideally to improved effectiveness of the organization.

How Does one Describe and Assess the Culture of an Organization?

The common misunderstanding by some administrators and researchers is that culture is another word for climate. Early on, Schwartz and Davis (1981) make a clear distinction:

> Climate is a measure of whether people's expectations about what it should be like to work in an organization are being met. Measurements of climate can be very helpful in pinpointing the causes of poor employee motivation, such as unclear organization goals, dissatisfaction with compensation, inadequate advancement opportunities, or biased promotion practices. Culture, on the other hand, is a pattern of beliefs and expectations shared by the organization's members.

These authors differentiate on the basis of outcomes versus content. Their position is that beliefs (culture) produce norms that shape the behavior of individuals and groups in the organization. So, while climate measures whether expectations are being met, culture is concerned with the nature of these expectations themselves. Hence you can have 'good' and 'poor' climate depending on whether the employee's own view of life fits the prevailing organizational culture.

Dyer (1985) agrees with this definition and also considers culture to be a more basic and stable aspect of an organization than climate. To assess culture, he suggests collecting data on the following aspects: (i) verbal, behavioral and physical artifacts; (ii) perspectives; (iii) values; and (iv) assumptions. Examples of *artifacts* include verbal: language, stories, myths shared by members of the organization; behavioral: often-repeated rituals and ceremonies; physical: art, attire, physical layout, and technology. By *perspectives* Dyer means the coordinated set of ideas and actions a person uses in dealing with some problematic situation. *Perspectives* encompass socially shared formal and informal rules and norms applicable in a given situation and prescribe the bounds of acceptable behavior. *Values* are considered to be the evaluations people make of situations, acts, objects, and people; they reflect the organization's general goals, ideals, standards, and 'sins'. *Values* in this context are more generalizeable and permanent than perspectives. *Assumptions* are the tacit promises that underlie the overt artifacts, perspectives, and values. The questions that Dyer asks of assumptions are placed in five categories: the nature of relationships, human nature, the nature of truth, the environment, and universalism/particularism.

Several questions useful in understanding an organization follow from these assumptions. Are the relationships hierarchical, group oriented, or individualistic? Are humans basically good, evil, or neither? Are correct decisions (truth) revealed by external authority figures or are they determined by a process of personal investigation and testing? Is there a basic belief that human beings can master the environment, or that they must be subjugated by the environment, or that they should attempt to harmonize with the environment? Should all members be evaluated by the same standards, or should certain individuals be given preferential treatment?

Others have been more specific in their approach to assessing the culture. Deal and Kennedy (1982) list several ways to diagnose organizational culture: (i) study of the physical setting and company documents; and (ii) interviews and observations. These are some of the key questions they ask: (i) what is the history of the company (people communicate the mythology as they understand it); (ii) why is it a success (what people think is important in the company); (iii) what kind of people work here (who gets ahead in the long term); (iv) what kind of place is this to work in, what is the average day like, how do things get done (tells us rituals, meetings, bureaucratic procedures).

Further, they disagree somewhat with Dyer in that they refer to strong and weak cultures. Although they include some of the same elements of culture, that is, values, environment, rites and rituals, their definition indicates a premature bias in that they seem to know what constitutes a good (strong) culture. The 'strong' culture is a system of informal rules that spells out how people are to behave most of the time.

In the 'weak' culture, people are trying to figure out what they should do and how they should do it.

Sometimes it seems that there as many definitions of organizational culture as there are individuals writing about their use of the concept. Obviously the definitions indicated above, and there are many others, are at too high a level of abstraction (i.e., not stated in behavioral terms) to be of any immediate practical use.

It seemed to Musella and Davis (1989) that many of the methods and questions used in previous work in industry were too impractical to be of use in most situations. They believed that senior administrators and managers need more immediately applicable information (less generalized) to assist them in understanding the culture of the organization and in directing needed changes. Therefore, the focus of their search was toward a method of assessing the culture that would be practical in terms of time and resources, yet useful in terms of assisting administrators assess the culture of their organization. They believed that the values and norms represented most of the data necessary to assess the culture of an organization.

Further, the work of Allen and Dyer (1980) seemed, in part, to be more relevant to administrative work. In their attempt to describe and assess the norms, Allen and Dyer developed a questionnaire that identified seven areas 'found to be significantly related to the success of cultural change programs' (p. 194). Although interrelated conceptually with one another these areas can be viewed as separate focuses for organizational intervention: (i) performance facilitation; (ii) job involvement; (iii) training; (iv) leader-subordinate interaction; (v) policies and procedures; (vi) confrontation; and (vii) supportive climate.

The assumption was made by Musella and Davis that understanding of the culture was necessary before any assessment of the need for change and/or the initiation of change was undertaken. Hence the purpose of the study was to arrive at a method for appraising the culture of a school system. The method had to be practical in terms of the process for collecting data and useful in terms of the relevance of the data for understanding organizational culture and the need and direction for future organizational changes.

Methodology

The primary method used in their study was the case study of four large school boards. The data collection procedures included: (i) interviews; (ii) questionnaires; (iii) observation of trustee and staff activities; (iv) review of board documents; and (v) participation in professional development activities and selection and promotion procedures.

Four suburban school districts in Ontario, ranging in size from 25,000 to 50,000 students, were selected as the case study sites.

Interviews

An interview schedule was developed for the first case study and revised for each subsequent one. The questions were developed to obtain perceptions of the trustees and staff of the beliefs and values which are reflected in the standard operating procedures of that particular school system. One hundred and sixty-five individual interviews of approximately thirty to sixty minutes each were conducted with a variety of persons: school trustees, heads of staff associations, senior central office staff, middle management staff, other persons with system responsibilities, school principals, vice-principals, resource persons, and teachers. The final list of questions yielded the following categories of information about the school system as perceived by those participating in the study:[1]

- Most successful aspects of the system
- Least successful aspects of the system
- What the school system communicates as important
- The kind of place to work in
- Who gets ahead
- School system descriptors
- What the director (CEO) brings to the school system
- Orientation of new staff
- Professional development
- Organizational structure
- Interactions and relationships
- Desired role model
- Unsupported behaviors
- Desired changes.

Questionnaire

A questionnaire, The Norms Diagnostic Index (adapted from Allen and Dyer, 1980), was developed to assess the extent to which certain norms were in effect in each of the school systems. The questionnaire consisted of forty-seven statements of norms. The participants were ask to indicate on a scale of one to five the degree of agreement that the statement reflected practice in their school system.

The questionnaire was completed by 330 administrators (principals, vice-principals, superintendents, directors).

Each statement was found to be useful as a descriptor of practice. The following categories of information were obtained. Each category represents a collection of statements describing the perceived norms operating in the school system (see appendix a to this chapter for the complete list of statements.)

- Success
- Planning
- Orientation
- Support
- Satisfaction
- Quality
- Involvement
- Change
- Communication
- Cooperation
- Effectiveness.

Observation, Review of Documents, Participation in Board Activities

Observation involved attendance at formal meetings, informal discussions with trustees and staff, occasional visits to the board office, and occasional meetings with Board staff in other settings.

The documents reviewed included Board and committee minutes, CEO's newsletters, Board pamphlets, Board mission statements, administrator objectives, and various policy and procedural written documents.

The participation in Board activities included (i) facilitating at a trustee/senior administrator retreat for the purpose of improving role clarification and relationships; and (ii) conducting an assessment centre for the selection of vice-principals.

The purpose of the observation, review of documents, and participation in Board activities was to ascertain if these procedures could be useful in collecting data which reflected the culture of the organization.

Conclusions of the Study

The data collection methods found to be most useful in this study were the beliefs and values interviews and norms questionnaire. The question arises: what is meant by useful? The authors were interested in using the assessment of culture as a means for identifying the perceived need for changes which would provide direction to formal leaders concerned with improving the effectiveness of the organization. The assumption was made that the purpose of assessing the culture was to bring about changes leading to improving organizational effectiveness. The procedures did identify perceived beliefs and values held by those staff members interviewed and the norms perceived to be directing behavior by members of the organization. The need for change in these perceptions was in turn determined by the formal leader, in their case, the chief executive officer of the school system. The assumption was made that the formal leader now has data useful in directing the focus of change. One example illustrates the use of this data. One of the case study boards of education was experiencing rapid growth and hiring many teachers each year. One of their objectives was to improve effectiveness of performance by conducting orientation and inservice programs for all new teaching and non-teaching staff members. The results of the norms questionnaire indicated that it was not the norm to conduct effective orientation and inservice programs. The interviews confirmed the perception that little emphasis is placed on the quantity and quality of these programs. The data yielded a discrepancy between intent and perceived outcome. The responsibility of the formal leader then is to undertake activities to assess the extent of the discrepancy, identify the problem and propose solutions.

Can Organizational Culture be Changed; If So How?

Changing organizational culture has become a major concern of the corporate world. 'Transformational' programs have become widely used in an attempt to bring about corporate change. Although there are many advocates and critics of the varied strategies being used (Personal Report, 1987), the need for such change cannot be discounted. The solution is to develop ways which do indeed change an organization in such a way as to increase its effectiveness, however that may be defined.

The strategies for bringing about change are well known. The literature is replete with success and failure stories on the management of change (Beckhard, 1977; Bennis *et al.*, 1974; Lubin *et al.*, 1979; Morgan, 1986). The more basic question is, what works?

In defining and attempting to bring about cultural change, consideration must be given to the position that culture tends to be both a conservative, stabilizing force and an emergent force for any social system (Hansen, 1979). Many aspects of a culture have a deep sense of obligation attached to them. People act and think in certain ways because they feel strongly about keeping what they have and resisting change. In fact, attempts to force change in any part of culture can work against certain kinds of change. Culture is also emergent, that is, it changes as it comes in contact with or creates new ideas and values. Culture is largely a process — it is both static and dynamic. Challenge of cultural beliefs will often lead to conflict, dispute, disruption or concern about the change. Consequently, one can assume that most change will have some impact on the culture of the organization. Consequently, understanding the culture of the organization is critical prior to attempts at bringing about change. Further, one could also argue that one is changing the organizational culture when one is effecting behavioral changes of personnel within the organization.

Most administrators worry a lot about change, but too few of their worries focus on the cultural issues of changing. As a result, many times the changes they attempt do not happen. What follows is a set of 'common sense' statements taken from varied successful experiences with organizational change. These seem to be applicable to most organizations contemplating cultural change.

Build on a perceived and/or real need (problem or threat to present situation). If the problem or need cannot be communicated to those effected by the change so they accept and understand the need, problem or threat, entrenched resistance can be expected. Ideally, the answers to 'why change' must be credible in the eyes of those effected.

Select a 'hero' to lead the change. If possible, the 'hero' should be the chief executive officer. To those who are expected to follow, trust and credibility are essential characteristics of the leader. The source of the message is more important in many instances than the message itself. The leader's (hero) ability to influence is critical.

Involve many people in the change process. The bonding of those in the change process can lead to a temporary culture, one that will influence others to join. This in turn improves communication and understanding of the change and can prevent people from returning to the 'old' ways.

Provide transition education and training in the new values and behavior patterns. It seems rather obvious that all change must be preceded, accompanied, and followed with relevant education and training for those who are affected by and expected to change.

Bring in, at least for a time, trusted outsiders. Outsiders can play varied roles as expert information giver, trainer, facilitator, and catalyst. Further, the outsider often can be useful in showing how insiders can bring about the change. In other words, the outsider can provide very effective assistance in a focused, but limited, way.

Build in tangible symbols of the new directions. The symbols can be in varied forms, structural (for example, reorganization), personnel, communication procedures, and content. These serve as tangible reminders of the new direction, strategies, procedures, goals and behavioral changes.

Provide security in transition. To create unnecessary anxiety and frustration is to develop barriers to the change. All change brings with it some loss, either real or imagined. One way to create cultural transformation is to reduce the barriers to change. Security is a basic need.

Change leads to insecurity and loss. Consequently, the mystery of the change should be minimized or removed and replaced with hard evidence of security for those effected by or involved in the change.

Three types of cultural change seem to apply to most settings. One can be described as an evolutionary process. In this case new cultural elements are introduced as others are discarded. Change takes place but the participants do not perceive any radical change. The second type, the additive process, occurs when new assumptions arise which lead to changes that eventually modify an entire set of cultural beliefs or values. The third type is transformational. This is the result of deliberate attempts to change the culture. The situation in this instance can often be described as being in crisis.

On the basis of data reported earlier, Musella and Davis take the position that the factors affecting culture are constantly operating; hence, the main task is to assess the culture so that one can introduce an element of control in managing and directing the change. They suggest the process consists of three major sets of procedures. The first procedure is an assessment of the culture as perceived by the various members. The second is to identify and verify those areas in need of change. In other words, define the goal culture. How does the goal culture differ from the present culture? Are there aspects that can be maintained? What aspects are particularly antagonistic to the goal culture? Third, is to develop strategies for broadening support, for communicating the goal culture, and for making changes in those areas identified. Obviously organizational change is exceedingly complex. However, given what we know about change and what we now know about the assessment of organizational culture, the change should be less difficult to bring about and maintain. The reason is that the culture has shifted as a result of changes in specific aspects identified in the assessment.

What is the Role of the Chief Executive Officer in Fostering Cultural Change in the Organization?

To what extent is the culture of an organization a product of the leadership? There are those who say that the 'most important determinant of culture is the chief executive. He is the one responsible for shaping the motivations, commitments, and predispositions of all executives from senior managers to operators' (Sayles and Wright, 1985, pp. 1–2.). The evidence they use are examples from leaders of large corporations (for example, IBM, Watson; NASA, Webb; Cummins Engine, Miller; Allied Chemicals, Hennessey; GE, Welch) who have 'caused an entire organization to change its value and belief system'.

A recent body of literature suggests that an important function of leadership is the leader's[2] ability to change the culture of an organization (Smircich and Morgan, 1982; Firestone and Wilson, 1985; Weick and Daft, 1983; Purkey and Smith, 1982). The concept of leader in most of the literature refers to the most senior administrator of the organization. The concept of organization is used to refer to a variety of administrative units, for example, a corporation or a school system.

Smircich and Morgan see the leader as managing the interpretations that people within the organization identify. The process here is one of changing meaning (interpretation of intentions) to change behavior. Firestone and Wilson see the process of analyzing culture as central to understanding the organization, that is, its content, the behavior of individuals and groups and its climate. The assumption is made that analysis comes before any attempt to change the culture or any other aspect of the organization. Weick and Daft see the leader as making sense out of things and translating the meaning to others. They tie this process directly to organizational effectiveness models. Similarly, Purkey and Smith see the use of cultural analysis as leading to increased organizational effectiveness.

Sayles and Wright have identified the following components of culture as the target for reshaping through appropriate strategies: relative diversity, steepness of the hierarchy, resource allocations and rewards, degree of stability, and administrative practices. They claim that it is in these aspects of organizational life that the chief executive officer (CEO) has the most influence.

The ultimate objective of the CEO in any organization is to develop an organizational culture that results in less resistance in attempts at change in values, beliefs and behavior. In the following section some suggestions and propositions are offered which can increase the influence of CEOs in controlling cultural change in educational organizations. The reference here is specifically to school systems.

Decentralization and Diversity. Decentralization of decision-making, preceded by intensive professional development of middle management, and accompanied by increased involvement of personnel at the lower levels of the organization, and increased competition for resources should lead to increased diversity. This will produce a more open culture and increase potential for further changes.

Slope of the Pyramid. The less steep the hierarchy, the lesser the reliance on formal, channeled communication, and the greater the encouragement of lateral and informal contacts. This, in turn, will increase the potential for further change.

Resource Allocation and Rewards. He or she who controls resources controls the behavior of those others who desire and/or need the resources. The CEO who rewards behavior consistent with the desired culture will ultimately change the culture of the organization.

Stability and Change. Stability and change are present and needed in all organizations. Both are useful concepts to the CEO who wishes to change the basic values and beliefs of personnel within the organization. The greater the need for either one, the easier it is to bring about change in either direction.

Administrative Practices. The CEO has all the administrative policies and procedures at his or her disposal. The transmission of values is most obvious in the policies adopted and the procedures practiced. The greater the control over administrative policies and practices, the easier it is to bring about changes in values and beliefs commensurate with the desired culture of the organization.

Strategies for Managing Cultural Change

Schein (1985), Tichy (1983), Peters (1978), and Pfeffer (1981) identify strategies through which leaders define, influence, shape, and change organizational cultures. The key strategies are (i) leader attention to desired values and deliberate role modeling; (ii) shaping organizational systems to express cultural assumptions; (iii) interpreting the symbolic elements of organizations — the stories, myths, mottos, and symbols that both reflect and shape beliefs. Leader behavior provides direct evidence of what is important.

Organizational design systems provide leaders with opportunities to shape cultural beliefs directly and to alter traditional, habitual interaction patterns. The leader can take direct steps to 'unfreeze' the organization and create a climate of receptivity (Lewin, 1952; Schein, 1985). This can be done in a number of ways: changing structures, flattening the organizational hierarchy, redesigning committee work and membership. These are but a few examples of how the leader can alter traditional patterns of interaction, hence, change subcultural groups and alter those assumptions which are widely shared.

One can argue that the CEO's behavior reveals organizational culture because he is the most visible member of the organization and is perceived as controlling most aspects of the operation and most people's behavior. It is often said that if one had to make one personnel move to make the most change, one would change the CEO. Their personal behavior (for example, what is said, how and where they spend their time, what they reward, what questions they ask) and the organizational systems they create and support (for example, reporting mechanisms, personnel evaluation programs) are two significant ways in which they communicate their assumptions, beliefs and values. There is one caveat. The CEO must maintain a high level of credibility unless one has and can use considerable power effectively. In school systems the use of ultimate power decisions are rarely available. Hence the need for influence through other means — knowledge, expertise, credibility.

Summary

In spite of differences in definitions, the concept of culture has been of much use in improving our understanding of organizations. Further, the methods developed for assessing culture have provided new ways of undertaking organizational change. The role of the chief executive is paramount in diagnosing and using organizational culture as a means to improving organizational effectiveness.

Notes

1 Each Board of Education received the summary of responses from data collection for their Board only. Their final report is the property of each Board of Education. Further elaboration of the results of this study is limited to the method for assessing the culture of a school system.

2 Leader is used in this context as synonymous with chief executive officer (CEO).

Appendix Norms Diagnostic Index

Norms are expected or usual ways of behaving in groups or organizations.

This survey asks for your opinions concerning the norms that exist in your organization.

You are to circle the number that best describes your agreement or disagreement with each of the statements in the survey.

IT IS A NORM AROUND HERE:	Strongly Agree	Agree	Neutral	Disagree	Strongly Disagree	Don't Know
1 to maintain the progress that is made	1	2	3	4	5	6
2 for people to regularly plan their work goals and review progress	1	2	3	4	5	6
3 for people to be properly oriented and prepared for the job	1	2	3	4	5	6
4 for leaders to take time to follow up on the jobs they have assigned to people	1	2	3	4	5	6
5 for organizational policies and procedures to be helpful, well understood, and up-to-date	1	2	3	4	5	6
6 for people to confront negative behavior or 'norms' constructively	1	2	3	4	5	6
7 for people to avoid blame placing and concentrate on looking for constructive solutions	1	2	3	4	5	6
8 for people to feel satisfied with their pay	1	2	3	4	5	6
9 for people to feel that their work is important	1	2	3	4	5	6
10 for people to feel that the organization offers good job security	1	2	3	4	5	6
11 for people to feel satisfied with the benefits programs offered by the organization	1	2	3	4	5	6

IT IS A NORM AROUND HERE:	Strongly Agree	Agree	Neutral	Disagree	Strongly Disagree	Don't Know
12 for people to feel responsible for doing their own jobs right	1	2	3	4	5	6
13 for people to have some input on decisions that affect their work	1	2	3	4	5	6
14 for leaders to be equally concerned for people as well as results	1	2	3	4	5	6
15 to review policies and procedures regularly and change them as needed	1	2	3	4	5	6
16 for people to get feedback on how they are doing so they can develop as individuals	1	2	3	4	5	6
17 for people to feel 'turned on' and enthusiastic about what they are doing	1	2	3	4	5	6
18 for selection and promotion practices to be fair	1	2	3	4	5	6
19 for people to get good feelings of accomplishment from their work	1	2	3	4	5	6
20 not to have to rely on the 'grapevine' as their best source of information about the organization	1	2	3	4	5	6
21 to understand the organization's benefits programs	1	2	3	4	5	6
22 for people to help each other with on-the-job or personal problems	1	2	3	4	5	6
23 for people to follow through on programs that they begin	1	2	3	4	5	6
24 for training needs to be adequately met	1	2	3	4	5	6
25 for people to have an effective means of communication with peers and supervisors	1	2	3	4	5	6

IT IS A NORM AROUND HERE:	Strongly Agree	Agree	Neutral	Disagree	Strongly Disagree	Don't Know
26 for people to share responsibility for things that go wrong	1	2	3	4	5	6
27 for a spirit of cooperation and teamwork to be felt throughout the organization	1	2	3	4	5	6
28 for people to like the kind of work they are doing	1	2	3	4	5	6
29 for people to work together effectively	1	2	3	4	5	6
30 for people to take pride in their own work	1	2	3	4	5	6
31 for work loads to be evenly distributed	1	2	3	4	5	6
32 to care about and strive for excellent performance	1	2	3	4	5	6
33 to feel really involved in the work of the organization	1	2	3	4	5	6
34 to have a clear way of measuring results	1	2	3	4	5	6
35 for leaders to help their team members succeed	1	2	3	4	5	6
36 to point out errors constructively	1	2	3	4	5	6
37 for people working together to meet regularly on important issues	1	2	3	4	5	6
38 for improvement efforts to be based on facts	1	2	3	4	5	6
39 to use time and resources effectively	1	2	3	4	5	6
40 for leaders to demonstrate their own commitment to what the organization is trying to accomplish	1	2	3	4	5	6
41 for leaders to make a strong effort to involve and motivate people	1	2	3	4	5	6

IT IS A NORM AROUND HERE:	Strongly Agree	Agree	Neutral	Disagree	Strongly Disagree	Don't Know
42 to give and receive feedback in helpful ways	1	2	3	4	5	6
43 for authority to be delegated appropriately	1	2	3	4	5	6
44 for people to share responsibility for what happens in the organization	1	2	3	4	5	6
45 for groups to define goals clearly before a task is begun	1	2	3	4	5	6
46 for people to get whatever training is needed to help them succeed in their work	1	2	3	4	5	6
47 for people to feel that the organization keeps them informed on matters that directly affect them	1	2	3	4	5	6

References

Allen, R.F. and Dyer, F.J. (1980) 'A tool for tapping the organizational unconscious', *Personnel Journal*, March, pp. 192–8 and 223.

Beckhard, R. (1977) *Organizational Transitions: Managing Complex Change.* Reading, MA, Addison-Wesley.

Bennis, W.G., Benne, K.D. and Chin, R. (Eds) (1974) *The Planning of Change* (3rd ed rev). New York, Holt, Rinehart and Winston.

Beres, M.E. and J.D. Porterwood (1979) 'Explaining cultural differences in perceived role of work: An international cross-cultural study' in England, G. *et al.* (Eds) *Organizational Functioning in a Cross-cultural Perspective.* Kent, OH, Kent State University Press.

Deal, T.E. and Kennedy, A.A. (1982) *Corporate Cultures* Don Mills, Ontario, Addison-Wesley.

Dyer, Jr., W.G. (1982) *Patterns and Assumptions: The Keys to Understanding Organizational Culture* Office of Naval Research, Technical Report TR-ONR-7.

Dyer, Jr., W.G. (1985) 'The cycle of cultural evolution in organizations' in Kilmann, R.H., *et al.* (Eds) *Gaining Control of the Corporate Culture,* San Francisco, California, Jossey-Bass, pp. 200–29.

Evered, R. (1983) 'The language of organizations: The case of the navy' in Pondy, L.R., Frost, P.J., Morgan, G. and Dandridge, T.C. (Eds) *Organizational Symbolism*, Greenwich, CT, JAI Press, pp. 124–44.

Firestone, W.A. and Wilson, B.L. (1985) 'Using bureaucratic and cultural linkages to improve instruction: The principal's contribution', *Educational Administration Quarterly*. 21, 2, Spring, pp. 7–30.

GEERTZ, C. (1973) *The Interpretation of Cultures*, New York, Basic Books.

HANSEN, J.F. (1979) *Sociocultural Perspectives on Human Learning: An Introduction to Educational Anthropology*, Englewood Cliffs, NJ, Prenctice-Hall.

HERSKOVITZ, M.J. (1948) *Man and his Works*, New York, Knopf.

HIRSCH, P.M. and ANDREWS, J.A.Y. (1983). 'Ambushes, shootouts and knights of the round table: The language of corporate takeovers' in PONDY, L.R., FROST, P.J., MORGAN, G. and DANDRIDGE, T.C. (Eds) *Organizational Symbolism*. Greenwich, CT, JAI Press, pp. 145–56.

JELINEK, M., SMIRCICH, L. and HIRSCH, P. (1983) 'Introduction: A code of many colors', *Administrative Science Quarterly*, 28, pp. 331–338.

KILMANN, R.H., SAXTON, M.J., SERPA, R. and ASSOCIATES (1985) *Gaining Control of the Corporate Culture*. San Francisco, CA Jossey-Bass.

KLUCKHOHN, F.R. and STRODTBECK, F.I. (1961) *Variations in Value Orientation*. Evanston, IL, Row Peterson.

KROEBER, A.L. and PARSONS, T. (1958) 'The concept of culture and social systems', *American Sociological Review*, 23, pp. 582–3.

LEWIN, K. (1952) 'Group decision and social change', in SWANSON, G.E., NEWCOMB, T.N. and HARTLEY, E.L. (Eds) *Readings in Social Psychology* (Rev. ed.) New York: Holt, Rinehart and Winston.

LOUIS, M.R. (1980) 'Surprise and sense-making: What newcomers experience in entering unfamiliar organizational settings', *Administrative Science Quarterly*, 25, pp. 226–51.

LUBIN, B., GOODSTEIN, L.D. and LUBIN, A.W. (Eds) (1979) *Organizational Change, Sourcebook I: Cases in Organizational Development*, La Jolla, CA, University Associates.

LUNDBERG, C.C. (1985) 'On the feasibility of cultural interventions in organizations' in FROST, P. *et al.* (Eds) *Organizational Culture*, Beverly Hill, Sage.

MARTIN, J. (1982) 'Can organizational culture be managed?', presented at the annual meeting of the Academy of Management, New York.

MORGAN, G. (1986) *Images of Organization*, Beverly Hills, CA, Sage Publications.

MUSELLA, D. and DAVIS, J. (1989) 'A method for defining the organizational culture of school systems', Paper presented at AERA, San Francisco, 29 March.

PERSONAL REPORT FOR THE EXECUTIVE (1987) 'Transforming corporate culture', New York, National Institute of Business Management, December 15.

PETERS, T. (1978) 'Symbols, patterns and settings: an optomistic case for getting things done', *Organizational Dynamics* **9**: 3–23.

PETERS, T.J. (1979) 'Symbols, patterns, and settings: An optimistic case for getting things done', *Organizational Dynamics*, 7, pp. 3–23.

PETERS, T. and WATERMAN, R.H. (1982) *In Search of Excellence*, New York, Harper and Row.

PFEFFER, J. (1981) 'Management as symbolic action: The creation and maintenance of organizational paradigms' in CUMMINGS, L.L. and STAW, B.M. (Eds) *Research in Organizational Behavior*, (Vol. 3), Greenwich, CT, JAI Press.

PURKEY, S. and SMITH, M.S. (1982) 'Too soon to cheer: Synthesis of research on effective schools', *Elementary School Journal*, 83, 4 pp. 427–52.

SAYLES, L.R. and WRIGHT, R. (1985) 'The use of culture in strategic management', *Issues and Observations,* Center for Creative Leadership, November, 5, 4.

Schein, E.H. (1985) *Organizational Culture and Leadership: A Dynamic View*, San Francisco, CA, Jossey-Bass.

Schwartz, H. and Davis, S.M. (1981) 'Matching corporate culture and business strategy', *Organizational Dynamics*, summer, pp. 30–48.

Smircich, Linda. (1985) 'Is the concept of culture a paradigm for understanding organizations and ourselves?' in Frost, P.J., Moore, L.F., Louis, M.R., Lundberg, C.C. and Martin, J. (Eds) *Organizational Culture,* Beverly Hills, CA, Sage Publications, pp. 55–72.

Smircich, L. and Morgan, G. (1982) 'Leadership: The management of meaning,' *Journal of Applied Behavioural Science*, 18, 3, pp. 257–73.

Smith, P.B. and Peterson, M.F. (1988) *Leadership, Organizations and Culture,* Beverly Hills, CA, Sage Publications.

Sproull, L.S. (1979) 'Beliefs in organizations,' in Nystrom, P. and Starbuck, W.H. (Eds) *Handbook of Organizational Design*, New York, Oxford University Press.

Tichy, N.M. (1983) *Managing Strategic Change: Technical, Political and Cultural Dynamics*, New York, Wiley.

Trice, H.M. and J.M. Beyer (1984) 'Studying organizational cultures through rites and ceremonials', *Academy of Management Review*, 9, pp. 653–69.

Turnstall, W.B. (1983) 'Cultural transition at AT&T', *Sloan Management Review*, 25, 1, pp. 1–12.

VanMaanen, J. and Barley, S.R. (1985) 'Cultural organization: Fragments of a theory' in Frost, P.J., Moore, L.F., Louis, M.R., Lundberg, C.C. and Martin, J. (Eds) *Organizational Culture*, Beverly Hills, CA, Sage Publications, pp. 31–54.

Wallace, A.F.C. (1970) *Culture and Personality*, (2nd edn). New York, Random House.

Weick, K. E. and Daft, R.L. (1983) 'The effectiveness of interpretation systems' in Cameron, K.S. and Whetten, D.A. (Eds) *Organizational Effectiveness: A Comparison of Multiple Models*, New York, Academic.

Wilkins, A.L. (1983) 'The cultural audit: A tool for understanding organizations,' in Pondy, L. *et al.* (Eds) *Organizational Symbolism*, Greenwich, CT, JAI.

Wilson, B.L. and Corbett, H.D. (1983) 'Organization and change: The effects of school linkages on the quantity of implementation', *Educational Administration Quarterly*, 19, 4, pp. 85–104.

Chapter 13

Conclusion: Preparation for Becoming a CEO

Kenneth Leithwood and Donald Musella

Reflecting on the first six months of his experience on the job, a beginning CEO commiserated with us, near the beginning of our research:

> I had no idea that becoming the (CEO) meant being 'married' to the board chairman. There is not a day goes by when I'm not talking to him. I get calls on Saturday, Sunday, at night — there is no time that I am not on the job.

The ten other beginning CEOs in the same meeting nodded agreement. Like novices in most new positions, these people found themselves preoccupied with a set of tasks which they would eventually come to view as routine and managerial in nature; Allison's data (chapter 2) show such CEO — chairperson contacts to be quite common for most CEOs. As they matured in their role, their preoccupations would shift to the more technically demanding and organizationally complex functions which they needed to perform in order to cope smoothly with the role. Such stages of development have been described for those in many professional roles (for example, Huberman, 1988, outlines such a developmental model for teachers) and Torbert (1987) has provided a seven-stage conception of managerial development. As in other such models, however, people in the highest stages of Toberts' model transcend technical concerns. They begin to appreciate the importance of interpersonal relations and politics. The thinking of such people is flexible and complex and they have developed, as Tobert notes:

> . . . a capacity to generate new orders or organizations. (They) realize that all frames through which the world is seen are relative (and they have developed) — the capacity to explore a developing situation while acting on the priority of highest apparent

> importance and, if appropriate, simultaneously inviting a reframing or restructuring. (in Quinn, 1988, p. 7)

From the available evidence it is reasonable to infer, however, that only a small proportion of CEOs reach the highest stages of development. Because of this, organizations often suffer from a lack of senior leadership potentially available to them. In this concluding chapter, we consider what preparation would assist CEOs to fully develop their leadership capacity. Although of considerable importance, as well, the question of how such preparation might be provided is beyond the scope of this chapter.

Our data for identifying what preparation would assist CEOs come primarily from four sources. In chapter 1, a prior study of CEO practices edited by Boich, Farquhar and Leithwood (1988) was mentioned as a predecessor to the present book. The final chapter of that study analyzed the future implications for CEOs of a selected number of prevalent social trends. They were trends toward (a) an information-based society; (b) an aging population; (c) increased cultural diversity; and (d) greater attention to equal rights. Conclusions from that analysis provide one set of data for the present chapter. A second set of data consists of implications drawn from the eleven previous chapters in this book. Third, Musella (1989) carried out a series of three studies inquiring about Ontario CEO preparation needs as perceived by senior school system administrators. In one of these studies, forty-three CEO aspirants were asked to identify successful and unsuccessful characteristics and behaviors of CEOs with whom they had worked. Thirty-five second-level administrators (Ontario's superintendents) and eighteen CEOs provided opinions, in a second study, about the content of programs designed to assist in the development of CEOs. Musella also reviewed the criteria used for the evaluation of CEOs by nine school systems.

A fourth source of information was a broad ranging review of literature by Leithwood and Jantzi (1988). Adopting a 'multi-level' perspective on school systems, empirical research was examined which addressed the contribution to student outcomes of selected classroom, school and school district characteristics.

Taken together, data from these four sources are quite extensive and, as well, acknowledge the importance of both current and future demands on CEOs as a basis for determining their preparation needs.

Preparation for What? The Chief Education Officer as Organizational Designer

As a framework for considering the preparation needs of CEOs, we adopted and further extended a conception of the CEO's role proposed by Leithwood, Farquhar and Boich (1988) — the CEO as organizational designer. An organizational designer has a comprehensive appreciation of those elements within the organization that contribute to achieving its purposes. In addition, the designer understands (or seeks to understand) the relationships among such elements and how changes in one element affect other elements. The work of the CEO as organizational designer is to continuously fine tune organizational elements so that they work in greater harmony to achieve (possibly dynamic) ends that are valued by both the organization's clients and members. The process involved in such fine tuning has been characterized by Jones and Leithwood (1989) as 'persistent, reflective problem solving' (p. 244) Of course, CEOs cannot accomplish such fine tuning by dint of personal effort alone. In particular, they require active support of elected officials and those other administrators with whom they have direct contact. Very little is known about how CEOs succeed in gaining support. Insights gained through research in a corporate context by Prahalad and Doz (1984) seem useful to explore, however. Results of this research suggest that CEOs work through key administrators to accomplish changes in their organizations' designs by 'management of the cognitive maps, the consensus process, and the balance of power' (p. 369) among those key administrators whose commitment is essential for implementing design changes.

This conception of CEOs' work attributes considerable importance to the ability to influence the thinking of other key individual administrators in the school systems. As well, it encompasses Hodgkinson's (1978) notion of generalism, discussed by Allison in chapter 2. As a generalist:

> (the CEO) is naturally more concerned with ends than means; with the broad co-ordination of effort, rather than handling of specific functions; with the future than the present, and with planning rather than reacting.

Allison cites evidence of these concerns in Ontario CEOs' efforts to integrate the three sectors of their work environment — the board, the school system and the community. Leithwood and Steinbach (chapter 6), as well as Allison (chapter 2), report efforts by CEOs to develop a broad picture of their systems and how they function. Townsend's (chapter 3) data indicate that the CEO's interactions with other groups in the organization often is for the purpose of helping those groups (including other key individual administrators) see the relationship between their activities and the activities of others so that both sets of activities can be developed harmoniously. Organizational work places considerable pressure on the CEO's ability to think abstractly. This ability becomes increasingly important, hypothesizes Allison (chapter 2), as the size of the CEO's organization becomes larger. But thinking abstractly is not enough. The CEO as organizational designer must be able to reshape the thinking of other key administrators in the direction of a shared vision of a preferred design for the school system.

Conceiving of the CEO's work as organizational design provides a useful basis from which to identify, in more detail, the preparation needs of CEOs. Indeed, even in the limited form developed to this point, such a conception signals the need for CEOs to:

- be able to integrate large amounts of information from a wide variety of sources
- be able to evaluate rapidly the relevance of that information for their own purposes
- be able to assist individuals and groups to see the relationship between their work and the work of others inside and outside the system
- detect sources of incoherence among components of the organization
- reshape organizational components in order to achieve greater coherence (or coherence to some optimum level which still acknowledges the importance of the stimulus for change to be found in diversity).

In addition to these skills, an organizational design conception of CEOs' work suggests the need to develop (or possess) several crucial dispositions:

- tolerance for the ambiguity inherent in a continuously evolving and dynamic system
- a willingness to persist at the design task over the protracted periods of time necessary to achieve substantial increases in organizational harmony or coherence. (Prahalad and Doz (1984) suggest that strategic redirection in a large corporation may take from two to eight years. Jones and Leithwood's 1989 data suggest comparable changes in school systems may take considerably longer).

Additional insights about CEO preparation depend, in part, on a more fully elaborated model of both the content and process of organizational design. Figure 13.1 visually represents the version of such a model which we use in the remainder of this chapter. The large box in the figure includes components of an organization which we considered to be central in understanding how school systems function. These components originated with Galbraith (1977) and subsequently have been adapted and

Figure 13.1 Components of a School System Organization and Relationships with CEOs' Processes and Practices and the External Environment

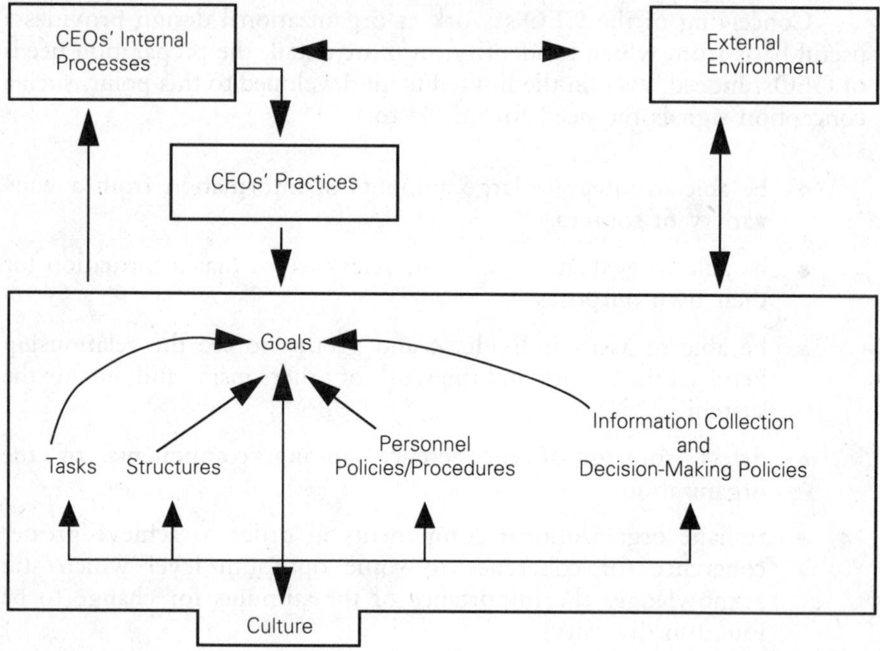

applied to help better understand school systems by Jones and Leithwood (1989), Leithwood (1988) and Leithwood and Jantzi (in press).

This model assumes that members of a school system are capable of holding collective goals for their students (which some would argue). Six highly interdependent elements of the school system account for the extent to which such goals, which may also change, are achieved. Each of these elements is considered an area of choice, controllable in varying degrees by members of the school system. There is, however, no single best array of choices within the six. Assuming the choice of tasks potentially capable of producing the goals, the likelihood of achieving the goals depends on the extent to which choices made within each element are mutually supportive (coherent); it also depends on how appropriate the choices are to the school system's size, stage of development, wider environment and educational 'technology'.

The model in figure 13.1 offers a set of categories for organizing information about CEO preparation needs. It also conceptualizes the relationships that exist among CEOs' internal processes and practices (the central focus of much of this book), components of the school system and the external environment (for example, the community 'sector' referred to in chapter 2). Put differently, whereas a good deal of the research reported in earlier chapters of this book clarified *how* CEOs think and act.

Figure 13.1 also suggest *what* it would be useful for them to think about and act on. A more detailed explanation of figure 13.1 will be provided throughout the remainder of the chapter. The main purpose for this chapter, however, is to identify significant examples of CEO preparation needs in relation to each component of the organization design model using the four sources of information discussed earlier (i.e., Musella, 1989; Leithwood, Farquhar and Boich, 1988; chapters in this book; and the Leithwood and Jantzi, 1988, review).

Each component of the organization identified in figure 13.1 will be addressed. This involves defining each component and justifying the claim that each component makes a potentially significant contribution to the effects school system's have on their clients. Whenever possible we adopt a multilevel perspective on the school system in presenting such justification: that is, we examine the contribution of each component as it is manifest at the classroom, school and system levels. Finally, based on such evidence, inferences are drawn with respect to the CEO's role as organizational designer and examples of what that means for preparation needs.

This is an ambitious strategy for identifying CEO preparation needs and we make no claim to have completed it in a comprehensive way. We do believe, however, that the range of preparation needs identified through our analysis provides a useful point of departure for further, more detailed efforts aimed at CEO preparation.

Organizational Culture

Organizational culture consists of the mechanisms of integration and coordination of a subjective and interpersonal nature. These mechanisms include patterns of behavior, usages of language, symbols, rites and rituals which serve to unite school system members and provide a unique identity (Schein, 1984). Such external manifestations of culture spring from shared norms, beliefs and values; they set implicit, if not explicit limits on organizational design choices members of the school system are prepared to consider.

System or district and school cultures impact on students to the extent that they influence the teaching culture and in turn that culture shapes the physical and social environment directly experienced by students. Some teaching cultures appear to make a much greater contribution to student growth than others. Traditional teaching cultures have been described by Feiman-Nemser and Floden (1986) in terms of norms of interaction with students, teachers, administrators and parents. Norms of authority and discipline along with a competing need for close personal bonds characterize teachers' interactions with students. Typical norms act to isolate teachers from asking their peers for, or offering to their peers, professional advice. Teachers, it has been said, have peers but no colleagues. School administrators are valued by teachers when they act as buffers from outside pressures and maintain school discipline, but not if they interfere in daily routines or instructional decisions. Parents are valued as supports for the teacher's plans and practices but are not expected to 'interfere' in those plans. As a whole, these traditional norms of interaction create a highly autonomous professional culture, one that is clearly adaptive under some conditions such as: traditional expectations for student outcomes; administrators unable to provide instructional leadership; little public interest in accountability and modest expectations for the contribution of schools to society with few external pressures for change; prevailing images of teaching as a craft (or art) based on limited technical know-how; and traditional contributions by the family to the development of students.

Since most of these conditions no longer prevail in many schools, it is not surprising to find evidence of a different teaching culture emerging, most notably in research on effective schools (for example, Little, 1982; Rosenholtz, 1986; Rutter *et al.*, 1979). The teaching culture of such schools is student centred and based on norms of interaction with students that are supportive and positive. While discipline is maintained it is obviously to serve the interests of learning rather than an end in its own right. Teachers have a shared, technical culture, built on norms of collegiality, collaborative planning and continuous improvement. Staff and the student body are cohesive and have a strong sense of community. There is a reciprocity between and among staff and students. Administrators are expected to offer instructional leadership and parents are considered co-partners in the education of students wherever possible. Such a culture appears to be adaptive to increasingly prevalent conditions, such as: new and more complex expectations for student outcomes; administrators able to provide instructional leadership; high expectations by the public for its schools and many associated, external pressures for change; a rapidly expanding body of technical know-how concerning instruction; and changing family environments. This culture is central to the 'second wave' of reform in the United States (for example, Bacharach, 1988). Gideonese (1988) characterizes it as a 'revolutionary transformation' in the teaching profession and Fullan and Connelly (1987) use it as the basis of their recommendations for reforming teaching education in Ontario.

While much less evidence is available concerning school district cultures, several recent studies suggest strong parallels between the culture of 'effective districts' and the culture of effective schools (Peterson, Murphy and Hallinger, 1987; Berman and McLaughlin, 1979; Wissler and Ortiz, 1988; Rozenholtz, 1987; Coleman and LaRocque, 1987). Furthermore, effective districts are not the 'organized anarchies' (Cohen, March and Olsen, 1976) or 'loosely coupled' systems (Meyer, Scott and Deal, 1983) depicted in research which is insensitive to variations in district effectiveness. On the contrary, curriculum and instructional decision-making in effective districts is carefully coordinated. In chapter 5, LaRocque and Coleman refine our understanding of the characteristics of effective district cultures and, in particular, show more clearly how effective CEOs are able to shape the district culture in ways that encourage the development of effective school and teaching cultures. These CEOs demonstrate, in multiple and persistent fashion, a strong commitment to a vision of what their organization should provide to students. When an ethos of service (and accountability) to clients thus developed is combined with norms of mutual respect for other members of the educational community, the CEO is able to negotiate a 'master contract' agreed to by all members of the organization to serve the vision. Such action on the part of the CEO presupposes a close knowledge of existing organizational culture, especially aspects of the culture in need of change. Townsend in chapter 3 focusses on one CEO's language for building an organizational culture and in chapter 12, Musella and Davis provide further specific advice about how such knowledge may be acquired. With respect to organizational culture, then, significant examples of CEO preparation needs include:

- being able to develop a clear vision of what the school system should provide to students and how such service can be delivered (see also Musella, 1988)
- being able to justify that vision with skills in argumentation;
- being able to diagnose the school system's existing norms values and beliefs
- being able to develop or refine organizational policies so that they are consistent with the preferred norms, values and beliefs of the school system
- being able to create an organizational ethos based on service to clients through interactions characterized by mutual respect and mutual influence.

This dimension of the CEO's work might be referred to as Normative or Cultural Leadership.

Organizational Goals

School systems are asked to address four broad goals: the provision of custodial care for children; assistance in maintaining or reforming existing social structures; assisting in the economic development of society; and the socialization and education of individual pupils. To help clarify CEO preparation needs in relation to this component of a school system's design, we focus on only the last of these goals, the goal for which the public is most demanding of its schools. What characteristics of this goal, in particular, have implications for CEO preparation? There are six such characteristics according to organization design theory: ambiguity, complexity, and breadth of the goals. Also important are the instability of any statement of goals over time as an adequate expression of what it means to be educated, uncertainty at any single point in time about the extent of public support for a given set of goals and the universality of goals. Why are these characteristics so critical to the success of a school system in contributing to student growth?

First, to claim that typical educational goals are ambiguous is to say that people may hold quite different understandings of what they mean. Such ambiguity has political advantages since people with different interests may see those interests potentially reflected in the goal, or at least not ruled out. But whereas agreeing on *what* to do sometimes is aided by goal ambiguity, deciding *how* best to accomplish the goal is severely hampered. The clarity that a school system is able to bring to its goals for students determines its success in identifying the tasks in which its members need to become skilled and to carry out.

Complexity is the second critical characteristic of a substantial portion of typical educational goals. Indeed as socially shared images of the educated person reflect the need to master increasingly complex skills, bodies of knowledge, social functions and the like, traditional educational goals (such as basic language skills) assume a subordinate, instrumental and supportive role. This is significant since it places demands on members of the school system not only to appreciate and agree on this more complex mission but also to master the new tasks required to succeed. The skills and knowledge on which these new tasks are based are often not part of the repertoire that can be assumed among a school system's professional members. A great deal of new learning on their part may be required. The new learning is of two types. One type involves expanding one's individual instructional repertoire. The second type involves altering the traditionally autonomous teaching culture, in the school particularly. Many of the more complex goals demand collective action. The criteria and standards used in the socialization and selection of new members may also need substantial revision. Hence the complexity of educational goals impacts not only on the tasks that members of the school system will have to carry out but also demands changes in the culture and personnel policies and procedures which support such tasks. Changes may also be required in traditional structures or forms of organization to facilitate the carrying out of new tasks.

The breadth of goals for school systems, especially in light of the other functions expected of such systems, is daunting. Responsibility for many of these goals traditionally has been shared by the family, the church and other social institutions. But schools are being asked to shoulder an increasing share of the responsibility as some of these institutions, most notably the family, undergo radical transformations. At the same time, schools are not receiving any larger share of society's resources for the task, nor do they seem well suited as they are presently structured, to address a sizeable portion of the goals. In order to avoid attempting more than they can possibly accomplish, school systems need to be able to clarify their purposes in relation to other social institutions and sometimes to assist those institutions in contributing to educational goals which they are better suited to help students achieve. School systems also need to define a manageable set of priorities on which to focus their efforts. These requirements are met through a school system's information collection and decision-making processes.

Two other characteristics of educational goals challenge the contribution of school systems to student learning through the demands they place on information collection and decision-making processes. As Leithwood, Farquhar and Boich (1988) note, changing social values (for example, equal opportunity for women) and changing demographic characteristics (for example, greater ethnic diversity) of the student population have eroded the consensus about goals of education that prevailed several decades ago. Indeed, in chapter 4, Holmes drew attention to the possible conflict between CEO goals and those of the groups which they serve. He raised questions about how suited were CEOs to pursue educational goals which they did not personally hold. Further, the speed of social and technological change now being experienced stimulates changes in prevailing social images of the educated person that are difficult for members of a school system to capture adequately (Leithwood, Farquhar and Boich, 1988). Since such images constitute the roots out of which educational goals grow, school systems have greater difficulty being sure their espoused goals will serve their students well in the future.

Universality is the final characteristic of educational goals to be considered. Sometimes this goal is expressed as equality of opportunity, usually meaning equality of access to educational resources. More recently however, universality has been interpreted as equality of access to the knowledge, skills and dispositions fostered by schools among those best served by schools. This interpretation has significant implications for the restructuring of schools — 'destreaming' of schools and classes being the currently most evident focus of restructuring — in efforts to address the needs of a far greater than usual proportion of young people.

Leaving aside the implications of these six characteristics of education goals for other elements of a school system's design, what CEO preparation needs are there with respect to such goals? It seems reasonable to claim, for example, that CEO's should:

- possess a robust philosophy of education themselves
- be able to assist school system stakeholders with diverse interests to find a common set of aspirations for their schools
- be able to assist in the identification of emerging and changing goals for the school system
- be able to help clarify their school system's goals and priorities (see also Musella, 1989)
- be able to persuade staff of the value of the more complex mission with which schools are now charged and the need to acquire the new practices required for such a mission.
- be able to design working environments which allow staff to develop mastery over the accomplishment of their more complex mission.

Leithwood, Farquhar and Boich (1988) refer to the CEO's work in relation to the goals component of school systems' designs as Ethical Leadership.

Tasks

In order to accomplish the goals of the school system, its members must carry out certain tasks. The tasks themselves are not central in decisions about organizational design, however. Rather, the design choice rests upon expected levels of task performance and the extent to which members of the school system view the tasks as uncertain, difficult to perform and diverse or variable. Different degrees of 'subjectively experienced' task complexity (if someone *thinks* the task is complex, it *is* complex) and different performance expectations create different demands within other elements of a school system's design. For example, as task uncertainty and complexity increase so, too, does the need for rigorous information collection and decision-making processes. High levels of task performance expectations also seem to require more discriminating personnel policies and procedures.

Our previous examination of the complexity of goals facing school systems now and in the foreseeable future suggests that many school system members are likely to believe that the tasks they are being asked to carry out to accomplish such goals are indeed difficult and uncertain. Expectations for the performance of teachers and principals have risen dramatically over the past fifteen years. Possessing managerial skill and 'running a smooth ship' was considered the apex of effective principal practice fifteen years ago, for example. Today, however, such practice is both assumed and subsumed within a much more demanding image of the principal as instructional leader.

What do these conditions of task uncertainty, diversity and difficulty signify for the preparation needs of CEOs? In particular, what qualities will CEOs need to possess or develop in order to exercise a positive influence on the 'technical core' of their systems — the tasks performed especially by school-based staff in delivering service to students? The response to this question appears to have two parts. One part concerns the CEO's influence on the technical core indirectly, through reshaping other components of the school system's design; for example, see the previous discussion of organizational culture. The other part of the response concerns means available to the CEO for directly influencing the technical core. In order to illustrate the nature of these means for direct influence, we consider two task categories which have unambiguous and substantial effects on student growth, as well as some future trends likely to impact on the technical core of the school systems. From these considerations, we identify examples of relevant CEO preparation needs.

One task category includes setting and communicating specific objectives for instruction. Clear objectives for instruction communicated by teachers provide students with an unambiguous basis on which to develop their own internalized objectives for learning. Evidence suggests that, when teachers stress some types of objectives rather than others (for example, recall vs. application), there tends to be a noticeable effect on what students learn (Arehart, 1979). Effective elementary and secondary schools achieve an unusually high degree of clarity about instructional objectives (tending to emphasize cognitive objectives). Such objectives are used for decision-making. They also provide a web of identification and affiliation which inspires loyalty to the school among staff and students (Leithwood and Batcher, 1988).

Procedures for setting and communicating board and school objectives help determine the certainty that school staffs have about what they are trying to accomplish at the classroom level. Evidence suggests that these procedures foster such certainty when school staffs participate in setting board objectives when the board specifies procedures to be used in clarifying school objectives and when senior administrators have a set of clear beliefs concerning such objectives (for example, Louis, 1987; Rosenholtz, 1989). Certainty regarding objectives is also fostered by clear and direct communication of district objectives to school staffs and support for such objectives by parents and the wider school community. A relatively stable policy environment and (as noted previously) coherence across policies in the objectives which such policies support increases certainty. District support for norms of risk-taking and professionalism in pursuit of such objectives also increases certainty.

A second task category concerns the forms of instruction used in the classroom. Variations in teachers' instructional practices account for a very high proportion of variance in student achievement (Walberg and Fowler, 1987; Walberg, 1984). Peterson, Murphy and Hallinger's (1987) study of twelve effective school districts found that the majority of these districts prescribed a preferred model of instruction. This model, based on considerable research conducted in the 1970s and early 80s, increased the focus and specificity of teacher selection and training, eased principals' supervision problems and increased the likelihood of feedback to teachers about their instruction. Used in this way, such model prescription provides considerable direct control over teacher practices. And the specific model chosen in these districts (apparently some version of direct instruction) seems likely to increase achievement of basic skills. But this instructional model is also likely to restrict the types of student outcomes accomplished in the classroom. Indeed, as Resnick (Brandt, 1988-1989) points out, some features of this model conflict with the goal of teaching thinking. Districts wishing to exercise direct control over instructional practices through policy, therefore, would contribute more successfully to the full set of outcomes they are likely to hold by taking a different approach. That approach involves focusing such policy on teachers' acquisition of a large repertoire of instructional models and the skills required to match models in that repertoire to the particular instructional goals, students and other aspects of the contexts which they face.

Effective schools are reported to stress carefully planned instruction (Leithwood and Batcher, 1988). This means: a limited focus within a single lesson; actively structured and directed classroom activities; establishment of a clear framework for pursuing sub-themes and small group or individual activities; emphasizing opportunities for competence and achievement; and provision of diverse experiences for students. Specific teacher-student interactions reflect defensible learning principles including clear communication of goals; promotion of extensive interaction in class; use of factual questions to establish a foundation followed by higher order questions requiring more interpretation; and efforts to keep discussions concrete and to demonstrate the relevance of curriculum material to the everyday world of students.

Finally, Leithwood, Farquhar and Boich (1988) examined how a selected set of social trends are likely to impact school systems and CEOs in the future. They suggested that the combined effects of an increasingly information-based society, an aging population, increased cultural diversity and greater attention to equal rights will place four demands on tasks required at the technical core of schools. These are demands for greater efficiency in the delivery of instruction, more flexible forms of instruction, greater client control over the choice of instruction and the elimination of discriminatory instructional practices (for example, practices which may conflict with the values or norms of behavior held by a particular social, religious or ethnic group). Responding to these demands will require school systems to improve their capacity in assessing both the cost-effectiveness and social acceptability of instructional methods. School systems will also have to provide a political environment which respects the choice of such methods using procedures sufficiently systematic and rational to prevent excessive conflict.

Based on such considerations, important examples of CEO preparation needs in relation to the task component of the school system's design include being able:

- to develop systematic, relatively rational procedures for determining preferred practices at the technical core of their systems
- to marshall support among different stakeholders' groups to adhere to such systematic rational procedures
- to devise means for clearly communicating preferred practices to all those who are responsible for their implementation
- to establish a reasonably stable policy environment in support of the preferred practices.

Leithwood, Farquhar and Boich (1988) have referred to this dimension of the CEO's role as Technical Leadership.

Organizational Structure

Organizational structure involves choices concerning size, the division of labor and ways in which the activities undertaken by different members of the school system will be coordinated. Decisions about structure also include choices about how power will be distributed in the school system (for example, degrees of centralization/decentralization) and how people will be grouped to carry out their work (for example, departments, divisions). To evaluate CEO preparation needs in relation to this component of a school system's design we first review research evidence bearing on questions of optimum size and organization. Then we consider the likely impact on structure of the four social trends examined by Leithwood, Farquhar and Boich (1988).

With respect to organizational size, smaller is definitely better. This is the case for districts, schools and classes. Smaller school districts, defined in terms of student enrolment have consistently outperformed larger school districts, when other relevant variables such as student socioeconomic status (SES) are taken into account (Walberg and Fowler, 1987). The reason for these findings, it is speculated, is the effect of smaller size on variables mediating student learning: greater district awareness of community preferences, less administrative complexity, greater teacher involvement in decision-making and closer home-school relations. In chapter 2, Allison identifies significant implications for CEOs' work of the size of their school systems including the likelihood that CEOs of smaller systems remain more directly involved in decisions about the technical core of their systems. Considerable evidence also suggests that smaller schools contribute more than larger schools to important aspects of student learning (Haller and Monk, 1988; Hamilton, 1983). In addition to the reasons for greater effects by small districts, smaller schools are believed to foster greater student participation in extracurricular activity, better self concept and lower levels of alienation. They also tend to function in a more collegial manner.

Similar results are found in research on class size (Glass and Smith, 1979; Hedges and Stock, 1983) in that smaller classes generally lead to higher achievement than larger classes. This relationship is stronger in elementary than in secondary schools but appears not to differ across school subjects or among students of different ability levels. Between class sizes of forty and one lie more than thirty percentile ranks of achievement (for example, a student normally at the fiftieth percentile on an achievement test in a class of forty would be at least at the eightieth percentile in a class of one). Class size differences at the low end (between one and ten students, for instance) have quite large effects on achievement. Differences at the high end (20 vs. 40 students, say) have very small effects that are probably educationally insignificant. These results present a strong case for small class sizes, while, at the same time, raising serious questions about the likely advantage of lowering class-sizes within the parameters that are normally practical.

A negative relationship has been reported between district financial resources, however measured, and student outcomes, once district size and SES are taken into account! Nor does there appear to be a significant relationship between student outcomes and specific spending on such things as class size reductions (within a feasible range), physical facilities, teacher salaries, library facilities and the like. Walberg and Fowler (1987) explain these results by pointing to the large corpus of studies in educational psychology supporting the view that what teachers do determines how much students learn and that some behaviors contribute much more than others to such learning. Coleman (1986) extends this basic argument beyond teachers in suggesting that high achieving boards have a 'norm of frugality' (p. 519) and a focus on instructional improvement that reduces their tendency to spend money on unnecessary administrative staff or ineffective but costly organizational policies.

Little evidence is available concerning the effects of district-level organization on student learning. However, in a study of variables influencing the implementation and continuation of curricular innovations, Rosenblum and Louis (1981) suggested that:

> In general, the more a district's schools were isolated from each other and from the district office, the less densely populated the district was — the lower the district scored on our implementation and continuation measures. (p. 237)

Effects of these variables were explained in terms of the difficulty in developing coordinated, homogeneous action among widely dispersed schools.

At the school level, decisions concerning the allocation of students to teachers, the between-class grouping of students and team teaching have been shown to affect student learning. Modest research support is available for the positive effects on students of appropriately matching teachers' preferred instructional methods with students' preferred learning styles (Hunt, 1981). Such effects arise from individual differences in the way students learn. Because of these differences, a student is likely to have greater aptitude for learning from one instructional method than from another. Most teachers are predisposed toward a restricted range of preferred methods and such preferences are relatively resistant to change. Hence, it makes sense to maximize the congruence between teachers' preferred instructional methods and students' learning styles when assigning students to teachers.

A great deal of evidence is available concerning the effects on students of a particular type of between-class grouping. Such grouping, variously referred to as tracking or streaming is standard practice in the vast majority of North American schools (Goodlad, 1984). It is usually based on academic ability and aims at greater homogeneity of such ability within classes. While there are many reasons for homogeneous, between-class grouping, as Dar (1985) points out, fostering student growth is not one of them. Such grouping has negative effects on the intellectual and social growth of students in the lower tracks and also perpetuates cultural, ethnic and social divisions. The reasons appear to include, for example, slower pace of instruction, concentrations of behavior problems, low morale, student norms which do not value learning and absence of appropriate academic role models (Kulik and Kulik, 1982; Slavin, 1984). The domination of homogeneous, between-class grouping policies has had such a powerful effect on especially secondary school programs, cultures and stuctures that 'destreaming' now constitutes a major problem for which there are few successful solutions available.

At the classroom level, within-class mixed-ability groupings have been shown to be of some advantage to low-ability students in some subjects, perhaps due to the faster pace of instruction, which they experience as teachers attempt to keep their pace similar to progress of other students within the class (Slavin and Karweit, 1985). Although some evidence shows that within-class tracking leads to favorable outcomes there are many studies that reveal negative effects similar to those associated with between-class grouping practices.

Research on team teaching suggests that this method of organizing teachers within the school has positive effects on student outcomes. In summarizing this evidence, Rosenholtz (1989) describes team teaching as:

> a vehicle for greater instructional interaction, as teachers discussed and challenged each other's ideas about students, grouping arrangements, the curriculum, and classroom management. Unlike isolated settings, work arrangements and communications in team teaching related directly to the nature of instruction; teachers held greater decision-making rights, collaborated more with principals about those decisions and markedly increased their own exchange of advice and assistance. (p. 45)

Through an examination of the four prominent social trends discussed previously, Leithwood, Farquhar and Boich (1988) predict several likely changes to the structure of school systems. School systems, they suggest, are likely to become structurally more diverse: this seems likely given, for example, the ease of access to information and the need to address equal rights concerns. School systems may also decentralize more of their decision making also because of ease of access to information (Lawton and Scane, chapter 11, offer additional reasons for this trend). Efforts to engage an aging population may require school systems to collaborate more with other agencies and to become more market oriented. And increased cultural, religious and other forms of social diversity seem likely to result in schools with less heterogeneous student populations as each group strives to protect itself from assimilation in the mainstream.

Significant examples of CEO preparation needs implicated in this examination of organization structure are fourfold. The CEO should:

- know about alternative organizational structures at the district, school and within school levels (assuming such 'levels' are appropriate)
- be able to locate, or help staff locate information about the consequences of implementing each of these structural alternatives
- be able to assist staff in choosing or creating structures which facilitate the achievement of organization goals and reflect demands placed on the system by significant social trends
- be able to assess or help staff assess the value of existing organizational structures in contributing to organizational goals.

Leithwood, Farquhar and Boich (1988) label this dimension of the CEO's work as Managerial Leadership.

Personnel Characteristics, Policies and Procedures

In this section we are initially concerned with the amount and nature of contribution made to the achievement of a school system's goals by the background characteristics of staff and students as well as policies and procedures directly governing their practices. We then consider how the CEO may act, as a designer, in relation to these elements of the organization and the preparation needs that such actions imply.

Background Characteristics

Personnel background characteristics include factors potentially influencing behavior. Age, experience and socioeconomic status are examples of such characteristics. With respect to these characteristics of staff, our attention is limited to principals and teachers. A relatively large amount of evidence supports the claim that school principals are able to have significant impact on students' acquisition of basic skills, attitudes toward school, absenteeism, vandalism, retention in school and possibly other outcomes, as well (Leithwood, 1988). Such impact, however, results from particular patterns of practice that have come to be labelled 'instructional leadership'. These patterns of practice are characteristic of a growing number of principals, but still the minority in North America. Background characteristics of principals affect student outcomes through their influence on the patterns of practice in which principals engage. Evidence suggests that the probability of instructional leadership is greater among those with longer classroom experience prior to the role and a more nurturing attitude toward students. Both characteristics are more likely among female than male principals, at present. Instructional leadership is also associated with: greater formal education, as well as specific curriculum or policy-related knowledge; adequate on-the-job training as a vice principal; and openmindedness. Age and length of experience in the role does not appear to be related to instructional leadership (Leithwood, 1988; Salley, McPherson and Baehr, 1978).

One characteristic of teachers which affects student learning is experience. More experienced teachers appear to have greater inputs on student achievement than their less experienced peers. More experienced teachers have been associated with increases in the number of secondary school students that have been successful in passing state examinations as well as elementary student gains in basic skills achievement. There is likely a ceiling on this effect, and some evidence suggests that it varies with student ability level. Centra and Potter's (1980) review, for example, concluded that high ability students benefit most from more experienced teachers. Low ability students appear to benefit more from the fresh enthusiasm of relatively new, inexperienced teachers.

Some staff may well be suited to some instructional assignments than others. For example, the tendency of junior high school students (11 to 14 years) to form cliques in class and sometimes to be more antagonistic toward each other has been observed. This observation has led to the recommendation that teachers of such students should possess special skills in coping with negative affect and diffusing friction in the class.

Higher social class, greater education, both general and professional, and higher verbal achievement are other teacher background characteristics known to affect students. An intuitively plausible link exists between teacher performance in the classroom and all but the first of these variables; this supports the 'common-sense' claim that teacher characteristics influence student behavior and learning only as they affect teaching performance (Centra and Potter, 1980).

Student characteristics influencing what they learn are of two sorts: socioeconomic status (SES) and attitudes. With respect to SES, as it is usually measured, high levels of student achievement are strongly correlated with higher parental occupational status, greater numbers of family possessions, more years of parental schooling, more ambitious educational aspirations on the part of parents for their children and fewer people living in the home. Student attitudes, in particular, high locus of control, self concept and academic aspirations also explain a significant amount of achievement variance (Glasman and Biniaminov, 1981; Monk, 1980; Centra and Potter, 1980). In fact, it has been suggested, that attitudes are stronger determinants at least of verbal achievement than is SES (Monk, 1980). It is likely more meaningful, however, to consider students' SES and attitudes as highly interdependent.

Student characteristics are usually treated as highly stable 'givens' and the relationship to decisions about the organization of schools or school boards is not considered. James Coleman's (1987) concept of 'social capital', however, offers considerable promise in better appreciating that relationship. Building on this concept, SES, as it is normally measured seems likely to be a (somewhat misleading) proxy for the quality of contributions made by traditional families and communities to the socialization of children. These contributions Coleman describes as attitudes (for example, locus of control), effort (for example, academic aspirations) and self concept, contributions requiring the close, intimate and persistent environment available in the stable 'traditional' community around the school and the 'traditional' family. When such contributions or social capital are available, children are better able to take advantage of the contributions typically associated with schools. Coleman characterizes these school contributions as opportunities, demands and rewards. The problem of concern to Coleman is a policy or a school system redesign problem: how best to respond to the erosion of the social capital available to children as a consequence of significant community and family changes. Considered in these terms, it seems evident that the effects of a school system on student learning are highly dependent on student background characteristics. But such characteristics, while not easily changed, need not be considered insurmountable barriers when they limit student outcomes. As Hawley (1988) suggests, restructuring the relationship between schools and families may be an appropriate goal for school redesign (for example, involving parents more in their childrens' education and strengthening families). Such a goal takes on added significance when the effects on schools of the trend toward greater multicultural diversity is considered (Leithwood, Farquhar and Boich, 1988). Many school systems currently serving such diverse populations have long since discovered the value of such strengthened relationships for ensuring appropriate services to their students.

Personnel Policies and Procedures

Personnel policies and procedures encompass activities for socializing, selecting and promoting, training, and supervising and evaluating staff. These policies and procedures have, at their core, a set of decisions about the criteria to be used in selecting, transferring, compensating, promoting and developing members of the school system. Central determinants of such criteria are the tasks people are to perform and levels of expected performance. What is the contribution of these policies and procedures to student growth? Available research does not permit a comprehensive answer to this question; that is, an assessment of the impact of each set of policies at each level of the school system. As a consequence, we illustrate the probable nature and extent of impact, using the most reliable of the evidence available.

Personnel policies and procedures affect students indirectly to the extent that they shape the practices of teachers and administrators. In general, such policies and procedures are still in a relatively primitive state in most school systems, as compared with their state in other, mature organizations (Leithwood, 1989). Their impact on students is usually minimal and in some cases negative.

Few school systems give explicit, systematic attention to the socialization of their members. Yet most of the superintendents' preparation for the role appears to be a function of such socialization (Crowson, 1987). Further, the values and dispositions requisite to the adoption of an instructional leadership image of the role by principals depend primarily on the nature of their socialization experiences prior to being in the role

(Leithwood, 1988). And, as Lortie (1975) has pointed out, the individualistic nature of most teachers' socialization lays the base for traditional, intuitive approaches to teaching — approaches antithetical to the norms of collegiality found in effective schools. Based on recent research on principals (Leithwood, Steinbach and Begley, in press), socialization appears to shape practices in ways most likely to foster student learning when the person receives active, sustained encouragement to enter a role, many opportunities to exercise on-the-job leadership, continuous feedback and support once in the role and is exposed to models of effective practice. Opportunities for interaction with a network of peers concerning the substance of the job and support by a mentor are also features of 'good' socialization. School boards contribute to such socialization, as well, by consistently reinforcing and rewarding merit.

Evidence suggests that typical selection and promotion policies and procedures are fraught with features which seriously jeopardize the likelihood of their actually identifying candidates most likely to contribute to student growth. Data concerning such policies and procedures as they relate to principals, for example, (for example, Baltzell and Dentler, 1983; Morgan, Hall and MacKay, 1983: Musella and Lawton, 1986) identify absence of explicit policy, the use of unwarranted criteria and unreliable evidence among their major limitations. When such limitations have been addressed, selection and promotion processes are perceived to be fair and to identify the most important candidates.

Supervision and evaluation of principals has been the subject of little research and has not received much attention by school systems until quite recently (Peterson, 1986). Where this function is performed well, however, the majority of principals report being influenced by it (Lawton *et al.*, 1988). In this context 'well' means: 'the use of criteria which are clearly defined and relevant to instructional improvement; focus on coordination of classroom, school and district goals; provision of on-going feedback', and active involvement of the superintendent (Cousins, 1988; Murphy, Hallinger and Peterson, 1985).

With respect to teachers, Rosenholtz (1987) in summarizing effective supervision and evaluation practices, claims that student achievement is influenced by teachers' certainty about their practices and the behavior resulting from such certainty. This certainty, in turn, is developed by a form of teacher evaluation by principals that she terms 'active monitoring'. Such monitoring involves the provision of clear guidelines for what teachers are to emphasize and frequent observation and feedback. Such monitoring also involves well understood, valid criteria; and the speedy provision of any needed assistance uncovered through the evaluation.

It seems clear from our examination of personal background characteristics, policies and procedures that this element of most school systems has received less attention than it deserves. Furthermore, the CEO has an especially crucial role to play concerning this element since few others in the organization are likely to have the formal authority to act. With respect to preparation needs, therefore, it is reasonable to claim that the CEO should:

- know about the characteristics of effective policies and procedures for selecting and placing as well as evaluating and supervising staff
- be able to develop and implement such policies and procedures through processes that encourage their widespread acceptance among staff
- be able to monitor the consequences of such policies and procedures, refining them as evidence warrants
- be able to provide socialization experiences to staff which contribute significantly to their development
- be able to work effectively with the school community in order to optimize the combined contributions to student growth of the family and the school.

This dimension of the CEOs work was referred to by Leithwood, Farquhar and Boich (1989) as Leadership in the Empowerment of Others.

Information Collection and Decision-making Processes

Decision mechanisms and the degree of formalization of data to be used are part of the design element labelled 'information collection and decision-making processes'. Also included is the scope of the data base, the frequency with which information is collected and the decision taken based on such information. A central assumption of our organizational design framework is that many design decisions and much organizational activity can be effectively carried out through rational processes. Information collection and decision-making processes need to become more systematic as tasks become more uncertain and as school systems become larger and more mature.

Information Collection

Information collection is a standard part of what school systems do. In a non-standard way, the CEO in Townsend's portrait (chapter 3) bypassed his bureaucracy's hierarchy to seek out data informally across the system. But the extent to which this function contributes to student learning depends on the quality and the amount of such information and its relationship to those aspects of the system which impact most directly on students. The impact of information collection also depends on its eventual use. Whether at the district, school or classroom levels, information collection has its greatest impact when effects are made to collect adequate amounts of valid information about both 'inputs' (for example, staff performance) and 'outputs' (for example, student achievement) and to use that information in formative ways; that is, to help decide how to do things better in the future.

Research on effective school systems reveals a commitment to the collection of information about principal and teacher performance as well as the extent to which school and classroom goals are consistent with school system goals. Teachers are monitored in order to assist in more skillful implementation of district-endorsed instructional practices. Principals are monitored in order to improve their skills in assisting teachers. Student achievement data are usually part of the data base for evaluating staff. Effective districts establish quite precise and explicit performance expectations for students and staff, as we have already noted.

Effective schools research identifies some systematic methods for frequent monitoring of students' classroom progress as a conspicuous part of what effective schools do. This practice is largely missing from less effective schools. Multiple methods for collecting data are used by teachers in effective schools. These include, for example, teacher-made tests, samples of student work, mastery skills check lists, criterion-referenced tests, and norm-referenced tests. 'Spot checks' often are made of student assignments, and the marking of homework is common. While the recording and managing of such data presents a potentially major drain on teachers' time, effective schools help teachers keep such time to a minimum. Sometimes a school computer is used for this purpose.

All teachers collect information about students in less systematic, more spontaneous ways, as well. But more effective teachers are more sensitive to the moment-by-moment cues available to them as students respond to classroom events. Teachers who are more 'with-it' in this sense are better able to make meaningful adjustments in their responses to students as instruction proceeds.

Two major purposes are served by the data collected and recorded by effective teachers. Instructional planning and revision by the teacher is one purpose. Such data indicate to teachers how much progress has been made, where remediation is required, and how appropriate is the pace of instruction. The clarity and specificity of the teacher's instructional objectives are central determinants of just how valuable frequently collected data are for purposes of instructional planning. Reinforcement of student learning is a second purpose. This is the use about which the bulk of available research is concerned, a concern fostered by findings which consistently show extremely large effects of reinforcement on student achievement.

Decision-making Processes

Research on effective districts, in particular, suggests considerable involvement of school staffs and 'experts' in system-level decision-making. Involvement or participation of this sort is both recommended and rationalized by LaRocque and Coleman's (chapter 5) consensual norms for decision-making in effective districts. Musella and Leithwood (chapter 4) uncovered a strong desire by school system personnel to participate more fully in decisions many CEOs reserve for themselves. And respondents to Musella's (1989) survey identified delegation as an important skill for CEOs to possess. In effective school systems, such delegation usually occurs within a strong, centrally developed framework which may take the form of a strategic plan. Feedback channels are developed which permit central coordination, monitoring, and long term planning activities.

Decision-making in effective schools parallels the description of effective boards. That is, teachers are involved in school-level policy decisions often including, for example, the assignment of students to classes. Effective schools have considerable school-level discretion for determining the means to be used in addressing problems of increasing academic performance. As McNeil's (1986) study points out, for example, effective secondary schools are not primarily organized and managed to keep them running smoothly, although they do tend to run smoothly. Such schools are organized and managed to support the purposes of the curriculum and the requirements for instruction implied by the school's philosophy of education.

What is reasonable to infer from these data regarding the preparation needs of CEOs? CEOs, we suggest, should:

- develop a strong commitment to the systematic collection and use, by themselves and other staff, of appropriate information about all significant aspects of their school system's functioning
- be able to develop and implement effective procedures, informal and formal, for the collection and use of appropriate information
- be able to use a wide range of decision-making procedures and know how to select those procedures best suited to the task and the setting
- develop a strong commitment to consensual and participative forms of decision-making where possible.

Leithwood, Farquhar and Boich (1988) refer to this dimension of the CEO's work as Reflective Leadership.

Conclusion

In considering the preparation needs of CEOs we have argued, in this chapter, for the usefulness of conceptualizing the work of the CEO as an organizational designer. In order to clarify specific examples of such preparation needs each of seven components of a school system's design were examined. Evidence was presented for the contribution of each component to student growth, either directly or indirectly. Inferences were drawn from this evidence about the skills, knowledges and dispositions to be developed by effective CEOs. Such inferences at least exemplified the character and range of objectives that would serve as an appropriate direction for systematic CEO preparation opportunities.

This conceptualization is not the only one that could have been adopted. Some would argue that in seeking a good leader with a clear vision, a school board should not anticipate that the person they choose will be either skilled or interested in all aspects of school administration and management. This counter argument would favour a diversity of leadership styles and foci, rather than an attempt to turn all CEOs towards some idealized role description. Thus Holmes (chapter 10) envisages a CEO of the future as being prepared to head an organization offering a variety of educational opportunities and thrusts, with only some of which the CEO would be likely to be personally engaged. Analogously, one CEO might be particularly strong on financial management, another in the arts, another in instruction in the basic skills. Every CEO would choose staff to complement rather than reflect his/her own competencies. By this view, the idea that one can train people on the basis of a model of an ideal leader is misguided and may lead to a similarly-minded set of consensual supervisory officers who will be ignorant of history and unable to imagine futures. By this alternative account, CEOs should be expected to be widely read, well aware of positions different from their own and should have strong backgrounds academically and in experience.

The view taken in this chapter, however, is that the CEO should be prepared to deal with the characteristic responsibilities and problems of the approved role description.

An organization design perspective on the role, like any other perspective that might have been adopted, highlights some important aspects of the CEO's work and casts shadows on others. Our perspective has not, for example had much to say explicitly about such matters as the CEO's interpersonal and communication skills or relationships with trustees. Attention has not been paid to the other side of that coin, trustees' respectives of CEOs (on this, see, for instance, Townsend, 1988). Nor has much been said about the demands on CEOs to acquire, maintain and manage their systems' fiscal resources. These are obviously important aspects of the job, especially in the minds of those anticipating entry into the role (Musella, 1989). While we do not deny that this is so, we believe that issues of design which take achievement of organizational goals seriously and require attention to organizational harmony and coherence have been seriously underestimated in importance, if not largely overlooked by most to date. And yet signs of the debilitating effects on school systems of incoherence are everywhere: achievement tests fail to cohere with valued curriculum policies; personnel selection criteria are discordant with personnel evaluation criteria; staff development objectives are unrelated to the new tasks staff are being asked to perform; budget allocations are unrelated to program priorities . . . the list seems endless. And, as Jones and Leithwood (1989) claim, the best single explanation for the failure of school systems to institutionalize promising new practices is the inattention given to redesigning key components of the system so they support rather than kill off efforts to continue such practices. For all these reasons we are convinced that the needs of CEOs, inferred through the analyses in this chapter, warrant the attention of anyone seriously interested in CEO preparation.

This chapter would be incomplete unless we addressed, at least briefly, the problem of how the preparation needs which have been identified could be delivered. In chapter 1, we acknowledged the absence of opportunities for CEOs to systematically prepare themselves for their roles, either before entering the role or during the course of living out the role. There are several simple explanations for this state of affairs. As we also pointed out in chapter 1, the formal knowledge base regarding the role is meagre, at best. This has made it difficult to build systematic preparation opportunities, the validity of which could be defended with confidence. But there is also an economic explanation for the current state of affairs. In contrast to teachers and school principals, for example, there are very few CEOs in any given jurisdiction — a province or a state, for example — and there is only one per school system. So the most common strategy for funding professional preparation opportunities, recovering at least a significant portion of the costs directly from the client, results in a prohibitive price tag for the service. Program development, implementation and evaluation costs, for example, remain constant whatever the size of the client base, but there are relatively few CEOs to share the burden. Indeed the size of the 'market' is one plausible explanation for the lack of research about CEOs. Those who do research require an audience for the results of their work. The potential audience for CEO research is not only relatively small but, just as significant, not one likely to consume its products through such traditional vehicles as graduate university courses. This is a significant disincentive for university-based researchers who typically use their on-going research activities to inform and enrich their teaching. In any event, constraints surrounding graduate instruction are shockingly discordant with the work patterns, interests and incentives of CEOs and those in immediately preceding roles. If CEO preparation is to be pursued successfully through graduate instruction, it will need to be dramatically restructured.

Any promising vehicle for stimulating development of knowledge about the CEOs role and the systematic preparation of CEOs would have to solve these two problems, in our view: small market size and the incompatibility of delivery mechanisms with the work patterns, interests and incentives of aspiring and incumbent CEOs. As the beginning of a response to these problems, it may be useful to consider the establishment of an organizational structure with broad jurisdictional responsibilities. In Canada, for example, a centre for leadership development with a national mandate seems like a promising part of the solution. Such a centre is likely to be able to attract the critical mass of resources and clients necessary to carry out the research and offer the sort of preparatory experiences which the contribution of the CEO's role to the quality of education received by the country's young people deserves.

References

AREHART, J.E. (1979) 'Student opportunities to learn related to student achievement of objectives in a probability unit'. *Journal of Educational Research*, 72, pp. 253–59.

BACHARACH, S. (1988) 'Four themes of reform: An editorial Essay', *Educational Administration Quarterly*, 24, pp. 484–96.

BALTZELL, D.C. and DENTLER, R.A. (1983) *Selecting American School Principals: A Sourcebook for Educators*. Washington, DC, Abt Associates Inc.

BERMAN, P. and MCLAUGHLIN, M.W. (1979) *An Exploratory Study of School District Adaptation*, Santa Monica, CA, Rand Corporation.

BOICH, J., FARQUHAR, R. LEITHWOOD, K. (1988) (Eds) *The Canadian School Superintendent*, Toronto, OISE Press.

BRANDT, R. (1988–89) 'On learning research: A conversation with Lauren Resnick', *Educational Leadership*, 46, 4, pp. 12–16.

CENTRA, J.A. and POTTER, D.A. (1980). 'School and teacher effects: An interrelational model. *Review of Educational Research*, 50, 2, pp. 273–91.

COHEN, M.D., MARCH, J.G. and OLSEN, J.P. (1976) 'A garbage can model of organizational choice', *Administrative Science Quarterly*, 17, pp. 1–25.

COLEMAN, J. (1987) 'Families and schools', *American Educational Research Journal*, 16, 6, pp. 32–8.

COLEMAN, P. (1986) 'School districts and student achievement in British Columbia: A preliminary analysis'. *Canadian Journal of Education*, 11, 4, pp. 509–21.

Coleman, P. and LaRocque, L. (1987) *Reaching Out: Instructional Leadership in School Districts*, mimeo Vancouver, Simon Fraser University.

Cousins, B. (1988) 'Factors influencing knowledge utilization: Principals' use of appraisal data concerning their own performance', unpublished dissertation, University of Toronto.

Crowson, R.L. (1987) 'The local school district superintendency: A puzzling administrative role', *Educational Administration Quarterly*, 23, 3, pp. 49–69.

Dar, Y.(1985) 'Teacher attitudes toward ability grouping: Educational considerations and social organizational influences, *Interchange*, 16, 2, pp. 17–28.

Fieman-Nemser, S. and Floden, R.E. (1986) 'The cultures of teaching' in Wittrock, M. (Ed.) *Handbook of Research on Teaching*, New York, Macmillan.

Fullan, M. and Connelly, F.M. (1987) *Teacher Education in Ontario: Current Practices and Options for the Future*, Toronto, Ministry of Education and Ministry of Colleges and Universities, Ontario.

Galbraith, J.R. (1977) *Organizational Design*, Reading, MA, Addison-Wesley.

Gideonese, H.D. (1988) 'Practitioner-oriented inquiry by teachers: Meaning, justification and implications for school structure, *Journal of Curriculum and Supervision*, 4, 1, pp. 65–76.

Glasman, N.S. and Biniaminov, I. (1981) 'input-output analysis of schools', *Review of Educational Research*, 51, 4, pp. 509–40.

Glass, G.V. and Smith, M.L. (1979) 'Meta-analysis of research on class size and achievement', *Educational Evaluation and Policy Analysis*, 1, pp. 2–16.

Goodlad, J.I. (1984) *A Place Called School: Prospects for the Future*, New York, McGraw-Hill.

Haller, E.J. and Monk, D.H. (1988) 'New reforms, old reforms and the consolidation of small rural schools', *Educational Administration Quarterly*, 24, 4, pp. 470–83.

Hamilton, S.F. (1983) 'The social side of schooling: Ecological studies of classrooms and schools', *Elementary School Journal*, 83, pp. 313–34.

Hawley, W. (1988) 'Missing pieces of educational reform agenda: Or why the first and second waves may miss the boat', *Educational Administration Quarterly*, 24, 4, pp. 416–37.

Hedges, L.V. and Stock, W. (1983) 'The effects of class size: An examination of rival hypotheses', *American Educational Research Journal*, 20, 1, pp. 63–85.

Hodgkinson, C. (1978) *Toward a Philosophy of Administration*, Oxford, Basil Blackwell.

Huberman, M. (1988) 'Teacher careers and school improvement', *Journal of Curriculum Studies*, 20, 2, pp. 119–32.

Hunt, D.E. (1981) 'Teachers' adaptation: "Reading" and "flexing" to students' in Joyce, B.R. *et al.* (Eds) *Flexibility in Teaching*, New York, Longman.

Jones, L.B. and Leithwood, K.A. (1989) 'Draining the swamp: A case study of school system design', *Canadian Journal of Education*, 14, 2, pp. 242–60.

Kulik, C. and Kulik, J. (1982) 'Effects of ability grouping on secondary school students: A meta-analysis of evaluation findings', *American Educational Research Journal*, 19, 3, pp. 415–28.

Lawton, S.B., Leithwood, K.A., Batcher, E., Donaldson, E. and Stewart, R. (1988) *Student Retention and Transition*, Toronto, Ministry of Education.

Leithwood, K.A. (1988) 'The nature, causes and consequences of what principals do: A framework for research and review of recent literature', Paper presented at the Annual Meeting of the American Educational Research Association, New Orleans.

LEITHWOOD, K.A. (1989) '*School system policies for effective school administration*' in HOLMES, M., LEITHWOOD, K. and MUSELLA, D. (Eds) *School Policies for Effective Schools*, Toronto, OISE Press.

LEITHWOOD, K.A. and BATCHER, E. (1988) 'A review of research concerning characteristics of exemplary secondary schools', mimeo, Toronto, Ontario Institute for Studies in Education.

LEITHWOOD, K., FARQUHAR, R. and BOICH, J. (1988) 'Future projections and conclusions' in BOICH, J., FARQUHAR, R. and LEITHWOOD, K. (Eds) *The Canadian School Superintendent*, Toronto, OISE Press.

LEITHWOOD, K. and JANTZI, D. (1988) 'How present educational policies and practices influence what students learn: A brief review of current research', mimeo Toronto, OISE.

LEITHWOOD, K. and JANTZI, D. (in press) 'Organizational effects of student learning' in POSTLETHWAITE, N. (Ed.) *International Encyclopedia of Education: Supplement 2*, Oxford, Pergamon Press.

LEITHWOOD, K.A., STEINBACH, R. and BEGLEY, P. (in press) 'The nature and contribution of socialization experiences to becoming a principal in Canada' in HALL, G.E. and PARKAY, F.W. (Eds) *Becoming a Principal: The Challenges of Beginning Leadership*, New York, Allyn Bacon.

LITTLE, J.W. (1982) 'Norms of collegiality and experimentation: Workplace conditions of school success', *American Educational Research*, 19, 3, pp. 325–40.

LORTIE, D. (1975) *School Teacher: A Sociological Study*, Chicago, University of Chicago Press.

LOUIS, K. (1987) 'The role of school districts in school innovations', paper prepared for a conference on Organizational Policy for School Improvement, Toronto, Ontario Institute for Studies in Education.

MCNEIL, L.M. (1986) *Contradictions of Control*. New York, Routledge.

MEYER, J.W., SCOTT, N.R. and DEAL, T. (1983) 'Research on school and district organization' in BALDRIDGE, J.V. and DEAL, T. (Eds) *The Dynamics of Organizational Change in Education*, Berkeley, CA, McCutchan

MONK, D.H. (1980) 'Towards a multilevel perspective on the allocation of educational resources', *Review of Educational Research*, 51, 2, pp. 215–56.

MORGAN, C., HALL, V. and MACKAY, H. (1983) *The Selection of Secondary Headteachers*, Milton Keynes, Open University Press.

MURPHY, J., HALLINGER, P. and PETERSON, K.D. (1985) 'Supervising and evaluating principals: lessons from effective districts', *Educational Leadership*, 43, 2, pp. 78–82.

MUSELLA, D. (1989) 'Training needs of chief executive officers', mineo, Toronto, OISE.

MUSELLA, D. and LAWTON, S. (1986) *Selection and Promotion Policies in Ontario School Boards*, Toronto, Ministry of Education.

PETERSON, K. (1986) 'Principals' work socialization and training: Developing more effective leaders, *Theory into Practice*, 25, 3, pp. 151–5.

PETERSON, K.D., MURPHY, J., HALLINGER, P. (1987) 'Superintendents' perceptions of the control and coordination of the technical care in effective school districts', *Educational Administration Quarterly*, 23, 1, pp. 79–95.

PRAHALD, C.K. and DOZ, Y.L. (1984) 'Managing managers: The work of top management' in HUNT, J.G., HOSKING, D., SCHRIESHELM, C.A. and STEWART, R. (Eds) *Leaders and Managers: International Perspectives On Managerial Behavior and Leadership*, New York, Pergamon Press.

QUINN, R.E. (1988) *Beyond Rational Management*, San Francisco, CA, Jossey-Bass.

ROSENBLUM, S. and LOUIS, K.S. (1981) *Stability and Change: Innovation in an Educational Context*. New York, Plenum.

ROSENHOLTZ, S. (1987) 'School success and the organizational conditions of teaching' in LANE, J.J. and WALBERG, H.J. (Eds) *Effective School Leadership*, Berkeley CA, McCutchan.

RUTTER, M., MAUGHAN, B., MORTIMORE, P. and OUSTON, J. (1979) *Fifteen Thousand Hours: Secondary Schools and Their Effects on Children*. Cambridge, MA, Harvard University Press.

SALLEY, C., MCPHERSON, R.B. and BAEHR, M.E. (1978) 'What principals do: A preliminary occupational analysis' in ERICKSON, D.A. and RELLER, T.L. (Eds) *The Principal in Metropolitan Schools* Berkeley, CA, McCutchan.

SCHEIN, E. (1984) *Organizational Culture*, San Francisco, CA, Jossey-Bass.

SLAVIN, R.E. (1984) 'Team assisted individualization instruction in the mainstreamed classroom', *Remedial and Special Education*, 5, 6, pp. 33–42.

SLAVIN, R.E. and KARWEIT, N.L. (1985) 'Effects on whole class ability grouped and individualized instruction on mathematics and achievement', *American Educational Research Journal*, 22, pp. 351–67.

TORBERT, W.R. (1987) *Managing the Corporate Dream: Restructuring For Long Term Success*. Homewood, IL, Dow Jones-Irwin.

TOWNSEND, R.G. (1988) *They Politick for Schools*, Toronto, OISE Press.

WALBERG, H.J. (1984) 'Improving the productivity of America's schools', *Educational Leadership*, 41, 8, pp. 19–27.

WALBERG, H.J., FOWLER, W.J. (1987) 'Expenditure and site effectiveness of public school districts', *Educational Researcher* 16, 7, pp. 5–13.

WALLBERG, H.J. and SCHAFFARZICK, J. (1974) 'Comparing curricula', *Review of Educational Research*, 44, 1, pp. 83–113.

WISSLER, D.F. and ORTIZ, F.I. (1988) *The Superintendents' Leadership in School Reform*. Lewes, Falmer Press.

Index

abstract modes of thought, 39, 308
  see also spectrum of abstraction
acceptance: and educational policy, 251
accommodation: in educational policy, 249, 262
accountability, 98, 102, 103–5, 107–9 *passim*, 254
  of board superintendents, 220–2
  and decentralization, 273
  focus, 113
  norm of, 106, 114
achievement testing, 165
actions: in problem solving, 146
active learning, 246, 249, 255
activities, orchestration of: and CEO influence on, 88, 89, 109, 110
administration: beliefs in, 7, 154
  Canadian *externa* and *interna*, 223
  centralized system of school —, 24
  educational, study of, 219–20, 229
  and organizational change, 298
  see also school system administration
administrator evaluation practices:
  professional development, 93, 94
  selection and promotion, 81
  and student learning, 81
  and trustee relations, 81
administrators: and loss of influence, 97
advice role, 31
affect: in problem solving, 149
affirmative action: in educational policies, 256–7
Allison, David, 226
alternative causes: and problem solving, 138
analysis: of data, 26, 135, 179
anecdotes: in problem solving, 137, 139
argumentation: from analogy, 70
  categories of, 44–5
  diagrams, 46, 50, 69
ARIDO, Association of Registered Interior Designers of Ontario, 203
artifacts: of organizational culture, 290
assessment: and student learning, 80, 165
ASSU, American Sunday School Union: control by, 212
assumptions: in organizational culture, 290
authoritative mode, 66
authority: of CEO, 3
  decentralizing, 247–8

backing: in policy arguments, 45, 46, 50, 52, 54, 69
'balance of life': in education, 253
Beevor, Wally, policy administrator, 47–9
behaviour: controls, 12
  overt, of effective principals, 128
  roots of, 128
beliefs, of CEOs: educational, 154, 155
  personal, 154, 155
bias: in policy arguments, 58
board superintendents: accountability, 220–2

in Canada, 230, 232–4
as chief executive, 217–18, 222, 234
in US, 215–16
boards: activities, participation in, 291, 293
— community relations, and student learning, 81
corruption in, 217
documents, review, 291
management difficulties, 32
powers of, 209
work with, 29, 30
Braun, Hank, Director, Brock Board of Education, 256–8
Brendel, Peter, Director, Caswell Board of Education, 251–4
brokerage administration, 266

Canadian CEOs, 2, 209–13, 222–35
caring focus, 13
cause: arguing from, 57–60
CEO, Chief Education Officer, in Canada:
basic tools of, 186–7
centrists, 242
characteristics, 242, 244
as chief executive, 234
effect of decentralization, 274–86
influence on subordinates, 111
non-materialistic values of, 202
and organizational change, 294–305
preparation of needs for, 15, 306–32
delivery of, 331
restructuring, 332
public, 168–70
qualities of, 330
research on, 331–2
role of, viii–ix, 2–5
evolution of, 1, 209–38
separate, 168–90
small number of, 331
spousal occupation, 160
work of, viii, 3
working life of, 170–3
chairpeople: relationship with, 30
change processes, viii
and executive leadership, 98–9, 252
focus, 113
management of, 298–9
in organizational culture, 294–305
training for, 295
change strategies, 4
chief provincial school officers: in Canada, 223–6, 227
city schools: boards, 234
and corporate model, 217–18
locally employed superintendents, 232, 234
and small-town superintendents, 218–19
claims: in policy argument, 44, 46, 50, 65
clarity: as function of problem, 136, 146
Classic North American Model of Geographic Community, 264–7
Classic Model Decentralized, 267–9
classroom management: and CEO influence, 86, 87
and size, 320
and student learning, 79–80
climate: and organizational culture, 289–90
cognitive: flexibility, 9
images, 9
commitment focus, 113
communication: CEO influence on, 88, 89, 92, 93
tools for, 187
in work pattern, 27, 171
community: in CEO educational policy, 250, 257, 260
and decentralization, 284
focus, 113
influence of, 110
local — schools, 264
professional, 36–7
relationships, and student learning, 80
work with, 29, 35–7
comparative: administration, viii
cases, arguing from, 62, 74
comparison groups: with CEOs, 157
conflict: management of, 11, 34
congruence: notion of, 111
consensuality, 103–5, 107–9 *passim*
and CEOs philosophy, 241, 265
problem of public, 262–3

in program of education, 154, 168
norm of, 105
constraints: in problem solving, 132–3 *passim*, 144–5
consultation process, 51
corruption: and city boards, 217, 220
Costello, Sean, Director, Melton Roman Catholic Separate School Board, 248–9
Council of Public Instruction, 224
CSSOs, chief state school officers, 213–14
Cubberley, Ellwood, P., Superintendent, San Diego schools, 216–17, 219, 233
cultural: development, 173
philosophy, 163, 168, 169, 246, 249, 254, 257
culture (ethos): folk, in CEO offices, 177, 196
as leadership tool, 100
popular, in CEO offices, 177, 196
see also organizational culture
curriculum development, 246, 313
school-based, 94

data: analysis, 26, 135, 179
collection, 133–4, 294
for research, 25, 48, 84, 307
decentralization, 115–16, 118, 267, 273–86, 297
and autonomy, 275
degree of, 279–80
goals of, 277–8
information on, 277
level of involvement, 280–2
research sample, 276
decision-making, 7, 8, 27, 34, 315, 327, 329–30
and consensual norms, 96
and decentralization, 281, 297
delegation by CEO, 92, 93, 94, 329
instructional, 313
principal involvement in, 115, 117
deferring salaries, 47
delegation: as CEO skill, 329
demographic characteristics: of CEOs, 154, 162
Diderot effect: in CEO offices, 198–200
direction: sense of, 88, 89
district: ethos, 112–13
groupings, 114–15
task, 113
Dodds, Evelyn, Chair, Lakehead Board of Education, Thunder Bay, 261, 262
Dutton, Samuel, administration reformer, 219

Edmonton: public school board restructuring, 274
education: 'franchising', 285
prime purposes of, 173–4
educational: administration, study of, 219–20, 229
beliefs, 5, 6, 8, 154
and decisions, 8
goals, *see* organizational goals
philosophies, 5, 6, 154, 163–8
and CEO educational practices, 241–72
ranking, 164
policy, 156
and CEO philosophies, 242–72
issues, 165
research, 167
effective districts, 312–13
effective schools movement, 78, 100
and information collection, 328
and planned instruction, 318
and teaching culture, 312
effectiveness: of CEO, 15
efficiency ideologies, 68
Egalitarian philosophy, 163
Entry Plans: and policy administration, 61, 73
equality of opportunity, 315
ethics: arguing from, 54–6
as warrant, 64
ethnic make-up: of student body, 14
ethos: ratings, by district, 111, 112
see also productive ethos
evaluation of information: by CEOs, 309
executive leadership: of CEOs, 97

existing procedures: in problem solving, 138
experience: in problem solving, 137, 138, 150
  of teachers, 323–4
expert-invoking rhetoric, 66
explanatory warrant, 64
externa school administration: and local school boards, 223

fairness: in problem solving, 143
'fiefdoms': in schools, 114–15, 118
fiscal leadership, 89, 90
'folk wisdom', educational, 164, 165
framework: of CEO role, 5
functional leadership, 100
funding: independent schools, 166
  public, and consensus, 262–3
    models for, 264–71
  and student learning, 82
  and student outcomes, 320

gender: of CEOs, 26, 162
  and CEO offices, 190, 202
  of inspectors, 235
geographical setting, of Ontario, 24
general command systems, 39
generalism: theory of, 37–8, 308
goals: ambiguity in, 314
  breadth of, 314–15
  complexity of, 314, 316
  organizational, 313–16
  university of, 315
goal settings, 51
  number of, 140
  in problem solving, 131–3 *passim*, 139–41
  process, 139
  product, 140, 150
Goggin, David, 226
grade-level surveys, 64–5
groundwork: in policy arguments, 52–3
guidance role, 31

Halton Board: and meta-process, 51
hierarchy: and organizational change, 298
human values, 141, 142

ideas and initiatives: CEO influence on, 88, 89
ideo-technic function: of objects, in CEO offices, 177, 198
immediate effects: in problem solving, 137, 138
impact of CEO: magnitude of, 4
improvement: meaning of, 4
inclusion: as educational policy, 247
individual identity: and CEO offices, 195
Individualistic philosophy, 163, 164, 174, 250, 252, 254, 257, 259
influence: of CEOs in school effectiveness, amount of, 85–6
    nature of, 86–8
  loss of, by administrators, 97
  strategies, 11–13
  see also mutual influence
informal channels: in policy administration, 58
information: channels, 57
  collecting, 37, 38, 214, 315, 327–9
  exchanging, 37, 60
  see also relevant information
information processing theory: of problem solving, 127, 129, 138, 149
input controls, 11
inspectors, in Canada, 227–34
  access to, 230
  gender of, 235
  qualifications for, 228–9, 234, 235
  recruitment, 229
  supervisory practices, 230
  work of, 227, 229–30
instructional: leadership, 323, 325
  model, 318
  objectives, 317
integration of ideas: CEO influence on, 88, 89, 309
interactions: of administrators, 110, 308
  norms of, 312
interior design: Rorschach test, 182
Interior Designers of Canada, 203
interna school administration: and provincial authorities, 223, 226
internal processes, 10

interpersonal skills: and policy administration, 67, 306
interpretation: in problem solving, 131–3 *passim*, 135–9
interviews: of CEO educational philosophies and policies, 245–6
 and decentralization, 276
 and organizational change, 287, 291
  schedule, 292
intuition: arguing from, 53–4
involvement: CEO influence on, 88

Jessop, John, 226
job functions, 10, 11

knowledge: and problem solving, 129

leadership, 43, 66–7, 69, 248
 and CEO influence, 88–91 *passim*, 93
 development of, 307
 in empowerment of others, 327
 ethical, 316
 impact of, 43
 institutional, 43
 managerial, 322
 normative/cultural, 313
 and organizational change, 295, 297
 potential for, 15
 properties of, 82
 provincial, and decentralization, 285
 reflective, 330
 technical, 319
 see also functional; shared; transformational
learning, factors affecting student —, 79–82
 classroom, 79–80, 86
 provincial, 82, 86
 school-wide, 80–1, 86
 system factors, 81, 86
learning focus, 113
liaison: interagency, 36
liberalism: of CEOs, 162, 168
 and Roman Catholics, 170
limitations: of research, 26
LMS, local management of schools, 273, 274, 277
lobbying, 70
loyalty: in problem solving, 143
LSS, large school systems, 25, 33, 34, 38

Mackay, A.H., 226
Mackenzie, Jim, Director, Suffolk Board of Education, 254–6
managerial and executive work, 11, 27, 171, 306
 and CEO offices, 178
master contract, 96, 97, 313
 negotiation of, 119–20
 and transformational leaders, 101–3
materialism: in problem solving, 143
materials and resources: and student learning, 80
MBO, Management-By-Objectives, 62
mediator: role as, 11
meetings: breakfast, 57–60, 67, 72
 internal, 33
 and policy administration, 51
 scheduled, 11, 27–8
 and system size, 28
 Meilleur, Dr Jean Baptiste, chief provincial school officer, 223–4
 meta-process, of policy administration, 51, 53, 54–6, 70–2, 73, 118
 flexibility, 55
method: arguing from, 49, 51–3
Ministry of Education: role in decentralization, 284
mistakes, by CEOs, 15
modelling, 108–9
 in problem solving, 151
mood: of CEO offices, 182
moral values, 141, 142
morale, system: and student learning, 81
motivation: arguing from, 60–2
 as warrant, 65
multiculturalism: and educational choice, 263
Murray, Rev. Robert: chief provincial school officer, 223–4
mutual influence: and accountability, 99

negotiated beliefs, 101
Norms Diagnostic Index: and
  organizational culture, 292–3,
  299–303

OAEAO, Ontario Association of
  Education Administrative Officials, 79
objectives, instructional, 319
objects, in CEO office: function and
  meaning, 176, 190–2 *passim*, 201–2,
  207–8
  and successors, 194
O'Brien, Ross, Director, Swansea
  Roman Catholic Separate School
  Board, 250–1
observation: in organizational culture,
  291, 293
offices, of CEOs: adjacent facilities,
  183–4
  decoration, 175–6
  and household objects, 190
  impact of succession, 192–4
  and individual identity, 195
  personal touch, 187–92
  religious symbolism in, 196, 201
  renovations, 179, 182
  sample study, 178–9
    interview guide, 204–6
  and school systems, 180–1, 197
  size, 197–8
  special objects in, 188
  storage, 200
  typical layout, 185
  work areas, 164, 200
Ontario: geographical setting of
  research, 24–5
  inspectors in, 228
  study of CEOs educational
    philosophies
    and policies, 241–72
    unrepresentation of, 271
open enrolment policy, 257, 268
options: in pluralist model, 269
organizational: context, 13
  ethos, 96, 313
  goals, 100, 313–16
organizational culture, viii, 13, 96,
  311–13
  change in, 287–305
  and climate, 289
  concept of, 287–9, 299
  definitions, 291
  method of appraising, 291–4
  and transformational leadership, 100
  programs, 294
organizational designer: CEO role as,
  307–32
organizational structure, 319–23
  and size, 319–20

pantries: in CEO offices, 184
parallel cases: arguing from, 62
parents: choice of, 258
  relationship with, 36
  role of, 106, 325
  and teachers, 312
participation: in problem solving, 143
performance: appraisal, 254
  level, 112
  rank, by district, 111
person: in policy evaluation, 62
personal: beliefs, 158, 159
  involvement, 110
  judgment, and policy arguments, 53
personnel: leadership, 89, 90
  policies and procedures, 325–7
perspectives: in organizational culture,
  290
philosophies: *see* educational
physical environment: and student
  learning, 80
Pinkham, William Cyprian, 226
planning: as CEO educational policy,
  252, 254, 255
  forward, in problem solving, 146
    action, hierarchical model, 147
  backward, 147
  opportunities, 148, 150
pluralism: interpretations, 270
  and local school autonomy, 268
pluralist model, 269–70, 272
policy: administration rhetoric of,
  42–77
  and CEOs philosophies, 242–72
  cycle, 46–7
  developments, 51
  formulation, arguments in, 46,
    49–56

further research in, 68–9
implementation, arguments in, 46, 56–62
leadership, 91
revaluation, arguments in, 46, 62–6
see also educational policy
politics: of CEOs, 158, 160–2 *passim*
power: in problem solving, 144
practicality: of CEO offices, 182
practices, CEO, 4, 6, 10
preparation needs: of CEOs, 15, 306–32
principals: autonomy, 117, 248, 267–8
characteristics, 323
as instructional leader, 317
interaction with, 34
and problem solving, 130–4
and CEOs, 143–4, 147, 149–50
and shared leadership, 101, 115–18
principles: in problem solving, 131, 132
priority: and CEOs time, 172
setting, in problem solving, 138
problem solving, 5, 6, 8–10, 34, 127–53, 308
categorization, 69
methods, 130–1, 133–5
models, 151
research, 128, 151
problems: context of, 130
definition, 135
difficulty, 138
finding, 138
rephrasing, 137, 138
structured, 129, 136, 150
types of, 134
un-structured, 129, 132, 136–7, 150
process: in policy evaluation, 62–3
policy manual, 70–1
product: in policy evaluation, 62
productive ethos, 96
district, 111–15
and master contract, 119–20
professional values, 141, 142
program: leadership, 91
and student learning, content, 80
evaluation, 81
integration, 80
objectives, 79
program: content, and student learning, 80
evaluation, and student learning, 81
integration, and student learning, 80
Progressive philosophy, 163, 167, 169
and CEOs, 241, 246, 249, 250, 252, 257–9 *passim*, 261, 266, 276
provincial authorities: and central control, 223–6
provincial factors: and CEOs influence, 86, 92–3
and fiefdoms, 115
and student learning, 82
Prussian school system, 209, 212, 213
public authorities, 43
public relations role, 35–6, 38, 90, 171
publicly funded independent schools model, 270–1

qualifiers: in policy arguments, 45, 46, 50
quantitative models, 68
Quebec: inspectors in, 228
questionnaires: in organizational culture, 287, 291, 292–3
response, 157
use of, 83–4, 154, 156–8, 243

race relations: and educational policy, 256
Rand, T.H., 226
range: of CEO, 106–11
rational approach: and intuition, 54
reach: of CEO, 111–15
rebuttal: in policy arguments, 45, 65
reform: of secondary education, 165
regional superintendents: in US, 214–15, 227
relationships: and CEO influence, 88–9, 310–11
classroom, and student learning, 80
difficulties in, 35
and organizational culture, 290, 308, 309
in policy administration, 51–2, 67

relevant information: in policy arguments, 45, 46, 50, 65
religion: of CEOs, 158, 160, 161
  and CEO offices, 196, 201
Report of the Commission on Private Schools, Ontario, 275
representativeness: and CEOs, 97, 98
research project: on CEO role, 1, 25–6
resources: and organizational change, 298
restructuring school systems, 273–86, 315, 322
rhetoric: in policy administration, 42–77
role, of CEO, viii–ix, 2–5, 25–6
  decisional, 27
  evolution of, 1
  informational, 27
  interpersonal, 27
  as secretary, 25
Roman Catholic separate CEOs, 168–70
Ryerson, Egerton, chief provincial school officer, 224–5, 227, 228, 234

sample: in CEO influence, 83–4
SBB, school-based budgeting, 273, 274, 277
SBM, school-based management, 273, 274, 277
school: autonomy, 117, 248, 267–8, 272
  — based planning, 94
  committee, 275
  effectiveness, viii
    and CEO influence, 78–95
  factors, and CEO influence, 86, 87
    and student learning, 80–1
  as field of opportunity, 173
  local community, 264
  responsibility, 173
  visits, 34, 92, 110, 230
school district consolidation, 231
school system administration, 309–10
  and CEO offices, 180–1, 197
  framework for understanding, 1–19
  future of, 331
  interaction with personnel, 32–3
  official control, 211, 212
  and public view of, 260–1
  work in, 29
  see also restructuring
school system culture: effective, 14
school system factors: and CEO influence, 86, 92, 93
  and student learning, 81
school system size, 14, 23, 25–6, 33, 38–9
secondary schooling: organization and availability in Canada, 231
  and pluralist model, 269
segregation: social 264
selection of CEOs: and educational philosophy, 271–2
SES, student socioeconomic status, 319, 324
sexual equality: in education, 166
shared leadership, 101, 102, 115–18
single-team bargaining, 47–8
situational analyses, 51, 55–6
size: and organizational structure, 319–20
small town superintendents, 218–19
social: capital, 324
  equality, 174
  and political values, 141, 142, 143
  progress, 68
  trends, and school system impact, 318
socio-technic function: of objects, in CEO offices, 177, 195
solution processes: in problem solving, 131–3 *passim*, 145–8, 150
SOs, supervisory officers: interaction with, 32, 33
specific role responsibility, 141–2
spectrum of abstraction, 39–40
SSS, small school systems, 25, 33, 34, 38, 39
stability: and organizational change, 298
staffing decisions: and decentralization, 281
state: autonomy of, 43
  policies, 44

strategic opportunism model: in problem solving, 148, 150
Strayer, George, administrator reformer, 219
streaming, 321
  superintendents, in US, 213–14
student learning, 79–81, 320, 328
  characteristics, 319, 324–5
style: of CEO offices, 182–3, 201
superintendent: board, in US, 215–16, 220–2
  chief provincial, in Canada, 223–7
  evolution of, 210–11
  as factotum, 216–17
  regional, in US, 214–15, 227
  rise of corporate model, 217–18
  state, in US, 213–14
  see also CEOs; inspectors
system: job descriptions, 25

tail-gating: in policy administration, 74
tasks: complexity, 316
  for school system goals, 316–19
teachers: accessibility to, 92
  characteristics, 324
  consultation, 92
  and decentralization, 281
  efficacy literature, 102
  'freedom', 102
  instructional practices, 317, 321, 325
  selection and promotion, 326
  socialization, 325–6
  — student interactions, 318
  and student learning, 79
    development, 81
    evaluation practices, 81
    relationships, 81
    selection and promotion, 81
  supervision and evaluation, 326
  trustee relations, 81
teaching culture, 312
team: building, by CEO, 92
  teaching, 322
technical competence: of CEOs, 97
technocratic philosophy, 163, 164, 169, 246, 249, 252, 254
technomic function: of objects, in CEO offices, 176, 195, 196
thought processes: rational, 5, 6, 8, 9
time: CEOs, 172
  lines, in problem solving, 138
  spent in offices, 186
tracking, 321
  within-class, 321
Traditional philosophy, 163, 167, 169, 248, 250, 259
transformational leadership: and productive ethos, 96–123
trustees: and decentralization, 284
  divisiveness, with CEOs, 260
  election, 227
  interaction with, 30–1
  leadership, 91
  office space for, 198

US: CEOs, 2, 209, 213–22
  see also under superintendents

value-criticism: arguing from, 49, 54, 56
  in policy evaluation, 63, 68
values, of CEOs, 5, 6, 155
  choice of, 7, 8
  and educational policies, 241–72
  and executive action, 6–7
  in organizational culture, 290
  and principles, in problem solving, 131, 141–4, 150
    categories, 141, 142
    classification, 132
    definition, 131
  and use of controls, 8
verbal communication, 11
vision-strong convictions: of CEOs, 103–6, 313
visual art: in CEO offices, 187, 189, 191, 194, 196, 202
VLSS, very large school systems, 25, 33, 34, 38, 39

warrants: cause-effect, 61
  motivational, 61, 65
  in policy arguments, 45, 46, 50, 54, 69
washrooms: for CEO offices, 183–4
Weir, Ruth, member, Etobicoke Board of Education, 261, 262
Wilmot, Grant, Director,

Northampton Board of Education, 246–8
work: of CEO, viii, 23, 170–3
consequences of, 3
environment, 23, 110
sectored, 29–31
patterns, 27–8
hours in week, 27